CROP CIRCLES, JUNG, and the Reemergence of the ARCHETYPAL FEMININE

CROP CIRCLES, JUNG, and the Reemergence of the ARCHETYPAL FEMININE

GARY S. BOBROFF

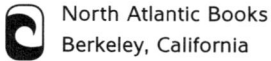
North Atlantic Books
Berkeley, California

Published by
North Atlantic Books
P.O. Box 12327
Berkeley, California 94712

Cover art © 2010 by Regina Allen (www.ReginaAllen.com)
Paintings by Irene Champernowne appear courtesy of Julian David
Cover and book design by Claudia Smelser
Printed in the United States of America

Crop Circles, Jung, and the Reemergence of the Archetypal Feminine is sponsored by the Society for the Study of Native Arts and Sciences, a nonprofit educational corporation whose goals are to develop an educational and cross-cultural perspective linking various scientific, social, and artistic fields; to nurture a holistic view of arts, sciences, humanities, and healing; and to publish and distribute literature on the relationship of mind, body, and nature.

North Atlantic Books' publications are available through most bookstores. For further information, visit our website at www.northatlanticbooks.com or call 800–733–3000.

Library of Congress Cataloging-in-Publication Data
Bobroff, Gary S., 1971–
Crop circles, Jung, and the reemergence of the archetypal feminine / Gary S. Bobroff, M.A.
     pages cm
Includes bibliographical references.
Summary "Gary S. Bobroff's book Crop Circles, Jung and the Reemergence of the Archetypal Feminine offers an enthralling exploration of a real-life phenomenon—crop circles—as an expression of the divine feminine"—Provided by publisher.
ISBN 978-1-58394-735-7
1. Crop circles. 2. Jungian psychology. 3. Symbolism (Psychology) I. Title.
AG243.B535 2014
133.9'3—dc23
                                                                    2013041694

1 2 3 4 5 6 7 8 9 SHERIDAN 19 18 17 16 15 14
Printed on recycled paper

FOR KATE

CONTENTS

FOREWORD

I first met Gary Bobroff about two years ago at a conference in North Carolina. I was immediately struck by his easy charm, the depth and authority of his reading and intellect, and the unpretentious way he spoke of mysteries he had, quite obviously, experienced. I thought to myself, "This is a rare and gifted man who will be one of the authentic teachers of his generation."

Gary is a stunning writer—graceful, eloquent, subtle—and the skill with which he weaves together his fascination with Crop Circles, the return of the Divine Feminine in our time, and Jungian psychology in what is a kind of "spiritual mystery" exhilarates me, and confirmed my experience of him as a person. This is a work of high originality, one whose tone and structure incarnates Gary's knowledge of the cosmos and our role in it as an open-ended, endlessly unfolding, seductive display of the Mother's wisdom, passion, and love. There is no other book quite like it, and its publication announces the arrival of a remarkably accomplished and fresh new voice who demands to be heard.

There are two things I especially love about this book. The first is the way that Gary dances in, out, and around his central themes, so magically that the reader is enchanted into the book, only to discover that he or she, along with the author, is on a voyage of profound discovery. The second is that both in the sinuous and suggestive way he explores and opens up his material and in the glowing depths of the work itself, this book is a celebration and manifestation of the Divine Feminine. The return of the Divine Feminine, in both miraculous and subtle ways, is the single most important aspect of our time: only though Her, and with Her wisdom and grace, can we possibly hope to restore our devastated world. What I find sacred about Gary's style and intellect is that they are both dedicated to the Mother. He brings his masculine brilliance, clarity, and robustness of intellect and lays them at Her feet in a prolonged and gorgeous act of devotion. As a man who has attempted to do the same over decades of work, I salute him and learn from him.

This is an original masterpiece of a book. Savor it richly, slowly, and gratefully, and many interlinked secrets will be revealed to you, and in you.

—*Andrew Harvey*

PREFACE

Sparked by their curiosity, thousands of people have contributed to the study of Crop Circles around the world. Individuals throughout the United Kingdom, Europe, Canada, Australia, Japan, the United States, and elsewhere have given their time freely to the documentation of this phenomenon. They have measured, marked, photographed, and taken the samples that constitute an abundant archive of data from which we may now seek to draw our own conclusions. As a researcher, I have been delighted to discover the wealth of materials on the physical science and mythological context of the Crop Circle phenomenon that they have collected. This book is consequently built upon the product of their efforts.

This work is an attempt to sketch a framework for deeper consideration of the question of Crop Circles. If you are looking for an answer or a solution to this phenomenon's riddle, best look elsewhere. At best, I hope to offer a direction—a route by which to begin tracking something very elusive (that seemingly wants us to follow it). For those who have engaged with this mystery for some time, it is a source of deepening wonder and it is to that experience that you are invited.

From sixteenth-century England to 1970s Saskatchewan, Canada, through to its explosion in frequency in the last thirty years, some of those who have encountered Crop Circles have followed their curiosity and chosen to study it; honoring their own inner sense of wonder, they have become engaged with this new discovery.

A particularly dedicated group of Crop Circle enthusiasts have produced a number of outstanding publications and online resources on the subject. Their efforts have made my attempt to understand this phenomenon possible. It should be mentioned that, with only the rarest exceptions, even those who have produced the most brilliant and popular of these works have given more to the study of this subject than they are ever likely to recover financially.[1] Nonetheless, they persist in their efforts of their own free will. I would like to recommend your use of their media as an additional support for your own investigation of Crop Circles. A selection of recommended choices follows at the end of this book.

This book has been written to be accessible to the general reader. It is meant to serve as an introduction to both Crop Circles and Jungian psychology, and no familiarity with the concepts or jargon of either subject is assumed. I strongly believe that the significance of this phenomenon is available to all of us, and that engagement with it should not be reserved for experts, academics, or only those with the financial resources to travel abroad. I believe that the meaning of the arrival of Crop Circles in our time is as within reach or hard to grasp for the intellectual as it is for the farmer in whose fields these formations arrive. Its arrival challenges us all equally and its mystery is open to us all. However, this subject does introduce readers to ideas that may be new to them. It brings up wide categories of thought and poses broad questions—questions that stretch the imagination and our preconceptions. Answering these questions necessitates a labor on the part of the reader, but the argument made here is intended to appeal to common sense.

Primarily, I believe that this subject asks of its investigators (and you now are one) an actively engaged participation—not a simple reading, but a "dance for two." Each of us responds differently to new things and whether we bring to this topic a skeptical brow or a wide-eyed enthusiasm, we do not come to it empty-handed. It is in how we engage with our own first responses to this phenomenon that the burden of our work in response to it lies. Meeting this task involves a willingness to play with our own responses—to be in process with them, rather than attaching and identifying with our own initial reaction. I have yet to meet two people who feel exactly the same way about Crop Circles. I have also found that, over time, our engagement with the facts and theories that surround them changes and deepens. Given time, this labor yields its own fruit for each of us. Tending to this harvest begins by resisting identification with our first reactions to this material. This task is only possible if you accompany your reading by observing and according value to your own thoughts in response to it. Write down your own responses as you read this book or look at Crop Circle images. Your first responses are often the most valuable here. Flashes of response, no matter how brief, offer the possibility of glimpsing something within us that is truly fresh and genuinely new. Participation in this engagement hosts what is evoked in us by the phenomenon and thereby brings a mirror to the new possibilities that are inherent within us.

Rather than placing value upon what you find written here and looking at this interpretation for answers, please place as much or greater value upon your own curiosity, insight, and questions—note your responses, your feelings, and your thoughts. Make room for your own disagreement with what is written here. It was engagement with my own dissension that produced some of what I believe are the most valuable arguments presented here. In your own writing, try not to judge the process as it happens; simply record it as it comes. After some time, you may want to write past your initial responses and notice what else comes to mind. After following the open road of your own responses and writing down whatever comes up, watch throughout the rest of the day or night for new thoughts or feelings. Noting these responses encourages an inner dialogue and works a muscle that most of us have forgotten how to exercise.

As the products of a culture that prizes certainty, in the act of inner dialogue we reengage that part of ourselves that remembers how to wonder and values sometimes *not* knowing. Jung felt that following this voice led to the true growth of the personality, and that "the creation of something new is not accomplished by the intellect but by the play instinct acting from inner necessity. The creative mind plays with the thing it loves."[2] In reading this book, if you examine your own reactions as much as you think about what you are reading, then you are consciously choosing to participate creatively with Crop Circles. Treated in this way, the material presented here offers itself as a framework for deepening your participation with the mystery of this phenomenon.

In the hope of facilitating this process, this book is constructed in a particular manner and with exceptions to some of the usual writing rules. Each chapter is *rich,* so please take your time proceeding through them. Throughout this work, consideration is given to Crop Circles in general, as opposed to the particular meaning of any single formation, as the latter has been addressed very well in many other publications. In order to emphasize the importance of keeping the mystery alive in our pursuit of this phenomenon, I have chosen to capitalize the term Crop Circles throughout the publication. In capitalizing the name of the phenomenon I run the risk of seeming to conflate it with a divinity—which I do not intend to do. To leave this term uncapitalized would enable the phenomenon to be more easily minimized as simply an intellectual puzzle or a concept that can be conveniently labeled (in line with modern sensibilities, which tend to be uncomfortable with the reality and unknown quality of what is being met here).

For the same reason, I have chosen to capitalize the term Nature throughout. The dominant paradigm of our culture tends to encourage us to view Nature as entirely mechanistic and without mystery. This psychological error is being challenged by many new phenomena and discoveries that are emerging today (including Crop Circles). A thorough and honest consideration of these new developments opens our view of Nature beyond the neat and tidy (and mystery-free) boxes foisted upon us by our culture. I capitalize these terms with the hope of helping you to remain present with the unknown nature of what we are encountering here.

Crop Circles, Jung, and the Reemergence of the Archetypal Feminine is an exploration of the circle and grain symbols, each of which has a strongly defined place in Jungian psychology. The circle is the most fundamental symbol of the Self archetype, Jung's term for the force within us that holds us together through the process of change, reorients us toward balance, and guides our growth into higher forms and greater wholeness. Grain is among our most ancient mythological symbols and is associated strongly with our wonder at the process of life as embodied in female form. Goddesses, whether carved in prehistoric times or painted as medieval saints, express our fascination with existence itself, with the seed emerging from the "dead" ground of the earth, with that animating force that flows through all life. That both of these symbols should be presented to us in mysterious form at a time when we are, as a culture, both profoundly out of balance and estranged from the miracle of life should give us pause for thought. And perhaps what is most profound about Crop Circles, when seen through the Jungian lens, is not the particular meaning of these symbols, but rather how precisely that meaning draws out a clear view of the psychological illness afflicting our culture. In the living context of our moment, this strange and beautiful mystery offers a mirror through which we can more clearly see our shadow—the evil and good that we are denying in ourselves.

In the final chapter, I introduce the remarkable dream images of Irene Champernowne, an English art therapist and clinic director living in the English countryside in the 1950s. She was fortunate enough not only to have a remarkable series of dreams that seem to clearly presage our modern encounter with Crop Circles, but to also have Antonia "Toni" Wolff, a close companion of Jung's, as her analyst. Irene's dreams included images of UFOs, swirled grain, and female figures, and she painted these dreams and sent the paintings to Toni for analysis and comment. Their dialogue around these images is deep and profound and focuses upon the nature of the Feminine and its essential reemergence in our era. In 1951, as she was sitting with Emma and Carl Jung, Emma told Irene that "your pictures have impressed me very deeply indeed; I feel there is something extremely important and valuable [in them] for woman in general."[3] Carl was so struck by them that he used the UFO image from her first painting as the cover for his 1959 book on the topic. Their thoughts open a window to what all three might have said about our modern encounter with Crop Circles.

INTRODUCTION TO JUNGIAN INTERPRETATION

Throughout human history different cultures have revered particular symbols. Mythologies are the product of our identification with an image and its meaning to us. In the context of the history of a particular group, a symbol appears that resonates so much that it is carried forth as emblematic of their culture. Likewise, in our personal lives, dreams appear whose symbols are found to be meaningful for us. However, it is not the image itself that carries meaning, but the symbol's relevance to our life. We are moved by dreams precisely because they address our life so appropriately at that moment. It is the context of our life—of our history and culture, of certain moments in time or of certain places—that comes together to generate particular insights and ways of thinking that we grow to identify with as our own. The symbols of our lives (those from dream life and waking life) are intimately related to our history, our culture, and our biography. Such symbols can only be recognized and understood in the dynamic context of the facts of our lived experience. Likewise, there is a personal history to each of us that provides the context for our dreams. Meaning is then generated through those symbols, only by making our engagement with them conscious. Dream interpretation looks at the relationship between these forces and how our real lives fall together to create a context in response to which symbolic insight emerges.

Jung repeatedly noticed in the fantasies and dreams of his patients that images seemed to be pulled not only from life experiences, but also from something seemingly deeper as well. In their material, he recognized obscure and esoteric images from foreign cultures that he was certain his patients had never seen—an observation only possible before the presence of today's television and Internet. He first spoke of these as primordial images, considering them to represent the most basic patterns of intelligence within the psyche, shared by all humanity. Eventually, he called these forms "archetypes," from the Greek term whose root terms are *archein,* meaning "original," and *tupos,* meaning "impression" or "model." These are the patterns and themes that we recognize as being fundamental forms within our imagination. For the Greeks, archetypes constituted the basis of their worldview. For common citizens, as well as for Plato, Socrates, and Aristotle, such "original impressions" were:

> An ordered expression of certain primordial essences or transcendent first principles, variously conceived as Forms, Ideas, universals, changeless absolutes, immortal deities, divine archai. . . . Archetypal principles included mathematical forms of geometry and arithmetic; cosmic principles such as light and dark, male and female, love and hate, unity and multiplicity; the forms of man and other living creatures; and the Ideas of the Good, the Beautiful, and the Just, and other absolute moral and aesthetic values . . . as well as the more personified

figures such as Zeus, Prometheus, and Aphrodite. In this perspective, every aspect of existence was patterned and permeated by such fundamentals.[4]

For Jung, "the concept of the archetype . . . is derived from the repeated observation that, for instance, the myths and fairytales of world literature contain definite motifs which crop up everywhere. We meet these same motifs in the fantasies, dreams, deliria, and delusions of individuals living today."[5] Affecting and structuring cognition, emotion, instinct, feeling, and thought, archetypes link both body and mind, conscious and unconscious. As Jungian analyst Ann Belford Ulanov describes, "just as birds submit to forms that force them to build their nests in a certain way, so we humans find our instincts taking specific forms because 'unconscious thought expresses itself mythologically.'"[6] "[Archetypes] act like magnetic fields which, though unseen, arrange responses, emotions, and actions into specific patterns expressed in the form of symbolic images. If the ego can relate to these archetypal centers of energy through their symbolic expressions, the use of instinctive energy can be consciously guided for the ego's purposes."[7] Seen in their wealth of reference in myth and fiction, and their dynamic activity in the psyche, archetypes are paradoxical and multivalent—many-sided. We can know their type without knowing how that type will manifest in a particular case. Operating both nonlinearly and nonliterally, they are able to affect us in body, heart, and mind simultaneously. They speak at once to our conscious mind and to the unconscious depths within us.

Although the archetypal form necessitates the idea of a type, a definite form or set of characteristics that make one type unique from another and provide a recognizable pattern, in practice it is often only through an archetype's activity in our lives and the "particularly strong feeling tones" that it evokes in us that we begin to notice them.

Archetypes have the power to entrance us. Both individually and culturally, an archetype can emerge into the forefront of our imagination and captivate us. When a particular archetype resonates for us, we react strongly to it: it may strike us numb, we may become animated by it, identify with it, or overreact against it and reject it; but when we are in its grip, it will always "impress, influence, and *fascinate* us."[8] For better or worse, we are pulled by our heartstrings and lifted toward a new (or old) direction when the wind of its voice blows upon us. Archetypes enfold us into a *partici-pation mystique*—inside of which we become bound, enthralled and over-whelmed. Sometimes we may feel exalted. An archetypal dynamic takes us on a roller coaster of possibilities, inflating us, making us feel on top of the world, or deflating us and removing all hope.

In the background, looming like powerful gods, our archetypal complexes sit enthroned. Our capacity to become entranced by a particular archetype speaks to a kind of background-foreground switch, in which the particular complexes that we have confuse for us the personal with the cosmological in a somatically felt, emotionally experienced way. In our lived experience, this background image (the archetypal, transpersonal content in our psyche) becomes reversed with a foreground image when we come into contact with someone (or something) who ignites that archetypal image for us. At that time, winning such a person, object, or issue, or losing them, is felt to be a world-constituting or -destroying reality. In this way, an experience with a single person can become a world-negating or world-enlightening event. If this seems difficult to believe, think of all of the teenage suicide over love and the feeling of "the world will end if I can't have this person." We know that an object has enchanted us when we become deflated by its loss. In such situations, the background archetypal image becomes reversed with the literal foreground truth of the particular person, object, issue, value, etc. This dynamic is also experienced in repetition compulsions, where an often-overwhelming desire for a literal object is a concrete substitution made for a pull toward an elusive archetypal content (like a hopeful sacrifice made to an unknown god). Whether experienced in interpersonal relations, pol-itics, addiction, or consumerism, there is often a substitution of a concrete object for an intimate healthy need or higher symbolic ideal. In all of these ways, archetypal fascinations redirect our energy, sometimes positively—moving us toward psychic health—and sometimes negatively, damning us into the dead-end of trying to literalize regressive fantasies. This inverted dynamic illustrates how, in day-to-day life, we may be unable to grasp on to an archetype's positive values and end up finding ourselves subject to its un-healthy dominance. One may feel out of control when exposed to it, or con-trolled by it—neither able to separate from a negative archetypal content, nor attach ourselves to its positive form.[9] Yet psychologically, redemption is always possible. Where there is a negative pole there is always a positive pole too—a way out, if we have the strength to grasp it. Doing so requires making our participation conscious, a process that is begun by an honest recognition of our own fascination. Overcoming passive captivity in an archetype begins with a move toward active conscious engagement *with* it. This process makes it possible to *look at* an archetype, complex, or emotion, rather than continue to *lay caught* in it. In this way, we serve "the goal of psychoanalysis [which is] to help a person gain his or her own capacity to relate to the unconscious."[10]

Jung found that symbolic associations could be used to break us out of entrapment within an archetype. In a process called amplification, images, myths, and stories relating to the symbols of the dream are presented in order to "make louder" the link between the conscious mind and unconscious content. Amplification through symbols aims for conscious recognition of such an archetypal pattern. In this search to bring the hidden unconscious source of a difficulty into the light, the cognitive, often intuitive, search for symbolic identification goes hand in hand with an attentive awareness of our affective state. We find out whether an archetypal symbol has resonance by the measure of our felt response to it, or lack thereof. Sometimes dramatically or at other times very subtly, we respond emotionally to archetypal contents that are particularly active for us, or fail to respond when it would be healthy to do so. If we are attentive, our feeling guides us toward the recognition of such potent content in our psyche. However, in doing so, it quite often does not point to an immediate literal solution. In making such a recognition, we place our finger upon an active dynamic and frequently find something beyond a simple one-step corrective. Becoming cognitively aware of the relevance of an archetype for us—perceiving consciously what had previously been unconscious to us—is only a first step. The next step brings us toward a whole-body integration of the reality of the new content. While the therapeutic bond of trust enables the subject to slowly, but consciously, begin to listen to the symptom's quiet whisper and start to accept mentally what had previously been intolerable to awareness, healing is ultimately found by becoming able to tolerate an emotional experience of the symptom's root.

In the ancient theater of Greece, a play ideally moved the audience toward a felt catharsis, a *metanoia,* a "change of heart." To serve this purpose, the play's action needed to address something that was often unspoken in the audience. Plays were written to make conscious ills within the community and to connect the audience with the questions of its own hidden, inner community. Great playwrights, such as Shakespeare, address the human necessity to "speak what we feel, not what we ought to say." Giving voice to such ills—to those who needed to hear them—is risky and requires real courage; our history is full of obituaries for those who dared to do so. Likewise, at night, in our dreams, similar unspoken questions are put forth to our conscious mind's dominance. In our sleep, we are led like the play's audience, toward contact with something in ourselves that needs expression. Unfortunately, oftentimes the pain of recognizing such truth is too much and all that is left is for symptoms to express "the unspeakability of the problem."[11]

Psychological conflict is often the expression of a fundamental one-sidedness in our conscious relation to the world. It is a natural function of the psyche to seek to bring about a compensation for this imbalance. Yet while compensatory archetypal images are brought forth from the unconscious in order to correct for such imbalances, because the new quality often comes in opposition to a dominant conscious attitude (often made into a tightly held value system or lack thereof), the adjustment toward healing is often not easily made.

> This compensation is accomplished by means of the constellation and stressing of material which is not infrequently simply complementary and which assumes archetypal forms of expression [the goal of which is to] the correct [the] relation to the surrounding world.[12]

Encountering the deeper healing functions of the psyche always means discovering something that is authentically new. Reaching the moment at which a symbol "clicks" for us and meaning is realized is not an intellectual exercise, but a journey often through a suffering "of the whole person."[13] This demand for a change of the whole person is typified in the Old Testament struggle between Moses and the hard-hearted Pharaoh. Only through repeated signs, warnings, and threats did Pharaoh come to believe in a God more powerful than his own and free the slaves as Moses had asked of him. Even after releasing the slaves, Pharaoh returned once more to his old ways, sending his army to recapture them and thus leading his soldiers to their destruction when the miraculously parted waves of the Red Sea crashed in all around them. While very frequently a symbol can be easily understood as an antidote to an imbalance—we have a dream, we wake up and say "Yes, I see"—and such occurrences are blessings, more often, if given time, signs unfold over time into symbols of greater depth. Like Ukrainian dolls, each one enclosed within a larger version of the next, a symbol's meaning can unfold repeatedly anew with the events of our lives. In such cases, we continue to rediscover a symbol in greater meaning and depth.

Recognizing the nature of such archetypal dynamics, through the use of amplification, myths, symbols, and the like, offers a first step toward the possibility of being able to depersonalize our sufferings. Seeing our own plight reflected in a mythological context helps us to realize that "it's not just me" and to let go of some of our identification with our pain. And while healing sometimes asks us to bring new passion and strength to holding on to what we know we value, there are also times when it asks of us a courageous letting go—a consciously chosen vulnerability. Rather than a simple change in conscious attitude, what is demanded is the recognition of a symbol's ability to give us a *picture of the whole*—the *larger version of ourselves that we are being asked to become*. Because a symbol must compensate for a particularly vast expanse between a consciously held attitude and a deeply unconscious new value, its bridge across consciousness cannot be simply informational; it must extend past literal limitations and open us up to a greater whole living within us. Seen as such, a symbol is not one-dimensional data, but rather like a quantum hologram of today's new physics, capable, even in its smallest part, of lighting up within us a three-dimensional image of the greater whole. In this light we can understand Jung's definition of the challenge posed by our movement into the psyche:

> In many cases in psychiatry, the patient who comes to us has a story that is not told, and which as a rule no one knows of. To my mind, therapy only really begins after the investigation of the wholly personal story. It is the patient's secret, the rock against which he is shattered. If I know his secret story, I have a key to

the treatment. The doctor's task is to find out how to gain that knowledge. In most cases exploration of the conscious material is insufficient. Sometimes an association test can open the way; so can the interpretation of dreams, or long and patient human contact with the individual. In therapy the problem is always the whole person, never the symptom alone. We must ask questions which challenge the whole personality.[14]

What defines depth psychology today, in contrast to other forms of psychology, medical psychiatry, and pharmacological approaches to healing, is its emphasis upon participation with symptom beyond resolution of health. The goal is not only the abeyance of symptom, but rather it is the pursuit of that symptom to its unknown point of origin. "Why did that feeling come upon me in the way it did?" "Why did I act that way?" "Why can't I change this?" This journey does not end with the relief of symptoms, nor with the achievement of mental recognition of a symptom's root, but extends beyond these end-points to our eventual emotional participation with the truth such that it transforms us, providing a change of heart on the other side of which we look anew at ourselves and our relationship to the world in which we live. The depth psychological approach is also significantly different from other psychological methods (and most modern methods in general), in that it goes around the content, the dream, the image or symptom, rather than slashing head-on into it. In repeatedly circling around an image and amplifying it through the introduction of related myths and symbols, one hopes to catch sight of an unconscious element that is hidden from the conscious view.

It is this approach, a nonlinear, multi-turned consideration that is undertaken here in pursuit of Crop Circles. This approach may be taxing for some readers, but such a slow, circuitous advance would seem to be of particular value in looking at something whose very nature is mysterious and unknown to us. This mode of approach leads much of the content of this book to be about things other than Crop Circles and this may be frustrating or seem odd to some readers. Please keep in mind that such a roundabout approach serves a deeper purpose: to amplify its nature and provide a meaningful context for this mystery.

For thousands of years, traditional cultures placed value upon the function that the unconscious serves in regulating this transforming movement within our psyches. The Jewish Talmud instructs a multiplicity of ways to interpret dreams. The Old Testament tells the story of Joseph in Egypt, who successfully interprets the Pharoah's dreams, illustrating the importance of dream interpretation to the ancient Hebrews and Egyptians. The ancient Greeks revered dreams and other signs, as do Native North and South American, African, and Australian aboriginal traditional cultures today. Nearly all Asian cultures have a historical attachment to such beliefs, as does the Islamic faith. Jung used the breadth of these traditional forms of interpretation to complement our modern perspective. In addition to ancient modes of dream interpretation, the rich wealth of our stories, myths, rituals, beliefs, and literature all stand before us as routes by which to understand and attend to our inner calling, exemplifying the operation of archetypal dynamics. No culture before ours has had access to such a broad array, or seen reflected more brightly, the psyche's abundant depth of pageantry.

> Concern with the psychology of primitives, with folklore, mythology, and the comparative history of religions opens the eyes to the wide horizons of the human psyche and in addition it gives that indispensable aid we so urgently need for the understanding of unconscious processes. Only when we see in what shape and what guise dream symbols, which are apparently unique, appear on the historical and ethnic scene, can we really understand what they are pointing at.[15]

The depth psychological method opens up the possibility of healing, as did previous cultures' attendance to the images of vision and dream. In doing so, it enables us to reconnect with what has been cut off by our cultural identification with conscious awareness, allowing our participation "with the unconscious that nourished our ancestors—[with] dream, vision, ritual, and religious experience—[which] are largely lost to us, dismissed by our modern mind as primitive or superstitious."[16] However, it does so at a *whole new level.*

Our modern awareness offers us the objectivity to participate with a symbol or symptom, without necessarily getting lost in our personal history, our society's collective experience of that symptom or symbol, or losing it in other outside factors. Today, we possess the steely separation of awareness necessary to view the symbols of our lives plainly in their own truth. Benefiting both from the scientific method and from modern self-consciousness, today we can participate with the same living unconscious that was revered by our ancestors. Yet, we can do so with less danger of falling victim to it and with a greater possibility of engaging with it constructively. The strength of our modern self-awareness offers us the capability of relating to our unconscious contents objectively. However, such participation requires a voluntary sacrifice of our ego's certainty and a willingness to proceed into the unknown inside of us—a chosen release of the illusion that we know what we'll find there. Through such voluntary "not-knowing," we make room for something new to emerge from the fertile bed of the unconscious. Through such participation, today we are able to combine the first strand of human impetus—the drive to know consciously, accurately, and objectively—with the second strand of human impetus—the need to participate with the unknown depths in the world and in ourselves, which we find in myth and in the presentations of the unconscious.

Because a symbol, active in our psyche, reaches across the barrier from consciousness to unconsciousness; because it exists for us simultaneously cognitively and emotionally, abstractly and concretely; because it dominates our conscious will and intention and affects us in ways often beyond our control; in its process, we witness the living truth of a symbol's capacity to contain within it things that would otherwise be opposite. Its paradoxical nature bridges across the entire plain of our psyche: rooted in the unconscious—in an archetypal base; budding in the "unspeakability" of the symptom and through our attendance to it; blooming forth as a new awareness. Here something almost inexplicable happens. What we once were completely unaware of becomes known to us and lived by us—a truth we once never knew is suddenly a part of us. Like a quantum jump, when something clicks, awareness leaps across from unconsciousness into consciousness within us, and we are no longer the same.

The possibility of such growth has, for the mystics of many cultures, pointed toward the realization of the transpersonal and unifying ground of the psyche. In modern times, such questions are regarded philosophically and usually reduced to intellectual puzzles about the physical constitution of our world, or the relative merits of our perception of our relationship to it. However, in this witnessing of the stunning capacity of psyche for transformation (not just cumulative growth), we can begin to realize why the inner world has often been regarded as pointing us toward a mystery that exceeds the grasp of the rational strand of consciousness, ultimately directing us toward age-old philosophical, religious, and moral questions.

Like a snowflake or a fingerprint, each one unique, a dream occurs only once. Each night the world gives birth anew through us, and our task is one of attendance to this arrival. Hosting our dreams requires both our linear, scientific-minded conscious discrimination and also something more difficult for us today. If we are to allow the mythic amplification of a symbol to really impact us, we must allow ourselves to become *subject to it*. As the poet Rilke wrote, "the continuity becomes everywhere apparent, and where some obscurity remains it is of the sort that demands not clearing up but subjection."[17]

> None of us asks to be confronted in the night with mysteries, oracles, and conundrums, to have something barge into our inner lives that we did not invite. . . . A dream will help us if we are willing to dwell for a time within its ambiguities without resolving them, to sink into its depths without always knowing when—or where—we shall surface. . . .[18]

Now—in this moment—we are presented with something new. Crop Circles are a mystery in our response to which we continue to be able to draw upon the strands of both science and mythology—their form and image seems to point us toward both. The scientific study of its qualities enables us to feel grounded in the authenticity of its reality and genuine mystery. Yet, by their very nature, Crop Circles speak to our imagination's capacity for deepest wonder; their images and new appearance both delight us and bring us face to face with tremendous awe and perhaps even fear (or other challenging psychological states). As a Jungian interpretation, this book examines the symbols associated with Crop Circles, both within the universality of their imagery and within the context of those images being set into our modern moment. It is only in this way that we can place their particular symbolic reference into a dynamic, meaningful arrangement. Attendance to this setting enables our placing the world "dream" of Crop

Circles in the context of world reality. In looking not only at the phenomenon but at its context too, we expand the framework of our consideration of its mystery to the appropriate scope, for Crop Circles do not arrive at some random time or place but before us now into our present moment. When we engage with the whole of its qualities, we must necessarily place ourselves into context with it, and in doing so we begin the process of making its meaning real for us. In this way, in searching for its story, we may discover a story of our own that is not yet told.

ONE

BODY OF EVIDENCE

There are two ways to be fooled, one is to believe what isn't true; the
other is to refuse to believe what is true.

—SØREN KIERKEGAARD

For those farmers and countryfolk who first came upon the flattened, wide
areas in their field, the way in which Crop Circles appeared allowed each
discoverer to make of them what they would for themselves. The formations have been occurring for centuries, especially in England, coming from
spring to fall and peaking in frequency in late summer before the harvest.
Initially only circles, Crop Circles came to prominence in the late 1980s,
partly due to their sudden explosion in frequency and increase in geometric
complexity. But this sudden appearance overshadows a longer historic record that serves to refute the dismissal of the phenomenon as a hoax. Archival records of the phenomenon are numerous: an infamous woodcut from
1678; American anthropological records as early as 1853; an 1880 *Nature*
magazine article from England; and newspaper reports from Australia in
the 1960s and the Canadian Prairie in the 1970s. Farmers in Europe and
North America have recorded their observance of them during the 1920s,
1930s, 1940s, and 1950s onward; Air Force pilots and others reported seeing them during World War II.[1] Crop Circles occur in nearly every kind
of cereal crop and grain, including wheat, rye, barley, rape, oats, and corn,
as well as in grass, rice, and other vegetation. While predominantly found

in England, they appear regularly in Canada, Australia, New Zealand, the United States, throughout Europe, and elsewhere. Occurring much more frequently since 1989, Crop Circles are usually found in numbers from 100 to 250 annually worldwide.[2] Today they are often hundreds of feet in diameter, complex, intricately woven, and geometrically precise, and the majesty of each one's appearance makes it singularly striking to witness. While developing into more complicated forms, the formations continue to be individual and unique. As with Nature's creations, no two are ever the same, and perhaps what is most interesting about the phenomenon is its continuing evolution.

This chapter presents an overview of the phenomenon and an introduction to the modern scientific evidence for its authenticity, both of which have been documented extensively. This evidence consists of physical, chemical, biological, cellular, and germinal changes to the plants themselves. Electromagnetic changes have also been reported in some of the affected formation areas. Additional evidence, including historic documentation, the scope and intelligent nature of their design, and other extraordinary factors (which have been reported repeatedly) all serve to augment the overwhelming evidence for the existence of this phenomenon as a genuine mystery.

Although scientific evidence is available today to provide a clear awareness of the authentic mystery of the phenomenon, this evidence leaves us with the same question that faced the farmers who were the first to discover them: what to make of it for ourselves. While the scientific facts enable the possibility of a more conscious appreciation of the phenomenon, this knowledge leads to deeper inquiry rather than to a solution. In looking at this evidence, we know that we are dealing with something special, but the question of how to make sense of that specialness remains for each one of us. Carl Sagan has famously said that extraordinary claims carry the burden of extraordinary evidence. However, in the case of this phenomenon as it is before us today, it is not the lack of evidence that keeps us from engaging with it, but rather our psychological and culturally reinforced unwillingness to look directly at that evidence. Combined with our own natural self-doubt, our tendency to disbelieve the extraordinary is reinforced by cultural conditioning that implies an expectation of shaming for believing "in the impossible." Overcoming this blockage is both a psychological and moral challenge. However, today we are aided by the presence of scientific evidence that establishes a clear division between genuine formations and human-made hoaxing incidents, validating the authentic mystery of this phenomenon. In the face of these facts, our continued dismissal of the phenomenon is simply a form of Kierkegaard's latter condition—foolishness through refusing "to believe what is true."

What gave Crop Circles validity to the farmers who discovered them and looked at them closely enough was the presence of physical changes in the plants themselves. Uniformly worldwide, the flat appearance of the circle is generated not by the stems of the plants being broken down or forced over, but by a ninety-degree bending of the plant itself at the root node (the first node above ground) in many of the affected plants. In the area of the design plants show: bent rather than broken stems (the plants constructing the design are not pushed over as they would be in a hoax, but rather anatomically altered), stretched plant nodes (the part of the plant at which its sections are joined together are extended) and expulsion cavities (the appearance of being blown out from the inside at lower nodes). In the formation's construction, the grain itself is woven together flat along the ground, with one layer beneath the next set at cross angles, fans of wheat one below the next, folded gracefully together and hidden beneath the formation's top surface. Despite these anatomical changes, plants remain fully alive and will continue to grow. Within days they will begin to reorient themselves toward the sun, and slowly, one by one, once again stand up. Also noticeable to farmers is the fact that the plants themselves are left unbruised, even crops that bruise easily or snap when bent by force. While these anatomical changes alone distinguish Crop Circles from human-made hoaxes, the farmers, who most often discover the formations, also attest to the formation's authenticity. Speaking to the lack of evidence of intrusion found, they argue that if there had been anyone on their land they would know, often noting the absence of broken stems and the lack of footprints in their chalk, dry or wet, muddy fields. Often to their own continuing astonishment, farmers continue to report this, following their discovery of a Crop Circle in their fields. Despite their testimony and the presence of this physical evidence, it was only with the discovery of additional scientific evidence that the phenomenon began to be recognized as authentically enigmatic.

The anatomical anomalies in the affected plants, described above, were first publicly documented in a scientific journal by biophysicist W. C. Levengood in 1994. Between 1994 and 1999, Levengood published three peer-reviewed scientific papers on the study of the changes to the plants in national and international journals (he is the author of forty-seven other peer-reviewed papers). Published in 1994, his first article documented the anatomical anomalies in the formations, including the expansion of the stem nodes. Levengood and others have since documented that changes in node length are found to be present with linearly decreasing effect from the center of the formation out into the surrounding crop. Even plants left standing within the formation and surrounding plants outside of the formation show the presence of this effect. Since that time, further research has found that changes in node length follow the widely applied Beer-Lambert principle of physics.[3]

However, along with externally visible physical changes, Levengood also noticed two less obvious yet startling categories of change to the plants themselves: cellular and germinal. Utilizing an optical microscope, in hundreds of international plant samples tested, Levengood observed an alteration of the cellular walls within the bract tissue in affected plant nodes: "On the microscopic level, abnormal enlargement of cell wall pits in bract tissue (a thin membrane which surrounds the seed-head and through which nutrients pass to the developing seed) were found."[4] This change, which reflects sudden heating from inside the plants, enables easier nutrient transfer to the developing seed embryos. This change in cell structure, including expanded and elongated cell wall pits, is clearly evident in microscopic photo images.[5] In addition, and likely in connection to these changes, changes to the appearance and germinal qualities of the seeds were also found. Nancy Talbott (a co-researcher who later worked with Levengood) summarized the three categories of change to the seed: the absence of seeds in normal-appearing seed-heads, stunted and malformed seeds in normal-appearing seed-heads, and a marked alteration in seed germination and growth patterns (both depressed and increased). When a Crop Circle formation has arrived early in the plant's life cycle, later growth in seed-head size is reduced dramatically, or the seeds themselves may be stunted. Further, Talbott describes, "however—and this is terribly interesting—if a crop formation occurs in a much more mature crop, then what we see is extremely energized seeds, so that they then reproduce at five times the normal rate. . . . Now, whatever in the world is doing this, I should think would be of great interest to anybody."[6]

As one might expect, these changes to the seeds and to their growth rates are reflected in changes to later plant growth. New growth in the following years seem to mirror, either by overgrowth or by lack of growth, the shape in which the previous year's Crop Circle appeared. Brilliant photo illustration of this effect can be seen online.[7] These changes have been noted repeatedly by farmers and researchers: Burke, Levengood, and Talbott (BLT) describe a 1999 formation at Barbury Castle, England, in which "as the new crop began to grow in the field, the 'ghost' of the 1999 formation could easily be seen, in spite of the fact that the field had been tilled and re-planted as usual . . . the areas which had been flattened in 1999 were both a darker green in color than the rest of the crop, and they were at least 6–8 inches taller."[8]

In 1995, Levengood added to these findings with an article in which he noted the presence of iron magnetite deposits on the plants. These particles, which seem related to micrometeorite dust in the atmosphere, are also found to be present in the soil beneath the formations themselves. This iron magnetite becomes fused with the wheat and earth within the formations—occasionally to such a degree that the wheat itself can be picked up with a magnet. One can view an example of the presence of metallic particles within the affected crop online and in the documentary film *Quest for Truth* (2002)—which along with Suzanne Taylor's *What on Earth? Inside the Crop Circle Mystery* (2009) is highly recommended. As with the changes in node length, these mysterious magnetic particles also follow a linear distribution pattern outward from the center of the formation into surrounding crops, and are also found to be present on non-flattened crops present within the formation.

Levengood and the BLT team pioneered the vast depth of scientific research that has been performed on samples from the formations, and they continue to do so today. (If you find this research as fascinating as I do, I encourage you to support their nonprofit organization with a U.S. tax deductible donation: www.bltresearch.com.) Other studies continue to confirm these initial findings, adding new evidence, corroborating, and building upon them. Like many others, Haselhoff (2001) has confirmed the node length and germination tests and also performed an interesting hypothetical analysis of node lengths in the hopes of learning more about the causation of the formations (further discussed in Chapter Eight).

Changes in electromagnetic radiation have also been frequently reported in the area of formations. A newspaper report from Manitoba, Canada, describes a 1970s account:

> With a radiation detector they went over the field and discovered four or five patches where radiation counts were four times higher than the count for the rest of the field. Checks with scientists revealed these radiation jumps were not found naturally in the area. Two weeks later, the men returned with the radiation detector to the same spot, and a provincial geologist. Even though heavy rains had fallen, and the field had been ploughed since the first check, the increase in radiation in the same patches was easily detectable. (Brandon *Sun*, July 11, 1975)

Andrews has claimed to have found evidence of changes in the electromagnetic radiation levels in genuine formations, as well as a variance in the magnetic field around them—consistently off true north by five degrees.[9] Vigay finds this regularly, including a reported eight-degree variance[10] and pilots have reported this as well.[11] These findings echo the description of Roger Sear, who found a "Witch's ring," as they were sometimes called, swirled into grass near Cissbury Ring, England, in July of 1927 or 1928:

> [He] considered it not too out of the ordinary, as he had seen and entered other such circles during the same era in the countryside around his home village. Unusual effects had been noticed in his previous encounters, including the magnetization of a knife stuck into the soil at the center, a tickling sensation in the feet, the refusal of a dog to enter, and the magnetization and hence effective destruction of an Ingersol pocket watch.[12]

Sear also reports a compass going haywire, animals refusing to enter the circles, grass and bicycles being electrically charged after being left in a formation for a time, as well as the presence of an electrical burning smell and experiencing headaches after visiting a later formation.[13] Thomas observes that similar electromagnetic effects have been observed in formations in the same fields in the 1990s.[14] These electromagnetic energies are thought to account for the frequent reports of electrical equipment failure and other anomalies within formations. Nearly every book, film, and experienced researcher relates such accounts, which include the sudden draining of previously charged batteries (including new ones), upon entering the circle, and photo, video, and sound equipment failing to operate within formations, yet functioning normally again outside; even BBC video equipment has been damaged by such effects.[15] Hein (2002) recounts the common phenomenon of magnetic compasses losing their direction and, more rarely, watches slowing down or speeding up. Pringle reports car and tractor engines cutting out around formations, which may somehow be explained by the presence of unusual electromagnetic energy in the formations. "Work with electrostatic volt meters has [shown] distinct anomalies in natural electrical fields at circle sites."[16] Vigay's research concluded with the observation that "whatever is making the corn circles is draining electrical energy away from corn inside the formation. It is as if the corn has been 'earthed.'"[17] There are innumerable incidents of electric anomalies and electrostatic discharge experienced in and around genuine formations by visitors.

In addition to these changes, biochemical changes in affected plants have also been found throughout the history of research into the phenomenon. Pringle reports changes in both plants and soil taken from inside formations and compared to control samples, having a 2:1 variation in the nitrate/nitrogen content of samples taken from genuine circles.[18] Thomas describes a 1995 study, conducted through a British government services office—the Agricultural Development and Advisory Service, a division of the Ministry of Agriculture—in which an increase in the nitrogen/nitrate ration was found to be present.[19] Sadly, despite this study being paid for, the agency was shut down shortly afterward, apparently due to a Member of Parliament's complaint about "wasting resources on such nonsensical frivolities."[20] Early Crop Circle researcher Pat Delgado describes a 1990 study of crop and soil samples examined using radionics analysis at Delawarr Laboratories in the U.K. Compared to control samples, samples from a new crop in the affected area shortly after a formation had occurred showed depletion and elevation of nutrients, including, again, a 2:1 loss of nitrates, phosphates, and sulfur and an excess of cobalt, carbon, plutonium, and zinc These effects were thought to have occurred as a result of a rapid, extreme heating process.[21]

In 2002, BLT Research, funded by Lawrence Rockefeller, completed a study into X-ray refraction within clay and mineral materials in the area of a formation. Their completed report can be viewed online.[22] Diane Conrad, a geologist in Logan, Utah, conceived of the experiment in 1996 while listening to a local radio interview with Nancy Talbott. A formation had recently been found nearby and she had visited it. Having completed her thesis on heat effects on clay minerals, Conrad knew that heat effects would leave evidence in the form of changes in the degree of crystallization in soil minerals.

In conducting this experiment, samples were taken from a formation in Edmonton, Alberta, Canada, in 1999, and in order to avoid previous forms of criticism, outside agencies and scientists were used exclusively throughout this project. "These scientists were carefully chosen, not only for their specific expertise, but because they were unaware of the phenomenon, thus ruling out any potential assertions by skeptics of 'experimenter bias.'" They included Dartmouth College geologist and mineralogist R. C. Reynolds, who completed the mineralogical review. Reynolds is "described by his colleagues as 'a brilliant scientist and without any exaggeration . . . the best known expert in the world of X-ray diffraction analysis of finely-dispersed layer compounds . . . of clay minerals.'"[23] After examining the experiment's results, Reynolds concluded, "in short, I believe that our present knowledge provides no explanation for the observed decrease in peak breadth with respect to proximity to the center of the Crop Circle."[24] A further study by BLT Research shows that the decrease in KI (Kubler index) value correlates with the node length changes at 99 percent certainty. Thus, it is certain that whatever caused the changes in crystallization of soil minerals also caused the plant abnormalities.

Analyses made of Crop Circle locations in England in 1989 and 1990 by Grist (1991), and ten years later by Page and Broughton (1999), point out that formations occurred exclusively in areas where groundwater lay close to the surface. It is believed that the presence of water may be related to the process by which the formations occur, as electrical charge is generated as water recedes away from the surface.[25] Broughton and Page noticed that the timing and location of formations follows the summer's slow recession of the aquifer. As the water recedes in the summer months new Crop Circles are only found within that new smaller area,[26] and 93 percent of formations are discovered within the aquifer area or in chalky soil (or near limestone in North America). It is also frequently reported that formations occur the night of rainfall or shortly thereafter.

Although one might begin to imagine possibilities, physical, biochemical, cellular, electromagnetic, and germinal changes to physical objects simply cannot be counterfeited. Any single one of these factors would alone be sufficient ground to authenticate the phenomenon's mystery. However, taken in concert, each discovery reinforces the results found in the next, constructing an authoritative argument to refute the explanation of hoaxing as the cause of the phenomenon. Changes to the seeds inside a grain plant's seed-head cannot be faked, nor can germinal changes to those seeds be counterfeited. Can one forge a bend in the root node of a still-growing plant to a ninety-degree angle? Can stretched or blown-out plant nodes following a perfect linear distribution outward from the center of each formation be faked? Can a hoax change plants on a cellular level?

It is simply not possible to fake changes to the plants' biochemistry or cellular structure, or the often-reported changes in electromagnetic radiation. The presence of iron magnetite particles infused into the plants, and node length changes following the same linear distribution, offer additional certainty. While the dismissal of Crop Circles as a hoax is perhaps the most common response to the phenomenon, and is an automatic first response of modern human nature, such an explanation does not withstand the test of further examination. As *each one* of these changes is, *in itself,* simply not possible to fake, this scientific body of evidence constitutes an insurmountable challenge to the dismissal of this phenomenon as a hoax.

Since the late 1980s, some percentage of Crop Circle formations have been produced by human hoaxers (more so in Britain than anywhere else). Beyond the simple fakes often found in North America to be the works of teenagers, in the U.K. there is a well-organized hoaxing system that produces elaborate and even beautiful formations. However, these hoaxes display none of the scientific alterations described herein. The history and psychology of hoaxing is considered further in the next chapter.

Prior to this century many of the great discoveries in science were made by amateur researchers—even Einstein was working as a patent clerk when he wrote his most important work. If you are somewhat skeptical, yet open to finding out the truth (no matter how strange), I encourage you to try to *discover* this evidence *for yourself.* A great many of these experiments can be done on your own. Anatomical changes can be viewed (and photographed) on your own; radiation gauges and electrostatic meters are not too expensive. So get creative! As this chapter illustrates, thoughtful researchers have come up with their own approaches, to provide experiments to investigate this phenomenon. This can be done not just in England, but in many countries around the world. There is something about our moment in time (as will be discussed further) in which *the onus is being placed upon the individual* to become his and her own authority, rather than relying upon institutions to tell us what we should or should not believe. Crop Circles are one more example of this, and the way in which they exist offers us the opportunity to participate in one of the most incredible and important phenomena of the ages for ourselves! Take a chance and strike out on your own (or bring some friends).

The skeptics who have attacked pieces of this scientific evidence have tended to question a particular experimenter's method. By attacking a particular experiment or experimenter, skeptics avoid having to face the sum total of all the collective evidence and the fact that it is now clear that this evidence fits together more and more as it is added to and refined. Along with our own inspection of anatomical changes to the plants, and scientific investigation of the factors listed above, as well as potential new ones, Pringle suggests an additional method by which to, at least partially, determine a Crop Circle's authenticity for ourselves. She notes that there is a film present in virgin crops that, when rubbed against, disappears. "So, if you have the privilege of entering an immature crop circle and observe this grey film intact, not just at surface level but right through all levels down to the ground, you have every right to be excited over the prospect of being in a genuine formation."[27]

Today, one of the hallmarks of authenticity in Crop Circles is the depth and quality of the weaving and crop lay that is evident in genuine formations. While modern hoaxers are creating large, elaborate formations in England, their works lack all of the anatomic changes noted above. Additionally, they also lack the interior quality of construction found in genuine formations. Nearly every Crop Circle expresses in the lay of its wheat the spiral, the most common design element in nature. Most of the floors of the formations spread out in a radial weave from the center of the circle. Unlike the hoaxes, the wheat in most (but not all) authentic formations is flattened, smoothly level with the ground. The wheat in these formations is not simply pushed over, but rather woven together, layer beneath layer, often in a tiered spiral fan. Perhaps the most astonishing demonstration of this quality came in the three-dimensionally woven Breadbasket formation in 1999. It was harvested nearly immediately after its discovery, but luckily captured on video and film.[28] This amazing woven construction is part of the hallmark of many genuine formations and can be seen in a great many of them (for examples, see U.K., East Field July, 2009[29] and Ohio, U.S.A., 2005[30]). However, this woven quality can be found to a lesser degree in almost every genuine formation floor, where the overlapping stalk layers are laid at cross-angles. These layers are often placed together so tightly that they glint from the air—their smoothly flattened surface made reflective . This complexity and intricacy of construction is also displayed in the "seamless curves"[31] of the perimeter walls of formations—the outer edges left standing around the flattened design and the consistently precise geometry often oriented around central standing stalks.

The size of many modern formations is also considered to be an impediment to hoaxing. The 2001 Milk Hill circle covered an area of 700,000 square feet, containing 409 circles, laid perfectly smoothly and woven beautifully, across a diameter of 900 feet. It was suggested that this would have taken weeks to hoax and it appeared overnight, during a heavy rainstorm. Such scope speaks to the difficulty of creating huge formations in a short amount of time. The 1996 Julia set formation found at Stonehenge was formed less than a hundred feet from a busy highway and numerous witnesses cannot account for its sudden appearance in less than forty-five minutes, in broad daylight.[32]

Early in July 1996 a pilot flew a light aircraft over the field opposite Stonehenge at 5:50 p.m., and saw nothing in the field. Half an hour later, a second pilot spotted the enormous and spectacular Julia Set in the previously empty field, measuring some 915' by 508' in the wheat. A gamekeeper and a security guard at the monument both confirm that the formation was not there in the morning, but had appeared by the evening, and there is evidence from the police that the pictogram formed in under 15 minutes.[33]

I have spoken with a Canadian tourist who was at Stonehenge on the day that this formation was discovered and he reports asking the staff there about Crop Circles. They replied that they hadn't had any there recently, to which he responded, "Well, then what's that?" pointing out the recently arrived formation. The pilot's account can be verified due to the presence of the nearby British Air Force base that requires that all flights passing through be registered. Their passage both coming and going was monitored and recorded by both the air base and by air traffic control. The specific time of their departure was 5:15 p.m.; their return, when the formation was now visible, was 6:00 p.m. (Sunday, July 7, 1996).[34] In this case, the passenger and second witness was a medical doctor.

Along with the issues of scope, size, and time, the frequently reported presence of strong physical effects, bodily sensations, and even strong emotional responses among visitors to the formations also serve as evidence. Reports of such physical sensations are much more frequent among visitors to authentic circles visited in the first few days after their discovery, but most visitors to Crop Circles report either little or no bodily sensation. Experiences can vary strongly, even within the same circle. Other generally reported effects vary from an experience of joy or a sense of increased well-being, to negative feelings including headaches, disorientation, nausea, and a sense of being overwhelmed or afraid. Spatial or directional disorientation is also a particularly common effect. The strongest positive physical effects include reports of spontaneous healing.[35] Pringle has also documented changes in hormone levels to an unexplained degree in the endocrine system of visitors to Crop Circles.[36] Some people also report having had the urge to meditate or lie down in a particular spot. This effect has even been noticed in animals. Dogs, birds, and other creatures have been noted avoiding the circle area or acting strangely inside of them.[37] Perhaps most commonly, as one English farmer described it to me, there is simply "a feeling of a presence."

Even more curious, however, are the reports of photographic distortions, which seem to echo the electromagnetic changes that are reported with a subtle or slight distortion of time (these are considered in greater detail in Chapter Eight) and the sighting of luminous spherical objects called Balls of Light (or BOLs) in and around the formations, both during the day and at night. Such evidence was considered entirely secondary until observers began catching moving pictures of luminous Balls of Light near the formations on video. These sightings can be viewed online or on documentary videos, and are also discussed further in Chapter Eight. Such sightings are echoed historically in the names given to two common locations for Crop Circle discoveries and Ball of Light sightings: Golden Ball Hill and Silbury Hill (meaning "Hill of the Shining Ones"). The latter site is recognized as one of the largest Neolithic mound dwellings of human construction of its type in European prehistory.

Today, a strong correlation is evident between such ancient archeological sites and Crop Circles. The majority of formations are found in an area of English countryside covered by stone circles and ancient mound dwellings—places of continued human worship across thousands of years. Megaliths or henges (raised-stone sites) and chambered tombs have been built in this area since at least 2500 BC and perhaps even before the construction of the Egyptian pyramids. It is on top of these sites, or in reference to them, that Crop Circles frequently appear. Stonehenge, Avebury, and other less well-known stone circles and mounds are frequent homes for the formations. Noted authorities on stone circle design and sacred geometry John Martineau and John Michell have observed that the formations will take the design of these stone circles into precise account in their orientation, pattern, and geometry.[38] They are often found integrated into the position and design of formations, such as England's great chalk White Horses, gigantic rock icons carved into hillsides.[39] However, today, Crop Circles not only appear in reference to ancient English landmarks and early sites of worship and habitation, but also at or near modern religious sites and communities worldwide.

Crop circles in Canada and the United States are often found near religious communities, churches, native religious sites, graveyards, and burial grounds. In 1925, on a farm in Leeshore, Alberta, Canada, small circles were found in wheat, flattened right down to the ground. Paul Anderson interestingly points out that Leeshore, the tiny farming community of Lamont County, has the oldest Ukrainian settlements in Canada (dating back to 1894) and the greatest number of churches per capita in North America. One of the most well-known ancient human dwelling sites in America is Serpent Mound. It was the location of a formation in August 2003. In 2003 and 2004, formations near Fairfield, California, occurred in a field directly across from a church and nearby cemetery.[40] The proximity of Crop Circles to sacred sites is a relationship also reflected in the evolution of the phenomenon's imagery.

Prior to 1978, shapes other than circles were found only rarely.[41] In 1983, one of the first evolutions of the phenomenon into more complicated forms was discovered by British scientist Colin Andrews. He was astonished on the morning of June 19, when he discovered a five-circle formation, one large central circle with four smaller surrounding circles in the form of the Celtic cross—a local religious symbol incorporating elements of both pagan and Christian influence. On that morning, he witnessed one of the first evolutionary steps of the phenomenon beyond its characteristic circular shape. Andrews, an engineer and one of the earliest dedicated researchers, was also deeply touched by this discovery, as he had been hoping for a formation near his home. He was "utterly amazed," because the night before he had been picturing just this shape.[42]

From then on, a steady increase in complexity within the circle and ring form took place annually. In 1989, circles and rings were supplanted by pictograms—bars appeared between circles and clearly new shapes occurred, such as keys in 1990. The nineties saw the "beginning of life" designs, including insectograms, DNA-like string images, and solar systems. In 1991, formations began to incorporate the Mandlebrot set and Julia sets—the modern mathematical equations behind fractal computer imagery. In the late nineties, the phenomenon blossomed into a string of breathtaking images, large precision shapes of intricate harmony and elegance. As a part of this evolution, coherent symbols appeared that had meaning within the world's religious and mythological traditions. Images representing and containing the Jewish Kabbalah's Tree of Life,[43] Star of David,[44] and

Menorah;[45] the Christian Vesica Pisces (with its connection to Glastonbury Tor)[46] and numerous Celtic crosses; the Buddhist Wheel of Dharma[47] and symbols recognized universally within Christian, pagan, Hindu, Native, and other world cultures.

This growth in complexity within the phenomenon is present both chronologically and geographically. While each year the circles appear more advanced, they evolve from a center of sophistication in the U.K., outward toward the rest of the world. Despite the continuing evolution of the phenomenon globally, the formations in England remain more complex and intricate than those found elsewhere.

Within the evolution of the phenomenon, each new formation emerges original and unique; each one has its own singular aesthetic quality and emotive effect. Yet, common to all Crop Circles, and perhaps what is most impacting about them, is their explicit meaningful and intelligent design. The modern phenomenon shows symbols that are explicitly intentional—images such as those from the Mandlebrot set and iconic images from religion are clear, intelligible, and direct forms of communication. More subtly, however, intention is also displayed in the construction of the formations themselves. Often single flowers of another species are left standing untouched in the midst of grain laid flat and woven together; center stalks are often left standing together and bird's nests can be found untouched. In genuine formations, the pattern often weaves in and out, with the grass laid exactly at cross-angles, blooming forth with perfect geometry. Some are constructed so tightly and woven so precisely that they reflect the sunlight when seen from the air. Beneath the explicit coherence in symbols and past the visible symmetry of construction lie an innate harmony and an intentional perfection of design. Gerald Hawkins (a former chairman of the Astronomy Department at Boston University) discovered the presence of diatonic ratios (the ratios found in musical scales and elsewhere) within the formations. In their construction, there exists an inner self-reference and a correspondence to geometric theorems, which many believe to be an additional standard by which to authenticate genuine circles.

Hawkins noticed that some of the most visually striking of the crop circle patterns embodied geometric theorems that express specific numerical relationships among the areas of various circles, triangles, and other shapes making up the patterns.[48]

It is now recognized that, in the construction of genuine formations, there is a multilayered adherence to the rules of sacred geometry. Sacred geometry is exemplified by the presence of the golden section, a harmonic ratio of design in which the lesser part is in an equivalent ratio to the greater part, as the greater part is to the whole. Found throughout Nature, including within our physical anatomy, this ratio is often illustrated using the image of the nautilus shell, the growth of which repeats this ratio. This school of design precedes ancient Greece, and its images illustrate the ratio while reminding us of the sacred harmony in Nature's own design. The presence of this harmony within a creation was cited by the ancient Greeks as "proof of the sacred intention" of the artist. Within the design of genuine Crop Circles this same ratio abounds. The perfection and creative use of sacred geometry within the formations continues to astound those who study it. Geometer and author John Martineau notes that not only is sacred geometry found in the Crop Circles themselves but also in their orientation to stone circles around them: "the geometrical characteristics of crop circles can be extended to stone circles and even the solar system. Whoever the circlemakers are, they know their stuff!" The depth of complexity found in the formations is best understood visually, and further descriptions of this material can be found in Martineau's excellent book, *Crop Circle Geometry*, as well as in the documentary *Crop Circles: Quest for Truth*[49] and in other sources on Crop Circle geometry.[50]

Among the earliest formations examined by Hawkins, sixteen out of twenty-five contained diatonic ratios (a coincidence statistically possible only once in 400,000).[51] He also observes that formations of several hundred feet were conforming to the principles of this geometry "within a few inches of accuracy." This same precision continues to this day. Hoaxes, on the other hand, consistently fail to display the degree of inherently harmonious geometry found in authentic formations.

Through further in-depth analysis of the phenomenon's geometry, Hawkins found that Crop Circle design incorporates innovative and previously unseen use of mathematical principles. Examining the ratios present in Crop Circle construction, he discovered the use of principles that fit in with Euclidean theorems, but were not present there nor anywhere else in geometric theory. "Proving a theorem is one thing . . . but creating one is altogether a much harder proposition."[52] Hawkins put this to the test, taking out advertisements in popular math and science magazines seeing if anyone could come up with the theories he had found to be present in Crop Circle geometry. Given the first new theory that he discovered, respondents were supposed to figure out the second theory (which he found by accident). None did. While displaying these profound geometric complexities and ingenuity, the formations are also consistently beautiful and display an artistic sensibility, each new formation an original work within an ever-increasing evolution of the overall phenomenon in form and design.

Inclusion of the observation of such qualities within the nature of the formations opens up our participation with the Crop Circle's essential mystery, rather than closing it. What does it say about the agent of this phenomenon that they design using sacred geometry? Does this not require us to open up our view of them? Looking closely at the facts of the phenomenon's physical evidence begins a broadening process, one in which our preconceived notions about the phenomenon may begin to seem too small. Each of these qualities opens the imagination's possibilities and yet simultaneously constricts the phenomenon into a definite reality: the universality evident in its symbols and geometry; its occurrence near ancient and modern sites of worship and burial; its construction using Nature's methods of design; our witness of the Balls of Light and photographic anomalies; the phenomenon's evolution and geometric ingenuity; its concentration in England and the historical and geographic associations found to it there; its emotional and bodily effects; the feeling of "a presence" experienced by some. As we become aware of each one of these qualities, it raises a new post upon which to unfold the tent of our own consideration. Each new element of understanding ignites a new torch in the nighttime of our not knowing. Yet, while our imagination may begin to take flight through consideration of the phenomenon's various aspects, the reality of the scientific evidence grounds our consideration.

In this phenomenon, we are not coming upon the events of a science fiction novel, a fantasy, an old folk tale, or a myth. Crop Circles exist as a *living mystery* and their source is *unexplained*. In the phenomenon's physical authenticity—the body of evidence of its science—we meet the first hurdle to overcome in facing it and the basis upon which our process of further investigation rests. In providing us with such grounds, the phenomenon offers us its merit for pursuit—a kind of safe haven to which we can return if we begin to question the value of our journey of inquiry. And such a safe haven is necessary because considering this phenomenon may open a stormy and untamed sea of mixed emotions—fear, denial, and even anger, as well as joy and wonder. To accept the physical reality of the scientific evidence is to venture toward uncharted territory and discover oneself facing what the German theologist Rudolph Otto dubbed, in his work *The Idea of the Holy,* a mysterium tremendum—an existence that is awe-inspiring and overpowering, sublime and fascinating and yet bewildering too; a presence that is wholly Other. Jung used Otto's term "numinous" to describe experiences of this kind:

> Numinous is either a noun or an adjective used to describe a dynamic agency or effect not caused by an arbitrary act of will [that] seizes and controls the human subject . . Archetypes are also quite often described as being numinous.[53]

In pursuing our curiosity into these unknown waters, we may find ourselves thrown back and forth between doubt and certainty, conclusion, loss of faith, and reengagement. Consideration of this phenomenon is often experienced as a back-and-forth process, one of speculation, disillusion, and return. Yet, throughout this process the physical evidence stands as a rock—a stable landmark speaking not only to the reality of what we are considering, but also to the value of our own pursuit. Rooting the phenomenon in a scientifically accessible media, in grain and other cereals and grasses, brings its question down from the imagination and into reality—making its petition a moral one. If we can recognize and admit into our awareness the truth of its existence, we can begin to face its importance as a living question.

Despite Crop Circles' dazzling symmetries, this annual spectacle remains mostly unheralded. As a culture we have failed to receive it—failed to respond to it in fullness or even with proper curiosity, and this can be explained in part by the fact that the phenomenon's mystery cannot be solved simply by any one of our diverse modern worldviews. Our failure to receive Crop Circles must ultimately lie in the nature of our modern character—the wide variety of our diverse points of view speaks to our fragmentation and essential uncertainty: we have come so far but really don't know what to make of the crises and mysteries that we face. Our media sources reflect this difficulty back to us. Today's media is fragmented and tentative, seemingly allergic to in-depth reporting and averse to drawing any conclusions. Sometimes media report the discovery of new formations with genuine curiosity and wild-eyed enthusiastic interest[54] and other times their uncertainty in the face of the truly astonishing nature of the phenomenon lets them slip too easily into denial and amateurish skepticism.[55] In these ways and many more, our culture at times feeds the voice within us that would prefer to leave this mystery's reality neatly to the side, unconsidered.

In the face of this resistance, the appearance of the phenomenon's question in a way that allows each *individual his or her own participation* demonstrates a profound subtlety. In its artistry, it appeals to our eyes and hearts; in its design and construction to our mind; it can be touched, walked in, and felt within our bodies. And in the reality of all of these facts, there lies the possibility of fascination. Presenting broad metaphysical questions in the form of a beautiful, embodied physical phenomenon necessitates *authentic individual* moral struggle. In its combination of concreteness and mystery, it defies simple categorization. In its artistic sensitivity and technical innovation, one-dimensional solutions are made insufficient in response to it. In its defiance of our normal modes of understanding, impersonal, easy answers are revealed to be morally inadequate. In the nature of these qualities, we glimpse the dynamic, even intimate relationship between ourselves and Crop Circles—a finely balanced question posed precisely, seemingly spoken in order to receive our response.

While such questions might feel overwhelming and may be difficult for us to accept, being able to consider the possibility of something beyond what we take for granted going on around us can be pleasing—as one friend of mine said upon first seeing pictures of Crop Circles, "What a relief."

The next chapter presents the history of our theories and responses to the Crop Circle phenomenon. There is a very wide range of possible responses to this phenomenon and each of us will be sparked uniquely and originally in response to these theories. These first sparks, our own genuine, rough, and rugged first reactions, are the most valuable elements we can draw from such a consideration. We are struck authentically the first time we encounter something new—and in that moment we are offered a glimpse of the truth of our own genuine response. Conscious awareness of that response and acceptance of it—no matter what its quality—begins a process of honest participation with this new mystery.

TWO

WITCHES' RINGS AND DEVIL'S TWISTS

Everyone stumbles over the truth from time to time, but most people pick themselves up and hurry off as though nothing ever happened.

—SIR WINSTON CHURCHILL

Examining the truth of the scientific evidence tells us much about the nature of the formations and rules out the dismissal of the phenomenon as a hoax, but it does not answer questions about why the phenomenon is occurring, or what it might mean. Crop Circles evoked strong responses from those who first came upon them, and the way in which they occur allows for a host of theoretical interpretations. The theories put forth in response to Crop Circles echo the mindset of the time. As David Fideler has noted, they are a kind of Rorschach test reflecting the psyche of the day and telling us more about the nature of the observer than the observed.[1] The earliest historical accounts of the discovery of formations attributed them to nefarious spirits. Even as late as a hundred years ago, Crop Circles were referred to by the farmers of the English countryside as "Witches' rings" and "Devil's twists." Nearing modernity, theories sprang up emphasizing the possibility of natural causation of the phenomenon by weather or wind—theories that were more suitable to the new scientific palette of the day. Today, our wide variety of explanations reveals the diverse and fragmented character of modernity. Our historical responses to the phenomenon reflect the way in which human psychology responds to the new and unknown. They offer us a mirror of our psyche and demonstrate qualities of *our own* nature.

The history of modern theoretical responses to Crop Circles includes: mathematical,[2] musical,[3] environmental or Gaia/Earth energy,[4] alien,[5] alien-technological,[6] government-military, spiritual,[7] geometric,[8] and even biblical interpretations.[9] These theories represent attempts to respond to the phenomenon following an honest examination of the scientific evidence. Each of these theories points to what the phenomenon might mean, but, as of yet, does not prove definitively that one particular point of view is the only valid one. The Jungian-oriented psychological and symbolic interpretation included here need not be taken to be any more or less valid than any other mode of approach. One might imagine how several of these theories could fit together well, or how those not seeming to fit together now may be found to do so in the future, if further developed or seen in a different light. It is possible that several of these theories could coexist as representing the true nature of the phenomenon. Overall, these theories reflect differing partial views. Most important, we should remember that they are our words for describing our response to something that we *do not yet understand.*

The first medieval descriptions of the phenomenon were vivid and intense, even fearful.[10] In an English pamphlet from 1678, a woodcut shows a field of oats flattened into a circle, being reaped by a "Mowing Devil." The accompanying text describes its words as being the "true relation of a farmer," who upon being asked too high a price by a mower swore that:

> The devil should mow it rather than He. And so it fell out, that very Night, the Crop of Oat shew'd as if it had been all of a flame: but next Morning appear'd so neatly mow'd by the Devil or some Infernal Spirit, that no Mortal Man was able to do the like. . . . But not to keep the curious Reader any longer in suspense, The inquisitive Farmer no sooner arriv'd at the place where his Oats grew, But to his admiration he found the Crop was cut down ready to his hands; And [as] if the Devil had a mind to shew his dexterity in the art of Husbandry, And scorn'd to mow them after the usual manner, he cut them in round circles, And plac't every straw with that exactness that it would have taken up above an Age for any

Man to perform what he did that one night: And the man that owns them is as yet afraid to remove them.[11]

This woodcut's text provides an amazing echo from the past. Astonishingly, it reflects perfectly what is seen today. Its words could be taken from a modern farmer's description: each straw "placed with exactness" that would have "taken an age"; the field having been seen "all of a flame" echoes the strange lights often seen in and around Crop Circles and its occurrence overnight. The pamphlet's accompanying text's reference to the formation being the work of the "Devil," or "some Infernal Spirit," reflects the era's belief in the world of spirits. The farmer's fear to touch his own crop speaks to the same awe that we sometimes feel today in encountering the phenomenon. This same fear is found in the use of "Devil's twists" or "Witches' rings" as names for Crop Circles. Imagine that a Crop Circle appeared in your farming field, a field that you have known well for your whole life— might you not be scared when you discovered it?

Because such experiences are actually frightening, we seek to keep our distance from them; labeling them becomes a method by which we can gain a foothold against our fear. Through such a categorization we may also enact a kind of dismissal, enabling ourselves to deny somewhat what was seen and to establish a false sense of control over an overwhelming, numinous experience (which, by its very nature, is something that is wholly other and beyond our control). As one early-twentieth-century witness of the phenomenon, who discussed what he saw with the older farmers around him, was told, "You don't want to worry about them boy, you often see them— the old men used to call them 'Devil Twists'. . . . The farmer then gave me a pitch fork and told me to try to raise the fallen corn. I stood in the circle but I faced a futile task, as fast as I raised the corn stalks they sprang back into place."[12] In attributing the formations to the work of devils, witches, or other "Infernal Spirits," we find our first, natural, fear-based attempt to avoid meeting the phenomenon head on.

Another less explicit variation upon this theme relates the devilish figure, Robin Goodfellow,[13] to the formations. Robin Goodfellow is related to Robin Hood, whose green garb depicts their mutual association with the green of Nature's feminine principle and the Goddess. Countryside tradition, to this day, dresses the May Queen in green and has Robin, Jack the Green, King of the May, or the Green Man dancing ahead of, or with her. In his role as trickster, Robin Goodfellow is a figure resembling the Roman god Mercury or the Greek god Hermes (alchemical Mercurius). A god of communication and symbol, Hermes acts as an interpreter and messenger from gods to humans. His province is the in-between, places of both and thresholds: "human and creature, wild and cultured, male and female."[14] Hermes gives us our word "hermeneutics" for the art of interpreting hidden meaning. In Greek a lucky find was a *hermaion*. The Homeric hymn to Hermes invokes him as the one

> of many shifts, blandly cunning, a robber, a cattle driver, a bringer of dreams, a watcher by night, a thief at the gates, one who was soon to show forth wonderful deeds among the deathless gods.[15]

As Harpur[16] and Michell[17] have noted, there is a long-held association with mysterious goings-on in the English countryside, and Mercury "is identified with the wandering, nocturnal spirit of the earth, whose mysterious flickering flames were known in old England as 'Hermes lights.' He is a trickster, specializing in the deflation of human presumptions, and Crop Circles bear his hallmark."[18] Michell sees a Mercurial hand behind the phenomenon, Hermes as Nature's messenger and also as something more powerful: "the being that inscribes mysterious symbols on cornfields is no mere rustic imp . . . we can neither control it nor discover its methods . . ."[19]

In rural communities worldwide, belief in the spirit world extended through to modern times, including in the English countryside that today is the home of Crop Circle formations. At the turn of the last century, Walter Evans-Wentz traveled the Celtic regions of the British Isles and France gathering the tales that compose his classic *The Fairy Faith in Celtic Countries* (1911). Many of their fairy tales include descriptions of rings on the grass, which can be matched to a mushroom spore that produces a blue-green-gray ring in a circle around it.[20] Shakespeare describes the fairies responsible for producing such rings: "you demi-puppets that by moonshine do the green sour ringlets make, whereof ewe not bites; and you, whose pastime is to make midnight mushrooms."[21] However, some of the references to fairy rings in Evans-Wentz describe a flattening of the crop that we know is not part of the effects of the fungal ring phenomenon:

> Sometimes the fairies helped human beings with their work, coming in at night to finish spinning or . . . thresh a farmer's corn or fan his grain. (p. 88)

> In Sennen country, within a mile of the end of Britain, I talked with two farmers who knew something of the piskies . . . [they] gave the following evidence: Up on Sea-View Green, there are two rings where the piskies used to dance. (p. 181)

> Piskies always come out at night, and in marshy ground there are round places called pisky beds where they play. (p. 184)

References here to flattened rings and spun or threshed grain clearly distinguish these accounts from the natural mushroom spore phenomenon—which is not known to ever have similar effects. Whether such tales of fairy rings refer to sightings of Crop Circles is uncertain, but the mushroom spore theory is certainly an insufficient explanation for the characteristics described. Gardner (in Silva) has also noted a related distinguishing account in the writings of John Leyland, a chronicler appointed by Henry VIII. In Leyland's writings he describes the origin of the traditional English maypole dance this way: "we go out in the early hours and we learn the patterns that appear on grass overnight."[22] Creating dances from fungal ring patterns seems nonsensical in comparison to the opportunity for physical participation offered by larger Crop Circle formations. In addition, one cannot imagine people being moved to dance by fungal rings, whereas such a socially celebrated and repeated ritual in response to the discovery of a Crop Circle in one's field reflects the numinousness—the psychological power—present in the phenomenon still today. From Leyland's description it is easy to imagine that the early formations in the British Isles were also given a reverent response in the construction of the stone circles that adorn its landscape. If the "patterns that appear on the grass overnight" were being commemorated in dance, would it not also seem likely that earlier folk may have commemorated the phenomenon in stone? Would such an act of demarcation not have been an appropriate response to the wonder they felt in facing such a marvel?

The discrepancy between fairy rings and Crop Circle formations is given further advancement in the extensive account made by a professor of chemistry at Oxford and first keeper of Oxford's Ashmolean Museum, Robert Plot, L.L.D. In 1686, Plot recorded his observations of Crop Circles in a work entitled *The Natural History of Staffordshire*. Plot's description is identical to the modern phenomenon and notes that these rings found in the grass are commonly spoken of as "fairy circles."[23] His crisp drawings illustrate the same geometric forms characteristic of the earliest modern Crop Circles, including rings, spirals, and squares within rings. The size he describes, "near fifty yards," and the downed area of crop defining the ring, "from the least to the biggest, seldom broader than a yard," both fit with what we see now. Additionally, Plot found the presence of the same germinal improvement in the affected area that we find today: "the earth underneath having been highly improved with a fat sulpherous matter . . . ever since it was first stricken, though not exerting its fertilizing quality till some time after." In mature onset formations, crop yields are improved, and this fertilizing effect continues to be found today in the year following the appearance of a formation in crops worldwide.[24] Through his account, Plot provides early scientific documentation of the phenomenon and allows us to know that at least some of what was referred to in English folklore and the testimony of country folk as "fairy rings" were, most certainly, the same genuine phenomenon of Crop Circles that we see today.

Plot theorized that the formations were caused by natural storm phenomena and he illustrates his hypothesis as a trumpet-like effect coming from the clouds. Today, formations continue to be found the night after tremendous thunderstorms—the 2001 Milk Hill formation, consisting of 409 individual circles and spanning 1,000 feet across—being perhaps the finest example of this correlation and possibly the best Crop Circle of its day.

Another historical account of Crop Circles as being caused by windstorms comes from an August 1880 edition of British *Nature* magazine:[25]

This account provides unique details that fit precisely with the construction of modern formations; references made to crisp wall edges and standing center stalks stand out in this regard. Capron also notes the phenomenon's location in sandy loam, which is the most common soil in which the modern phenomena occur in England. Talbott and others have observed that sandy loam has a composition that, in combination with water, allows for great electrical conductivity. This is an effect also found in the limestone that sits beneath the most common North American locations of the phenomenon. In Plot's and Capron's categorization of the phenomenon as storm effects, we see the transition toward the modern worldview and away from the medieval attribution of the phenomenon to spirits. As Western culture's beliefs changed, we began to categorize Crop Circles in ways that reflect our new perspective. Capron's keen interest in hearing whether anyone else had found such a thing speaks to the same not-knowing that we feel today. His openness to his own ignorance of this topic displays a genuine curiosity, and his attitude might be regarded as the best and most open-minded psychological form that science can take. Causation by atmospheric forces is one of the earliest forms of modern response. It was developed in the 1980s by G. T. Meaden and continues to be a part of Levengood's explanation today.

Causation by windstorm is one of the nine first categories of interpretation recognized initially by researcher Colin Andrews.[26] However, since this theory fails to explain the intelligent complexity of the modern formations, it is no longer considered sufficient. But some still argue that causation by weather effect is a legitimate argument, citing the presence of complex forms in Nature as a defense for this position. What this approach removes is the conscious agency that is seemingly present in the clear communicative design and intention of the modern formations. Further evidence presented here will also make the weather effect hypothesis untenable. This being said, there continues to be legitimate scientific evidence for atmospheric elements in the production (if not the agency) of formations.

Modern theories, such as that of weather causation, tend to be much more emotionally neutral than their predecessors. Gone are the devils, witches, and fairies and the exalted dances of our ancestors, replaced with distanced observation and flat affect. Roger Sear considered what he called "Witch's rings" to be "not too out of the ordinary, as had seen and entered other such circles during the same era in the countryside around his home village." This despite the fact of the unusual effects that went along with it, such as "a tickling sensation in the feet, the refusal of a dog to enter, and the magnetization and hence effective destruction of an Ingersol pocket watch."[27]

Typically, in the twentieth century, the characteristic response is often virtually no response at all:

> A Mrs. Jean Songhurst, for example, writing in *Country Life* earlier this year, tells us that she had seen circles in Donegal more than sixty years before but that the farmers kept quiet about them.... Her uncle in Scotland had also seen circles on his farm at Thurso in the 1890s.[28]

There is a curious lack of curiosity in many of the descriptions of formations found in the last century—especially in its middle fifty years. Why do we "keep quiet about them"? Certainly in this time period, there was an expectation of being shamed for speaking of "fairy circles" or UFOs (another modern form of response). At this time, one was expected to think oneself crazy for believing in such things and certainly you could never claim to have seen them. As will be considered more fully in Chapter Five, the modern worldview has taken into account all the mystery that was formerly cast out into the world in wonder and awe. No longer do those who witness such marvels have the right to describe the vivid strangeness and fantastic power *(numen)* of what they have seen that was afforded to those in previous eras. No longer allowed "fantasies" of devils or witches, in fact not allowed to encounter the strange at all, today one is subtly taught to deny such experiences altogether, or to blame it on others, as one unfortunate young man's story shows us:

> During World War II, I was evacuated to Wales from Birmingham as it was being heavily bombed. I lived on a farm in the village of Arddleen near Llanymynech. One day in the late summer of 1941, I was given a good hiding by the farmer's grown-up son for allegedly damaging the corn (damage to food crops was very serious then as food was in short supply and rationed). I was taken to see two corn circles I was supposed to have made. They were some way into the field and could only be seen by standing on the field gate (a typical barred farm gate). They were about 15 metres in diameter. I did not make them and we never found out who did. Was I blamed for some of the earliest corn circles?[29]

For the modern mind, the easiest response is to deny what was seen altogether, or attribute it to other people. While since the late 1980s some percentage of the annual Crop Circles found have been produced by human hoaxers (more so in Britain than anywhere else), somewhere further back in local history denial had already become a part of the tradition. As the older farmers told the young man mentioned earlier, "You don't want to worry about them boy, you often see them. [We call] them 'Devil Twists.'" "Don't worry about them" is not only what we are often told, but also what we are *subtly conditioned to tell ourselves*. Denial happens unconsciously and it is thus that for many, before consideration of this phenomenon is begun it is already ended. For many who see or enter into a formation it is immediately a hoax, because "what else could it be"—or they insist that "something is wrong."

> What psychologists call psychic identity, or "mystical participation," has been stripped off our world of things. But it is exactly this halo of unconscious associations that gives a colorful and fantastic aspect to the primitive's world. We have lost it to such a degree that we do not recognize it when we meet it again. With us such things are kept below the threshold; when they occasionally reappear, we even insist that something is wrong. (Jung)[30]

Jung recognized that, as a condition of the modern mind and as part of our journey into a strong sense of self and ego identity, we have lost our mystical participation with the world around us. When we meet something fantastic, something truly beyond the norm, we not only can't participate with it, we may not even be able to see it or accept its reality. The unconscious plays a far greater role in our resistance to meeting the new than the rational person would like to admit. The way we respond to any given situation is influenced profoundly *before* we think of it consciously (Gladwell's *Blink* does a good job of introducing this fact from a non–depth psychological perspective). Even before we can come to rationally consider this phenomenon, our impression of it is influenced by our unconscious. Because of this fact, we can accept that it's *natural* for people to have differences of opinion on this topic and that, for a large portion, it will be difficult to accept its reality at all, just as for others every formation is genuine despite contradictory evidence. Patience is the hoped for by-product of accepting this fact. However, what can be brought to attention is the way in which the particular qualities of the modern psyche play a part in this. We can point out that, for example, the preference of the modern psyche is to remain detached and experience only the *idea* of what was seen, felt, or experienced. Unconsciously, this act of psychological diminution reduces our experience to something smaller so that we can tolerate it more easily. Doing so may help us to avoid coming into contact with something that may be uncomfortable for us to feel or consider. Thus today, when we are faced with numinous or overwhelming experiences with which we do not feel grounded, our first response is to protect ourselves from a true emotional experience of it and, either overtly or subtly, to "increasingly detach [the phenomenon] from its dynamic background and gradually [turn it] into a purely intellectual formula. In this way it is neutralized, and you can then say one can live with it quite well."[31]

There is a host of ways in which we do this, only the most obvious of which is clinging to the hoax solution. But it also plays into the various categories of response and the choices that we make as to which agency we want to believe is behind the formations. In each of our personal responses there can be room for subtle reduction via intellectualization—the phenomenon is simply less scary if we can fit it into a broader category that works for us. Of course, most folks, especially those who have not given much thought to the topic, deny it completely, thinking to themselves, as Jung observes, that "something must be wrong," or that something must be wrong with those who are researching it or their data. Denial is the fastest road to the psychological security of the current mindset. Yet all of us may find some measure of intellectual reduction in our choice. Although we look for objectivity in the science of the phenomenon, we must look at the subjectivity in our psyche to begin to generate authentic meaning in regard to it. It is authentically new, and as Tolstoy wrote there is in all of us there is a deep, profound, and predominantly unconscious investment in our current beliefs about the world:

> I know that most men, including those at ease with problems of the greatest complexity, can seldom accept even the simplest and most obvious truth if it be such as would oblige them to admit the falsity of conclusions which they have delighted in explaining to colleagues, which they have proudly taught to others, and which they have woven, thread by thread, into the fabric of their lives.[32]

Alongside the difficulty of admitting something genuinely new into our lives lies the challenge of placing this new material into a context within the framework of our understanding. Crop Circles do not come with a guide or instruction manual. It is very difficult to admit something into our frame of reference if it exists in fundamental contradiction to that frame or lacking any context at all; there is "nowhere to put it." The profound diversity of modern perspectives on reality makes knowing how to think about this mystery even more difficult—the fragmentation of thinking that is characteristic of our time separates us from the part of us that can place our experiences into lived context. Hoaxing plays upon this fragmentation and inability to find context, enabling us to not think further about the phenomenon. It allows the status quo to be upheld, avoiding personal moral struggle altogether. This is especially true when the media grabs onto and runs with such an explanation. It has been observed that the microfocus of our media dialogue—focusing on very short amounts of time—fundamentally disables our capacity to see ourselves within a context, or to generate insight.[33] Such a shortsighted focus only allows for quick answers despite our need for complex solutions and processes of inquiry.

While at times some media sources have been open to Crop Circles and presented them with open-faced awe,[34] most commonly they are shown with a mocking air and without context or any of the scientific data. Most media stories are only knee-jerk restorations of an unquestioning status quo. Incredibly shallow articles published by major national magazines epitomize this trend; ignoring the scientific data presented to them, they choose instead to sensationalize the phenomenon and its researchers. Particularly disappointing is the commissioning of hoaxes in the U.K, and a dreadful article, by *National Geographic* magazine.[35] The best reporting on the subject has been done consistently by local newspapers and television stations in Canada and the U.K.[36] Jungian analyst and author Thomas Moore notes that the media participates and advances a kind of cultural sleep, by avoiding issues which demand something of the viewer: "the media co-operate[s] in this cultural narcosis by 'dumbing down' discourse on world events and promoting a lifestyle that is passive. More now than ever, they appeal to the lowest common denominator of education and intellectual curiosity."[37]

Such media stories reinforce our psychological tendency toward denial in the face of the new.

Like Pharaoh, in the biblical interchange with Moses, the condition of the modern, well-developed ego is such that it repeatedly seeks that its own vision of reality be reinforced regardless of the truth of the events around it. Our media culture enables the ego's resistance to new visions of the world and ourselves, facilitating our denial of the "fantastic." It is only through our own choice to participate consciously with the phenomenon (as you are doing right now) that our tendency to avoid looking for a context is overcome. Furthermore, in this case we are offered a very direct route for overcoming all of these impediments and asking better questions. We are able to enter into the formations for ourselves.

> What is it about these circles? People either seem to get all starry eyed about them, or else they get very irritated. There is now a third group, who thanks to some farmers being more generous in letting people into their fields, have come away with a genuine curiosity or interest in what this strange phenomenon is all about.[38]

Unfortunately, today it is not only the public that is being let into the farmer's fields. Beyond the simple fakes often found in North America to be the work of young people, in the U.K. there is a well-organized hoaxing system that produces elaborate and beautiful formations. The advanced level of commitment necessary for the production of such complicated hoaxes speaks to an agency beyond that of sneaky teenagers. It is well-known around the parts of England in which most formations are discovered that some farmers are now being paid to allow the creation of fake circles on their property. Such a well-developed, and apparently well-financed, hoaxing operation implies a broader resource and motivation than that of drunken pranksters. One explanation that seems to fit this degree of motivation and resource is the involvement of governments in hoaxing. Considering the legitimate mystery and scope of the formations, one can imagine that they perhaps feel responsible to do so (a motivation discussed further in the next chapter).[39] Rather than viewing such an involvement along the lines of an "out-there" conspiracy, it seems reasonable to believe that concerned governments faced with the scientific evidence maintain a policy of hoaxing, in order to muddy the waters around the phenomenon and take advantage of our natural inclination to disbelieve the extraordinary and turn away from it before looking closer. The U.S. government's decision to undertake a very similar course of action is a matter of historic fact. A 1953 report by the Scientific Advisory Panel of the CIA (known as the Robertson panel) recommended that the UFO phenomenon be actively discredited by "re-educating" the public to believe that such stories always had an explanation other than aliens. To accomplish this end, it would seem that the *National Enquirer* magazine was employed, as its founding editor had been a psychological warfare specialist for the CIA.[40] It then went about producing stories that paint alien encounters and UFO sightings as too silly to ever be taken seriously, very effectively "re-educating" the U.S. population.

One of the earliest indicators of the presence of British government involvement in hoaxing comes from their involvement with setting up Crop Circle researcher Colin Andrews in 1990. Andrews's and Pat Delgado's first book, *Circular Evidence,* was a best seller, and in 1989 chosen by Her Majesty Queen Elizabeth II to be on her highly regarded summer reading list. The following year, the British Ministry of Defense involved themselves in a research project funded jointly by Nippon and the BBC, called Operation Blackbird. After the unplanned involvement of the British Army, the project was leaked to the press. A hoaxed formation was then secretly produced by military personnel. Awoken in the middle of the night and forced to comment on the formation under false pretenses, Andrews was made the fool on worldwide television and the phenomenon was discredited for the first time. This dismissal occurred despite no change to the scientific or historic data that establishes the existence of the genuine phenomenon. This is a powerful example of the media's ability to discredit something, or someone, without needing to discredit its facts—a tactic used regularly in political campaigns.

The second successful discrediting of the phenomenon in the media came with the introduction of a new "scandal" in 1991. Two old Englishmen were put forward as being responsible for producing the entire Crop Circle phenomenon, and this explanation was lapped up by the media. Britain's newspaper *Today* ran the headline "The Men Who Conned the World" on September 9, 1991. These men claimed to have produced the phenomenon with boards and string and other primitive contraptions and did not have half a clue about what they were talking about. When questioned about their methods they described leaping out from the center of formations and other such feats of strength. Again, no change in the evidence for the phenomenon was found. Simply an offer of an easy solution was handed to the media and they accepted. It was an easy story to put together and one well-suited to a twenty-four-hour news cycle—unlike the truth, which requires actual investigative journalism, which if done would have discovered that the public relation firm that put together the worldwide effort to promote this nonsense had a direct relationship to the MI-5, the British equivalent of the CIA.[41] Although the hoaxed explanation has no merit, it nonetheless achieved its goal: "the immediate purpose of the scam appears to have been the continuing discrediting of the research community."[42] Interest in the genuinely mysterious phenomenon quickly died down.

There is a long history of military and government interest in Crop Circle formations. Andrews found that government interest in his, as well as others', research of the phenomenon came right away: "some of the first people to respond to my research findings were representatives from intelligence organizations in the United States, Germany, and the U.K. Many of them infiltrated research groups, and some even visited researchers' homes and spoke to their families in an effort to acquire information about the burgeoning crop circle mystery."[43] A Canadian military investigation into a 1967 Camrose, Alberta, three-ring formation describes circles that were thirty-two to thirty-five feet in diameter, each with a six-inch outer ring that was perfectly flat. The report concluded that: "I do not see how the hoaxers could have produced these marks in isolation without leaving some evidence of their approach to the area and departure from it . . . the marks were sufficiently unique in my experience for me to state categorically that if I saw similar marks elsewhere my tendency to treat the matter as a hoax would be sharply reduced."[44] In the 1980s, a farmer from Sarnia, Ontario, Canada discovered a donut-shaped formation in grass that had appeared overnight. He reported that "'government men' took samples at the site but no conclusions were published."[45]

U.S. Army personnel have been seen as recently as 2003 monitoring those investigating Crop Circles. On July 4, 2003, Art Rantala watched a Crop

Circle form across from his property in Horicon, Wisconsin. At approximately 7:40 A.M.he noticed that the strength of the wind and rain was ripping bark off of the hickory nut tree ten feet outside his workshop window. Leaning out of his window, he noticed that the trees in the field across the street had "started swinging every which-way." He then watched, one by one, three circles form in the wheat, by no apparent means, right in front of him. It all took less than twelve seconds. Three weeks later, a team of researchers arrived to investigate the formation and were greeted by a military helicopter and U.S. Air Force personnel—who noted their vehicle license plates—and claimed to be part of a U.S. Air Force Crop Circle task force (view photos and report online[46]). Regardless of whether or not what these witnesses were told was true, government agencies have demonstrated a consistent interest in the phenomenon, were among the first institutions to make contact with early researchers, have made attempts to discredit the phenomenon and its researchers directly, and continue to demonstrate an interest in the topic today (as is shown in later chapters), despite making no official statements about the phenomenon.

Finally, there are some who believe that governments may be involved in the construction of *genuine* Crop Circle formations. As with the weather causation theories, this theory fails to account for many of the anomalous facts, both intrinsic and extrinsic, to the formations: the various changes to the plants and the presence of Balls of Light; but more important, it conflicts directly with what we *do* know about government involvement in hoaxing. If governments are involved in producing the phenomenon why would they also be involved in discrediting the phenomenon? Such a theory leads down the path of absurdity and creates many more questions than answers. While hoaxers are producing high-quality formations (in the U.K. especially), hoaxing and/or government involvement as a theory of causation for the phenomenon fails to deal with its facts. The presence of anatomical, chemical, cellular, germinal, and electromagnetic changes to the plants themselves cannot be explained through this agency either. This theory also fails to offer any account of motive nor *even the possibility of explaining* the phenomenon's more challenging elements—as we will see. Furthermore, even British circle-hoaxers themselves have testified to going to a spot to produce a formation only to find the circle that they planned on creating already present in the field, or later having unplanned elements added to their designs (both bearing genuine hallmarks).[47]

Today, there are three general categories of causation that seem to best accommodate these facts.[48] While there are other theories that have been, and could be, proposed, these three categories provide a useful division for discussion. They are the most commonly discussed among those interested in the phenomenon and are seemingly the most relevant to its causation and inherent nature. Each of these categories addresses the presence of intelligent, consciously intended design; the careful precision in construction and scope; the attendance to sacred geometry and creativity within geometric theory; and its essential mystery. These theories of causation include attendance to both the scientific and the numinous quality of the formations. However, it is important to note that while all of these categories reflect different elements of the modern psyche, each directly challenges modern assumptions about the nature of reality. The categories of agency introduced here are considered in further depth throughout this work.

> We begin with the theory that Mother Earth herself is actually involved in some way in the construction of crop circles. The Gaia Theory proposes that our planet is not simply a mass of lifeless rock flying through space, not simply a lucky accident in the cosmic scheme of things.[49]

The first of these broad categories of response is related to the Gaia Hypothesis. Gaia, or Ge, is the primordial creatrix of Greek mythology, born of the "infernal" deity Chaos. It is believed that, through her, matter began to emerge into form out of disorder. Among the earliest great mother goddesses, Gaia was the giver of life to grain and the fertilizing essence of Nature's abundance. Her name is synonymous with the Earth itself; the prefix "ge" in geography and geology stem from this Greek root. In 1979, James Lovelock put forward the Gaia Hypothesis, which proposes that the Earth itself is a living, self-regulating system. It is both a proposal and a response to the observation of the vast complexity, interrelativity, and ability to self-organize and self-correct the natural systems of the planet. As Andrews, among others, have observed, Lovelock's book profoundly changed the way scientists, and ordinary people, look at life *on* Earth and the life *of* the Earth.

The relationship between [Earth] and man, a dominant animal species in the complex living system, and the possibly shifting balance of power between them, are questions of obvious importance. . . . The Gaia hypothesis is for those who like to walk or simply stand and stare, to wonder about the Earth and the life it bears, and to speculate about the consequences of our own presence here. It is an alternative to that pessimistic view which sees nature as a primitive force to be subdued and conquered. It is also an alternative to that equally depressing picture of our planet as a demented spaceship, forever travelling, driverless and purposeless, around an inner circle of the sun.[50]

One of the few most commonly expressed opinions about Crop Circles is that they are in some way a response to our degradation of the environment. In this view, the phenomenon is understood as a communication from the planet itself, perhaps as a warning signal that we are endangering its, and our own, survival. This is one of the most commonly shared interpretations of Crop Circles.[51] In this view,

[The Earth] can no longer support the anti-life tendencies and continuous disregard the human populations have shown, and seeks to readjust all forms of consciousness to its new directive. The crop circles are a "spiritual nudge" which is designed to awaken us to our larger context and milieu, which is none other than our collective earth soul.[52]

While it is hard to extract causal understanding of the role of earth energies in the construction of the phenomenon, the nature of its construction and the fact of our ever-increasing damage to the planet give merit to the inclusion of this point of view within our search for answers. As the first general category of response, this theory and its popularity among both researchers and the general public seems at least to address a motivation for the phenomenon's occurrence. It speaks to why it is happening now with such frequency, yet it leaves us with questions of mechanism left unanswered—how can the Earth be seen to be actually creating the formations? Furthermore, can we believe that the Earth is capable of being conscious of itself, and us, in this way? In leaving the question of the phenomenon's actual physical construction unanswered, it is very unlike another prominent category of response, that of alien causation.

In the modern era, causation by extraterrestrials is the second most common first response to Crop Circles (after belief in the hoaxing theory and psychological denial). Extraterrestrial life is a possibility that has fascinated us for a long time, but perhaps never more so than in this last century. With the popularization of science fiction, interest in extraterrestrial beings exploded in popularity. Many of these stories involve the theme of first contact, the first meeting of aliens and humanity. Under this thematic influence, Crop Circles are thought of as calling cards placed before us as we begin to approach a time of meeting with other beings who are now trying to ease us into the reality of their existence.[53] Alternately, as the movie *Signs* depicts, Crop Circles can be thought of as the work of alien creatures who are ultimately hostile. The category of alien causation opens up a great variety of possibilities of intention, and many different scenarios within this category are available in print and online.[54] Causation by aliens directly addresses (at least hypothetically) the method, or agent, by which Crop Circles are constructed, and offers a broad width of possibilities to the imagination.

In 1966, when Crop Circle formations were found in Australia, they were thought of as being the wake, or afterimage, of alien spacecraft that had landed and therefore labeled as being "saucer's nests." This explanation was also popular on the Canadian Prairie in the 1970s:

UFO's left nothing but their footprints. (*Brandon Sun,* Manitoba, September 1974)

A probable U.F.O. landing near Estevan was reported Tuesday. (*Estevan-Mercury,* Saskatchewan, October 1974)

The Fairies must have got confused at Landenburg . . . the circles were slicked down like hair on a wet dog, but still fresh and green. (*Regina Leader-Post,* Saskatchewan, October 1974)[55]

One reason the alien-UFO theory is so popular as a causal explanation for the phenomenon is the frequent sighting of Balls of Light in correlation with the discovery of Crop Circles. Although there have been many eyewitness accounts of Crop Circles being made,[56] only a few directly claim to have seen a UFO-type object involved in their formation.[57] What has been seen with great frequency near Crop Circle formations both prior to and after their formation, and documented on video on many different occasions, are white Balls of Light (or BOLs). These orbs are described as being one foot in diameter and luminous, in white or yellow-orange color.

While an alien causation theory allows us to imagine possibilities of construction more easily than theories emphasizing the planet, alien causation—by the diversity of scenarios that it is capable of hosting—in itself, offers little *direct* insight into the meaning of Crop Circles' arrival. Broad terms such as alien (or Gaia/Earth energies) are simply labels. The term "alien" has different meanings and possibilities to different people—and this diversity allows this term to be used lightly at times, thus avoiding truly participating with the mystery before us. What are aliens? What image does that term conjure up for you? Many of those who speak about Crop Circles do not refer to aliens as being a kind of B-movie extraterrestrial from another planet, but rather as something closer to spiritual or dimensional, a description which has much in common with the third broad category of theoretical response to the phenomenon.

The third category ascribes a spiritual source as agency. Under the banner of this broad category is included the idea that spiritual or extra-dimensional beings, or God or Spirit itself, is causing them; and the possibility that the formations are caused by souls or human spirits living after death. Here, Crop Circles are seen as "vessels of communication between two worlds."[58] While the modern condition often disables us from immediate participation with such ideas, the category of spiritual causation is made more accessible to us through the appearance in Crop Circle formations of images and symbols from the world's religious and spiritual traditions. From the beginning of the modern era of the phenomenon's discovery, religious imagery has been a part of what has been seen. This notion is furthered by the frequent appearance of forms of sacred imagery and the frequent discovery of formations at or near human religious sites. The ancient ritual sites near to which Crop Circles are found annually in England regularly include Stonehenge, Avebury, Glastonbury, and many other stone circles and Neolithic burial tombs. This correlation is not limited to the British Isles, as Crop Circles have been found near ancient burial grounds and religious sites, particularly devoted rural religious communities and churches, in North American and Europe.[59]

Additionally, a spiritual response also makes room for the frequent reports of psychic coincidence between researchers and the appearance of new formations. In a documentary film,[60] Andrews describes his praying for a clue to the mystery and for a formation close to his home because he could not afford to travel. The next morning, he awoke to a neighboring farmer reporting his discovery of a new, nearby formation. Researcher and pilot Busty Taylor describes flying and talking with Andrews about a hoped-for new design, only to find that exact design the following day on the very spot over which they had been flying while discussing it.[61] Strangely, nearly every researcher, including the least flaky among the lot, has eventually found themselves facing such psychic coincidences or synchronicities. Many researchers record such interactions, including group meditations upon an image that was then found to appear in monitored fields, and the fact of "such interactions [having] a habit of following the people closely associated with the phenomenon, as if [to offer] reassurance."[62] Does Jung's idea of the collective unconscious play a role here, as many have wondered?[63] Whether such psychic interaction can be considered evidence of a spiritual agency behind the phenomenon is up to each one of us.

The visual evidence of Balls of Light can also be seen to fit within a spiritual category of explanation. The balls are often described as energy, not matter. In many of the world's religions and mystic traditions, the Spirit is associated with light. As well, light is often associated with near-death experiences and the ascent toward heaven. Popular descriptions of the luminosity of the human spirit when it is separated from the body might allow one to imagine Balls of Light as being related to souls. "The soul, too, according to tradition has a round form. As the Monk of Heisterbach wrote, it is . . . 'furnished on all sides with eyes' *(ex omni parte oculata)* . . . 'globes of light' . . . with remarkable consistency, are regarded as 'souls' in the remotest parts of the world."[64] This is an ancient notion. Considering that belief in the survival of the human soul after death in some form is the basis of many of the world's religions, this explanation is quite natural. Widespread also is belief in the capacity and interest of these departed souls to aid us or do us harm. In Chinese culture, they are spoken of as ancestors and their assistance is gained, or punishment comes, based upon the morality of our behavior. Belief in such spirits is nearly universal among human populations, most commonly the belief that deceased loved ones watch over and protect us. Could such entities have a role in Crop Circle formations, and if so, what would their motivation be? English psychic Isabelle Kingston refers to the agency creating the formations as "The Watchers," a form of "universal consciousness."[65] Her interaction with the Watchers began during a meditation focused upon Silbury Hill in 1982, and in the years of that decade they conveyed to her their intention to raise the consciousness of humanity and that the sacred sites around Wiltshire would be a locus of their efforts.

There are many people who see possibilities that overlap between the Gaia, alien, and spiritual. Some, while not identifying the source of causation, somehow speak simultaneously to all three. Having been shown images of the formations in the early 1990s, elders from the North American Hopi tribe saw significance in them *both* as a spiritual sign and an environmental warning: "the Hopi were aware of this too when they reacted to a picture of one particular crop formation: 'Mother is crying, the Earth's blood is being taken and her lungs choked.' It is not by chance that the sudden worldwide proliferation of Crop Circles coincides with a phase in the Earth's history when its natural systems are threatened with ecocide."[66] They spoke of their belief that the earth is being poisoned, and that it, and we, are in profound need of a period of purification. Throughout their discussions with elders from the Hopi, Ute, Lakota, Mayan, and Hawaiian nations, Holden and Scott found them emphasizing that what spoke to them in the images of the formations was the criticalness of returning to a view of ourselves, both within ourselves and in relation to the world around us, that is broadened to a wider vision. Within this broader vision, they themselves speak of the Earth as Mother and as a Spirit, and are able to include as well (as do many other indigenous traditions) the idea of aliens or "Star people."

We can also examine the existence of sacred geometry in the formations as we take into consideration the three main theories of agency. In the documentary *Quest for Truth,* Martineau explains how geometric harmony is folded deeply into the construction of each authentic formation. For example, where five-fold geometry is found, that form is reflected in the constitution of every part, the size of the outer circle finding a relation, following the Golden Mean, to the larger ring around it and to the area of the whole

Circle itself. Furthermore, each formation "obeys the same rules"[67] in the construction of sacred art that we see worldwide. Including:

1. The balance of line and curve.

2. The balance of light and dark.

3. Two-ness [balance] between laid and standing crop.

4. No signature, no ego attachment to the work.

5. Integrity of material ("green, clean, and holy") [nothing inorganic].

6. Impermanence of form [as with the Navajo and Tibetan sandpaintings for example]; one does not make the work into an idol.

While following these rules, the design of authentic formations often relates to, or seems to point out, ancient stone circles or other sacred sites in the landscape. Often the geometry of the formation will directly fit into the sacred geometry already present at the nearby site. In my own experience, time spent viewing formations allows for a felt appreciation of this quality.

Karen Alexander has observed that there is an essential harmony to be found within the geometry of the formations. The presence of the Golden Section's sacred measure throughout Crop Circle construction speaks to an inherent harmony within the designs—they are an expression of harmonious relationship.[68] These subtle harmonies of construction speak to the mystery of the phenomenon. Such observations take us somewhat farther than just the question of why are they forming. They lead us to wonder, more subtly and perhaps even intimately, why are they forming in a way that is fundamentally harmonious?

They also express this harmony eloquently in the universal language of symbol. The circle itself is recognized throughout worldwide indigenous and mythological tradition as a symbol of relativity—of the essential interactivity between part and whole. It has been used throughout those traditions to convey a vision of the larger world around us and of ourselves in relation to it. "Regardless of the origin of Crop Circles, their fascination, their hypnotic effect, comes from their geometry. What is it that exerts this magical effect and attraction, even in the simplest geometric forms?"[69] Jung observed that present within the psyche is a fascination with circular and concentric forms, a pattern that he noted extends worldwide in ritual use: in the concentric placements of images around a central point in iconography and symbolism; in their use as yantras or instruments of contemplation (seen, for example, in the sandpaintings of Tibetan Buddhist and Navajo traditions); and "in the sphere of religious practices and in psychology it denotes circular images which are drawn, painted, modeled, or danced."[70] Jung saw in our preoccupation with concentric form not just an aesthetic attraction, but something deep within the nature of the psyche revealed:

> In studying the mandala as it appears in the drawings of patients, it is noted that the very expression of the symbol also produces a unifying effect, bringing the patient back to the inner unconsciousness that is the source and goal of the psyche.[71]

We recognize such forms and respond to them powerfully because of their connection to psychic factors beneath the mantle of conscious awareness. Both in their conscious use in religious iconography and as they occur naturally within the psyche, mandalas serve to effect an "inner 'refounding' or reorganization."[72] Within the psyche, it is the function of such imagery to reconnect us with the greater whole of who we are, readjusting the conscious attitude to include more of ourselves that was formerly repressed in the unconscious. The appearance of mandala imagery in the products of the psyche come as an "attempt at self-healing on the part of Nature, which does not spring from conscious reflection but from an instinctive impulse."[73] Usually appearing in situations of "psychic confusion and perplexity," mandala imagery "represents a pattern of order which like a psychological view-finder . . . [enables restoration to be] brought into being."[74] Images of this kind also frequently accompany peak states and what are termed religious experiences. Jung strongly believed that we have lost awareness of our connection to this natural function within the psyche as a consequence of achieving the capacity for disjunction that is characteristic of the modern self, and that the rediscovery of our natural movement toward wholeness was of the greatest necessity.

Psychologically, dreams, images, and other products of the unconscious are often understood as speaking for a correction that is needed, for the reclamation of something of ourselves that is missing from consciousness.

With this in mind, one may say, as with Alexander and taking their construction with sacred geometric precision as a metaphor, that Crop Circles encourage our participation with that part of ourselves that knows itself as inherently related to a greater whole. "Symbols are the highest effective powers of nature, which are enclosed in the simplest possible form."[75] In this context, the formations arrive with the intention, at least in part, to serve as a "communicating door" not only between ourselves and something out there but also between ourselves and something inner that we are missing or have forgotten.

What might we be missing of ourselves that Crop Circles could reawaken us to? Why might they use beauty to do so? In the psyche, dreams can point us toward a missing component, but they can also herald that within us that is new and emergent, something growing inside of us, a new stage of who we are. 'One of the functions of dreams appears to be a preparation for some approaching phase in life. Life is full of thresholds. . . . Where a new adjustment to life, a change in attitude, is called for. Dreams prepare us for this change."[76] Many Native leaders see this function as a part of the message of Crop Circles. Beyond categories of agency and causation, they see the arrival of the phenomenon speaking to the moment in which we live as one of profound change,[77] and that the formations may be understood as "being forerunners of that change."[78] Hawaiian elders "felt the Circles were part of the coming changes,"[79] and there are many people today who share the belief that we are at a profoundly important moment in history. Given the variety of crises that we are facing simultaneously, including the readily apparent changes to the global climate, this seems clear. Writing in the late 1950s, near the end of his life, Jung offered his own version of this sentiment:

> There is a general feeling today, to be sure, that we have reached a significant turning point in the ages, but people imagine that the great change has to do with nuclear fission and fusion, or with space rockets. What is concurrently taking place in the human psyche is usually overlooked.[80]

If we do live at a "significant turning point in the ages," then surely no better sign of it could be provided than what we have before us in Crop Circle formations around the world. However, such a conclusion remains for each one of us to reach on our own. Through the ages, the history of our responses to the phenomenon shows us not a truth about Crop Circles, but rather a truth about ourselves. While the scientific facts of the phenomenon's physical changes to the plants constricts it into a definite reality, our theories about it open us up to vast possibilities within our imagination and reflect the psychological truth that lives unconsciously within us. As Fideler first said, Crop Circles are a kind of Rorschach test, and our responses to them show a clear trend across the centuries—as time has passed, our responses to them have been less vivid, less colorful, less invested with awe, and more abstract, diminished, and intellectualized. Their numinous power and their ability to inspire dances and devils (and perhaps stone circles too) has gone from us for the most part. Most of the time, we are left with only theories and ideas, thoughts and "solutions." Increasingly, our responses to Crop Circles have had less passion and been less emotional. Our imaginative participation is absent, replaced with an automatic unconscious denial of mystery and, for the most part, a rational-minded reduction of our experience. Might this lost capacity also be tied to the environmental crisis we face? Might our inability to look upon Crop Circles with awe reflect our inability to look upon the world around us with awe too? If so, then consciously looking upon the history of our responses to Crop Circles, and unraveling the story of how we can respond to this great mystery with so little passion, may help us to successfully pass through this "turning point of the ages."

The history of our theoretical reactions to the phenomenon by its age and quantity provides an additional piece of evidence, which along with the scientific facts helps us to rebuff the notion that it's a hoax and aids us in overcoming our denial of it. Perhaps, just as important, considering the history of our cultural responses and looking at our own personal reactions may offer the possibility of unfolding *something further of ourselves*. Whether one prefers to take a spiritual, extraterrestrial, Gaia-oriented, or other theoretical response, or one prefers to not respond at all, each reaction can lead to a deeper questioning and provide an opportunity for self-exploration, if one is open to it. The history of our theories should remind you that our reactions are imperfect and that this is a work in progress. Can you make room for your own work? What do you think is behind all this—aliens, spirits, something else? When you read about each of these how do you *feel*? Where is there passion and emotional power? Are you angry, sad, happy, or relieved? What is your honest reaction?

> The Crop Circles are part of a process, not an end in themselves—and they should never be regarded as such. . . . [They] are an integral part of the thread which binds us all together in the tapestry of life, woven from the finery of the universal plan. . . . It is within ourselves that we find the means to solve the Crop Circle enigma, and to realise that they involve a greater quest than a three-dimensional search for meaning.[81]

Can we give ourselves permission to go on such a search? Can we allow ourselves the space to not know right away? Can we look at Crop Circles without immediately lessening its mystery? Might an open imagination be able to rejoin scientific facts to their ground in bodily experience? If we were able to break through the diminution of our emotional involvement that is characteristic of our culture, without losing our capacity for accurate distinction, what might we feel inside ourselves as we look at Crop Circles? Awe? Wonder? Invigoration? Or would we say quietly to ourselves, as that friend of mine did, "What a relief," feeling within her a gratitude for something more existing in the world. Does all of this leave you wondering whether we *actually are* living in a time of profound transition? Could it even be possible that we might find the Rorschach test looking back at us, that somehow through looking at Crop Circles we could be led to look anew at ourselves and at the world around us?

> In this way the mystery of the crop circles can never be an insular thing, it cannot be solely a matter of investigation and physical evidence. It is something much more wide reaching and requires of us an ever-opening mind that is able to seek out new directions and possibilities; and a realization that the crop circle is only the beginning, and where we go from there is, as always, up to us.[82]

THREE GREENING CIRCLES

The history of our responses to Crop Circle formations could be said to be a story of our relating to a stranger, an Other. While some may have danced and commemorated finding them, at some point they became feared too and like "the 'other fellow,' who in his strangeness is always suspect,"[1] were cast as a Devil. With the advent of a culture of science, we began to imagine natural causes for their formation and dropped the magic from our reaction. They became just another phenomenon to be studied, and in doing so known and mastered like all the rest. Here the stranger holds no wonder and is neither a blessing or a curse. As with so many strangers we pass every day, our predominant response is a not-seeing, no interest, no curiosity. In each case of our responding to them, Crop Circles are "pulled into the already existing trend of consciousness."[2] What can we understand about ourselves in viewing it as Devil, wind, or weather? What can we see of ourselves in the movement of our theories and in their development and direction? What can these reactions tell us about who we are and have been?

What too can we tell of its essential symbol—of its nature as being birthed from a circular form? Crop Circles are prototypically, though not exclusively, circular. Historically, the phenomenon originated around the world in circular form, and psychological significance also lies in the fact that the phenomenon is referred to as Crop Circles.[3] From a Jungian perspective it is remarkable that the emergence of the phenomenon into greater complexity, while maintaining its concentric form, is a progression that mirrors the expressions of the Self archetype.[4] Both in the spontaneous productions of his patients and throughout the world's religious iconography, Jung observed a coherent unifying purpose. In each case, "through the ritual action [of drawing the circle], attention and interest are led back to the inner, sacred precinct, which is the source and goal of the psyche and contains the unity of life and consciousness."[5] Throughout mythology and religious representation, the circle is regarded as a symbol of "undivided completeness" and of our essential "freedom from distinction or separation."[6] In the symbols of the Self archetype, Jung saw Nature's miraculous ability to evolve into something new, while maintaining its form. It is in this sense that the circle embraces "both that of eternity and that of a perpetual series of fresh beginnings."[7] Yet even as a symbol of this kind, how do Crop Circles remain a stranger to us, a kind of Other?

The German philosopher Immanuel Kant (1724–1804) warned that one could never know the "thing-in-itself" but only our experience of that thing. Objective reality is never known by us in its essential truth; rather, we have only our subjective knowledge of it. Jung (and Freud) observed the profundity with which this truth influences human experience. Beneath the conscious strata of our awareness lies a burgeoning cauldron of unconscious instinct and archetype, which affects our perception of everything that we encounter. Often, through what they termed projection, we are moved to experience the reality of someone or something with a special twinkle, tinge, or taint that is not necessarily a quality of that "thing-in-itself." Such automatic responses are natural and occur unconsciously, and, as such, they are both "ubiquitous and inevitable."[8]

Coloring our experience of the world, unconscious projection can have us feeling, thinking, and believing that someone or something, is better, worse, or somehow different than it actually is. We can believe that someone is invested with good qualities that we do not possess ourselves (as cult followers believe of their guru), or that "those people" are the source of "all that is wrong with the world" (often accompanied with the belief that my group is the source of all that is right in the world). The power of such beliefs cannot be underestimated: the great horrors of the past century, and this new one, stand as a testament to the power of the psyche to have us believe with utter conviction that heaven can be brought forth through the elimination of "them." It is this dynamic that allows the other group to be dehumanized in one's experience—known not as a subject, but as an object, devoid of the quality that makes us human. We continue to witness the malevolent power of this dynamic today. Yet, projection plays some role, both positively and negatively, in all of our relating to people, objects, and ideas—it is part of the currency of our psychological interrelating. Falling in love is influenced strongly by projection and it greases the wheel of our day-to-day view of others. "So long as the libido can use these projections as agreeable and convenient bridges to the world, they will alleviate life in a positive way."[9]

"We don't make projections, we meet with them,"[10] says Jungian analyst Daryl Sharp, and one of the most common projections that we meet is that of the shadow. Jung defined the shadow as "utterly different from the conscious ego"[11] and from who we think of ourselves to be. It is "the thing a person has no wish to be,"[12] as well as the unconscious repository of what is unacceptable to our conscious self-image. It is our darkness, our feelings of inferiority, our woundedness, and parts of our primitive and instinctual self. It is everything about ourselves that we seek to keep hidden from others, and often from ourselves as well. Most often, we come to experience the shadow in a "strong, irrational projection, positive or negative, upon one's neighbor"[13] and "to the extent that I have to be right and good, he, she, or they become the carriers of all the evil which I fail to acknowledge within myself."[14] The shadow does not consist only of repressed formerly conscious elements, but is broader and deeper. The shadow exists in contrast to the ego's bright self-image. In Jungian psychology, the shadow is understood as including the instinctive and creative parts of ourselves that we have not yet integrated. Because "the shadow is the repository of what is unacceptable to consciousness. It is therefore ripe for projection."[15] It is also the darkest aspects of our humanity and our worst selves. In this sense the shadow is related to evil and finds itself ultimately personified as the Devil. In looking at the medieval characterization of the agent behind Crop Circles as the Devil, it is easy to see the projection of the shadow. But there is also something deeper going on.

For the medieval farmer, the world was filled with spirits. The descriptions of Crop Circle formations as "pisky beds" and "fairy circles" points to the prevalence of this magical worldview.[16] Historical evidence makes clear that even after the introduction of Christianity across Europe, pagan belief and tradition survived. Farmer and wife practiced ancient rituals to ensure the fertility of their land. The rituals they undertook reflected their living psychological and emotional connection to Nature's dark mystery: the miracle of the seed emerging from the ground; the magic of the moon's cycle; the wonder of the newborn child arriving out of the void of the womb. In contrast to the earthy, downward focus of this kind of spirituality, which was most often Goddess-oriented, the arrival of the Patriarchal God image brings an upward-directed spirituality to the pagans of Europe. Suddenly divinity is light, revelation can be found in reason, and God is a Father "up there." Christianity introduced European medieval farmers to a wholly new view of spirituality, themselves, and the cosmos. Nature was no longer the source of the world's profound wonder. Instead, there was a righteous and loving God who existed outside of the world and provided for humanity (Chapter Five looks at this further). But this new view stood psychologically in opposition to all that had come before. To some extent, the Church tried to smooth the transition by Christian-izing pagan rituals and locating religious holidays on the same dates as these celebrations (e.g. Christmas near winter solstice, its symbol made a tree, and the name of the Easter celebration taken from the Goddess).[17] However, imagine that for centuries you and your family have celebrated in a certain fashion and are suddenly instructed that your beliefs and rituals are entirely wrong (and bad) and that a new way is required of you. While this transition may have been easy for some, for most it meant uprooting practices and an entire psychological shift in self-understanding. For medieval Christians (especially farmers), it must have been an immense psychological challenge to let go of rituals that had celebrated the land on which their survival depended. As well, it was a way of understanding the divine that celebrated their interaction with the living spirituality of the land. Of even greater difficulty was the challenge to live up to a vision of themselves in which Christian goodness is equated with rational choice, an upward movement out of Nature and a bright Solar spirituality. Especially when so much of their previous culture and natural selves were tied up in the psychological dark of Nature, the moon, and the libido. This transition epitomizes the shift from an archetypal feminine psychology to an archetypally masculine one.[18] The new religion required a new way of seeing oneself and of relating to the community. A new measure of goodness was offered in Christianity, and while there was great depth to this change for some, for many new believers it meant only adoption of a new public face, a new persona, or outer image.

Standing in direct contradistinction to the shadow, the persona is our public mask. The persona is who we think we should be, how we imagine we should behave, and our idea of what we should be thinking. Clearly there is a great difference between a Christian persona and a pagan one. The persona is often associated with our profession or gender role (and the lack of one can speak to a maladjustment to society).[19] There is often a great deal of difference between the way we are seen by coworkers and colleagues and how our family and friends know us. The persona, seen by the outside world, can be very different from who we actually are, and even centuries after becoming Christian the culture of European farmers remained a mishmash of pagan pageantry and priest-led piety. This split lived as much within the individual's psyche as it did in external ritual and rite. There is intense inner conflict between a persona equated with the new Christian view of God as rational and light, and the primitive, dark, primal natural self of our prehistory. This conflict remains with us today and the problem becomes what to do with the conflict engendered with Christianity's introduction. It is always easier to project the conflict outward onto others than it is to hold it ourselves. Chaotic influences threaten an unstable self-image, and as Jung writes, "everyone carries a shadow, and the less embodied in the individual's conscious life, the blacker and denser it is."[20] Given the presence of this preexisting conflict, the medieval Christian farmer's tentative attachment to his new faith and new self-image must have been radically challenged by the extraordinary experience of discovering a Crop Circle formation. At this stage, when one encounters something powerfully numinous but unorthodox, seeing it as the Devil is natural. A collective value demanded not only restriction of our response to the phenomenon, but also recrimination of our urge to respond to it differently. Projection enables this effect through the characterization of what was seen as unholy and demonic. The medieval witness of a Crop Circle could not allow himself to be carried by what was seen there and had to say no to it. The voice inside himself may have, in some way, wanted to say yes to it, just as it had carried his ancestors to call such things "pisky beds" and "fairy circles." The newly Christian farmer was asked to cut himself from such dark impiety, to see himself in the light of God's righteousness and to name what he saw as the work of the Devil. Jung observed that "to the degree that we identify with a bright persona, the shadow is correspondingly dark."[21] These feelings had to be "cast out" and projection effected relief for this anxiety. Standing with one foot in the old darkness of the magical pagan world and with one foot in the new light of Christianity, the medieval farmer who stumbled upon a Crop Circle was between a rock and a hard place—it could only be the work of the Devil—"or would I be made to blame?" His grasp on his self-image as a worthy Christian is already tenuous by his proximity to his own pagan heritage, and the shadow is projected onto the phenomenon to reduce his inner distress. In casting the Devil as the agent behind the phenomenon, one can gain sight of the tremendous complexity in the experience of the profound struggle between modern and primitive humanity. History has witnessed this dynamic—inability to admit even the possibility of one's own fallibility in endless variations. The Inquisition, anti-Semitism, and witch burnings all exemplify how the Other constellates an encounter with all that is rejected in oneself. In these examples, the early Christian's own conflict and feelings of unworthiness are projected onto the unfortunate nonbeliever, Jew, or "witch."

As we move toward becoming civilized in the modern world, our conscious mind is taught to control certain responses and actions. Instinct is curtailed to the benefit of society, and we are taught to restrict our thoughts ("How could you think that way?"). Like a child conditioned by his parents to behave a certain way and not to "act like that," culture strongly influences our automatic unconscious responses. This same operative mode acts within the psyche, keeping our self-image intact and our ego healthy. However, also like a child, the ego is often insistent upon ruling its dominion, and seeing parts of the psyche existing outside of our current self-image can be threatening to this drive. Coming into contact with something existing outside of the illusion of itself brings a defensive reaction from the ego and often even a "censoring and denying of inner experience."[22] "In order to protect its own control and sovereignty the ego instinctively puts up a great resistance to the confrontation with the shadow; when it catches a glimpse of the shadow the ego most often reacts with an attempt to eliminate it."[23] Repression, or the blocking out of psychic facts, enables a continued preservation of the ego's self-image and keeps us insulated from what lies below. Attempts to eliminate the shadow can be made in a variety of ways. One can project the shadow onto an outer other, repress it, or even deny it altogether. Each of these reduces the anxiety produced by seeing it in ourselves. Equally effective is to intellectualize it, as Jung says, and "then one can live with it quite well." Each of these defenses reduces the emotional content of what was experienced and, in doing so, neutralizes its impact on our psyche. By virtue of being born into the time and place in which we live, each of us experiences struggle between our higher and lower self. Regardless of our religious creed, most Westerners live with conflicts between aim and urge, reason and craving. "We are Christianized in the higher levels of the psyche, but down below we are still completely pagan."[24]

Such psychological conditioning is important in our consideration of Crop Circles. As we began to approach the modern worldview, changes in the way we viewed the world were reflected in the response that we had to formations. Where they had suggested pixies, dancing rings, and Mowing Devils previously, now they brought forth images of "wind action." This change reflects a new relationship of ego to shadow, where imagination and instinct have given way to something more objective in the psyche. In the psychological conditioning begun in the era of the Enlightenment and the scientific revolution, we have developed defense mechanisms that both inhibit us and enable us to function in society by the time adulthood is reached. Projection, repression, and intellectualization are defense mechanisms that enable our escape from inner conflict. Each of these is well developed in our individual ways during our childhood and adolescence. In each of these defensive reactions, our capacity for feeling experience of the content before us is diminished, or even neutralized. To some degree, in each of us, these defensive responses form an adaptive pattern of reaction that reduces our feeling responses and shapes how we think. Branden provides a metaphor for how repression can affect us globally: "When one is given an anesthetic in preparation for surgery, it is not merely the capacity to experience pain that is suspended; the capacity to experience pleasure goes also—because what is blocked is the capacity to experience *feeling*."[25] Our unconscious defenses inform not only how we think about the formations but whether we respond to them at all. It is our defenses that inform how much weight we will give to the matter. To the degree that psychological defense impedes our capacity for feeling response to something, its *value* to us is limited:

> Phenomenon cannot be grasped in its totality by the intellect, for it consists not only of meaning but also of value, and this depends on the intensity of the accompanying feeling tones. . . . [T]he feeling value is very important criterion which psychology cannot do without, because it determines in large measure the role the content will play in the psychic economy. . . . [T]he affective value gives the measure of the intensity of an idea, and the intensity in its turn expresses that idea's energic tension, its effective potential.[26]

Although the Enlightenment era's responses to Crop Circles demonstrate sophistication, they also show the first stages of the modern loss of "energic tension" and "effective potential" that we see so clearly today. In comparison to those who saw in it the Devil, a pixie, or a miracle to be commemorated in stone, when the phenomenon is met by the distanced, scientific eye something of its vivid character is lost. This form of response provides the psychological security of an *illusion of control* over the phenomenon, but it does so through the *restriction* of our response to it. Here the observer mistakes measurement for mastery, and in deluded grandeur loses the numinous quality of what is being observed. In facing the phenomenon in this way, loss of control is avoided and fear and frustration skirted, but missing too is exhilaration, joy, and wonder. The writings of Sir Francis Bacon (1561–1626) depict perfectly the attitude taken toward phenomenon through the scientific lens of this time, and remain present in the perspective of our culture today: "I am come in very truth leading to you Nature with all her children to bind her to your service and make her your slave. . . . You have but to follow and as it were hound Nature in her wanderings, and you will be able, when you like, to lead and drive her afterwards to the same place again."[27] Bacon's words illustrate the psyche's loss of the ability to perceive mystery in the world around it. Nature and the phenomenal world are rightly to be made a slave, a position that precisely mirrors the ego's increasing grandiosity within the psyche that characterizes the modern era. In this approach there is an absolute privileging of the quantitative, objective dimension of reality over and above any of its qualitative aspects. Here, the stranger is considered as an object to be studied, measured, and reported upon, as the assumption is made that we need not look any further in order to know what he is about. Here, mystery has been neutralized emotionally.

> In the last paper he wrote, Jung pointed out that this is a great temptation for the intellectual type because intellectuals overlook the emotional and feeling factor, which is always connected with an archetypal image. An archetypal image is not only a thought pattern; it is also an emotional experience—the emotional experience of an individual. Only if it has emotional and feeling value for an individual is it alive and meaningful.[28]

In facing Crop Circles through the lens of this distanced, scientific approach, the living dynamism available to us within our experience of it is compromised. Without any felt connection to what is viewed, one's psychological involvement is curtailed as "affect reveals the locus and force of psychological values."[29] Without a measure of felt relatedness to what we experience *(eros)*, we can sit without a care for the world. Feeling values reflect part of the truth of who we are and, typically, whether or not we care about something is shown in the intensity, or lack of, our feelings for it. While the scientific responses to the phenomenon provide us with tremendous objectively valuable information, the objectivity of this response reflects an impeded ability to participate subjectively with the phenomenon, to find a feeling response to it and to come to a proper measure of its value to us. Both personally and collectively, Jung recognized that in those areas in which our feeling value is inferior, our moral judgment is impeded.[30] As examined further in later chapters, the degree of feeling absent in modern responses to the Crop Circle phenomena can be understood not only as denial, but as a product of the shadow at its most effective. Not requiring the gauche imagery of the Devil, the shadow achieves its goal of our nonparticipation with new content just as effectively today, if not more so, through the injection of the needle of emotional neutralization and subtle denial.

In this respect, the modern nonresponse is served very well by the production of hoaxed formations. Where the Enlightenment responses to the phenomenon fall into the illusion of mastery over it (removing the possibility of any Other from its agency), with the introduction of hoaxed formations in the last twenty years this rational-minded denial of it is given a final stamp of approval—"see, the Other wasn't real all along." Removing the possibility of an Other as agent is appealing to the ego, because it saves us from having to actually think about what it would mean—*for us personally*—if the phenomenon were real. Each of us has a vast set of beliefs and opinions from which we construct our identity, and perceiving the reality of something of this magnitude threatens all that our worldview is based on. Even those interested enough to look more closely at the facts, history, and newly arriving formations have their unconscious pressure to participate more fully with it reduced by the doubt introduced by hoaxing. We are also likely to have a strongly assembled set of beliefs about the phenomenon's agency and purpose that may reflect or reinforce a preconceived self-image. Hoaxing is the ego's soothing salvation, because it allows us to doubt, to deny, and to feel little emotional discomfort in doing so. Through hoaxing we are let off the hook and allowed to believe that the whole thing is fake, thereby enabling us to keep our involvement at a distance.

If one chooses to believe that the most likely root source for the production of the intricate hoaxes constructed in England (since approximately 1990) is governmental, then they can be seen to be acting in the same way that the ego does when something genuinely new is introduced into consciousness: very often it represses it by any means necessary, even by automatically making one go unconscious.[31] (And perhaps governments think that they are right to do so and that they are protecting the populace from a truth they can't handle.)

One can understand hoaxing and denial as another stage in our response to Crop Circles: a series of reactions that reflect the psychology of the time and that could not have been other than they were. But it is also clear that in our current moment there is a bidirectional course that can be discriminated in the history of our responses. On the one hand, there is *increasing objectivity* in our responses, from pixies and Devils to wind and weather (and even hoaxing), that demonstrates a more consciously chosen and less projective series of responses. On the other hand, however, there is a *lessening of our emotional participation* with the phenomenon, a decreased ability to respond with feeling to what we see before us. And so we have an ever-more-detached relationship between what we know and how we feel about it. We are able to discriminate its details with greater precision, but *less able to place value on what we conclude* about it. This dichotomy does not only apply to Crop Circles—it is one that can be understood as defining our modern present moment. The movement from primitive projective responses to discrimination and denial is one that mirrors Western culture's larger psychological journey. In each, we see consciousness gained and something vital lost. We know the facts, but cannot tell the story as those before us did, to achieve "a vivifying effect and a satisfactory reaction [that brings] one into peace with one's unconscious substratum, just as the telling of fairy tales always did."[32] To tell the story of our discovery of Crop Circles in a way that achieves a "vivifying effect" and produces a satisfying, peaceful accord with the unconscious, it is necessary to look more closely at the meaning of its essentially circular nature. Perhaps, in doing so, we will have to open ourselves to *both* discrimination and imagination, and permit ourselves to wonder about what it might mean that Crop Circles' concentric evolution mirrors the way in which the Self archetype unfolds in the psyche, and that we seem to share something essential of our nature with the phenomenon.

The circle is among the oldest known pictographic symbols, and from our earliest attempts at expression the circle has been used to voice our awe for Creation. Related to the forms of sphere and spiral, symbols of this kind offer a way by which our ancestors could express their identification with, and sense of containment within, the natural world's cyclical majesty— their wonder at life energy itself: "Parkin observes in his *Prehistoric Art* that no ornamental motif seems to have been more attractive than the spiral."[33] Circular forms predominate throughout the natural world. To begin to consider the circle symbolically is to discover its nature as an emblem of relatedness and relationship of the inclusion of the parts within a greater whole. This is an understanding expressed in the native greeting of 'All my relations' and embodied in their sacred hoop.

Everything the Power of the World does is done in a circle. The sky is round, and I have heard that the earth is round like a ball, and so are all the stars. The wind, its greatest power, whirls. Birds make their nests in circles, for theirs is the same religion as ours. The sun comes forth and goes down again in a circle. The moon does the same, and both are round. Even the seasons form a great circle in their changing, and always come back again to where they were. The life of a man is a circle from childhood to childhood, and so it is in everything where power moves. Our teepees were round like the nest of birds, and these were always set in a circle, the nation's hoop, a nest of many nests, where the Great Spirit meant for us to hatch our children.[34]

Nature protects the egg with a shell, the fruit with a peel, and the bubble by its shape. Geometry provides its sphere as the most perfect distribution of stress around an object. The circle illustrates the process of life that brings us to maturity: in the womb we grow, by the parent we are held, and in the family we bond. However, as we mature we separate, first from our mother and then our family. From within an enclosed safety we emerge, as instinct compels us out of our old shells; we gain self-awareness and the strength needed to transform ourselves in the next phase of our development. Yet, even as we grow, separate, and make new bonds, we remain bound in affection to our family. Nature provides each of us with these just-right processes—by them we are afforded Her gifts. They are the matrices of our lives, we live in them both physically and psychologically, and our physical and psychological selves grow within them.

The spiral form too expresses the energetic qualities of Nature's growth. In the turning flow of the spiral, often depicted with outreaching buds of plant growth, anthropologist Maria Gimbutas sees an image of the joyous sensation of the triumph of life. Often such dynamic symbols are shown as either energy incarnate, or as the stimulators of the process of becoming. The circular, spiral form is displayed throughout Nature in the forms and patterns of life's development:

> The life-force power within the spiral is demonstrated pictorially when spirals transform into plants, as leaves branch off from their outer turnings. The spiraling force affects the germination and growth of trees and plants. Beautiful examples of these spiral/plant combinations come from the art of Malta and Minoan Crete. In human life, the umbilical cord is itself a serpentine connection between the mother and new life. (Gimbutas)[35]

Taken a step farther by our ancestors, the spiral comes to represent both life and afterlife. We see this for example at Ireland's Newgrange site, where the spiral is used as funerary monument and as a symbol of spiritual journey. Such circuitous symbols also point to death's regeneration in the renewal of Nature—movement from the point of death to life, from dark to full moon, from winter to spring, and through our cycles of birth, menstruation, fertility, and death. One sees this association in the stone circles of the English countryside—the landmarks that mark the observance of cyclical time and infuse life's rhythms into human worship. Traditional Celtic knotwork also displays this same symbolic relativity; as Canon Martin Wallace explains, "untying" Celtic knotwork reveals how "the interwoven patterns emphasize that everything in Creation is connected. We live as interconnected people not isolated units. . . . The process of ever deepening reflection can never cease, just as the patterns themselves have no end."[36]

> The Celtic imagination loved the circle. It recognized how the rhythm of experience, nature and divinity followed a circular pattern. (O' Donoghue)[37]

The circle is a symbol that gives voice to our innate sense of interrelatedness, to our reverence for Nature and our embeddedness within it. It points toward Nature's rhythms, reminding us of the direction to the center and of all those ways in which we are held in larger circles and contained in living cycles. As individuals, we are our own whole being, yet we are always also only a part. In our families, we are a part of biological and historic greater wholes. The circle depicts the protection and safety, sustenance and nurturance that our communal bonds can offer. To encircle means to include and surround, suggesting ancestors, community, our connection with others, and our circle of friends and bonds of marriage with its symbol a ring. The circle can stand for the kinship group, the clan, and the tribe.[38] Inside of the circle, we find safety, home, harbor, and shelter. Such limitations define who we are and who we choose to join. All of nature uses such boundaries in order to grow: "in order to manifest, we must limit."[39]

> The circle encloses a space. That which is inside the circle is protected, strengthened, and delimited. The circle recalls the matrifocal village, of ancient sacred spaces, and of countless forms in nature. (Fincher)[40]

As Nature provides a perfect habitat for growth externally, internally too our conscious mind exists within a living system that allows for both continuity and growth. Our conscious selves grow, change, and transform; yet our personhood remains intact. Whole new beliefs and ways of feeling emerge from somewhere inside us, yet we remain who we are. Within the psyche, the ego is contained within a greater psychological foundation out of which it develops. In Jungian psychology, the circle is understood as representing that in which the ego is contained. It is an image of this greater whole—as the person is symbolized in relation to the natural world, the ego symbolized in relation to the unconscious foundation from which it develops. In the circle, the whole structure of the psyche is represented. All different elements and parts of consciousness together are seen in their natural relatedness.

> The circle is a symbol of the Self. It expresses the totality of the psyche in all its aspects, including the relationship between man and the whole of nature. (Jung)[41]

The term "Self" refers to the psychological principle within us that directs our growth and toward which we are unconsciously striving. "[It is] the principle of coherence, structure, organization that governs balance and integration of psychic contents."[42] The activity of the Self archetype, and its image as circle, is an expression of the instinct that all living systems have to continuously renew themselves, and regulate this process in such a way that the integrity of their structure is maintained. Like the Nautilus shell whose spiral repeats the same pattern while simultaneously growing into larger physical size, the Self archetype preserves our inherent harmony while allowing for our growth into greater consciousness. It is the energy within us that draws together a healthy ego, and it is both the container in which, and from which, this growth occurs.

The relationship between the ego and the Self is expressed such that the Self usually seeks the expansion of consciousness and the ego clings tightly to the mode of consciousness that it has already developed. Most often, the ego holds the current view, while the Self offers the possibility of a new way of responding. If given room inside us, the tension between the two eventually produces a new way of seeing the world. This is a natural process in which what was formerly paradoxical to us suddenly makes sense. We see this regularly in children. For example, the child psychologist Piaget describes a stage of learning at which a taller glass can be made to appear to have more liquid in it than a shorter glass of equal volume. As the child grows, they are no longer fooled by this vertical illusion—what previously tricked us no longer does.

> The tension between opposites is a conflict that, when held in a dialectic relationship of allowing influences from both sides, can resolve into a "uniting third" or new synthesis. This function [is] the center of growth. (Eisendrath-Young)[43]

While we are drawn toward this force for growth within us, we simultaneously have an innate resistance to its process. Our egos resist recognition of new material because it conflicts with their current way of making sense of the world. Coming from a direction that we are not used to looking toward, in our experiences with the new we discover something emerging that was previously left out of consciousness—a blind spot in our psyches. Therefore, such experiences are like greeting a visitor for whom we are not prepared, and our reception of them becomes a delicate matter to be handled with care. In our experience of this process, the new thing is never what we expect it to be. It is an expression of the total personality, an unintegrated piece of the whole of all the possibilities unconsciously present within the individual. From this whole place, an element appears that is far removed, if not opposite to, our current conscious way of understanding the world. If we can open up to this process, we are often presented with new pieces of ourselves, and perhaps even a new sense of the world. One of the goals of psychotherapy is the advancement of this natural process within us. Jung called this process "individuation" and said its by-product is a greater sense of wholeness, the achievement of which is always qualitative rather than quantitative; to even speak of it as an achievement is incorrect since it cannot be sought directly. It does, however, involve attempting the honest realization of further qualities of ourselves, even those qualities that we are afraid of and dislike. Wholeness is not perfection, flawlessness, or social normality, and our developing of it may require us to move in opposition to each of these. We might find it in our mistakes, rather than in our triumphs. We also might find it in a strength that we did not know we had. It brings to us change, and our engagement with it might only begin after our own wounding. All of Nature's living systems seek to balance stability and growth, and in order to integrate a greater depth of ourselves this process always requires the introduction of something new and unexpected into our lives. How likely are we to look at ourselves until we see that our vision of ourselves as complete no longer holds water? Without our vulnerability there is little room for the new. Wholeness brings a stronger connection to our personal authenticity; it is a coming to fruition of our individual, imperfect, and genuine selves. Such development is always a unique flowering, and it is only ever begun by our choice to make a place within us for a seed to grow.

When symbols of the Self occur in our dreams and other forms, such images often point us toward this new direction, reminding us of our need for it or demarcating our arrival there. Often appearing at times of confusion, they can act as a light in the darkness. Symbols both of the destination and the route to get there, they are instruments that help to bring order into being.[44] Producing dreams and fantasies of concentric images in the mind's eye, they act as healing vehicles during periods of dissociation and conflict. Images affecting this function are most basically circular or concentric and their centrality reflects their *reintroduction of a containing and unifying principle.* While the shape's arrangement around a focal point offers a coherent orienting image, the shape's outer edge (its boundary) also serves a purpose. As living creatures exist through the presence of a boundary (the cellular wall in biology), likewise the boundary of the Self's image reflects the psyche's capacity to repel invasion. Such a symbol shows chaos held back, even if only momentarily, and the provision is offered for the creation of a new foundation. Symbolic cities or cell walls may appear and reorient us in concentric fashion, while illustrating natural boundaries. Rings or crowns may enter, reflecting the royal nature of the function that the Self serves in blessing the entry of the new and lesser into the greater sanctum of the whole. Inner castles, tents, and temples may be found, demarcating and consecrating a space that permits entry only to that which serves the forward motion of growth. Arriving spontaneously in moments of disorientation as a compensatory unifying symbol, these symbols offer the possibility of real healing, and our experience of them is not abstract.

Jung found [such] symbolism occurring spontaneously in the dreams and visions of many of his patients. Its appearance was incomprehensible to them, but it was usually accompanied by a strong feeling of harmony or of peace. (Fordham)[45]

Clinical research shows that, even among children, images of the Self archetype appear spontaneously in response to threatening internal or external psychological conditions, acting as protective forms at times when the ego is threatened by disruptive forces. Fordham cites several occasions with children when the drawing of a circle was associated with the word "I," which led to some effective action the child had previously been unable to take.[46] Such observances are not simply intellectual, as they point to experiences that are lived in our whole bodies. The emergence of such images mirrors our reconnection to the whole, or help to affect that reconnection, and point us toward that larger part of ourselves beyond the conscious mind and greater than the ego.

Concentric images exemplify the peaceful, centered experience of the Self's arrival within us: flowers—radial petals extending from its bud and gardens arranged, containing and protective. For thousands of years, mystic traditions have used similar images for contemplation and the productions of the Self, and the images of religious devotion overlap with them to a great extent. While these images represent and serve a natural self-organizing function within the psyche, in the same way such images have been used from our earliest history as aids for spiritual contemplation. Within traditional practices, the circular form is often carried into greater and more complex designs, commonly referred to uniformly today as mandalas (Sanskrit for "magic circle"). Such symbols are used worldwide to represent our conceptions of the divine and to help us reconnect with the sacred. Internally these symbols reflect that part of ourselves that is capable of rediscovering the whole within us and redirecting the psyche toward health.

Through the ritual action [of drawing the circle], attention and interest are led back to the inner, sacred precinct, which is the source and goal of the psyche and contains the unity of life and consciousness. (Jung)[47]

Jung recognized the special power of the images of the Self to demarcate a *temenos* (Greek for "sacred space"), that was "set apart either by circumambulation or by drawing a circle." Set off, it excludes entry to what is without and protects and concentrates what is within. As von Franz describes, the word "*temno*, to cut . . . indicates being cut out from the meaningless, profane layer of life—a part cut out and isolated for a special purpose."[48] We find this same meaning in the concentric form, given to the divine in worldwide religious tradition. Cultures as diverse as Buddhism, Western and Eastern Christianity, and Latin, African, and North American indigenous traditions use this form to express the same inner compulsion toward realignment in the psyche. For Westerners, the quadrate stained-glass windows of churches and cathedrals serve to exalt the soul toward peace and inner contemplation. Zen Buddhists employ drawings of concentric circles to symbolize the stages of inner perfection and the progressive harmonization of the spirit.[49] Navajo sandpainting is used as a vehicle for both ritual and healing, and the ill person is sometimes even placed into its center, symbolically re-creating the desired return to harmony. In the process of Tibetan sandpainting, the mandala serves to place the mind into the right perspective and reflect a universal view—the Mandala's center is the center of the cosmos.[50] The use of such forms as a device for cosmological reorientation is ubiquitous in religious and mythic symbolic tradition.

To the ancients, the observed cosmos presented itself inescapably as

> circular—not only the planets themselves . . . but also their cyclical movements and the recurring cycles of the seasons. . . . The ritual of walking around a sacred object, or defining and sanctifying a space by making a circuit of it, imitates solar and astral cycles, and pays homage to celestial forces and the protective symbolism of the circle.[51]

Plato wrote that the Creator "made the world in the shape of a sphere, giving it that figure which of all is the most perfect and the most equal to itself."[52] Having no beginning or end, and no divisions, it is a symbol of eternity, of that which is timeless, from which the Greeks drew the conclusion that "the nature of God is a circle of which the center is everywhere and the circumference is nowhere." Therefore, they understood that, being "finished and perfect, the circle is the symbol of the Absolute,"[53] and thus it could be understood as "the most important and most universal of all geometric symbols in mystical thought."[54]

Philosophers and theologians would consider the circle as symbolizing the god-head viewed not only as immutable, but also as a goodness broadcast in the creation, subsistence and consummation of all things, or what Christian tradition would term the alpha and omega.[55]

Psychologically, the Self cannot be fully expressed. Although we can observe its patterning both intrapsychically and as it is expressed externally, we cannot bottle it: "it is a symbol, yet you can talk about it, you can explain it. But you can never explain what the Self is, because the Self in itself is unthinkable."[56] Jung's understanding of the archetypal Self within the psyche sees it as relating to both our capacity for growth as individuals and to our call toward the divine. However, it is important to note that Jung did not see this archetype as a replacement for religious practice or metaphysical truth, but rather, following the Zen saying that "the finger pointing to the moon is not the moon," our observance of the archetype is only the name of the Tao, not Tao itself. Observing the presence of the Self archetype does not leave us dissected from theological or metaphysical concerns, and should not be confused with the reality of God itself or the lack thereof. But we can see that in our participation with the images of the Self, they become the windows through which humanity touches the eternal in itself.[57]

Participation in religious and indigenous traditions of ritual dance, procession, pilgrimage, sandpainting, and other ceremonies using concentrically arranged form can be seen as offering a living experience of a symbol's pre-rational mystery. As Bachofen describes: "[it] is precisely the great dignity of the symbol, that it . . . leads from the truths of the physical life to those of a higher spiritual order."[58] Ritual participation with such concentric forms is made as a kind of physical sacrifice in the hopes of bringing oneself into harmony with the greater inside of us. Beyond their ceremonial purpose, such rituals are undertaken in the hope that participants may be able to forge a connection to Spirit within themselves. Like the mandala, walking a labyrinth, for example, invites "relationship and offer[s] a whole way of seeing,"[59] writes the Revered Dr. Lauren Artress of San Francisco's Grace Cathedral, who houses participation with this process through the provision of the permanent labyrinth in her church and workshops conducted abroad. Campbell has written of the great cathedral and labyrinth at

Chartres in France that it "talks to me about the spiritual information of the world."[60] Mystic tradition exemplifies this truth in practice. The great pilgrimage of the Muslim world focuses upon its holiest object, the Ka'ba, and its shrine at Mecca. There, the pilgrim proceeds around the holy object in contemplation, footsteps giving life to belief. One future mystic, Ibn Arabi (1201–2), walked as a pilgrim in ritual participation and describes his life-changing moment, an occasion of union spontaneously erupted:

> I see the building animated by those who circle round it. Behold the secret building before it is too late, and thou wilt see how it takes on life through those who circle round it and walk round its stones, and how it looks out at them from behind its veils and cloaks.[61]

Here, at the center of the pilgrimage, the sacred object becomes animated by the movement of the periphery. The pilgrims themselves and the relation between the two bring each to life. This precisely mirrors the life-animating force of the Self's ideal healthy relation to the ego. It is also clear that Ibn Arabi does not misrepresent the Ka'ba for the divine, but experiences the divine through ritual circumambulation of it. His religious experience is spurred into occurrence through his application to the physical contemplation of symbolic form. Few rites are as universally practiced as that of circumambulation, and the necessity of these rotations of holy pilgrimage as being deliberate, yet indirect, can serve to remind us of the importance of subtle attentiveness in our efforts to rediscover a proper orbit between our conscious selves and those deeper purposes of our souls, which are sometimes all too quiet.

Jung's understanding of the operation of the Self archetype within the human psyche is that it is simultaneously spiritual and individual, collective and personal. It is a natural force guiding our process of maturation and the unique form of its pattern. He observed that the urgent need for a relationship to this force within us usually arrives in the second half of our lives. It appeared most often as a religious question to be answered in our lived experience; it "is a fact of nature . . . [and] the great secret which has to be worked out."[62] While the first stage of life necessarily involves the establishment of the ego and the persona, the coming to know our own strengths and capabilities in a worldly sense, it is usually not until the second half of life that one begins the encounter between the ego and Self. While as children our Self and ego are tied together—just as a child's sense of self is initially undifferentiated from her mother—in adulthood the ego is separated and becomes strong and healthy, and such a development should not be confused with egocentricity. Johnson observes that there is a "tremendous difference between a strong ego and an egocentric ego; the latter is always weak."[63] Part of the weakness of the egocentric state of mind is its rigidity, defending itself against both the shadow and the Self; it does not stand on a firm foundation. The healthy ego does not fight the Self or the shadow but is open to meeting them, and thereby it is "not really diminished in the process of integration; it simply becomes less rigid in its boundaries. . . . Individuation, the attainment of one's real potential, can't take place without a strong ego." The ego and the Self are interdependent to each other, for "the Self provides the more holistic view and is therefore supreme, but it is the function of the ego to challenge or fulfill the demands of that supremacy."[64]

> The ego is a necessary vehicle for the expression of the Self, but you have to be willing to put the ego on the line. It's like Moses confronting the voice of God in the burning bush, and then going down to lead the people of Israel out of Egypt. That's the action of the strong ego. (Johnson)[65]

Not only is the healthy ego capable of confronting the Self, it is able to do so with a properly grounded humility and with a proper acceptance of its own relativity to the supremacy of the larger view. Thomas Moore notes how important the willingness to sacrifice the ego is in this regard, as he observed it in the "remarkable maturity"[66] of the young poet John Keats, who had "developed a philosophy of the soul by which he could live." Moore believes that Keats's maturity was on display in his esteem of the value of "negative capability"—the capacity of consciousness to remain present with the truth of experience, despite the lack of that truth's accord with the ego's belief. Keats described this quality in a letter of December 1817:

> Several things dove-tailed in my mind, and at once it struck me what quality went to form a Man of Achievement, especially in Literature, and which Shakespeare possessed so enormously—I mean Negative Capability, that is, when a

man is capable of being in uncertainties, mysteries, doubts, without any irritable reaching after fact and reason.[67]

Consciousness requires the permeability and vulnerability that Keats calls "negative capability," in order to permit the new to enter into it. Only with the capacity for holding doubt, living with uncertainty, can deeper parts of ourselves become conscious. Negative capability enables our first movement toward the containment of something larger than the current view; the "experience of containment expands with personality integration."[68] As we organically grow to become more of who we are, we integrate material that was formerly unconscious. The process of individuation allows deeper parts of ourselves to come into play.

> The symbolic dialogue between ego and Self, taking place through the medium of the unconscious, is a dialogue of opposites. Symbolic material wells up from within to compensate and balance the ego's view and values. The ego normally and inevitably has a narrower view than the Self. When consciousness is made even narrower by identifying with [our own first responses], dialogue with the Self is paradoxically more needed and less attainable.[69]

The process of transformation through the dialogue of ego and Self occurs in response to both internal and external events. Identifying with our first response to new content short circuits this process and limits our unfolding of it. It is, of course, "normal and inevitable" to do so, as most often we make "things seen into things as seen."[70] To meet the genuinely new means living with uncertainty, and the rarity of this ability is what makes it remarkable (as Moore observed of Keats).

Throughout the history of our engagement with Crop Circles we have identified with our first responses. Folktales telling of their construction by pixies or other beings reflect the superstitious beliefs of the time, but also demonstrate the open-minded "negative capability" of Keats' description; by according the phenomenon with a rightful degree of mystery, they do not, as we do today, presume mastery over the formations' origin. In the medieval view that a Mowing Devil is the phenomenon's source, the shadow's response is identified with, and both the formation and the farmer's experience of it is condemned. It is a shadow response to something larger than oneself. It should be noted too that this agency continues to accord the phenomenon a measure of mystery. The ego's response to something larger than itself is exemplified in the scientific assignment of the agency of the phenomenon to "wind action," or hoaxing, or its denial altogether—here, identification with an egoic response makes no room for mystery or doubt.

> Non-identification demands considerable moral effort. Moreover it is only legitimate when not used as a pretext for avoiding the necessary degree of personal understanding.[71]

Jung points out above how "negative capability" is demanding of moral effort, but also requires "positive capability," our willingness to seek truth in our personal understanding. The illegitimacy that he warns of is the sidestepping of discernment and the movement into mystery, without struggling with the factual reality of the difficult questions of our lives. While the earlier responses to the phenomenon demonstrate a failure of non-identification, many modern responses, such as categorizations that associate the phenomenon's causation with aliens, Gaia, or Spirit (each of which is considered later in greater detail), potentially close off our participation with the phenomenon prematurely. Today, we can choose to ask whether our attribution of the phenomenon to our own preferred theory is compelled by a thirst for a larger truth that will validate us personally—an unconscious drive to relate to the Self on our own terms—or not. We should keep in mind that if the phenomenon does not fit within our own idea of what Crop Circles are, this will be a defeat for our ego. There is a tendency to forget that this phenomenon is real unto itself and does not depend on our theories to exist.[72] It is easy to confuse function and form, cause and effect, and imagine that they exist solely to fulfill *our* theory for it. However, the depth of mystery that we witness in Crop Circles does not lie in our ability to construct complex theories about it; its mystery is present simply in its existence. "The eye goes blind when it only wants to see why" instructs the Sufi mystic Rumi, and if we want this phenomenon to fit into our preconceived explanation about it, not only may we be disappointed, but it would seem that something profound about its nature is missed. Pursuit of explanations offers a utility to the ego, but it may also keep us from being open to being affected in a genuinely new and unforeseen way by what we are facing. We can ask ourselves, in preferring one theory in favor of another, am I making the phenomenon bigger or smaller? Is it more comfortable to choose a label to place upon it that is less foreign to me? Can we still participate with this phenomenon without being guaranteed that we will be right? Can we look this phenomenon right in the eye and still see its mystery? A measure of conflict with our shadow is an unavoidable outcome of encountering Crop Circles. We can only choose whether or not to reflect upon that encounter with honesty and consciousness. Does the arrival of these formations open us up to confronting ourselves more honestly, more vigorously, and more deeply? Regardless of their actual cause or agency, how could such deep consideration be wrong? Only if we make them into an idol, investing them with our disowned hopes and fears, and cling to that image of them can they do us harm. And this can occur through denial, projection, or idealization. To be open to Keats's "negative capability" allows for space to exist between the phenomenon and our view of it. Without this openness we may not only be failing to "solve a puzzle," we may be failing to make room for the deepest growth within ourselves, for "the creation of space is what allows something new to happen."[73] Only if we can meet honestly with whatever comes up in ourselves, see what is there and not identify with it, can we exercise, to the best of our ability, both discernment and containment. To do so is to house the Other in ourselves.

> This process of coming to terms with the Other in us is well worth while, because in this way we get to know aspects of our nature which we would not allow anybody else to show us and which we ourselves would never have admitted.[74]

We have taken a circuitous route in our responses to this phenomenon. We have been suspicious of it and cast the Devil on it. We have studied it with the distanced eye and imagined it contained no mystery. Today, we certainly see it more clearly and with less projection, but are impeded in our affective reaction to it. In the M. Night Shyamalan Crop Circle–oriented feature film *Signs,* aliens are depicted as being responsible for the creation of the formations, as a precursor to an invasion of Earth. Shyamalan sets the film's action against the backdrop of a priest (Mel Gibson's character) who is in the midst of a spiritual crisis following the accidental death of his wife. Here, we see a recasting of the phenomenon's agent from Devil to hostile

Aliens, and so we can speak of this plot as another shadow projection. Yet the larger drama of the film points to the spiritual questions that are also a part of the innate dynamic of the Crop Circle mystery.

At first, this film focuses on the predominantly modern response of denial of the phenomenon's authenticity. Eventually, the presence of UFOs makes clear that "the nerds were right," and denial is left behind. But the film's focus remains on the struggle of Mel Gibson's character to understand who he is after his wife's death, and his subsequent loss of faith. Having lost his wife, he can no longer see God as all good and is forced to struggle to redeem his understanding of the world. Depicted in this film are two levels of the difficult struggle that we face in our encounter with Crop Circles. We are met with our own potential for denial and shadow projection at first—we say "it is nothing," or it is a hostile Other—and only after this are we left to confront the deeper issues that are brought on by the phenomenon. *Signs* presents a portrait of human response to the phenomenon where shadow is not squarely dealt with, but split into a fearsome alien agent of the formations and into Gibson's character's fears and uncertainties about darkness, faith, and God. Unlike this movie's fiction, in reality we are left with the moral challenge presented by Crop Circles. We cannot create a narrative to separate the phenomenon's questions from our own shadow, but must live with both together at once—if we are going to participate.

In the history of responses to Crop Circles, there has been a great deal of shadow, of the repressed Other in us, but very little of the Self, of our best potential. In fact, we might conclude that we *needed* to experience them as a provocateur of the shadow before we could respond to them with more of who we are. Where we have sought to keep the mystery of Crop Circles at bay and reduce its impact upon us, shadow projection, intellectualization, and denial have served this purpose. Each of these keeps the reality of the phenomenon at a distance. There is something in us that would prefer to keep the Otherness of the agent behind Crop Circles unreal and reduce the phenomenon so that our own fears can be kept in check. As long as the shadow remains unconscious in response to them, they remain insubstantial to us. To leave the shadow out of our consideration of the phenomenon is to continue to view the phenomenon in a cartoonlike fashion, making it a toy villain, a fairy tale bogeyman or something that is *more out of our imagination* than of the plain reality that we find in the wheat fields. Where we characterize the phenomenon in a cartoonlike fashion, we are leaving something out of the equation, not only from our view of it, but from our participation with it. By redeeming the shadow and taking back the projection—which means *changing* in some way *who we are*—we clear up our view of the phenomenon and give it both substantiality and reality. The seeing of the Other out there and the taking back of the Other into ourselves are, in this way, tied together. The task of personal shadow integration, in regard to the phenomenon, is necessary because as William Blake reminds us, "as a man is, so he sees."

What would it mean to bring our shadow into living consideration of the agent behind Crop Circles? Doing so requires granting the agent creating this phenomenon full, living reality as an Other, and this is a frightening proposition for many of us. It brings with it a personal psychological struggle and a batch of larger questions. Carrying our own shadow here requires us to reflect consciously upon our own reactions. How have you felt when you read about each of these historic responses to the phenomenon? Beneath your thoughts, what feelings exist within you, which theories do you react strongly to? In the emotional strength of our reaction (or lack thereof) we may find something of our shadow. Through observing our reactions without identifying with them—stepping outside of our personal attachment to them—we forge a vessel by which personal insight becomes possible. Reflecting upon our reactions unveils and transforms them and ourselves. If this can be done in any way and at any time, we may find that the shadow "does not consist only of morally reprehensible tendencies, but also displays a number of good qualities, such as normal instincts, appropriate reactions, realistic insights, creative impulses, *etc.*"[75] Particularly for us today, we may further find that our shadow "even contains childish or primitive qualities which would in a way vitalize and embellish human existence, but convention forbids!"[76]

In the vivid nature of the Mowing Devil response to the phenomenon, we can gain sight of a powerful and robust vitality. There is emotion and color in this response, even if it is negative. This insight is valuable because it points out that much of what is missing in the modern responses to the phenomenon is affect. We quietly deny it, we subtly intellectualize it, we forget about it and move on, illustrating why Jung knew that without connection to feeling, moral judgment is impeded. There is a great shadow element in such nonresponse, as it represents a misdirected, blocked, or impeded flow of life energy that is typical of our day—where something new might offer us the possibility for consideration and deep change, it is neutralized emotionally prior to our participation with it. For us today, to begin to integrate the shadow is to start to take back our vitality, our passion, and our moral strength. What would it be like to have the vivid fire of the Mowing Devil in our reaction without buying into its cartoon, integrating that fleshy passion into our modern pictures of Crop Circles' agent? Perhaps to do so would be to bring our hearts into engagement with it. This might also give us the strength to accept that our path could not have been otherwise and to finally meet this marvel before us in an entirely new way—wholeheartedly and unfettered, something extraordinary responded to extraordinarily. Perhaps then we might find ourselves, *rather than knowing the right answer,* giving voice to the question that needs to be spoken.

> I dreamt last night, oh marvelous error,
> that there were honeybees in my heart,
> making honey out of my old failures.
> —ANTONIO MACHADO[77]

Why does the seemingly intentional calling card that is Crop Circles come to us in this particular form? Why is it that we should have this image before us now? What might it mean for us, at this time, to be having this "dream"? Today, when we have consciousness enough to recognize this symbol and its home within us, do we remain incapable of relating to it? When in the past our shadow projection has kept us from being able to have a real relationship with this phenomenon, today our potential for shadow integration points not only to a clearer vision of the phenomenon itself, but also to the necessity of *our* proceeding somewhere further. Something more is being asked of us today. Symbols of the Self inherently point to our power to become something more, to grow into more of who we are. The Reverend Dr. Lauren Artress sees in the writings of twelfth-century Christian mystic Hildegard of Bingen an example of the potential that we have to unfold ourselves that is spoken of as the Self. Hildegard was the author of what Artress describes as:

[a] theology that knitted together nature and spirit, cosmos and soul. She described the Holy Spirit as the Greening Power of God. Just as plants are greened, so we are as well. As we grow up, our spark of life continually shines forth. If we ignore this spark, this greening power, we become thirsty and shriveled. And if we respond to the spark, we flower. Our task is to flower, to come into full blossom before our time comes to an end.[78]

To a great degree the modern psyche has lost contact with the deep Self that vivifies us, that brings us "to flower," in Artress's term. We are no doubt "thirsty and shriveled," needing contact with the Self so badly, but our way of being keeps us from it. Yet, just as shadow integration requires something authentic from each of us, actual change—even if small and subtle—in who we are, perhaps something beyond a simple causal curative, is pointed to in this "dream"'s symbol; not just correction, but a calling out of greater potential from inside us, a drawing forth of more of who we are. Symbols of the archetypal Self offer not only a corrective, but also the possibility of inner refounding or transformation.

> Mandala means "circle." There are innumerable variants of the motif. . . . Their basic motif is the premonition of a center of personality, a kind of central point within the psyche, to which everything is related, by which everything is arranged and which is itself a source of energy. The energy of the central point is manifested in the almost irresistible compulsion and urge to become what one is, just as every organism is driven to assume the form that is characteristic of its nature, no matter what the circumstances.[79]

Visually, the emergence of the Crop Circle phenomenon from the initial circular form seen throughout our history around the world into the diverse concentric complexity of the mandala mirrors the forms of the Self archetype's evolution in the psyche. This similarity does not provide the answer to the phenomenon's mystery, but rather casts a new and different light upon many of our current ways of thinking about it. In the coherent reflection between the formations and the Self archetype, no other theory is ruled out. We can still imagine ways that its causation might be related to numerous other possibilities. It may certainly include a relation to an environmental warning. Yet, as with Karen Alexander's notion of our intelligence of harmony being required in order to understand the phenomenon, its correlation with the Self archetype points to the *how* of the way we may come to understand it, rather than the *what*. While we should be cautious in drawing any conclusions about the phenomenon's agency, the accord between Crop Circles and the Self archetype within the psyche should inform our process of consideration, and perhaps point toward something of its agent's character and essential nature. Just as the presence of sacred geometry's Golden Section throughout the construction of authentic formations provides a suggestion of something harmonious within its nature, so too should we view the presence of the Self archetype as a good sign. This element of its constitution brings to mind the same symbolic message found in the Golden Section's relatedness of the lesser to the greater and the greater to the whole—an inherent natural harmony, an accord with the center. As Lawlor describes, "it can be said that wherever there is an intensification of function or a particular beauty and harmony of form, there the Golden Mean will be found. It is a reminder of the relatedness of the created world to the perfection of its source and of its potential future evolution."[80] The display of the images of the Self archetype in Crop Circles speaks not only to ideas of an otherworldly "perfection of source" and to those of "potential future evolution," but also to a more down-to-earth expression of something of Nature being included in its outward form and inward genesis. Perhaps in this way, it may serve to aid us in rediscovering something of our own deeper nature that we have lost touch with and that we need to reclaim, or perhaps there is a part of ourselves that we are growing into that we do not yet understand:

A few words about the functional significance of the mandala. Knowledge of the common origin of these unconsciously preformed symbols has been totally lost to us. In order to recover it, we have to read old texts and investigate old cultures, so as to gain an understanding of the things our patients bring us today in explanation of their psychic development. And when we penetrate a little more deeply below the surface of the psyche, we come upon historical layers which are not just dead dust, but alive and continuously active in everyone maybe to a degree that we cannot imagine in the present state of our knowledge. (Jung)[81]

FOUR

ANTIQUE PAGEANTRY

Where the first characteristic of this phenomenon, its shape, finds a coherent reflection in the psychological nature of the Self archetype, its second characteristic, its media, the living grains in which we find it, also has a clear archetypal association. Formed in the cereal crops that have sustained us for thousands of years, and constructed in living stock, Crop Circles echo the figures who have been celebrated across Europe and the world in association with the fruit of the harvest since before recorded history. Cultures around the world that have produced corn, rice, wheat, barley, and all of the staple grains of civilization have worshipped the divinities whom they believed protected and sustained their crops. Human adoration of these figures has traditionally been predominantly directed toward the form of feminine images, Goddesses of life and vegetation.[1]

> Though their specific characteristics differed according to period and geographic milieu, these female personifications of the earth express the common principles of abundance, protection and nourishment. . . . The deified earth in Greek mythology was Gaia, the universal mother of humankind. . . . In Homer she was especially honoured as the mother of all, who nourishes her creatures and pours rich blessings upon them. She was commonly identified with other goddesses such as Themis, Demeter and Hera, all of them maternal deities expressive of the creative, sustaining earth. (Berger)[2]

Dating as far back as 30,000 BCE, statues of figures whose shape emphasized the life-giving aspects of the female body were carved by early human beings from France to Siberia and Africa. Across Europe from the sixth to the third millennium BCE, female Goddess figurines, decorated with floral themes, were placed in vegetation-oriented shrines. Female figurines giving birth carved in the Neolithic period were found in grain bins or with heaps of grain attached to them in Anatolia (modern Turkey). Rituals such as these expressed a reverence for Nature's divinity that equated fascination at the Earth's abundance with fascination at women's maternal creative power. As early farmers planted and waited, watching for their seeds to grow, and as they watched and saw their bellies grow fat with children, they felt the source of life inside themselves and knew the association between the land's fertility and their own. And, as they, in their natural love for their children, nourished and cared for them, so too did they see, in the endless generosity of Nature, an expression of its love for us. Our ancestors' representations and rituals of the Goddess reflected this realization—not only our need for and benefit from the land—but that, in a fundamental way, in the symbol of grain, the Feminine and the miracle of life are entwined.

> The earliest human intuition of the sacred was that the earth was the source of all life and ground of being. (Gadon)[3]

Lacking the objective distance enabled by the modern mind's quality for separate self-awareness, our ancestors felt bonded to the world and sustained by it, one with it. Our distant forefathers and -mothers experienced themselves as living within and existing as one with the world around them. Anthropologist Lévy-Brühl termed this psychological enmeshment participation "mystique"—a condition in which the subject cannot distinguish itself from an object—in this case as the felt experience of oneself as living in an attached and dynamic relationship with the background of the world. Early humanity looked toward the world with awe, much like a child experiences its mother at a very young age—knowing it as a profound and powerful mystery, fearing its hostility or absence, yet sensing it all around them, as a part of them, being fed by it and supported by it, and feeling bonded to it—as something to which they naturally belonged. In these first acts of human reverence, their experience of captivation with life itself was given voice in Goddess images.

Goddesses are ubiquitous—they stood by the cradle of Homo Sapiens, as evidenced by the discovery in Aurignacian deposits, testifying to his earliest known appearance in Europe, some thirty to forty thousand years ago, of statuettes of nude women with enormous breasts and buttocks, and protruding abdomens. These figurines, representing highly stylized and exaggerated form women in an advanced stage of pregnancy, are usually referred to as Paleolithic Venuses—of Willendorf, Menton, Lesugne, Lausell, to name only a few ... are strikingly paralleled by finds ... unearthed in Mesopotamia and Syria, and dating from ... the fifth millennium B.C. Both the European Old Stone Age, and the Near Eastern, Halafian figurines served the same purpose: to ensure fertility and delivery; in all probability they served similar ends in relation to the animal and vegetable worlds as well. The earliest attested role of the goddess, therefore, was of the numinous mother who endowed her worshipers with her own mysterious qualities. (Patai)[4]

Around the world, in the carvings, texts, and oral traditions of the earliest human cultures, sit enshrined Goddesses whose divinity joined heavenly benevolence to earthly beneficence. The Roman goddess Ceres, from whom our word "cereal" is derived, was an adaptation of the earlier Greek goddess Demeter, the earth mother (in Greek *de* means "earth," *meter* means "mother"), and both Ceres and Demeter were deities of agriculture and plant life—their divinity was seen to constitute its growth, and staple grains were acknowledged as their gifts to us. The common Roman expression "fit for Ceres" referred to something that was splendid. In Japan, Ukemochi brought fertility through her own immolation, her body torn apart and spread across a field, a story also found in North and South American mythological tales of the Corn Goddess. The Earth Mother is "found almost everywhere in North American Native Tradition."[5] In India, the Hindu goddesses Parvati and Lakshmi provided abundant fertility and wealth, and throughout South Asia innumerable feminine village deities are worshipped and their protection is sought in times of crisis, famine, or disease.[6]

As goddess of earth and fertility ... the Great Goddess is everywhere the ruler over the food that springs from the earth, and all the usages connected with man's nourishment are subordinated to her. She is the goddess of agriculture, whether its product be rice, corn or wheat, barley, tapioca, or any other fruit of the soil . . . and Demeter, of Ceres and Spess, and of the Madonna, who in her character of Earth Mother is the "'Madonna of the sheaves." (Neumann)[7]

In the ancient Near East, in Sumerian tradition, the great Goddess was worshipped from approximately 3,500 to 500 BCE, as the giver of fertility, reproduction, and sexual love. Known by many names, first as Inanna and later as Ishtar, "the Green One," she was the verdant growth of the land itself, and the "Opener of the womb . . . [and] the one refuge of mothers in the pangs of childbirth. All life emanates from her; plants, animals, human beings are her children."[8] Her capacity to renew life itself was enacted through the rescue of her son, Tammuz, from death's underworld. She is one and the same with the processes of life's growth and its necessary decay into death's fecundity:

> When Lady Ishtar was away in the underworld, a time of terrible depression and despair fell upon the earth. For during her absence nothing could be conceived. Neither man nor beast nor plants nor trees could propagate, and worse than that they did not even want to propagate. The whole world is described as being sunk in a kind of hopeless inactivity, mourning for her return. (Harding)[9]

In the ancient Egyptian Nile river basin, the Great Goddess Isis was seen to guide nature's renewal out of inactivity—her divinity itself constituted the rising and annual reflooding of the river upon which all growth depended. In the most common myth associated with her, Isis wanders, lamenting, in search of the murdered body of her husband, Osiris. Collecting the lost parts of his dismembered body, her tears fall upon his body and renew his spirit sufficiently to conceive their son, Horus; as she is capable of giving birth annually to the Nile, restoring its water and with it life itself, so too is she able to reanimate Osiris and thus procreate a son. In symbolic parallel with the moon, Isis, like Ishtar, is present through all the stages—growth, decay, death, and renewal; existing from brightness to waning, to disappearance and return again.[10] For the Egyptians,

> Isis, the moon, is also Mother Nature, who is both good and bad. She tolerates all things . . . for nature consists necessarily in growth and decay. . . . The process

of life consists not in unchecked progress but in the conflict between growth and decay. For this that we call the "process of life" is not identical with the well-being of the form in which life is temporarily manifested. (Harding)[11]

One of the most potent expressions of this understanding of the "process of life," of Nature as Goddess hosting all things, comes in a Greek myth that stood "for a thousand years at the center of [their] inner religious life."[12] In the "Hymn to Demeter," as it is recorded by the famous epic poet Homer, a Goddess, who was the "bringer of seasons" and "giver of good gifts, lady of the golden sword and glorious fruits," has her daughter ripped away from her—abducted into the underworld. Persephone, "a bloom-like girl," daughter (in Greek, Persephone is *Kore*) of "Queenly" Demeter, wanders into a field, sighting in front of her the most marvelous and radiant narcissus flower. In the moment of her absorption in its beauty, Hades, God of the Underworld of the Dead, reaches forth, rising out of the earth, taking her, the object of his desire, to be his wife. Demeter is left alone to wander in search of her and agonize. Persephone's renewal to the daylight world is achieved only after a time of grief and anger, and Demeter's abandonment of both gods and humanity; only Her withholding of earthly fruits and growth forces Zeus to consent to their reunion.

> Demeter is the Great Mother of Life. Her grief reflects maternal anguish, but not maternal powerlessness. Awesome, majestic, personifying the Law of Life to which even the Gods are subject, she throws Mount Olympus into disarray, plunging the earth into drought because of her rage and grief. Zeus is forced to yield to her longing to be reunited with her daughter. (Baring and Harvey)[13]

In this way, Demeter illustrates the unique capacity of Goddess images to exemplify the irrepressible and unyielding life force of Nature, which, even through chaos, "destroys old forms [to bring] new ones into being."[14] Like Ishtar, Demeter's disappearance takes with it all outward movement of growth, leaving only winter's stillness; and her daughter Persephone's retrieval comes to represent nature's rebirth in spring and the miracle of the seed's emergence out of the silent earth. This myth would also come to be understood as addressing the human capacity, alongside Nature, to be reborn anew out the darkness of spiritual impoverishment.

As a nature myth, Persephone is the seed that splits off from the body of the ripened grain, the mother, when sinking beneath the earth, she returns in the spring as the new shoot. The etymology of her name "she who shines in the dark" suggests that the seed does not actually die but continues to live in the underworld, even though it cannot be seen above. (Baring and Cashford)[15]

The spiritual metaphor of this myth was ritualized in an initiation ceremony performed at Eleusis, near Athens, that was widely participated in by Greek society. Socrates, Aristotle, and other key figures in the development of the Western worldview undertook this initiation, in which the renewal of the spirit out of darkness was ritually enacted to create a cathartic rebirth in the initiate that was said to leave them no longer fearing death. They were led into an experience of unity with the Goddess and her daughter—made to feel the renewal that their bond expresses. This initiation and the story of Demeter and Persephone:

> Must have put all who listened to it in touch with their deepest feelings of grief and hope . . . [giving them] a deep sense of happiness and hope, trust in the survival of the soul and the reunion with loved ones after death. They were one of the most powerful ancient rituals ever devised for keeping alive the sense of relationship with the Divine Feminine as the eternal ground of life. (Baring and Harvey)[16]

The initiation process at Eleusis was not intended to transmit new intellectual dogma, but rather to lead the initiate to a feeling of union with the endlessly generative mystery of life itself. Here ritual acts serve as an entry point for emotional contemplation: witness of Demeter's suffering at the absence of her daughter enabled the initiate's experience of genuine grief; Persephone's rape opened the initiate to their own experience of violation; through Hades's sexual aggression they caught sight of their own libidinal desires; most important, however, they were led to feel Demeter and Persephone's raw anguish in not knowing why,[17] "why should this happen to me"—the inability to see any meaning in their suffering. This anguish, which is so readily understood as a part of the human experience, is shared by the initiate. It is only through such anguish that Persephone's return and her reunion with her mother can be simultaneously felt as a lived part of one's own experience and understood as *beyond oneself.* In the cycle of growth and decay, in the endless chain of birth, in the mirror of the Goddesses, the initiates saw themselves reflected in a vision of unity and came to view themselves as a part of Nature's miracle. In the moment of Persephone's return to Demeter, anguish was washed away and replaced by understanding.

> [Here the] idea lost everything confusing and became a satisfying vision. . . . Eleusis was the place of the finding of the Kore [Persephone]. In this finding something was seen—no matter through what symbols—that was objective and subjective at once. Objectively, the idea of the goddess regaining her daughter, and therefore herself, flashed on the experient's soul. Subjectively, that same flash of revelation showed him his own continuity, the continued existence of all living things. The not-knowing, the failure to understand that attached to the figure of the grieving Demeter, ceased. The paradox contained the living idea— that, in motherhood, death and continuity are one in the losing and finding of the Kore—is now resolved. (Kerenyi)[18]

In such moments, we become capable of an experience of feeling of infinity or immortality, which, metaphysics aside, we can know no other way. "As a transcendental idea, immortality cannot be the object of experience, hence there is no argument either for or against. But immortality as an *experience of feeling* is rather different" (Jung).[19] Drawn through the mourning process of grief and darkness at the ceremony's climax, the participants, men and women alike, knew themselves identified with the Goddess and felt reborn with her child. In some instances of this ceremony, ritual rebirth was signified simply by the display of an ear of corn.

> The mown ear of corn . . . is a perfect symbol of immortality, of eternal rebirth. It is the fruit of life, the harvest which feeds and nourishes, it is the seed which must sink into the earth and disappear in order to give birth again. It was mown down in the moment of its ripeness, as Persephone was mown down and torn from her mother.[20]

Such a depiction gives voice to the capacity of corn and grain to represent our ability to reemerge anew, with deeper clarity and vision, following a period of darkness and descent. Rituals of this form emphasize the human capacity to grow beyond ourselves and the endless potential for renewal within the psyche. However, such renewal comes only following a period of loss, anger, and grief. Here a place is given to the value of decay; in order for something to be gained, something needed to be lost. Psychologically the "death" of knowing, the loss of the currently held conscious view, is shown to be necessary to this process. Finding the "lightness of heart" of the initiate required that their previously held way of looking at the world, their ego's personal and finite perspective, and its unconscious roots, be undermined.

For thousands of years of human history, ritual initiation was the method by which cultures "transmitted spiritual values."[21] Such practices almost uniformly begin with a period of ritual purification. Fasting, deprivation, physical or mental challenge all characterize this stage. Coming into contact with the "precariousness of life"[22] helped to lower adolescent ego-oriented states of mind and prepare the candidate for further revelation. Aristotle noted that "it is not necessary for the initiate to learn anything, but to receive impressions and to be put in a certain frame of mind."[23] In the mystic traditions of many religions and in indigenous traditions, purification techniques are used to help disintegrate the ego defenses of the candidate and begin the process in which the "profane man is being 'dissolved.'"[24] As the conscious mind's dominance is loosened, connections to lower parts of the psyche, both personal and archetypal, are opened. Through this connection, ritual acts are able to take on simultaneous objective and personal significance. The emotional truth of the shared purification flushes to the surface the candidate's unconsciously held pain and opens in them a deep and genuine vulnerability. Separated from familiar psychological points of reference and ways of making meaning, in the decay of this lost state, the initiate becomes ready for a "new Creation."[25] Through such a darkness one was made ready to see a light.

> Through initiation rites they felt different, behaved differently, and grew in new ways. No longer bound to the compulsion of adolescent states of mind, or to the flights into promiscuity that wasted their sexual energies, people in traditional cultures learned that they could "die" and be "reborn." And in their reborn form

they actually did see the world differently. They could, in fact, see in ways that they never could before. (Schwartz-Salant)[26]

While in the literal sense of these myths, farming, and its seeding, waiting, and growing are worshipped in relation to the female body, in their symbolic context these rituals are best understood as vehicles for speaking to the observance of something greater than one gender's particular biology. As an expression of a living awe, these Goddess images draw the observer up past the female sex's bounty of reproductivity and nurturance into the majesty of the archetypal Feminine, a category with which we each participate regardless of our gender.

> The mystery of the female body is the mystery of birth, which is also the mystery of the unmanifest becoming manifest in the whole world of nature. This far transcends the female body and woman as carrier of the image, for the body of the female of any species leads through the mystery of birth to the mystery of life itself. (Baring and Cashford)[27]

It is in this raw and undivided form that the Feminine archetype exists within us, looming large. In this way, the archetypal Feminine can be recognized as stretching from these first expressions of wonder at the "mystery of life itself," which literalize the profound miracle of life as witnessed in birth, into forms emphasizing the life-giving capacity of the female body, beyond personification in any gender into our most abstract questions about Nature's endless generativity and our place in that unfolding. As with any archetype, it has both an immediately apprehensible form, a recognizable quality that gives it its nature as a type, and deeper symbolic aspects that extend to forms that are less easily understood, are psychologically dynamic, and at their furthest extent become objects of wonder. It is in this expanse from literal to symbolic that the archetypal Feminine and its relation to grain and Crop Circles are best considered.

Uniquely charged for each of us, the archetype of the Feminine is the most potent association to the figure of grain in our psyche. While the Feminine need not always be associated with grain, grain is predominantly associated in mythology and in the unconscious with the Feminine, with the mystery of birth, and thus with the "mystery of the unmanifest becoming manifest in the whole world of nature . . . and the mystery of life itself." Therefore, to examine Crop Circles in regard to their media—their existence in grain crops worldwide—is to consider for ourselves one of the most fundamental fascinations that have preoccupied the human imagination since our beginning. Throughout our history, grain myths and rituals have expressed our engagement with this largest of questions and, very often, our gratitude. Sketching the imagination's territory in this regard, as it exists both in our personal and collective psyche, consciously and unconsciously, living within us in ways old and unendingly new, and watching what speaks within us as we consider this image, serves to provide a space for meaning to gestate within us, housing whatever it brings that may be new and as yet unborn.

At the same time as the rituals of Eleusis were underway, across the Mediterranean Sea a new and contrasting mythology to that of the Goddess was being born in the lands of Egypt and Canaan. Although male God-images had been a part of cultures worldwide, it is in the experiences of Moses and Abraham, as told in the Hebrew Bible, that a uniquely new vision of a single, unifying patriarchal God took hold. For the Hebrew Prophets, the God who commanded them and led them out of slavery was *the* God, the "One True God" and Creator of the World. The emergence of Judaism would come to be one of the most significant landmarks in human history, laying the framework for Christianity and Islam, and setting the course of Western development. This new faith developed in direct contradistinction to Goddess religions—Hebrew prophets would condemn worship of all prior objects of reverence, including Goddess images and animal idols (e.g., the infamous Golden Calf). In the coming of the Abrahamic paternal images of God, the withdrawal of the Goddess became nascent (a process also influenced by changes in the Greek pantheon, but fulfilled in the West through Christianity). Not simply a cosmetic gender change, the new God-image meant an abandonment of one way of life, an entire mode of human relation to life itself, and the introduction of a radically new point of view.

With the introduction of patriarchal God-images, humanity begins to replace cosmologies of process-of-life and relatedness to Nature with those of juxtaposition, distance, and hierarchy. As is considered in greater detail in the next chapter, this change is visible in both the Greek and Hebrew phi-losophies. In Judaism, an explicit covenant made between a singular omnip-otent God and the children of Abraham identifies them uniquely as God's Chosen People. Here a juxtaposition is explicit—this tribe is singled out above all others both for a greater affection and greater responsibility to God. In Moses's approach to God on the Mountain, we can see the begin-ning of divinity being regarded, not as immanent, but rather as existing "up there." Hierarchy (and patriarchy) are visible in the new and definite or-dering of reality, with God above humanity, humanity over Nature, and men over women. However, this new religion's emergence, coming in op-position to Nature idols and Goddesses, can be understood psychologically as an unconscious attempt to gain dominion over the tremendous power of the libidinal drives and chaotic forces within the human psyche. In this new view, demand is placed upon the ego to begin to restrict its response to Nature's instincts. The achievement of such a containment is necessary for the development of mature, conscious moral choice (this process is consid-ered further in the next chapter). Yet, despite the gains made in constrain-ing these drives through a new God-image (and thereby changing our image of ourselves), in achieving them our image of the divine as immanent, and of ourselves as living within the miracle of life, were sacrificed. Through this process:

> The peaceful Earth Goddesses were replaced by thunderous Sky Gods, the mira-cle of birth was supplanted by fear of death, the sacredness of sexuality repressed, and cooperative partnership was replaced by hierarchical control. With this change, the basic order of life—as it had been known since the dawn of human consciousness, perhaps even hundreds of thousands of years—was broken.... To the emerging patriarchal system, this meant a rejection and outright domination of the primary values of the previous Neolithic cultures ... the sacredness of the Earth, sexuality, emotion, women, community, and cooperation—essentially flipping all of these values into their opposites. (Judith)[28]

However, alongside the evolution of human civilization, the desire to in-voke the energetic quality of the archetypal Feminine and honor the bound-less generativity of her mystery would continue. As with all later developing religions, Judaism would indirectly incorporate elements of the previous faiths, and in particular, elements of reverent regard for an archetypal Feminine principle would continue to be found within its traditions. One example of this can be seen in Judaism's regard for the Sabbath as an aspect of God's feminine presence. Veneration of this aspect of the Creator is honored by a pause in activity—paralleling the seventh day of the Jewish creation story. However, the initial use of the term "Sabbath" referred to a local custom of honoring the land by letting it lie fallow for one growing season out of every seven, echoing the archetypal Feminine's connection to the land. In this way, the tie between the archetypal Feminine and gratitude for the gifts of the week and of the land are evident even in masculine-focused Jewish tradition. Witnessing such subtly intertwined tradition shows a borrowing from previous Goddess-oriented customs to be present within the very genesis of the Hebrew Creation story. The obscured face of the Goddess is glimpsed again later in the Old Testament Proverbs, where She is described as a feminine companion existing with Yahweh, the Hebrew God, as He created the world. She revels in His Creation and takes joy in humanity's existence:

> When he fixed the heavens firm, I was there, when he drew a circle on the surface of the deep, When he thickened the clouds above, when the sources of the deep began to swell, When he assigned the sea its boundaries—and the waters will not encroach the shore—when he traced the foundations of the earth, I was beside the master craftsman at play everywhere on his earth, delighting to be with the children of men. (Proverbs 8:26–31)[29]

A drive to acknowledge the divine Feminine persisted in the divergent Western traditions that followed, most often taking the form of harvest rituals that were performed nearly universally among our later ancestors. Tied in symbol to the land, celebrations of the Goddess, sacred dances, and rites of "antique pageantry," in Milton's phrase, would continue to be performed, even as male God-images began to overcome the earlier Goddess figures, and as humanity began to revel more and more in its own creative genius and its "dominion" over the land. However, across the centuries, She grew more and more disguised, unheralded, and obscure, and the voices of the Goddess were eventually lessened to a whisper.

It has been said that nothing is as valuable to those seeking to understand the feminine face of the God-image than the traditions of the world's First Peoples; Baring and Harvey note that "in them is preserved our original human relationship with Mother Earth in all her wisdom, humility and divine radiance."[30] The aboriginal worldview is one that is invested with a sense of the relatedness of all things, all life, and all happenings—there is no separation made between other creatures and ourselves, the land and its inhabitants, events and their place within the greater whole. They point out the profound humility that lies within such a view and note that, for our Native ancestors, their "unmediated intensity of connection" to this web of life made seeing themselves as only a part of it "as obvious as sunlight or the cry of a baby."[31] Rituals of the harvest and the hunt in indigenous societies demonstrate the attention paid to the relationship between themselves and the life that supported them. In the Americas, one form of such traditions was the ceremonial corn dance, performed as part of larger sacred rituals honoring the harvest. Many groups performed the Green Corn Dance, a feast of all "fat things" in which attendees brought all "their green corn, beans, pumpkins, squashes and everything that grew in the soil."[32] In some forms, this ritual was dedicated to the worship of a harvest Goddess or mythic ancestral figure known as "Our Grandmother" or "Corn Woman." Like their European counterparts, these Goddess figures embodied in themselves the power of Nature's renewal—a power unhalted even by death. Wilson describes the giving of thanks, acts of communal forgiveness and renewal, purifying rituals and mythologies that were a part of Southeastern Native traditions' enactment of the Green Corn Dance:

> For the Southeastern peoples, like Native Americans elsewhere, the year revolved around a series of sacred ceremonies. The most important, through most of the region, was the Green Corn Dance. . . . The roots of the Green Corn Dance . . . go to the heart of the Southeastern people's understanding of the world. Although the details vary from culture to culture, it invariably commemorates the gift of maize by an ancestral "Corn Woman" whose blood has the power to bring forth crops. . . . Even after death, the goddess continues to feed the people in the form of maize, but only as long as they continue to celebrate the Green Corn Ceremony. [But she warns] that there would be famine if they neglected her.

"If you forget to think of me . . . but make use of me without remembering my words, I will fling among you The Desolator!" (Wilson)[33]

Deidre Sklar, author of *Dancing with the Virgin: Body and Faith in the Fiesta of the Tortugas, New Mexico,* describes the Green Corn dance of the Rio Grande Pueblos as following a structural pattern with two or more dance groups alternating forming a circuit of the plaza. Men and women step differently in the ritual: the women's feet caressed the ground, they glided "without changing level, the women give the impression of continuity, without beginning or end; while the men's footfalls had more 'kinetic energy and rebound'. . . . Beating a light rhythm with the gourd rattles they hold, they seem to be running through the mountains."[34] Sklar points out that Robert Coles, who studied children in various different cultures for his work *The Moral Life of Children,* observed that Pueblo children had "learned to 'see' by metaphorically bringing themselves close to what they looked at. They were taught to notice in an empathic and participatory way, to capture a sight while at the same time giving themselves to it. There was 'a continuing willingness, passionate at that, to invest the mind's imagination in the world around it' and 'to consider its rhythms and demands of the highest consequence.'"[35]

In ancient Europe, the sites at which we now find Crop Circle formations served as host to similar ceremonies of worship. At Avebury and Stonehenge and other lesser-known circles across the English countryside, the circular dances were performed by previous generations, the process of life marked and celebrated, its rhythms joined in the dancer's feet. The Goddess—living as the land itself—was worshipped in their collective footfalls. Such early human ritual sprang from a desire, as Coles describes of the Pueblo children, to invest oneself in the mystery of the living cycle they saw unfolding around them and bring themselves closer to rhythms of Nature they felt within them (and as mentioned previously, such dances may have been done to honor the discovery of Crop Circles).[36] The act of dancing, its communal ritual, also served to bring each person physically closer and into tactile contact with one another. Such dances, which were held at key turning points in the year's growing cycle, therefore served to both honor the larger processes of Nature, and the human compulsion to be close to this wonder, and enacted such worship in a way that also drew them closer to one another. It is this capacity—the ability to bring ourselves into intimate participation and vulnerable empathy with the world around us and those in it, opening ourselves up to a feeling experience of the subjective nature that we all share—that continues to define the quality of the archetypal Feminine within the human psyche.

Places of standing stones—megalithic ritual sites such as Stonehenge, Avebury, and other similar sites across England and Europe—were constructed by a people who were invested with this form of consciousness, whose vision of the land was a living, participatory one. Stone risings, or henges, in intricate placement within the setting of the land, were an expression of this mindset, worshipful acknowledgment of a discovery of divinity in Nature. Those who created these sites and the later Celts saw the Goddess (whom the Celts called *Brigid* or *Bride*) as connected not only to the seasons and nature, but to the land's topography—she was alive there, intimately displayed in its hills and valleys.[37] Jones richly describes the presence of the Goddess in the soft curves, rises, and folds of the Glastonbury Tor and Avalon landscape.[38] The land surrounding Avebury, whose stone henge stood as the ritual center of an early human civilization, appears in the form of a woman's body. Sjoo and Mor observe that even prior to construction of these monuments, for thousands of years, "the entire landscape of the surrounding area, stretching for about 37 miles, had been seen as the outline of the body of the Goddess."[39] "The eighteenth century antiquarian, William Stuckley, whose field survey was the first comprehensive study of Avebury, made at a time when much more of the site survived, identified the temple as that of *Ertha,* the Northern European Goddess of spring and fertility after whom the Christian Easter is named."[40] Built by pre-Celtic farming people in 2600 BCE, Avebury is England's largest stone circle and is related in landscape to the nearby sites of Silbury Hill and West Kennet long barrow. Not only does its shape and chosen location reflect its association with the Great Goddess, so too does its practical use. Dames notes that the Avebury monuments, including the two gigantic barrows, together form a "condensed sequence of visual sculpted images within the center of a larger and more ancient presence. They express together the entire yearly agricultural cycle within the space of three fields"[41] and were built to "participate in dynamic processes—the fattening of the moon, the transformation of corn from green to gold and the stirrings of the unborn child."[42] This vision of the Goddess within the land is also to be seen in the nature of the rituals that took place at these sites.

> For us, as Professor Henri Frankfort observed, the phenomenal world is primarily an "it," but for the people who built the megaliths, "it" was a "thou." Wandering among the remaining stones of Avebury . . . it is not difficult to imagine the ritual dramas that took place during the year, the dances within the circles along the processional ways, imitating perhaps the cosmic dance of the stars, rituals of birth in spring, the marriage ceremony in early summer and rituals of death and rebirth in autumn and mid-winter. (Baring and Cashford)[43]

Ancient ritual dramas were performed each year at these sites, at the calendar points of the seasons. Each year at the halfway point between winter solstice and spring equinox, and in conjunction with seeding, *Imbolc,* meaning "in the belly" in Old Irish, was celebrated with a ritual procession around the first field prior to planting.[44] This field, seen as the belly of the Goddess, was honored as emblematic of that female transcendent power that brought "the rebirth of nature and new growth in the field."[45] Such a ritual, a movement around the field by those who would farm it, honored all of the relationships present—farmers to one another and to the land, the Goddess to the land in whose shape they saw Her, and Her gifts to them, the produce that kept them alive.[46] Such consecrations, made as solemn processions, communal dance, or less formalized celebrations as part of folk custom around first fields, were a traditional part of European pre-Christian practice. Virgil describes the Roman *Sementiva* rite:

> Chiefly pay fit worship to the gods. Make sacrifice each year to sovereign Ceres, when the grass is green and glad, and the winter making end and gentle Spring is in the air. . . . Let all the country youth of manly prime on Ceres call, bearing her tribute due of honey mixed with milk and sweet, new wine. Three times around the freshly bladed corn the blessed victim guide, while all the choir in gladsome company an anthem sing, bidding the goddess to their lowly doors. And let no reaper touch the ripened corn with sickle keen until his brows bind with twine of oak-leaf, while he trips along in artless dance with songs in Ceres' praise.[47]

Worship of the grain Goddess Ceres involved "going around the field" or *ambarvalia,* and this practice is mentioned by both Ovid and Tibullus.[48] Sementiva, the Roman holiday held in her honor, included "a purification of the fields by making a sacred circuit around them."[49] In Roman custom, the earth mother Goddess was venerated as protectress of the grain throughout its stages of growth: "She was invoked in one form or another at specific agrarian ceremonies throughout the year. . . . On some of these occasions, a *lustratio* (purification or lustration) was performed by circling around the fields. Part of the purification was a sacrifice to the earth mother goddess."[50] The honorary sacrifice, sheaves of wheat from last year's harvest placed into the empty furrows, was undertaken prior to a communal procession. The simple act of circling round a field was regarded as achieving this ritual purification; honoring the Goddess in this way made her present and sanctified the farmer's labors for another year.

The use of sheaves of last year's crop as consecrating sacrifice continues in modern traditions held on the same day. Christian celebration of both Candlemas and St. Brigid's day take place on the same day as Imbolc, and many of the day's traditions overlap. Shared rituals include the use of straw and grain from the previous year's crop to construct crosses (St. Brigid's crosses), which were then blessed with holy water and displayed prominently inside of homes or "set in the thatch of cottages."[51] Such practices parallel the ancient Corn Dolly tradition, in which the final sheaves of cereal crops are woven into female images ("corn" is a term synonymous with "cereal" in the U.K.). Known as Corn Dollies, the Corn Mother, the Corn Woman, or the Old Maiden, they were dressed as or made to depict a woman, or a female Goddess or saint, and were used in rites meant to honor the harvest and the fertilizing energy behind nature's abundance. Using the medium of the grain itself, as modern Crop Circles do, these rituals honored the phases of the land's fertility through the phases of the feminine fertile form. This custom is found worldwide but is particularly well developed in Europe, especially in the U.K.

The Mother-turning-into-Hag is still woven in rural England. As a symbol can, the Corn dolly functions through her ambiguity, taking two contradictory forms. The most common one was big-hipped, squatting; the other, long and thin, corresponded to the shape of the barrow. Like the Pregnant Harvest Goddess who, transformed into the Long Barrow, went into hibernation, the Corn Dolly was shut up in the barn every winter to be returned into the fields the following spring so that the eternal round could once more be renewed. (Gadon)[52]

Here Gadon points out the special relationship that these traditional Corn Dollies have to the barrows that characterize the area in which today we find the great abundance of Crop Circles. Gadon notes that like the landscape itself, with both full bodied monuments and old, long, thin burial tombs, the specific modes of construction of Corn Dollies illustrate the tripartite form of the Goddess Brigid (in this form also called *Brigitaine*) as Maiden, Wife, and Crone. This universal form of the archetypal feminine is found worldwide in mythology and parallels the phases of the moon. Throughout Eastern Europe corn dollies were constructed ritually, often using the last sheaves of wheat to make the doll, who was then, in some form, paraded into the community. She was brought home on the last harvest wagon or carried by two young men on a pole. In one tradition, the wheat from the doll is then turned into a wreath that is placed into a place of honor in the barn; and in another "the Corn-mother is placed on the top of a pile of wood, where she is the centre of the harvest supper and dance." Frazer gives an example from Mannhart's observations of the Corn Dolly tradition in Eastern Europe.

In Poland the last sheaf is commonly called the Baba, the Old Woman. "In the last sheaf," it is said, "sits the Baba." The sheaf itself is also called the Baba, and is sometimes composed of twelve smaller sheaves lashed together. In some parts of Bohemia the Baba, made out of the last sheaf, has the figure of a woman with a great straw hat. It is carried home on the last harvest-wagon and delivered, along with a garland, to the farmer by two girls. In binding the sheaves the women strive not to be last, for she who binds the last sheaf will have a child next year. Sometimes the harvesters call out to the woman who binds the last sheaf, "She has the Baba," or "She is the Baba." In the district of Cracow, when a man binds the last sheaf, they say, "The Grandfather is sitting in it"; when a woman binds it, they say, "The Baba is sitting in it," and the woman herself is wrapt up in the sheaf, so that only her head projects out of it. Thus encased in the sheaf, she is carried on the last harvest-waggon to the house, where she is drenched with water by the whole family. She remains in the sheaf till the dance is over, and for a year she retains the name of Baba.[53]

In these examples, we see the characteristic form of the ritual as it continues in the British Isles to this day. Women, either young or old, construct the Corn Dolly, which is then dressed or adorned and placed into a location of significance, above the door of the home, or in earlier days in a harvest-wagon, ceremonially shut up in the barn for the winter or laid into a ritual bridal bed, the latter form explicitly illustrating the ritual as a fertility rite. "Agriculture in the ancient world was nothing less than intimacy with the Mother Goddess,"[54] and these traditions express our previous reverence for this intimacy:

> Human survival depended on the spontaneous produce of the soil and ancient agriculturalists stood in awe of that life-producing power. When the hoe or plow entered the womb of the earth and the seed was sown, a new process of creation was initiated, all under the protection of the grain mother. (Berger)[55]

As pagan Goddess worship in ancient Europe met the newly arriving Christianity, the people's traditional rituals became an admixture—neither wholly one nor the other. In her definitive work, *The Goddess Obscured: Transformation of the Grain Protectress from Goddess to Saint,* Berger details the gradual transition of early Goddess figures into modern Christian saints. The form of Nature rituals performed by countryfolk, including celebrations of planting and harvest, would change gradually to include elements of Christianity. Across the centuries, legends of early Goddesses and patronesses would become intertwined with the stories of new Christian saints and with the Christ story itself. Although in some cases the church attempted to discontinue the practice of Corn Dolly rituals, in most cases traditions were simply given a new Christian framework in which to be understood. Communal rites performed at stone circles across England and smaller local customs made to honor the land and the gifts that it provided would begin to reflect this change in view. These words are from an Anglo-Saxon charm, spoken after an offering of baked meal loaf, kneaded with milk and holy water, had been laid beneath the first furrow prior to spring's planting, as their steps were made around a field:

Whole be thou Earth,
Mother of men.
In the lap of the God,
Be thou a-growing
Be filled with fodder
For fare-need of men.[56]

Berger notes the presence here of both male and female images of the deity, the earth as "Mother of men," who sits in the lap of the paternal father, God of Christian tradition. This intertwining of divinities is mirrored in the offering of not only the pagan meal loaf, but holy water as well. The charm continues:

Acre full fed,
Bring forth fodder for men!
Blossoming brightly,
Blessed become;
And the God who wrought the ground,
Grant us gifts of growing,
That the corn, all the corn,
May come into our need.[57]

Here blessedness and bounty are one, divinity manifesting on earth to meet our need. Not forgotten is the ancient way in which humanity looked upon the earth as Mother, the memory of a time when "human survival depended on the spontaneous produce of the soil and ancient agriculturalists stood in awe of that life-producing power. When the hoe or plow entered the womb of the earth and the seed was sown, a new process of creation was initiated, all under the protection of the grain mother."[58] In the charm described above, woven together are Goddess and God, as the Celts had woven their knotwork pattern into the Celtic cross—Christian linearity enjoined with the circle of the Mother. In the transition from Goddess worship to Christianity, not only did images of Goddess as Nature enter into the patriarchal Christian tradition—but Christian images became one and the same with the pagan traditions, in particular those related to Nature and grain. Pagan Imbolc would become Christian Candlemas, and its spring planting date seen as coinciding with the end of the Virgin Mary's period of traditional ritual purification following the birth of Jesus (as was observed in Judaism), a rite marked in Catholicism by the Feast of the Purification of Mary. Symbolically, both Mary and Jesus would become spoken of as, or analogized with, wheat. John would speak to the necessity of Christ's death as preparation for resurrection with these words: "Verily, verily, I say unto you, Except a grain of wheat fall into the earth and die, it abideth by itself alone; but if it die, it beareth much fruit."[59]

> Wheat germ was seen as a symbol of Christ, who descended into the underworld and was resurrected. To this day the Eucharist is symbolized on altar accessories by a head of wheat and a grape. The head of wheat is also a symbol of Mary, as it contains the seeds that yield flour for the Host. Mary (portrayed as a Madonna wearing a dress that has patterns shaped like heads of wheat) is compared with a field in which Christ, as wheat could grow.[60]

However, as one might naturally expect of a symbol so closely tied to feminine imagery, it would be predominantly Mary and other female saints who would carry forth the association of grain to divinity in Christian tradition. This is exemplified by the string of medieval folklore called "the grain miracle" that both predates Christianity and is tied up in it. Berger extensively details, through archeological, textual, art-historical, and anthropological evidence, the transformation of a pagan legend of a female saint's miraculous effect upon a farmer's crop,[61] into a story that would become a part of Christian belief and apocryphal lore about the nature of the holy family's flight into Egypt. The tale itself takes a general form in which men, often on horseback, are pursuing a female saint. Coming upon a farmer sowing seed in his field, she begs of him to tell her pursuers that he saw her "when he was sowing this field." He agrees and as she enters the field the wheat grows tall as to harvest. When her pursuers approach, he speaks, and she is hidden and saved (and he is blessed with this crop). Through this act "the forces of evil were foiled, and an abundant harvest would assure survival for another year."[62] In Christian tradition, this story would become blended into the virgin and child's flight into Egypt: fleeing Herod's murder of all the first-born children, they take cover in the miraculous growth of a farmer's field. This much-depicted scene also has another form, in which the holy family is shown in the "guise of beggars" resting under a fruit tree, which the baby Jesus brings to bloom and to bend toward them, and by which they are fed. The earliest versions of the Grain Miracle legend served to provide a crossover form for farmers whose ancient grain goddess rituals had no initial place in Christian ceremony. The long intertwining of folktales about these women saints across the centuries illustrates a push-pull between earlier practices, which the farm folk were unwilling to give up, and the new religion's struggle with the Goddess and the old ways; the earliest female Christian saints mythically took over the place of the pagan grain goddesses.

In pagan Ireland and throughout the Celtic world, the earlier Goddess Brigid would become nearly reborn in the later Christian Saint Brigid. "Saint Brigid shows an incredible likeness to the Celtic Goddess from whom she takes her name, Brigid, the great guardian of fertility and the land."[63] As discussed previously, customs made to honor the grain goddess include the corn dolly tradition being converted to a new form in St. Brigid's crosses, enabling satisfaction of both church authority and pagan belief. St. Brigid herself would be fashioned as a Christian embodiment of all the forms attributed to the earlier Great Goddess. Although she would be made virgin, she would remain synonymous with the land and become a "kind of symbolic matriarch of all Ireland."[64] "To this day pilgrims flock to wells, streams and ancient ruins associated with St. Brigid. . . . At one of her most important pilgrimage sites are found large stone tombs, underground passages and other prehistoric structures. It appears that as the old order passed away the Christian community reconsecrated the site, erected a stone cross, and set up a shrine with Brigid as patroness and heroine."[65]

> The Christian missionaries deliberately hijacked the old festivals and built their churches on top of the old sacred places. The effect was to fragment the ancient lore into a disjointed ragbag of isolated images and rites which became increasingly meaningless with the passage of time.[66]

Through the shattering of previous agrarian custom, energy attributed to the Goddess—her connection to the miracle of life—was redirected toward the new God-image. As with the sexuality of these female saints, the fruits of the Goddess were removed from her—her products, fruit, grain, and vegetative life were symbolically recast, taken into Christianity in some cases, in others made synonymous with sin. "Clearly, the resurrecting powers of the earth mother were completely subsumed by the Father in the context of Christianity."[67] While grain became a symbol of Christ, Mary, and other female saints, the apple, for example, would be become symbol of feminine sinfulness and of the evil of sexuality. While the social context of the elements of the Grain Miracle legend—a female saint being pursued by a hostile male, and a peasant farmer blessed materially by aiding her—reflect the reality of both a cruel social order and a sexually violent culture, the myth also speaks to a deeper, older image within the psyche, embodied in these:

> Special female saints who harbored within them an element of the divine. They were heir to the ancient powers of the earth mother.... [Using] the best weapon a female has against rape—trickery ... these Christianized substitutes for the antique grain goddess called on their ancient linkage with the land, and together with the good male sower brought about a subterfuge that saved them and also benefited mankind. (Berger)[68]

In drawing out the connections between the ancient Goddess rituals and Christian belief, neither is being undermined, detracted, or raised; rather, the history of their relating is brought forth in hope that we may gain insight into our present condition. Although predominantly misogynistic throughout its history, Christianity has for centuries also made a home for the Feminine in images of the Virgin Mary, which continue to be a source of the deepest reverence for believers worldwide—existing as the people's opportunity to connect to the divine Feminine. Today there is also renewed interest and debate about the role of Mary Magdalene and other figures associated with "the Black Madonna." The 1950 papal declaration of the *Assumptio Mariae,* which came in response to a petition signed by eight million people, stated that the Virgin Mary was "taken up body and soul into the glory of heaven,"[69] and her status was raised further with the 1954 proclamation of her being "Queen of Heaven." Jung saw this theological change as extremely significant in that it addressed, at least in name, the problematic psychological repression of the archetypal Feminine in Western consciousness. While continuing the split between body and spirit, this change reflects our continued calling toward female images of the divine.

Old customs of ritually relating Goddess and grain remind us of our previous connection to a view of the world in which we are related to the land, to each other, and to that invisible source that daily gives birth to the visible web of life. Giving consideration to the celebrations of Sementiva and Imbolc, and to ritual processions made round the fields in which sustaining grain was to grow, cannot but bring to mind the lack of such observance in our time. The sense of wonder in Nature's provision for us—symbolized through Her gifts of fruit and grain—and the sense of farmer as Her suitor today are gone. Like the female saint of the Grain Miracle legend, the Goddess was gradually put on the run and the farmer left without connection to the sacred merit of his labor, which had previously bestowed him with value and given him a sense of his own meaning. The modern mind had lost the sense of the sacred service of each for the other.

In the breaking of our association between the fruits of the land and the archetypal Feminine, it is not ritual for its own sake that has been lost; rather, we have abandoned our participation with the miracle of life itself. Today in the West, regardless of our particular creed, even if we should try to express our gratitude for the gifts of the land with sincerity, our culture has lost its sense of it as sacred. The fact that Crop Circles come right down into the very fields in which our food is grown makes our consideration of such psychological facts not arbitrary if we are truly seeking to understand the meaning of this "dream"'s arrival. The connection between grain and the archetypal Feminine is echoed in the history of the places in which the phenomenon is now found. Corn dollies made across the English countryside, tales of female saints, and the Grain Miracle all echo this association, a connection that is explicit in the old name given to Crop Circle formations in Belgium— *de Barende Vrouw,* "the woman giving birth."[70] This connection is also present in the occurrence of formations at ancient sites of worship and in seeming response to ancient burial tombs being uprooted. In looking at those traditional celebrations of "antique pageantry" that honored the connection of the Goddess to the land, we see a long forgotten intimate reverence expressed delicately and regularly, and room made for an experience of life's subtle yet pervading wonder.

How can we understand the history of our loss of this connection, of these values, both psychologically and culturally? As is examined more thoroughly in the following chapter, this psychological absence can be seen to have occurred due to much more than the imposition of Christianity upon Goddess culture and can be seen as a part of an unfolding dynamic within the human psyche—a movement out of unconscious identification with Nature toward conscious self-awareness, a moving away from the Mother psychologically, a movement toward the rationality of the modern mind, typified by the detached scientific viewpoint. Viewed in the context of the vast array of changes in the history of the Western mind, the loss of the Feminine can be seen as part of a larger archetypal movement. As Tarnas among others has observed, the journey of Western consciousness across the last three thousand years seems driven from underneath by a masculine imperative: to separate and increasingly distance ourselves from a self-image in which we are embedded within Nature, toward one in which we are separated from it; to establish a self-aware will that is liberated from unconscious drives through the development of the mind and reason, and the repression of instinct and the body; the seeking out of objectivity rather than subjectivity; the development of science; the rise of patriarchal religions and societies.[71] In each of these expressions we can see a pressing up against, a movement occurring in opposition to the archetypal Feminine, the depth of which Jung defines here in reference to "the Mother":

> "Mother" is an archetype and refers to the place of origin, to nature, to that which passively creates, hence to substance and matter, to materiality, the womb, the vegetative functions. It also means the unconscious, our natural and instinctive life, the physiological realm, the body in which we dwell or are contained; for the "mother" is also the matrix, the hollow form, the vessel that carries and nourishes, and thus it stands for the foundation of consciousness.[72]

Out of entrancement with Nature, Mother, and birth, our fascination transformed itself in this latest segment of our history, toward a new innate orientation. We have been driven, in the last three thousand years, toward understanding in opposition to the world rather than in relation to it. This movement into masculine consciousness has brought tremendous benefits to us, marvelous technological achievements and an incredible depth of objective knowledge about the world, but that knowledge has come at the cost of the loss of our sense of participating with a living world. Such an experience of participation lies at the root of Goddess and grain symbols, as a way of seeing that "metaphorically bring[s] oneself closer" to what is observed (as Coles observed in the Pueblo children) and stands in compensatory contradiction to the modern masculine way of looking at the world.

What our ancestors experienced in rituals of the Feminine was not something intellectual; they did not "learn anything," as Aristotle observed, but rather received impressions and were put into a "certain frame of mind."[73] The distanced observation of masculine-egoic consciousness and its division from experience was left behind; they were instead led closer to that around them and brought into participation with the events of the ritual drama:

> The myth of Demeter and Kore became contemporary once more; the rape of Kore, Demeter's laments, take place here and now, and it is by virtue of this nearness of the Goddesses, and finally of their presence, that the initiate *(mystes)* will have the unforgettable experience of initiation. (Eliade)[74]

At Eleusis, the initiate experienced ritual suffering that brought one not only into participation with Demeter and Persephone, but also enabled an embodied authentic connection to one's own personal suffering. Opening to this vulnerability allowed for a new cosmological understanding of life's taking-and-giving in a vision of suffering redeemed. Stemming from the literal act of nurturance or its absence, to the psychological experience of the personal mother, to the cultural expressions of woman and motherhood, a ritual that is begun by reflection upon spring and birth became a vehicle by which the whole cycle of birth, fertility, death, and rebirth *came to be seen as unified.*

> Mother divided from daughter, and the mown ear, are two symbols of something unspeakably painful that is hidden in the Demeter-aspect of the world; but also of something very consoling. Demeter contains this consolation in herself and reveals it in [her mysteries]. (Kerenyi)[75]

Here the sacred is met, not as light, but in the "revelation of something *still unopened, like a bud,*" as a dark yet ideal truth.[76] In contrast to the clear distinctions of patriarchal God-images, here the wonder lies in the "structure hidden in the abyss of the nucleus,'"[77] where one was brought to see the paradoxical truth of life that, as with the seed that must die to come into its flowering, the deepest spiritual possibility can be hidden in the darkness of suffering—that good can be found in evil. "The meaning of it—good concealed in evil—is immortality,"[78] wrote Kerenyi, and experience of this mystery was said to lessen the fear of dying. The poet Krinagoras describes the outcome of this experience as the achievement of a "lighter heart,"[79] and it is with this understanding that Aristides proclaimed, "Eleusis is a shrine common to the whole earth, and of all the divine things that exist among men."

> Happy is he among men upon earth who has seen these mysteries; but he who is uninitiate and who has no part in them, never has lot of like good things once he is dead, down in the darkness and gloom. (Homeric Hymn to Demeter)[80]

In rituals of the archetypal Feminine it is not that the mystery was simply equivalent to the female body but rather that these grain and Goddess images point toward the miracle of life and the possibility of "dead" matter giving birth to the new, and to that spark of the divine "greening power of God," in Bingen's words, which is somehow a part of organic life; and that through the "death" of our ego in suffering, we may gain sight of the connection to the transcendent within us. Here "the separation and reunion of the Mother and Daughter reappears as a story of the soul's separation from, reunion with, the divine ground of its origin."[81] In the fullest flowering of the archetypal Feminine there is a realization of the sanctity of spirit in matter. Describing an African female initiation rite, University of Chicago mythologist Mircea Eliade finds words to describe this mystery:

> It is not the natural phenomenon of giving birth that constitutes its mystery; it is the revelation of the feminine sacredness; that is, of the mystic unity between life, woman, nature and the divinity. This is a revelation of transpersonal order; for which reason it is expressed in symbols and actualized in rites. The girl or the initiated woman becomes conscious of a sanctity that emerges from the innermost depths of her being, and this consciousness, obscure though it may be, is experienced in symbols. It is in realising and in living this sacredness that the woman finds the spiritual meaning of her own existence, she feels that life is both real and sanctified, that it is not merely an endless series of blind, psychophysiological automatisms, useless and in the last reckoning absurd. (Eliade)[82]

At its most psychologically potent, the archetypal Feminine was experienced as "new, astonishing, inaccessible to rational cognition." The moment of insight in the Demeter-Persephone mysteries at Eleusis was conveyed through the image of an "ear of wheat growing and maturing with a supernatural speed,"[83] which was all at once "both origin and end, of mother and daughter; and just because of that it points beyond the individual to the universal, and eternal."[84] Nearing the end of his life, the Buddha gave a teaching that enabled a direct experience of a similar insight, simply with the holding up of a flower.

> The Buddha could equally well have held up something else, a stone or a bit of wood, with the same significance as the flower. But in Eleusis bud-like summings-up and goddesses in all their perfection form a single, unequivocal, coherent group. They set one another off and coalesce at the same time. And the thing that unites them like a common root is no less positive. Through all of them, through the grain of wheat, and the Mother-Daughter goddess, the same vision opens the vision . . . into the abyss of the nucleus. Every grain of wheat and every maiden contains, as it were, all its descendants and all their descendants . . . the infinity of supra-individual organic life. (Kerenyi)[85]

Although the Buddha's sermon was understood by only one of those in attendance, it expressed the teaching upon which Buddhism is founded. As with the stalks of wheat presented in silence in the Eleusian mysteries, the Buddha here sought to demonstrate the transcendent unity of spirit within organic life. As with the Greek experience of this revelation, *The Tibetan Book of the Dead* describes the wordless understanding of this truth to be an enabling passport for the successful passage after death. "Just as all men are Buddha, so are all things—plants, trees, the whole earth. . . . In his 'Flower Sermon,' words were finally transcended."[86]

> A mown ear of grain was presented, in silence, and the participants were made aware of "the continuity of life in the unity of maiden, mother, and child, a being that dies, gives birth, and comes to life again." Demeter was identified with grain, the grain that never dies but grows up from the earth continually. Demeter is thus a biological image of the Self. (Woodman)[87]

Woodman speaks of the flower-grain symbol as a biological image of the Self archetype. As discussed previously, the Self is that part of the psyche that seeks to unite our conscious self with our deeper aspects and fulfill the further unfolding of who we are. This process is open both to directing us in a spiritual, "upward" direction and a bodily, instinctual, "downward" direction. The latter is emphasized here:

> The Self may also symbolize itself as awe-inspiring natural phenomena such as wild animals, fish or trees, mountains and oceans. Here the instinctual or organic life of the Self is being stressed. This imagery tends to occur when the individual needs to re-establish contact with this level of being. (Corbett)[88]

In this way, we can understand the second characteristic of Crop Circles, their construction in the stalk of living cereal grains, as emphasizing the same Self archetype symbolism that is found in its composition in concentric geometric form. Here, however, the Self symbol's meaning is given direction: it is shown to be emphasizing the organic or instinctual aspect of our need of, and potential for, new and greater consciousness. Rather than a transcendent movement out of life and the moment's particulars toward abstract principles, as a symbol Crop Circles can be seen to call for a return of attention toward the immanent, toward the concrete, toward consciously apprehending what is present here. Implicit in such directionality is an emphasis upon the material, the organic, the bodily, and the earthly. We can, of course, move to consider such symbolic meanings on our own by entering physically into a Crop Circle formation for ourselves—they suggest our need for embodied inquiry and offer us an opportunity for it. Crop Circles are a symbol pointing "downward," a biological image of the Self. They point toward our need for greater contact with our organic and instinctual selves and echo a larger impetus that is emergent today. We live in a moment in history in which the quality of our innumerable crises and miraculous discoveries all direct us toward reconnection with the earth, the body, the immanent, the archetypal Feminine.

The journey of human consciousness out of unconscious participation mystique with Nature, out of unconscious identification with the archetypal Feminine, has been made out of psychological necessity (as will be considered further in the next chapter). However, the necessity of our growth out of such a state does not change the fact that in the course of achieving it we have repressed an aspect of ourselves and our understanding of the divine. Jung understood the Feminine in one aspect, as the foundation of the psyche, the unconscious basis from which consciousness develops, the fertile matrix of life itself within us. By definition, consciousness requires a turning away from this foundation and a movement into self-understanding through juxtaposition and separateness. In our turning away from identification with Nature, in the three-thousand-year journey of the West's directing of its attention "upward," much of what is "downward" materiality—instinct, the body, the planet (and our sense of interdependence with it)—have also become lost to us and even rejected by us. And so we have evil, femininity, and the body all tarred together in the vision of the sinfulness of Eve, for example. Where our ancestors lived in a participation mystique with Nature, which kept them primarily within the range of perspective of the Feminine, today we have come to look upon the world exclusively through the "narrow band of the archetypal masculine."[89]

Modern culture no longer gives thanks for what we receive from the earth; no longer do we see something divine in our daily bread, and lost to us is the miracle of life, the miracle of our own life. No longer do we make ritual procession around the field before planting, or do our own version of the Green Corn Dance, or see any intimacy in our participation with Mother Nature. We do not make the Corn Dolly, the Corn Mother, or the Old Woman; we do not place her above our doors or in our barns. Where is the consciousness of the Feminine for us? Gone underground, but unconsciously present as compulsive materiality—materialism, sexuality without intimacy, eating to fill an undefined craving in us or not eating to get a body that will fill an empty space inside us, neglect of the reality of our organic body and its healthy needs, neglect of the planet, even forgetting somehow that it is only within its environment that we survive. Existing outside of a view of life that is both "real and sanctified," we are left as Eliade describes it, living life as "an endless series of blind, psycho-physiological automatisms, useless and in the last reckoning absurd."[90]

> It is my belief that without knowledge of God as Mother as well as Father and without the conscious incorporation of the healing and balancing wisdom of the sacred feminine . . . the human race will die out and take a large part of nature with it. . . . Only a race in drastic denial of its interdependence with all things and beings could be devastating the environment as blindly as we are.[91]

Where environmental crisis and the other symptoms force our attention toward a "downward" direction, toward the Earth, the material, and the archetypal Feminine, Crop Circles in their breathtaking craft invite us to place our attention there. They are splendid, "fit for Ceres" in the Old Roman expression, and they lead the imagination up into wonder while still keeping our feet on the ground. In its most potent form, the archetypal Feminine is open to us as the experience of that same unitive vision that was known to the initiates of Eleusis, and that the Buddha pointed to in holding up a flower. Each of these revealed an "almost unfathomable mystery,"[92] "the infinity of supra-individual organic life" that is present in the "abyss of the nucleus." In such an understanding, each voice has value and each individual's actions are significant. With this in mind, we should remember that while we cannot return to an old form of consciousness, nor enfold ourselves once again in the breast of the Mother Goddess, we can, as the farmer of the Grain Miracle legend does, consciously choose to participate with this new mysterious visitor that we find before us. In choosing such participation, perhaps we might find ourselves feeling some small spark of the miraculous, or being moved to take a step toward dancing as our ancestors were, or even once again perhaps hearing Nature—no longer as just an "it" but a "thou"—with a voice who whispers to us.

> The inhabitant or soul of the universe is never seen;
> its voice alone is heard . . . It has a gentle voice
> like a woman, a voice so fine and gentle that
> even children cannot become afraid. What it says is,
> "Be not afraid of the universe."
> —NATIVE ALASKAN SAYING[93]

FIVE

REASON ALONE

Human consciousness has developed infinitely slowly out of nature. Before we knew ourselves as human, we were animal and plant, stone and water. For countless millennia, the potential for human consciousness was hidden within nature, like a seed buried deep within the earth. Then, very slowly, it began to differentiate itself from nature. Deep in our memory is the whole experience of life on this planet: life as hydrogen, oxygen, and carbon; life as the minutest particles of matter; life as water, fire, air and earth; life as rock, soil, plant, seed, insect, bird, animal; life as woman and man evolved from this eonic experience. Finally the point was reached where life evolved a brain that enabled us to speak, to formulate thoughts, to communicate with each other through language, to endow sounds with meaning, and invent writing as a way of transmitting thoughts. Over these billions of years life on this planet has evolved from undifferentiated awareness to the self-awareness of our species. All this can be described as an instinctive process, each phase blending imperceptibly into the next.

—BARING AND HARVEY[1]

As a part of this process, around the cultures of the world, where once a sense of wonder and containment within Nature's mystery filled human beings, our imagination turned slowly toward a new orientation. As Nature and the figures of the Goddess slowly fade from our awareness, as communities no longer celebrate Her charms and abundance, and as our conscious mind begins to lose sight of the archetypal Feminine, a simultaneous inflation occurs. Psyche, like space, abhors a vacuum, and as the Lunar mist faded from the consciousness of our ancestors, the bright light of the archetypal

Solar principle rose up to take its place. This transition of the human self-image, as reflected in our images of the divine, is important to our consideration of the "dream" of Crop Circles for two reasons. First, Goddess images and their archetypal connection to grain and Nature echo the medium into which formations occur. Second, and equally important, as we would expect in a personal dream interpretation, an inquiry into the context into which the dream falls is a necessary part of our task, and it is the absence of the archetypal Feminine from modern psychological experience that provides a key element of this context. It is the transition of our consciousness away from numinous participation with Nature toward investment in our own inventive, creative genius that defines to a significant measure the character of the modern mind. In order to understand why the "dream image" of Crop Circles comes to us in this particular moment, and what they reflect about our collective psyche right now, we need to see them within the context of the history of the "dreamer"'s experience.

> When we take up an obscure dream, our first task is not to understand and interpret, but to establish the context with minute care. By this I do not mean unlimited "free association" starting from any and every image in the dream, but a careful and conscious illumination of the interconnected associations objectively grouped round particular images. (Jung)[2]

> When . . . we seek a psychological explanation of a dream, we must first know what were the preceding experiences out of which it is composed. (Jung)[3]

What animates a dream into meaning within our own lives, as mentioned in the introduction, is the accord of that dream to the facts and challenges of our unique situation at that moment. What makes a dream meaningful for us is its acute representation, even if symbolic, of the specific personal conditions in which we find ourselves. It is not the dream images that generate power, but rather the relationship of those images to our lived experience. As a collective content—placed before us all today—how do Crop Circles relate to the current nature of the collective psyche? Why are we "dreaming" about Crop Circles right now? Only in relation to a context, to our actual living collective experience, can an answer to this question be discovered. Discovering insight here involves not only examination of the nature of the circle and grain as symbols, but also inquiry into the history of our development of consciousness and consideration of the actual psychological state of our collective culture at this moment in time.

Although a great deal could be said about the nature of the collective psyche as it is today, our current state is the end result of billions of years of evolution and does not exist in a vacuum. As Baring and Harvey point out in the epigraph of this chapter, before we knew ourselves in any other way, we knew ourselves as a part of Nature. The earliest human self-concept was a mirror of our entrancement with the dynamic mystery of the living world around us. On some level today, we carry within us the building blocks of our cellular and biological evolution; as they write, "deep in our memory is the whole experience of life on this planet . . . life as the minutest particles of matter; life as water, fire, air and earth; life as rock, soil, plant, seed, insect, bird, animal,"[4] or as the Persian mystic poet Hafiz wrote "once we were all tomatoes, potatoes, onions or zucchini."[5] There is a way in which we know ourselves that is rooted in the most mundane elements of Nature. Instinctively, in a way that is seemingly also a part of Nature, humanity slowly developed a consciousness capable of self-awareness and differentiation from the natural world. Prior to this achievement, early humanity lived psychologically tied and "magically" bound to the world around it, viewing each object as alive and seeing little difference between itself and the world around it. In this primal worldview, meaning is seen everywhere, and signs and spirits are omnipresent. "The primal person walks through a world that is experienced as continuous between inner and outer. . . . [He or she] sees and experiences a world in which the human soul is completely embedded in a larger being that is also ensouled."[6] It is out of this fascination, this participation mystique, that the earliest nature idols were carved, the first images of animals painted on the walls of the caves at Altamira, Spain, and that the ancient Goddess images were evoked and crafted.

The emergence of humanity out of this state of union with the natural world and into the initial phases of self-consciousness is represented psychologically in the West in the Judeo-Christian Creation story of the fall from grace—the banishment of Adam and Eve from Eden for eating from the Tree of Knowledge.[7] The story of the fall describes, metaphorically, the actual movement of human consciousness out of entrancement with

Mother Nature and into a self-awareness taking place within us at the time that these stories were conceived. The journey out of symbiosis with the Mother is a transition that we each make individually as children growing up; it was certainly also a shift that was made collectively across cultures and times throughout our history. Individually, at the age of about one and a half years, children begin to be able to understand themselves as a being separate from their mothers. One way in which this is evident is through their ability to recognize themselves in a mirror (an image that will continue to define this stage of development). Here the ego begins to emerge from the unconscious. With the achievement of self-recognition, the first steps are taken toward defining oneself and becoming aware of our ability to influence the environment around us. This movement of the child away from the mother, and of consciousness out of fascination with the natural world, is often regarded, for good and ill, as the beginning of a hero's journey.

> The mythological stages in the evolution of consciousness begin with the stage where the ego is contained in the unconscious, and leads up to a situation in which the ego not only becomes aware of its own position and defends it hero-ically, but also becomes capable of broadening and relativizing its experiences through the changes effected by its own activity. (Neumann)[8]

It is this ability—the ego's ability to broaden its awareness through recognition of the effects of its activity—that will define this next stage. From the first moment in which our ancestors grabbed hold of an object and used it as a tool, this process began. Rather than enchantment with and worship of Nature, here we have become fascinated by our ability to have an effect upon Nature. This orientation is described metaphorically as the hero's journey because in it one moves away from enclosure within the mother, the primary state of unconscious participation mystique, and begins to experiment with one's own autonomous capacities—to know oneself, to assert oneself, and to discover for oneself. This is the drive to have a will of one's own and it is a healthy and natural part of every individual's development. It is the instinct to strive to overcome the challenges and circumstances of our lives. It is the process by which our psychological state of unity with the environment, experienced as the primal I and Thou, or joined we, *is* broken and first experienced "as the 'You,' the non-ego, something different and strange."[9]

Establishment of this psychological capacity is a repeated process throughout our psychological development, but it occurs first, to the great frustration of parents, in the child's years known as the "terrible twos." What depicts this state, making it obvious, is the assertion of the child's will— through exclamation most often of the word "no." And it is precisely this saying "no" that illustrates the process that occurs every time in our life that a battle between ego and unconsciousness takes place. As we try to slip the regressive tendencies of instinct, even in our lives today, we constellate a re- newed combat between our conscious self-awareness and the unconscious matrix deep within us. At this stage, consciousness is defined by liberation through division:

> When we scrutinize the acts upon which consciousness and the ego are built up, we must admit that to begin with they are all negative acts. To discriminate, to distinguish, to mark off, to isolate oneself from the surrounding context— these are the basic acts of consciousness. Indeed, experimentation as the scien- tific method is a typical example of this process: a natural connection is broken down and something is isolated and analyzed, for the motto of consciousness is determinatio est negatio [determination by negation]. (Neumann)[10]

In the fallout after the breakdown of the paradisiacal unity, not only does consciousness discover itself as existing as separate from the Other to which it was formerly bonded, but it begins to experience (mainly unconsciously) a similar division within itself. Ego consciousness brings with it, and is de- fined by, the achievement of a separate sense of self that is distinct from the unconscious background from which it emerged. Yet this living background exists within us—achievement of ego consciousness only establishes an ini- tial point of separation, not emancipation. Lurking behind us, always both informing us and haunting us, lies the great unconscious matrix of instincts and archetypes, and regression into identification with unconscious content remains a very real threat throughout all of our lives. At the earliest stages of human development this threat was even more potent, and the first so- cially engendered taboos were a response to this danger. Shaming was, and is, used constructively to shore up our egos against this regression. Our re- ligious systems and moral codes (as well as psychotherapy) are attempts to bulwark consciousness against reversion to behavior driven by instinctual drives and the potential of being overwhelmed by the unconscious. Pushed away in this movement are the previously driving forces of instinct, body, the tremendous force of the cycles by which they endlessly regenerate, and all of the magnetic impulses of primal Nature. Development of this egoic capacity for resistance to the instinctual and unconscious forces within us is spoken of as our Solar conscience by Stein. It is a term "referring to an inner moral guide that represents the values within the thought and behavioral patterns which dominate the conscious life of the individual."[11] Solar values are readily available; they are drawn from one's culture and demand our responsibility to society. "They are 'in the light,' observed and recognized by all, and they shine on the individual with the brightness of the sun. Hence the term *solar*. . . . The ego is thus exposed to a bright light that can shine into its most secret corners and pass judgment in privacy. A violation of the norms upheld by solar conscience causes social anxiety in addition to guilt."[12] Solar conscience draws its values from the group norms, but then elevates them into perfect abstract ideals (for example, making the just act into justice). This act of elevation is then also turned inward and becomes a part of how we look at ourselves: "the ego now experiences an ego-ideal of abstract perfection and feels measured against that ideal."[13] Splitting off from the unconscious, the instinctual, and the body brings feelings of elevation (wonder at newfound independence), and the arrival of the inner critic, for, split off from a part of itself, it must guard against reversion and loss of self-control.

The myth of the hero becomes explicit in this transition, then, as the one struggling for the "self-emancipation of the ego, struggling to free itself from the power of the unconscious and to hold its own against overwhelming odds."[14] It is in this light that we can understand the tales of the hero against the Giant Beast. Throughout our religious imagery and myth, the snake and other animal images are made to exemplify the reality of bestial instinct inside of us, legends of great beasts and giants to be overcome by heroes; taken psychologically are metaphors for the light of consciousness's struggle against the dark interior of the human psyche. Only by the arrival of ego consciousness is such darkness made visible. In the previous state of consciousness, awareness was constricted within an undifferentiated unconscious self, and it is the danger of such reincorporation that threatens the ego. Tales of heroes caught inside great beasts, like the biblical Jonah in the whale, show literal fascination with this possibility—and emphasize the necessity of ego consciousness's ability to divide itself out from the powerful pull of regression into unconsciousness. In such tales, the hero is a personification of the ego as it is threatened with being engulfed within the overwhelming pull of regression. Although this danger is overcome in various ways throughout mythology, the symbolic weapon of the hero, which exemplifies the capacity of ego consciousness to differentiate, is the sword.

> The knight and his sword . . . represent the heroic attitude needed by the ego to deal with the dragon-chaos of the inner world . . . the world of conscious thought and discrimination, and the ego's ability to categorize, label, evaluate and discriminate. The cutting edge of the sword is the mind's sharpness, which separates experiences into their individual parts so that understanding may be gained. (Raff)[15]

The sword represents a quality of consciousness that divides, separates, and discriminates. In this way, it is in contrast to the character of the archetypal Feminine, which knows itself through relation *to* Other and to the world. By the nature of these qualities, this kind of hero-sword consciousness is more likely to be thought of as archetypally masculine, but in using a gender term as a descriptor one runs the risk of generating misunderstanding, mostly as the term "masculine" is confused with men in particular or patriarchal social systems in general. Psychologically, the archetypal masculine and Feminine exist within both sexes, as do masculinity and femininity. The polarization of nature into such complementary divisions is a fundamental part of our psyche's structure—regardless of our occasional modern preference to the contrary. "The fact of psychic polarities and the centrality of the masculine-feminine polarity is a basic structure of the human psyche."[16] masculine and Feminine are alive within each of us.

To view the ego as personified in the masculine image of the hero, a knight with a sword, therefore does not mean that women cannot or should not be heroes; rather, it points to the quality of a singular kind of heroic consciousness within all of us. Swords and heroes represent a mode of functioning that is evident within, and accessible to, men and women alike. In these myths the ego is personified as hero, or objectified as sword, and in their acts and capacities they represent the struggle of the ego to achieve its separate identity apart from the unconscious. At the stage of development being described earlier, psychological growth requires a heroic advance, as symbolized by the image of the knight with sword, and ego consciousness itself is often synonymous with this masculine mode. (While, by their nature, the images of hero and sword have a correspondence to the archetypal masculine, neither one exhausts its possibilities. Just as the sword has a range of interpretations that extend beyond the masculine, the masculine cannot be defined by a single image—and it is also not always equivalent with the ego.) Jungian analyst and author Edward F. Edinger describes this masculine energy as "the great agent of *separation* that brings consciousness and power over nature—both within and without—by its capacity to divide, name and categorize. One of its major symbols is the cutting edge that can dissect and differentiate on the one hand and kill on the other."[17] The archetypal masculine is that which divides the one out from the collective, strives to achieve autonomy and clarity. In contrast, as illustrated throughout Chapter Four, in the archetypal Feminine mode influence is served such that subject and object are not divided but brought into one, and relating and relationship are valued. Where Mother Nature, and the Goddess images representing her, symbolize the archetypal Feminine as Nature "hosting all things," good and bad both flourish in Her soil, none are turned away; archetypal masculinity, as symbolized in singular God-images, introduces juxtaposition, such as humanity over Nature. Under the latter influence, having an effect upon the environment becomes fascinating—he says, "Look what I can do!" In this way, its distinction from the archetypal Feminine is made clear[18]—where he explores the world around as set apart from him, she celebrates and values being a part of, and feeling related to it.

Each of us, at different times in our lives, will require the energy of each of these qualities in order to fulfill our developmental potential at that particular stage. Like the child who begins to assert its autonomy against the safety of the mother in the background, the ego pushes against the unconscious from which it has emerged. This movement is particularly associated with the son, as the male child in particular finds, in differentiating himself from the mother, an "Other" (the ego's view of the unconscious), whereas the daughter can see herself in the mother's reflection. Again, such a classic symbolic definition does not remove the necessity of female children's development of the ego (or their need for separation from their mothers), but rather offers a metaphor that is appropriate to this stage's growth. Neumann describes the stage prior to the ego's emergence as developing through centroversion—inward-focused movement, growth through concentration and unification, the desire of the organism to maintain itself as a whole (entelechy in biology).[19] Directionally this would be described as centripetal, energy spiraling inward toward a center, as one might imagine is necessary for the gestation and development of a baby or a child. Such movement has an obvious association to the Feminine. Contrasting this is centrifugal movement, spiraling outward away from center, as we might see, not only in the movement of child away from mother, but also in the movement of young males away from their herd, tribe, or community as they approach adulthood. Centrifugal energy, growth out from a previously developed center, has a correspondence to the archetypal masculine.[20]

At different stages of our lives, we will need to make room for one or the other type of movement—periods of both gestation and exploration are necessary for psychological maturity. However, breaking our habitual response patterns in order to make room for necessary changes in impetus is often difficult. How can we know what it is that we need when we are unconscious of that need? We may, at times, find ourselves making shifts toward one or the other without even knowing why or choosing to do so consciously. At such times, it would seem that life has its own plans for us. Likewise, at different stages of our cultural advancement one or the other of these can be seen to be present, driving and underlying our growth. In looking at the shift from Goddess to God images, many see such a transformation. For thousands of years, animal idol and Goddess worship, human reverence for Nature, expressed an interior-focused developmental process, a slow centroversion, in which psychic energy fed the psychological growth of our species. During this time, fascination remained locked in focus and adoration of the majesty of Nature as mother, and in awe of Her eternal primacy, as Bachofen explains:

> The mother is earlier than the son. The feminine has priority, while masculine creativity only appears afterwards as a secondary phenomenon. Woman comes

first, but man "becomes." The prime datum is the earth, the basic maternal substance. Visible creation precedes from her womb. . . . The female is primary, the male is only what comes out of her. He is part of the visible but ever-changing created world; he exists only in perishable form. Woman exists from ever-lasting, self-subsistent, immutable; man evolving, is subject to continual decay. In the realm of the physical, therefore, the masculine principle is of second rank, subordinate to the feminine. Herein lies the prototype and justification of gynocracy; herein is rooted that age-old conception of an immortal mother who unites herself with a mortal father. She is perennially the same, but from the man the generations multiply themselves to infinity. . . . The man appears as creature, not as creator; as effect, not cause. The reverse is true of the mother. She comes before the creature, appearing as cause, the prime giver of life, and not as an effect. . . . Everywhere the material, feminine, natural principle has the advantage; it takes the masculine principle, which is secondary and subsists on in perishable form as an ever-changing epiphenomenon, into its lap, as Demeter took the cista.[21]

Here the *cista* in Demeter's lap refers to a ritual phallic image crafted by worshippers out of clay and symbolically laid in the lap of the Great Mother Goddess. And appropriately so, as prior to the emergence of the ego, masculine energy laid in unconscious identification with the Mother and Nature. Only with its "second birth" into self-awareness does the masculine begin to invest itself with a degree of awe; only with a step into autonomy does the ego begin to feel its own separate sense of power and value. But taking this step has a profound psychological cost. Emerging from the vision of eternal splendor that is the Goddess as Nature and Creation as Her wonder, plunges one into awareness of death and loneliness.[22] Ego consciousness means attachment to a self that can feel pain. Losing connection to, and union with, a primordial psychological "we" that had been "constantly aware of its ties with, and dependence upon the matrix from which it sprang,"[23] like Adam and Eve flung out of Eden, the ego gains its terrible first achievement and its separation becomes real. "By discovering itself, the lonely ego simultaneously perceives the negative and relates to it, so that it at once establishes a connection between these two facts, taking its own genesis as guilt, and suffering, sickness, and death as condign punishment."[24] In this way, body, sexuality, guilt, sin, and death are conflated together—remaining so, in part, to this day. While psychologically "leaving the mother" has an equivalency to establishing a moral center beyond animal instinctuality,[25] doing so opens a Pandora's box of prejudices against what has been left behind. No longer enslaved unconsciously to animal instinct, ego consciousness enabled the distance required for moral choice. Yet this distance opened up the neuroses with which modern man now struggles. Having the choice to sacrifice instinctual impulse opened us up to fearing the phantoms that lurk in the psyche's darkness. In simultaneously discovering both his autonomy and mortality, he has lost that which he was once a part of and blames himself. Death comes as punishment for the separation that he has made—"through Adam's sin, which lay precisely in his becoming conscious, death came into the world. The neurotic who cannot leave his mother has good reasons for not doing so; ultimately, it is the fear of death that holds him there."[26] Not leaving the mother (literally and/or symbolically) enables a psychological denial of death and avoidance of combat with the great beast of our inner instinctual selves. In modernity, such battles are avoided by failing to participate in life itself and a "continual shrinking back from reality."[27] Taking on this battle, the hero leaves the Great Mother's house behind. Christian philosopher Owen Barfield described the pre-egoic state of unconscious union with Nature as the "original participation." Leaving this state was psychologically necessary, as Baring and Cashford describe, because:

> Human consciousness needed to detach itself from participation with the nature, in order to gain more space, more play between itself and the world.[28]

Achievement of the ego's self-conceptualization enables a perceptual distance to exist psychologically between the self and objects in the world. Consciousness represents a wedge between environment and our automatic responses to it. This capacity is expressed in the symbolic representation of objects through language. Language reflects the ego's existence, for one can now make symbols of objects—words, names, images—rather than only respond to them. This "room to move" enables choice, moral action, and resistance of temptation; it reflects the restriction of the instincts' natural response to the world—the first splitting off of body from mind. Psychologically, the "birth" of the ego introduces a barrier between thought and impulse that enables both self-knowledge and psychological denial. In its development is begun the process of the psychic energy's redirection from body to mind, the change in flow of psychic energy upward toward the head. Breaking the chains of enslavement to instinct opens up noble, life-enhancing possibilities of choice, discernment, and morality, but also the dangerous potential conditions of dissociation, denial, and the cloudy inner state in which body, emotion, instinct, and thought remain twisted together malignantly. The division in consciousness that enables morality also necessitates a split in which the body is rejected so that its drives may be overcome.

In early Judaism, the rejection of the Feminine, body, matter, and image were explicit. The Ten Commandments encoded a moral system designed to constrict the power of the instincts, and worship of the Goddess and Golden Calf idol were banned. Later on, with the introduction of the Psalms, and in other areas of scripture, a Feminine side to the Hebrew God-image would be reintroduced. In the beginning, however, God as Father was the clear image of the Hebrew deity. In the Hebrew image of God, He comes "as the Word," reflecting the achievement of the ego's capacity for symbolization. Yahweh's self-definition, "I am that I am" (of which the name YHWH is a tetragrammaton)[29]'speaks to the ego's ability to self-conceptualize its first statement of self-awareness: "I am." Echoing the ego's intrapsychic emergence, the God-image, in place of divinity as present and visible within Nature's majesty, offers a vision of the numinous as transcendent of the world. As the ego is no longer contained within its natural interior, neither is God to be viewed as being found there—He is *beyond Nature.*[30] The first act of Genesis, the separation of heaven and earth, defines this new cosmological view. Because of this, God Himself cannot be represented by an image—"Thou shalt not make unto thee any graven image or likeness of any thing that is in heaven above, or that is in the earth beneath"[31]—nor can any name be given to Him. Here, immanence is lost, the Goddess as divinity-near is nullified, and a transcendent and male God is gained.

The old imagery of the god as the son, lover and consort of the goddess has apparently vanished forever as if it had never existed. There is nothing to modify the exclusive and unrelated maleness of god. This absence of feminine symbolism in the image of God, as Pagels has pointed out, is to mark Judaism, Christianity and Islam in striking contrast to the world's other religious traditions. (Baring and Cashford)[32]

Simultaneously, this removed vision of the divine is also somehow male. While in no other way physically conceivable, the Hebrew God is referred to throughout the Old Testament as male. Here, looking into its reflection in the mirror of the suddenly strange world around it, ego consciousness envisions a masculine reflection. Like ego consciousness, this image of God is both without form (non-physical) and also archetypally masculine in its character. Not only does the Hebrew God-image resemble the ego, in its dissociation from Nature as instinct, body, and the unconscious, but it also reflects the patriarchal culture out of which it evolved.

The Biblical God-concept, intuitively grasped by the prophets and gropingly reached by the people, reflects the strictly patriarchal order of the society which produced it; this patriarchal society gave rise to a religion centered around a single, universal deity whose will was embodied in the Law, but who was abstract, devoid of all physical attributes and yet pronouncedly male, a true projection of the patriarchal family-head. (Patai)[33]

Surrounding the Israelites on all sides were tribes who worshipped other deities, often animal idols and Goddess-images. Reverence for such images stems from a level of consciousness that is associated with Nature and bonded to instinct. Accepting their God meant both a cultural rejection of those particular idols and a psychological rejection of the carnal energies that they represented and their rituals celebrated. Goddess worship was made punishable by death. A turning back toward such energies was incredibly tempting to the Israelites, as it always is to the ego, and they did not fail to fail. But, after a time, they came to believe that their God was *the* God, and not simply just another idol.

Legitimate Jewish faith, beginning with the earliest formulations of its belief system by the great Hebrew prophets . . . . has always been built upon the axiom of One God. This credo has its complementary corollary in the denial of the very possibility of other gods. [34]

The One True God has only one true people and they are the children of Abraham. They are special because of their unquestioning devotion. When Moses descended from Mt. Sinai, bringing with him the tablets bearing the Ten Commandments, the response of the Israelites is "We will do." They did not say, as Ulanov has observed, "We must know [first]," they responded with "a whole hearted loving of God so remarkable that in the New Testament Jesus took it as the first great commandment."[35] This relationship between a people and a God-image moves beyond a Nature cosmology in that it is more concrete, distinct, personal, unique, and one-to-one than the worship of the seasons or the cycles of life. Here the voice of a specific God, in Jewish faith *the* God, calls out to a specific people for the first time in history. Rather than an endless, repetitive circular view of time associated with Nature, here there is a breaking out of cycles into a cosmological view that has both a beginning and end of time. In Judaism, the flame of the divine is housed in a profoundly new way—God is present, involved in history, and promises the faithful redemption in the heavenly afterlife of the Promised Land.

Alongside the development of the Hebrew God-image, a similar unfolding was occurring in the psyche of ancient Greece. Their imaginations became seized by a curiosity with the operative principles orchestrating reality *behind and beyond* Nature. No longer were the various gods and Goddesses of the ancient pantheon sole recipients of reverence; rather, more and more, their culture invested itself in rational pursuit of divine "first causes." In his epic study, *The Passion of the Western Mind* (1991), Tarnas locates the beginning of our intellectual journey in the differentiation of the notion of "clarifying universals [existing] in the chaos of life."

> Despite the continuous flux of phenomena in both the outer world and inner experience, there could yet be distinguished specific immutable structures or essences, so definite and enduring they were believed to possess an independent reality of their own. . . . [In Plato's view these] archetypes form the world and also stand beyond it. They manifest themselves within time and yet are timeless. They constitute the veiled essence of things.[36]

Behind the form of the individual object or concept lies its archetypal form. In this worldview, equality, for example, can never be found, although things that are very near to equal can be. Equality exists outside of the manifest world; consciousness can know it empirically only in an approximate sense. Archetypes are absolute, transcending and superseding reality. In looking past appearance one found essence; looking beyond the particular, one came to the universal. For Plato, at the top of the pyramid of these values lie the Good, the True, and the Beautiful. Although there were great variations and contradictions in this worldview as it developed in Greece across the centuries, a common interest in this way of thinking was shared by Homer, Aristotle, Pythagoras, Plotinus, Aeschylus, and Sophocles.[37] It was birthed primarily, however, by Socrates and Plato. In it, emphasis is placed upon both rational inquiry and a kind of intuitive, holistic perception of reality that Plato equated with intellect. A critic of Plato once said, "I see particular horses, but not horseness," to which Plato answered, "That is because you have eyes but no intelligence."[38] In such a statement, it is clear that the kind of thinking that is valued here, while rational, is distinguished from the sensate-focused thinking that would soon branch off into the scientific view. Rather, what is considered as intelligence is the ability to attune ourselves to intuitive perception of the connections between things. "Archetypes reveal themselves more to the inner perception than to the outer."[39] Like the Hebrew God coming as the word, here ego consciousness looks into the mirror of the phenomenal world and sees on the other side of it a reflection of a divine transcendent order whose existence is absolute and unchanging.

In observing the similarities between the development of the Hebrew God-image, the Greek philosophic worldview, and the transition of the ego out of unconscious identification with Nature (both inner and outer), no statement about the metaphysical truth of either, negatively or positively, is being put forward. Nor are either considered to be only reflections of the psychological change taking place in the human mind at this time. To draw a parallel between our images of the divine and our psychological state does not invalidate any metaphysical truth—how could it? Rather, these parallels are cited in the hopes of presenting the seed of the hero's journey toward our present condition. In the flowering of this adventure in the stages that follow, it is hoped that the value of this metaphor will become clear, as will its relevance to the context into which Crop Circles have arrived.

Both worldviews, Hebrew and Greek, represent a psychological concentration of energy, now withdrawn from fascination with the world and redirected to the conscious rational mind—and through that shift given a new understanding of the redemptive transcendent. Divinity can now be found through the human mind's vehicle: heard as the word; seen in the form; responded to with devotion, thought, and curiosity; and served through courageous moral acts. All of these means illustrate and celebrate the birth of consciousness within the human psyche.[40]

Philo of Alexandria formulated a philosophical integration of the Greek and Hebrew worldviews, just after the time of Christ, in the year 40 CE. In the operation of archetypes, he saw a Greek statement of faith in the rational accessibility of spiritual meaning. In the Hebrew experience of God, he saw principles handed down in merit of faith and a promise made that principled devotion to that faith would ultimately be rewarded with eternal life in heaven. Both view the world as inherently ordered, see belief as capable of being grounded in reason, and access to profound spiritual meaning as being available through the application of thought. To describe this shared perception of "universal reason governing the world,"[41] Philo took a Greek word already in use in both cultures, *logos,* meaning word or reason. His recognition of this shared conception would influence later Neoplatonism and take on a more specific theological meaning within Christianity. However, this integration, and the change in cosmology at this time that it reflects, also serve to illustrate in greater definition the emergence of an archetypal masculine viewpoint into the world, which comes in direct contrast to the Feminine worldview as expressed previously in the Goddess religions.

The idea of logos points to a view of creation in which the sacred is accessed through objective, human discernment of the meaningful framework behind the world's chaos. By applying ourselves, *at a distance,* through rationality, we can receive insight. In contrast to this stood thousands of years of human experience of discovering the sacred through *participation with* Nature. Many of the world's ancient philosophical systems have observed these two opposing modes and enshrined them into terms that are most often in some form masculine and feminine. While not being identical, the Chinese philosophical *yin* and *yang* bear a resemblance to these two approaches, and medieval alchemy took the Latin names for sun and moon, *Sol* and *Luna,* to refer to a similar pair. Jung used the broad term of *Eros,* to refer to the Feminine principle here as being that which values *relation to* something, subjective connection to people and places; and *logos* to refer to that which values the distanced, objective, clarifying differentiation of the archetypal masculine. While there are significant philosophical differences between the definitions given to the masculine and feminine in each of these systems, they express a human fascination with the complement and opposition of these two modes. Campbell details the qualities of this pairing:

> The left, the side of the heart, the shield side, has been symbolic, traditionally and everywhere, of the feminine virtues and dangers: mothering and seduction, the tidal powers of the moon and substances of the body, the rhythms of the seasons: gestation, birth, nourishment and fosterage; yet equally malice, and revenge, irrationality, dark and terrible wrath, black magic, poisons, sorcery, and delusion; but also fair enchantment, beauty, rapture, and bliss. And the right, thereby, is of the male: action, weapons, hero-deeds, protection, the masculine virtues and dangers: egoism and active power, lucid luminous reason, sun-like creative power but also cold unfeeling malice, abstract spirituality, blind courage, theoretical dedication, sober, unplayful moral force.[42]

In the West, the birth of patriarchal God-images and Greek philosophy represent an initial psychological turning away from participation mystique with the Feminine toward an instinctive preference for the archetypal masculine and Solar consciousness. Where we had seen ourselves in Nature's reflection, now something new was being born through us, a quality if not uniquely, then at least particularly, human in the natural world. Here we see the origin out of which the entire human project will come to be "seen as pushing the differentiation between self and world, between humanity and nature, between autonomy and participation." (Tarnas)[43] In the Mother, we were united with Nature and the divine; the masculine sword would cut each asunder. Of the transition between the previous Goddess worship and the new patriarchal God-image that would characterize the next three thousand years, Rouselle wrote:

Animal cult, totemism, matriarchy have vanished. The bright day of the masculine spirit and its domination has begun. Its radiance still endures. The animals recede into the darkness and mystery of nature. The masculine mind sees the world in the bright—but at the same time dangerous and blinding—light, and believes that it can understand and regulate it.[44]

In its apperception of the "One True God," and that God's stepping over into history, the Judaic tradition not only brought the divine into view in a new way in human history, but it also brought to humanity a uniquely new significance. In both success and failure, the experience of the Hebrews emphasized that human action carried cosmological consequence—Creation's fall came from humanity's sin. The Chosen People were not only God's benefactors, but also recipients of His wrath. In both cases, the special place of humanity in relation to God was emphasized. Contrary to the Goddess cycles of endless death and rebirth, in this primarily masculine view both history and cosmology are linear—time has a beginning and an end, and the world consists of a spiritual heaven above and a punishing hell below, with humanity caught in the center between. When, in Christian belief, God became flesh in Christ, being human took on further spiritual significance. From the perspective of the evolution of human consciousness, one can see the Christian image of God (much like many other religious images) as a movement of awareness out from primitive participation mystique with Nature, past enslavement to unconscious regressive image and instinct, toward free moral choice. Like the hero with the sword, in Christianity the ego was again reinforced against the enchanting pull of the interior world of psyche and its powerful libidinal drives.

In its moral teachings, Christianity brought to the pagan world a new sense of the sanctity of all human life, the spiritual value of the family, the spiritual superiority of self-denial over egoistic fulfillment, or unworldly holiness over worldly ambition, of gentleness and forgiveness over violence and retribution; a condemnation of murder, suicide, the killing of infants, the massacre of prisoners, the degradation of slaves, sexual licentiousness and prostitution, bloody circus spectacles—all in the new awareness of God's love for humanity, and the moral purity that love required in the human soul.[45]

In the paradoxical combining of the God of the Hebrews as judging fa-ther, with the forgiving, openhearted vulnerability of the Son, Christ-ianity brought the good (which it identified with the divine) into greater relief against the darkness of the instinct, but simultaneously it split off the worldly, bodily, and material and identified it with sin—leaving the two unresolved. Exemplifying the archetypal masculine, here consciousness is aided against the "dragon-chaos of the inner world," and morality is made more possible. However, the sword cuts both ways. As Christ is made a sym-bol of the spiritual ascent of men, upward out of captivity to instinct and ig-norance of God, the other edge of this blade as it unfolded in the Western psyche was the pursuit of science—liberation through knowledge and rea-son, discrimination through objective investigation. Where one ascribed a mystical power to faith and gave voice to the light of God, the other would eventually swear off all faith and come to believe only in its own existence and in the tremendous power of the human mind.

In Europe, at the end of the fifteenth century and beginning of the six-teenth century, following the darkness of the period of the black plague and the chaos that brought down high medieval civilization, an unpredictable rebirth or Renaissance took place. Within just a hundred years, humani-ty's view of itself was radically altered: Luther posted his ninety-five theses and began the Reformation of the Church; Columbus discovered Amer-ica and Vasco de Gama discovered India (Columbus's intended aim); and the great artists of this period painted the masterpieces that continue to de-fine the era in our visual imagination. Capping this reblooming of civiliza-tion—in which many of the ancient world's boundaries of understanding had been transcended and a new vision of the power of humanity's genius had flourished—was the scientific revolution. Emblematic of this move-ment was Copernicus's reconstitution of the order of the heavens. Previ-ously, a geocentric universe (in which the earth is the steady center) had been taken for granted; it was seemingly supported both by Biblical verse and common sense. How could the earth be moving if we were standing still upon it? Yet Copernicus, in studying the clumsy and ever more com-plicated computations needed to understand the movement of the planets through this model, saw past common convention to a new view that we understand today to be common sense.[46]

In a world in which the authority of religious revelation was losing relevance to the pursuit of truth, philosophy, which had previously served to bridge the gap between reason and faith, now switched sides. Responding to the intellectual vacuum left by the break between Church and science, and the chaotic variety of new schools emerging in the century following the height of the Renaissance, Descartes sought to establish a firm basis upon which to move forward philosophically. We could be certain only of that which can be "clearly and distinctly conceived."[47] The world around us and even our own bodies could be "just a dream," but our self-awareness we could be sure of. He took our capacity for self-reflection, our self-evident ability to reason, as his new foundation. In his famous dictum, *Cogito ergo sum,* "I think therefore I am," he formulated the self-definition of the modern mind. Here recognition of the distinct importance of our self-awareness is reached. Understanding of the profound value of humanity's singular capacity for rationality is rightly regarded to be of immeasurable value.

> Rational beings have a unique dignity. They stand out against the background of nature, just in that they are free and self-determining. . . . Everything else in nature, conforms to laws blindly. Only rational creatures conform to laws that they themselves formulate. This is something immeasurably higher. (C. Taylor)[48]

Awareness of the significance of human consciousness, in just this way, could be taken to be a climax of purpose of the human journey under the influence of the archetypal masculine. Taylor's description of Descartes's view of the special role of humanity reflects the era's view that our capacity for reason gave us the ability to reflect the divine intelligence that permeated the world in the beauty of form, the elegance of physical law, and in the exquisite grace of mathematical, geometric, and intellectual perfection (a belief that Newton, among others, carried forward). But Descartes himself saw the Cogito as lending strength to belief in God,[49] and from this moment on humanity's self-understanding would be to a greater and greater degree characterized by a separation of consciousness and matter, subject from object, body from spirit. Where previously people had believed all living things shared a character of spirit (vitalism), now science opened the door to reductionism—the belief that all of Nature's fundamental principles could be understood as the operation of sums of smaller parts—reducing something to its elements, and mechanism, the belief that everything can be known through physical causation. Animals could be understood as biological robots and the world is denied that character that defined humanity—consciousness, spirit, or soul; matter is now *by definition* inert, soulless, inanimate; and humanity's greatest tool for understanding the world—reason—is given primary authority. "Infallibility, once ascribed only to Holy Scripture or the supreme pontiff, was now transferred to human reason itself. In effect, Descartes unintentionally began a theological Copernican revolution, for his mode of reasoning suggested that God's existence was established by human reason and not vice-versa."[50] The ancient patriarchal ordering of the cosmos was reversed, for now faith in reason was justified on its own, and reason the source of a justified faith.

Alongside the other pioneers of the scientific revolution, Descartes defined our modern worldview. Looking outward from its own singular interiority at a mechanistic inanimate world, and buoyed by the clearly evident and seemingly ever-growing fruits of its validity, science would subsume the authority previously accorded to the Church to define the truth about the world. Darwin would further propel the dislocation of humanity from its previous cosmological center. As a consequence of his theory of evolution, humanity was now only a sophisticated animal, and consciousness—our defining quality—was an accidental product of a randomly generating world. "Our ready-made individuality, our identity, is no more than an accidental cohesion in the flux of time."[51] Something profound was lost in this step forward, something that had previously been a part of our understanding of ourselves and had given foundation to our moral code. There was no longer a divine plan, only biology thrusting forward more complicated forms; the universe did not exist for our fulfillment, it simply existed.

> Despite any nostalgia for the venerable but now disproved cosmic womb, one could not go backward. . . . Man was a highly successful animal. He was not God's noble creation with a divine destiny, but nature's experiment with an uncertain destiny. (Tarnas)[52]

Left unassured by divine authority, humanity carried the keys to the kingdom nonetheless—no longer blessed by something greater than itself, it was free and independent on its own. Humanity now stood atop the universal pyramid by virtue of its possession of reason, no longer requiring God's grace for its progress and separated thoroughly from Nature as well. "Both the human mind and the natural world now stood autonomously as never before, separated from God and from each other."[53] The numinous gaze that humankind had previously placed upon Creation would become ever-more-focused upon its own capacity to create. Faith was now placed upon humanity's own self-education and insight, and it was these drives that would propel our curiosity, imagination, and hope. The potency of human genius was now unleashed, and to an ever greater extent, our consciousness became invested in its products. The world became viewed as a machine; ironically, as a machine is, of course, something crafted by our hand, and now we were the Creators. Symbolically, once we invented electricity, is was us who spoke: "Let there be light." Such powers were now ours and not God's, and this climate would lead Nietzsche to his famous declaration, "God is dead," which was printed on newspaper headlines worldwide; Fitzgerald would echo him in fiction, writing that "all the Gods were now dead."[54] Now humanity subsumed within itself all the psychic energy that it formerly directed out toward images of the divine, and the power of the Solar masculine and the rational mind soared into the twentieth century. Science predicting and controlling the natural world created innumerable scientific and technological wonders. Belief in the power of reason went hand in hand with a vision of endless future upward progression. In the brilliance of this light, history itself is understood as the heroic movement of the human self out of the darkness of unconsciousness and participation mystique with Nature, and into the sturdy self-awareness and objective thinking of the modern mind. We come to view ourselves through the "story of progress," in which history's direction is onward and upward, and is:

> Imaged, at least implicitly, as a masculine hero, rising above the constraints of nature and tradition, exploring the cosmos, mastering his environment, determining his own destiny: restless, bold, brilliant, innovative, ceaselessly pressing forward . . . forever seeking greater freedom and new horizons, discovering ever-widening arenas for self-realization.[55]

We can gain sight of the profound nobility of the archetypal masculine impetus in the wondrous achievements of the last centuries (artistic, intellectual, scientific, philosophical), in the courage of those willing to stand for the objective truth of the nature of our reality (e.g., Socrates, Galileo, Copernicus, Descartes), and in the valor of those who fought for freedom and self-defense. We see it too in all of our tremendous technological advances and we see it in the climactic splendor in our "touching the face of God," the Moon landing on July 20, 1969. A genuine epiphany, hailed with "Eureka!" shouted in the peak moments of our experience, displays the pure inspiration of this spirit within us.

The shadow of this story, however, is another part of our history and psychology. Our dispossession and "the story of the fall"—beginning with our loss of containment within the Goddess-image, the psychological loss of the paradisiacal unity of Eden—describes our loss of the sense of containment within Nature, the tragedy of our gradual alienation, and the increasing objectification of all of the contents of our experience. The juxtaposing "No!" of the ego has enabled the establishment of consciousness, a wedge between the world and our automatic response to it, but this division has left us cut off and isolated from the unity to which we formerly belonged. While our ego is strong, our view of ourselves is fractured. Modern consciousness in particular has disconnected us from much of what made the world valuable to us, what provided meaning, gave us self-understanding and ethical grounding, for, as Taylor writes, "what is the place of the Good, or the True, or the Beautiful, in a world entirely determined mechanistically?"[56] And here we begin to catch sight of how reason has led us forward and led us astray.

The masculine vision of an endless, bright horizon ahead points to the presence of an unconscious inflation and a correspondent detachment from psychological ground. Buoyed by the tremendous heights that it has achieved on the wings of this archetypal impetus, the modern psyche today displays an inflation in the *absolute* certainty with which it holds its belief—"My view is surely true." There is an equation made, morally and rationally, between our view and *the* right view. To the extent that this is an ego defense, it is defensive and rigid. "Intellectual rigidity which attempts to equate its own private truth or opinion with universal truth is also inflation."[57] Most often, under such a dynamic there is also a refusal to admit one's own dark side and an identification with our own goodness. Inflation rests upon the ego's imagining its partial to be whole and thus overstepping a natural boundary. Without the ability to acknowledge that there is some distinction between the personal ego and the transpersonal self, there is no possibility of genuine humility.[58] Pursuing our inflated ends can lead to justifying any means—with an appeal often made to rational necessity (we see this in our dismissive use of the natural world and our destruction of indigenous cultures). In a way that is hardly conscious in our culture, rationality and the Solar masculine has a dark side, a shadow side.

Pursuit of technological understanding and rational progress is never thought of as having a downside, but "doing the right thing," what we imagine to be demanded by reason, has led to some of the greatest horrors of the past century. Reason has answered innumerable questions in medical science, offered up the uncoding of the human genome, and taken us to the moon, but it has also made us capable of self-destruction with nuclear arms or by polluting the planet for the sake of economic progress. Acts of terrorism demonstrate how technology can and no doubt will be used against us. We like to think of atrocities committed in the last century as done irrationally, but the language of "Final Solution" is reason's dialect. Doing what we believe to be the right thing has led to both bad and good: both sides of nearly every civil war felt that they were just; it was the very orderly German soldiers and civilians who led millions to the gas chamber; aboriginal nations were placed on reservations and their children placed into abusive schools "for their own good"; modern nations continue to shed blood unnecessarily and justify their actions by appealing to abstract certitudes; and perhaps most dangerous of all, we continue to speed toward environmental apocalypse, chained psychologically as we are to the motor of perceived economic necessity. Lack of self-reflection and a refusal to admit one's own shadow, and the possibility that we may be wrong—one's identification with the good side of one's character—can lead to the greatest possible forms of malfeasance. John Ralston Saul observes that we automatically label such crimes as irrational when in fact they are committed under the guise of doing good, doing the right thing, the thing demanded by reason, and are in fact not irrational, but a shadow side of reason itself.[59] While the past century boasts spectacular accomplishments, it has a shadow side too, to which we remain unreconciled. It is tremendously difficult to bring together these two sides of our experience of ourselves without brushing off the bad as done by "them" and claiming the good always as our own. It is much more discomforting to look at our people's history of well-reasoned crimes, and there is rarely, if ever, a questioning of our driving mode itself— instead, as Mamet has written, we say, "more will cure it."[60] Writing in the years following World War I, and having yet to witness the rest of the twentieth century, Jung wrote that along with the heights that we have achieved:

> We are also the disappointment of the hopes and expectations of the ages. Think of nearly two thousand years of Christian ideas followed, instead of by the return of the Messiah and the heavenly millennium, by the World War among Christian nations and its barbed-wire and poison gas. . . . [We have] seen how beneficent are science, technology and organization, but also how catastrophic they can be.[61]

Insistent upon the correctness of its views and seeking their realization through force of its will, the masculine strives for perfection and cannot live with compromise, for to do so would be to have its feet touch the ground and end its inflation. Being identified with one's own goodness means having no place to put the bad within oneself, so its stain is painted onto "the Other" out there or in ourselves. We brand those people as "unclean" (racism, extremism) or demand perfection of ourselves, our children, or our bodies (body dysmorphia, anorexia, bulimia). Not seeing our shadow means never realizing the harmful effects that we are having on the world around us, and this dynamic can be understood as empowering an economic model that places no value in environmental costs or personal concerns. Yet today we are beginning to be able to see that where the masculine errs, in a certain direction: toward forgetting the nature of our own imperfect selves; toward believing that "we've got everything taken care of"; toward living under fantasies of our own omnipotence; toward neat, abstract principles that keep us from attending to the concrete good we could do nearby; toward identifying with the ego's voice inside us; toward excluding the images, whispers, and hints from the larger nature of the psyche within us.

As a function of Nature, the unconscious moves us toward a compensatory direction when our balance is lost, and while most of the voices in the history of previous centuries have been that of men, in the last century or so more voices have entered into the conversation, including those of women and minorities.[62] Furthermore, at this moment of the ego's ascent, the ground beneath its feet was simultaneously revealing itself to lack the firm foundation that the masculine had imagined for itself. Freud's and Jung's advancement of the discovery of the unconscious pointed out a disturbing lack of authority in human self-awareness. Psychoanalysis found beneath the sheen of rationality that, rather than being in full command of itself, there was a basis for thought, action, dream, and feeling that did not abide the ego's command. Here the third step of our dislocation from the center of Creation was made. Even Descartes's sacred interiority could not correctly be called our own: the world does not revolve around us, as our interiority has a depth beyond our conscious understanding of it. The freedom of reason was, in fact, illusory, for the direction of consciousness is in a constant negotiation with instinctual, infantile, imaginal, and archetypal voices inside us. The achievement of an ego strong enough to dialogue with these interior voices was of the greatest value because it enabled a negotiation and a fair fight, perhaps a dance even, but its dominion was not its own.

Underpinning the psyche of the modern person, there are three strands of historic self-understanding: the primordial understanding of our Goddess-worshipping ancestors, surviving today in indigenous cultures (kept alive in the West in the work of the Romantic thinkers, writers, and poets); superseding this view is the self-understanding of the patriarchal religious systems; and finally, the scientific view, which is the one most directly associated with modernity because it is, of course, unique to it, and with the advent of so much technological evidence (which is wrongly taken as evidence for a mechanistic worldview), this view has triumphed and become supreme: "Science is man's current authority. It's the one thing that is believable now."[63] Each of these perspectives believes its view to be the correct one: for the Romantic, there remains a unity present in the cosmos; for the believer in a patriarchal God, there is a just heavenly reward; and for the scientist, the only true reality is materially reducible and objectively discernible. These points of view would seem to be irreconcilable, yet the modern person is most often made up psychologically of an unresolved mixture of the romantic, patriarchal, and scientific views. Today there is an even greater multiplicity of worldviews from which to look upon the world, which led

Gertrude Stein to proclaim that "in the twentieth century, nothing is in agreement with anything else."[64] This diversity of perspective informs the modern psyche by making it difficult for us to find a foothold:

> The fact that the directions are multiple contributes to our sense of uncertainty. This is part of the reason why everyone is tentative today, why virtually no one can have . . . rooted confidence in their outlook.[65]

McLuhan notes that in an age of insecurity, one turns to specialization in order to "obtain some degree of confidence."[66] Saul, among others, has pointed out the profound disservice that fragmentation and specialization in the professional and intellectual world has done to us in this regard. While new and important views have been brought into the discussion in the last century, most of what has been added does not broaden our perspective but rather more narrowly refines it. We may know a great deal about our one field of expertise (whether it be academic, professional, or technical) but have little ability to seek conclusions beyond our scope, to integrate our views, or to discuss our perspective with others. There is an inherent danger in such specialization:

> Ten geographers who think the world is flat will tend to reinforce each other's errors. If they have a private dialect in which to do this, it becomes impossible for outsiders to disagree with them. Only a sailor can set them straight. The last person they want to meet is someone who, freed from the constraints of expertise, has sailed around the world.[67]

Such specialization is where our society has been headed, and investing ourselves in it protects our livelihood, but it is also has produced an institutional conditioning in which "the custodians of the Western, intellectual tradition—now devote themselves to the prevention of integrated thought."[68] Defense of one's territory motivates valuing one's specialized field to the exclusion of attention to other disciplines. Universities, now more than ever, place little emphasis on liberal education and the humanities and are becoming more like technical colleges; professional specialization and an ever-increasing materialism force the constriction of our focus and attention. Yet there is an assumption being made that somewhere, someone in our society is asking the questions that need to be asked:

"caught up in work and family . . . millions of people maintain a tradition of belief of the good intentions of their rational elites."[69] Unfortunately, the rational elites, while potentially well-intentioned, continue to fan out into the ever-multiplying areas of specialization, with no one turning back to look toward the unifying central point. Saul regards this as a failure to live up to the public trust.

The hero—sword in hand—divides the world into its constituent elements. Breaking the world down in order to understand it, we do not realize that sometimes its magic is killed off in the tearing apart. Mary Shelley's *Frankenstein* illustrates the monstrous illusion and inflation that we live under today. Identified with a view of world as "parts," we have no more illusions of our connection to a whole. Self-defined by the present moment and no longer seeing ourselves in the stories of the past, we do not experience ourselves as contained in any living history or myth; we have become, in Jung's term, "unhistoric."[70] Where the ancient Hebrews, Greeks, and Christians saw reason as a mode for the revelation of the divine in the world, steadily since that time we have fallen further and further into identification with this tremendous capacity within us—we *are* reason, Solarity, the ego.

> The patriarchal line of development of consciousness leads to a condition where patriarchal-masculine values are dominant, values that are often conceived in direct opposition to those of the archetypal Feminine and the unconscious. This development, directed by the archetypally conditioned canon and impressed upon the development of every male or female child in Western cultures, leads to the separation of consciousness from the unconscious, to the evolution of the independent conscious system with a masculine ego as the center, to a suppression of the unconscious, and to its greatest possible repression from the ego's field of vision. (Neumann)[71]

In order to achieve the ego's concentration of awareness, energy is required to be expended, to repress images of the unconscious, the feelings of the body, and nonrational thinking in general. Nietzsche railed against our fatal enchantment with our ideas of things to the loss of the world's true, living reality. Where the dark mysteries of life are made into illusion, the fractured modern psyche struggles to find itself in relation to the world it has created, and the moralist is made to look the fool where "the very

nature of the *objective* universe turns any spiritual faith and ideals into courageous acts of *subjectivity,* constantly vulnerable to intellectual negation."[72]
The bright light of Solar consciousness made the darkness disappear—or
so we believe. Where in the past we had known ourselves as oxygen and
carbon, water and earth, plant and animal (and "zucchini" too) and recognized ourselves in Nature's reflection; now, having invested all of the wonder that we had for the world in ourselves, we have become enchanted with
our own reflection.

> And the external shrinks into less and less.
> Where once an enduring house was,
> now a cerebral structure crosses our path,
> completely belonging to the realm of concepts,
> AS THOUGH IT STILL STOOD IN THE BRAIN. . . . (RILKE)[73]

Reason alone gets stuck in the illusion of its own magic. Like the ego,
Solar masculine consciousness can imagine that it requires no other and is
contained by nothing. Existing by its own cleverness, it relies on nothing for
its growth and was created by no one. Under reason alone, everything is a
function of brain circuits. "The rational hero . . . is ego unchained; god on
earth; the golden calf; . . . a new earthly divinity."[74] That function in us that
isolates things from their context has successfully appropriated itself out of
any context. This is, of course, the sin of pride. "Pride is recognized for what
it is—a 'sorting' gone astray, an urge for distinction that has become divi-
sive, split off and inflated with its own importance. . . . Pride must learn that
something else in the personality is strong."[75] Usually, it is through personal
suffering that ego's inflation is corrected. "We need the heavy hand of the
Self to crush the ego's boundless ambitions, a shock of fate to unseat it, even
the threat of death to dispel the ego's illusion that it stands at the center
of the universe."[76] Or a correction can be made through our own volition,
through the sacrifice of the ego, the surrender of which enables a return to
the ground of the real body, moment and predicament in which one is living. The recognition of what underpins it is the antidote to its inflation. In
its highest potential, the masculine does not to cling to his own certainties,
but rather opens itself to finding the truth, even at the risk of meeting his
own not-knowing. "The hero's survival is an accident, because the essence

of the heroic act is submission to unlimited risk. In other words the heroic act is perfectly irrational."[77] For these reasons, Jung understood that "reason alone does not suffice."[78]

In part, the difficulty is our persistent misidentification of things for our cognitive idea of them: "we affirm as true or real not what a thing really is, but how far it is representable in our mind."[79] Just as Nature has been "made our servant," our perception sees a world of objects whose meaning is found only in their use to us. "When the exact answers concerning the diverse realities are given, we become indifferent. There is nothing more to look for. . . . *Logos* becomes replaced by logic."[80] This conditioning underlies our psychological difficulty in facing the reality of Crop Circles. Having drained our imagination of its depth, we experience reality through "mental" thinking,[81] a form of consciousness separate and distinct from "lived" thinking. In "mental" thinking the personal thinker carries all the weight; in "lived" thinking context, relation to things larger than oneself are included. The difference here is likened to that between a geographic study and walking down the road to our childhood home, or simply eating bread and living on the land where the grain is grown and knowing that it is upon its growth that one's survival depends. "Without being open to what is greater than man . . . man is condemned to be small. Things which surround the small man in his artificial world, the suppressed things, are small. . . . Only by being subordinate to the realities which exceed him can man be great."[82] This can be seen as a third of three ways in which inflation upon the archetypal masculine impedes our participation with the phenomenon: first, our lack of rooted confidence in our outlook makes it hard to believe in the proof that we do have, and therefore susceptible to failure to believe something that is true (the second of the errors described by Kierkegaard previously); second, cultural inflation produces personal defensiveness to our participation with the phenomenon, because doing so necessitates a conflict with our shadows and the possibility of the ego's disillusionment; and third, having become used to asking only the small questions, we are likely not ready for the big ones. Psychologically we are very much used to a world that contains no other powers; having banished the darkness of spooks and spirits, we are unable to believe the possibility of their existence. At the deepest level, our over-rational conditioning impedes our capacity to bring ourselves to receive this question with the wholeness of our person, making it difficult to include our emotional selves or to pay attention to our fleeting momentary responses; and perhaps most important, as Nietzsche exclaimed, it impedes our full participation with the phenomenon by having robbed us of our vision for it.

> There cometh the time when man will no longer launch the arrow of his longing beyond man—and the string of his bow will have unlearned how to whizz![83]

Such psychological conditioning affects the ways in which Crop Circles are received—and not received—by us. It makes it difficult for news media to know how to consider and present such a profoundly "unbelievable" story. It encourages governments to believe in the necessity of restricting our access to the truth, for fear of our inability to handle it. It interferes with the ability of those in the scientific world to do research on the formations, due to the very realistic fear of ridicule, potential lack of promotion, and other practical concerns. Despite our assumptions that the academic world is well-intentioned and focused upon the most important questions of our day, in fact most would not want to touch this topic "with a ten-foot pole." If one is professionally and psychologically invested in the reductionist paradigm, Crop Circles are much like the sailor whom John Ralston Saul's ten geographers have very little desire to meet. It is investment in the ego's certainty and comfort that is risked in our participating with the new as we find it before us today in this phenomenon. In choosing to look closely at them with an open mind, we confront our attachment to the correctness of our assumptions, be they personal or collective, conscious or unconscious. Yet it is precisely this kind of courage that has led us forward at each new stage in the human journey.

Pursuing their genuine curiosity, courageous dreamers have brought before us world-changing new discoveries: we have discovered that the world is not flat, and that our planet does not lie at the universe's center; we have found proof of a theory of evolution that again removes us from an image of ourselves as existing as the center of God's creation; and in discovering the nature of the relationship of the unconscious to the conscious mind, found ourselves to be not even the "masters of our own house." We have discovered the existence of germs and atoms where such were previously believed to be impossible. We have learned to fly, gained sight of distant worlds, charted other heavenly bodies, and in what may be seen as our crowning glory thus far, touched the "face of God" in our landing on the moon. All of this accomplishment has had a dual effect: on the one hand, we have slowly turned toward ourselves the majestic eye with which our ancestors looked at the world—the wonder and mystery of the world is no longer awesome, rather only a puzzle that we have yet to solve; the energy that flowed out from us toward the divinity that we saw in the world is now caught in our own enamored view of ourselves. While the achievement of the Western heroic quest has inflated humanity to epic heights, it has utterly de-potentiated the world (as we know it) —and while this journey has been made of necessity, for our development, it is only now that it nears a breaking point that we realize that something may have been lost along the way.

SIX   A CALLING BACK DOWN

Little by little through the ages, as man's psychic life has become more and more symbolic. This is naturally a great step in advance, but it carries also a danger, for if the ritual loses entirely its connection with the instinctual sources from which it arose, it loses its power to renew or redeem, for it has become merely an abstraction and has lost its connection with the primal sources of life. In these days, when we have grown so far away from our humble beginnings, we need to contact again these life-giving symbols.

—ESTHER M. HARDING[1]

The movement of humanity out of enchantment with the natural world and into conscious self-awareness and the intellectual and scientific bloom in the modern era can be seen to be archetypally masculine. The characteristics that distinguish this masculinity from its complement, the archetypal Feminine, include a preference for objectivity over subjectivity, for rational thinking over feeling, for the exterior world over our internal one, for linear progress over circuitous transformational processes, and for clarity over the dark, sometimes irrational, world of the psyche. In its positive achievements, the heroic advance of the Western mind along its great masculine arc forms one aspect of the context of our moment; however, so too does its *negation*—what that journey has left behind—form another, shadow aspect. Alongside the technological gain that is well-known to us, there is something we have forgotten, something that has been lost along this spectacular and brilliant advance. In its bright face, the genius of human creativity has given us a profound capacity for knowing the universe in its objective sense, in its external forms, yet we have become so capable in this mode that we have come to identify and understand ourselves through it. Whereas our ancestors drew their view of themselves from a participatory relating to the world, today we are self-defined. Successfully applying the masculine mode of consciousness, we have "conquered" the world through scientific understanding. We look out and see the world and ourselves as a part of a grand machine—we look out at Nature and see nothing creative there, a perspective that expresses our unconscious infatuation with our own genius. Our inflated state of mind and bias toward masculine ways-of-being influence us unconsciously—*underlying* our thinking about nearly everything. It *shapes and informs us from within,* swaying how we respond to ideas (both old and new) and, just as important, affects what we—*without thinking*—choose to neglect. Because this mode overprivileges some aspects of consciousness and rejects others (just as the archetypal Feminine did in our prehistory), and because that which has been neglected around us and within us forms a shadow face of the context of our time—the context into which Crop Circles have arrived—it is necessary, in seeking the meaning of this phenomenon's appearance, to consider the quality and effect of this negation.

Perhaps the prototypical image associated with masculinity and with goodness too, in the West and particularly in America, is that of the cowboy, sun-drenched, strong, and self-sufficient—he is satisfied to know that his success is his own. Brass tacks are his stock and trade, in contrast to the Feminine, which "feels and transforms feeling into relatedness and understands this as accomplishment. For solar masculinity, nothing is of decided value unless it can be established."[2] Spiritually, he believes that "God helps those who help themselves" (a saying attributed by a majority of American Christians to Jesus, which was penned, in fact, by Ben Franklin).[3] Politically, this individualistic ideal is used to discredit the notion that much can be accomplished through "humanist co-operation" (Saul).[4] Psychologically, under this influence, the ego, the conscious self, is given the dominant role. Earlier in the stages of our evolution, the growth of the ego was necessary to help us to develop our autonomy, to enable our separation from the overpowering regressive pull of the unconscious and instinct, to enable our breaking free of our participation mystique with Nature, and to enable us to act with a consciously chosen free will. However, while at the early stages of our evolution the strengthening of the ego was necessary, today it has left our sense of self inflated, with the ego assuming itself to be the whole of who we are. In the modern mind, the ego lives as though it were itself whole, doing so by repressing any content outside of itself that conflicts with this vision, and denying the ground of its own inner nature altogether. Connection to aspects of the unconscious, including inner image, feeling, and dream, are denied value, and emphasis is placed upon what the ego can believe with absolute certainty—what can be "nailed down." Particularly in the U.S., value and goodness are associated with the external, with material goods, with concrete achievement and smiling productivity. Success is primary and is associated with clear, linear progress. Intuition, emotion, imagination, and introversion—all ways of naturally connecting with our inner life—are seen from this perspective as the pejorative daydreams, flights of fancy and "myth." Vulnerability, weakness, and failure—life's dark periods—are denied value, and mystery is robbed of its creative potential. "American life is, in subtle ways, so one-sided, so . . . uprooted," said Jung in 1957.[5]

> What is significant in psychic life is always below the horizon of consciousness, and when we speak of the spiritual problem of modern man we are dealing with things that are barely visible—with the most intimate and fragile things—with bowers that only open in the night. In daylight everything is clear and tangible; but the night lasts as long as the day, and we live in night-time also.[6]

The masculine has been described as a Solar form of awareness; like the sunlight of daytime, it enables precise clarification of that which is close to us, but which, by its brightness, obscures the deeper stars and bodies that can only be seen after dark.[7] Evaporated by the sharp contrasts of the daylight, the moon symbolizes the veiled, moist depths of the psyche's wellspring. Where the sun rules the daylight of rational thought, the moon is said to be ruling "the night of instinct and the shadowy perceptions of the inner intuitive world."[8] While the sword of masculine insight is of great practical use in pursuing that which is linear, that which is directly apprehensible, and that which we can know objectively, its conquering through division often cuts too swiftly through complexity and leads to oversimplification and "to the triumph of the one-dimensional reality over all contradiction" (Marcuse).[9] "Negative masculinity cannot think in metaphor,"[10] writes Woodman, and Jung saw in us that "it is still the case today that discrimination and differentiation means more to the rationalistic intellect than wholeness through the union of opposites. That is why the unconscious produces the symbols of wholeness."[11] He saw the psyche as holding the healing principle of balanced opposites within us—despite our own imbalance. Where the Solar consciousness may fall into inflated self-importance and hang on to belief in its own truth, the opposite part of our nature plays a role in consciousness as well, and the Lunar quality within us can help us to discover a cure for our bright grandiosity by rooting us in a truth that is dark, sometimes irrational or paradoxical, grounded in our body, in the instinctual, emotional, and archetypal energetic depths within us. Arising not out of linear, directed thinking, but coming seemingly without cause, the whispers of our Lunar consciousness "are not visionary, unreal imaginings; they are intuitively perceived *realities* . . . expressions of the feminine principle, the *Eros*."[12] The Lunar quality of our psyche exists beyond the ego's command, it can be inconstant like the moon, and yet it is a harbor for our hidden, inner processes of growth. Connected to the wider scope of the unconscious, it is the subtle, quiet voice of psyche, in which we may sometimes find that special something that we need, but did not know we needed. The moon symbolizes the psyche as "diffuse illumination."[13]

> The moon stands, indeed, for the great principle of transformation through the things which are lowest. That which is dark and cold and moist, which hides from the light of day and from man's enlightened thinking, holds also the secret of life. For life renews itself again and again, and when at last, through his repeated experiences, man understands, he will grasp the inner meaning which until that moment lies concealed within the very texture of the concrete happening. (Harding)[14]

While the development of the ego enabled consciousness to separate from participation mystique with Nature, it has today left us broken off from our own natural inner world. Where previously the whole range of intrapsychic activity could not be discriminated and was experienced as a magical flow between self and world, the development of the ego enabled the constriction of awareness to a narrow range, allowing one to objectively view images, thoughts, and feelings without attributing them to spirits or powers outside oneself. It is this separation from unconscious participation with the world that enables psychological self-awareness, but also enables the ego to mistake its perspective for the entire reality of consciousness. Jungian analyst and author Robert Johnson notes that "I is the center of the universe for a Westerner" and this perspective "cannot sit next to a dream. . . . It is a disdain for a level of intelligence in a human being which I consider superior to the ego." He says further, "Only his head, only his ego, only his thought, only the I, has validity for me. That brands a Westerner and dooms him to many of the ills which we have."[15] Our skewed view toward it leaves us with "the tendency to dichotomize and to attribute primacy to logical thinking, to technology and the *Logos* version of progress."[16] In the psyche of the West, the Solar masculine has come to identify itself with the light, both taking into itself a grandness that is not its own and denying the ground of Feminine dark around it.

> The separation of the spiritual and the vital spheres, and the subordination of the latter to the rational standpoint, is not satisfactory inasmuch as reason alone cannot do complete or even adequate justice to the irrational facts of the unconscious. . . . A materialistic view of the world ill accords with the reality and autonomy of the psyche. (Jung)[17]

Having denied the existence of other content within the psyche and diminished its relation to instinct, the ego is inflated, ungrounded, and out of contact with life and the Feminine. Here, the too-bright Solar influence has dried us out, sterilizing us psychologically, keeping us from touching the moistness of psyche's inner reaches, from experiencing the fecund potency for transformation in the unconscious, and from having the feelings that provide our existence with meaning.

> The life of today is empty and sterile and we look for renewal, whether we want to or not, from that source of spiritual awakening that lies within. For our science has proved itself strangely impotent in face of a threatened breakdown in our culture.[18]

O'Kane observes that today we believe "in the absolute superiority of technology and science . . . [and in] a unilateral adherence to rational progress," just as reason has "subjugated the psyche and the soul; technology [has] subjugated Nature."[19] In the modern mind, however, we do not experience these dichotomies as simply juxtaposition, but identified with one pole, we no longer believe in the reality of the other. Where consciousness had been a wedge, something for us to gain "play" between ourselves and the world, now all we see is the wedge—we can no longer see any sacredness in the world and we imagine, not that it is gone, but that it was never actually there to begin with. Exemplifying this negation, Dodson Gray notes that our relation to Nature parallels the relation of a child to its Mother.

> Because of that erroneous projection upon nature, male science and male technology always assumed that the bounty of nature was always there (like mother), was there to us and to use up (like mother), and was always going to be there to exploit (like passive women). This unfortunate projection . . . prevented male culture from understanding the actual place which human life has within the life-sustaining natural cycles of the biosphere. Whenever we are busy projecting inadequate or erroneous symbolic images of another, we are unable to discern the other's true character and identity.[20]

What Dodson Gray speaks to as "male science" and "male technology," I would suggest more accurately reflects the archetype of the masculine, as it is unbalanced in both men and women in our culture today. And while she observes that this external, masculine projection upon Nature prevents us from seeing both its "true character and identity," the same dynamic is present in our relationship to the psyche, to feeling and to our inner world. This provision of space for gestation—the sustaining, moist enclosing of the matrix of life itself—is taken for granted under the masculine vision as much in our inner world as in our outer one. In this condition, the Self archetype's drive toward individuation and greater wholeness is perverted into a fuel for our own grandiosity. Disconnected from instinct and the objective archetypal nature of the psyche, consciousness inflates and takes into itself properties of timelessness and immortality that are rightly beyond the province of the ego. Propelled by our masculine ability to distance ourselves from the world, we have become increasingly filled up with the awe and wonder that we used to project out into the world. The ego's mistake, in Woodman's phrase, is to insist upon making "temporal as perfect as the eternal it rejects."[21] Basking in the brightness of our glorious inventiveness, we are blind to the existence of any other centers of subjectivity in the world around us.

Lost from the world, not because of any change out there but because of a change inside of us, today "not only are we at the center of the cosmos, but we are alien to it: we are a singularity. The universe is strange to us, we are strange in the universe."[22] More and more we have come to see ourselves as living in a world without purpose or meaning; the only subject somewhere empty and cold. "Nothing has been purchased more dearly than the little bit of reason and sense of freedom which now constitutes our pride" (Nietzsche). Having given up our unconscious home in Nature inside of us, we can no longer root ourselves in the world around us and so instead we resent it:

> It is our ability to believe ourselves to be creatures apart—a deformation of the
> idea of consciousness—[which makes] us what Erich Fromm called "the freak of
> the universe." We alone "can feel evicted from paradise." What is this paradise?
> That of unconscious participation in the inner structure of the universe . . . That
> would explain our ambivalence to the planet on which we live. We love it, we
> moon over it, versify and paint it, yet we take great pleasure in raping it as if to
> teach it a lesson, as if demonstrating that the true beauty of the great synchronis-
> tic whole can be brought down to our level of psychic homelessness.[23]

In convincing ourselves that we are a "creature apart," we have come to feel a severe homelessness. As a result we have a tremendously anxious need to control the world around us. This condition is expressed in Bacon's proclamation that Nature is "to be bound to our service and made our slave" and in the restriction of contact with the larger contents of the psyche that characterizes Solar masculine consciousness.

Today, this now overused drive to split ourselves away from that which lies beneath has left us with a fragmentary consciousness that believes itself to be whole and constricts its awareness to suppress, as much as possible, intrusions from those natural, deeper parts of who we are that lie outside its field of vision. The ego that had formerly sought freedom from entrapment in the unconscious is now loose. Freed from "idols," it is high on the overflowing psychic energy, which is no longer directed elsewhere. Reason, that "divine instinct, immortal voice from heaven,"[24] has lifted and inflated us, and we are like Icarus ascending on wings of wax. Our capacity for Solar thinking is a profound advancement, but it carries a natural risk of loss of connection to that ground within us that joins us to the actuality of specific body, moment, and context. Here the myth of the progress and the myth of the fall are entangled with each other: we have tremendous energy for flight but no place to land; reflexively questioning, we are wired on objective truth and made frantic by the (unconscious) psychological fact that our genius ability to take apart does not help us to put back together. Saul notes that the lack of solid outlook or direction that permeates the modern psyche leaves us open to compulsively producing without purpose: "this rootless wandering is perhaps the explanation for the hypnotic effect which the idea of efficiency has upon us. Deprived of direction, we are determined to go there fast."[25] We can only try to fly higher and higher because we have lost the imagination for somewhere to land. Tarnas points out that while our primitive ancestors had known the entire world as being filled with meaning, today the human self exists as an "island of meaning and spiritual aspirations in a vast purposeless universe signifying nothing except what the human self creates . . . For quite literally, in a disenchanted cosmos, nothing is sacred."[26] Reason has banished all interior mystery, all soul from the world. The bright light of Solar consciousness has made the darkness disappear—or so we believe.

Having lost natural connection to the objective ground of archetype and instinct within us, those eternal, timeless qualities of the psyche that used to possess us wholly, we craft into our masculine inflation an unconscious relationship to those same qualities. Saul sees this psychological truth in our obsession with certainty and in our "devotion to absolute truths and linear progress [that are] actually a formalization of rather juvenile determinism; a determination to deny mortality and timelessness."[27] These pursuits are "aimed not at proving absolute knowledge, but at convincing ourselves that we are capable of absolute knowledge. In other words, it is the fantasy of a bastion against mortality." In our masculine-influenced mistaking of ourselves as a creature apart, we insist upon denying our essential connection to the ground of Nature inside us. Unbound from nature, we are left compulsively searching for the perfection we have denied inside ourselves. Without connection to this natural part of who we are, we are blocked from full, creative engagement with life. Woodman describes how we express this compulsion:

> Perfection belongs to the gods; completeness or wholeness is the most a human being can hope for. . . . It is in seeking perfection by isolating and exaggerating parts of ourselves that we become neurotic. Addiction to perfection is at root a suicidal addiction. The addict is simulating not life but death. Almost inevitably a woman addicted to perfection will view herself as a work of art, and her real terror is that the work of art, being so precious, may in one instant be destroyed. She has to treat herself as a rare piece of Ming porcelain or what Keats described as a "still unravished bride of quietness". . . . To move toward perfection is to move out of life, or what is worse, never to enter it. (Woodman)[28]

Under such an influence, we are more likely to remain in the abstract, in the theoretical, preferring to come up with insoluble intellectual puzzles for ourselves in order to avoid participating with the emotional truth of the dilemma we actually face. Here we are in danger of falling for what Ulanov calls the "Devil's trick," which is to "steer us off course into the turbulence of insoluble arguments. For even if we arrived at definitions, the actual situation of each individual person faced with interior struggles of this sort would prove an exception to the rule."[29] The Feminine can act as curative to the inflated ego of the modern masculine condition only through our conscious, emotional participation with life. In allowing ourselves to be pinned down, the heart suffers its way back into the equation and we are put back together by being torn apart. The ego is the locus for the experience and suffering that is inflation's eventual cure. As Ulanov reminds us, "The ego is the place where we register and suffer wounds, needs, problems and struggle to solve them. We never do this in the abstract, but always in most particular and personal ways."[30]

For centuries, Western culture's upward direction has subjugated the body to the spirit. Moral waywardness has been said to be located in following instinct, libido, and sensual desire. Across the vast history of human evolution such an inhibition may have been necessary for the achievement of consciousness and true free will, but today this continued overemphasis on separation from our bodies has come to impede our vitality and our spiritual and moral growth. Washburn notes that only to the degree that we are dynamically present in our physical feeling self do we participate authentically and vividly with experience; "when the power of the ground flows, experience quickens becoming alive and acute . . . when the power of the ground ebbs, experience slows, becoming pale, distant and dull . . . the absence of this power depotentiates experience."[31] Judith, among others, has observed that for most of the West's population energetic connection to the body is lacking.[32] Woodman and Johnson both note the heightened distance by which modern people seem to walk around above their bodies or off the ground energetically.[33] Such unconsciousness to our bodies gives reality a sense of being abstract and removes us from the actuality of our experience, keeping us from identifying with our feeling sense. This fact is in no way esoteric, as without the feeling sense our ability to make moral judgment is directly impeded. Where our aliveness is lessened through our non-participation with our inner tactile sense, we experience life with greater distance and more easily make abstract the moral quandaries of our lives. We can then "intellectualize something that we can live with it quite well," as Jung warns—the facts need not change where our dulled experience of them deafens us to their ethical calling.

Begun with the introduction of the patriarchal God-images, the repression of the body was perfected in the twentieth century. While the Enlightenment introduced us to the notion of our bodies as machine, today's psychopharmacology has made it possible to view every symptom, every neurosis as an expression of something being "mechanically" wrong with us. Again, because this belief is ingrained in us unconsciously, we are culturally resistant to accepting the notion that psychological complexes are something more than "brain breakdowns." This conditioning makes it difficult to accept the fact of the psyche's autonomous participation with the body. "The human psyche is in no way outside nature. . . . There is scarcely a disease of the body in which psychic factors do not play a part, just as bodily factors are also involved in so many psychogenic disorders."[34] Like a child disciplined too long, the body's voice is silenced in the Westerner to the point now that many must struggle to try to hear it again. One way in which we can witness this is in the restriction of the connection between material image (actual internal or external stimuli) and our emotional, in-stinctual responses to it—whether or not such a response would be healthy. Today our capacity to delay is so well refined that to some extent, we have lost such reactions altogether—in favor of abstract conceptualization about what is happening to us.

> The splitting of an unconscious content into its material and emotional compo-nents was originally in the interests of conscious development, but now is one of the critical features of a hypertrophied consciousness split off from the uncon-scious. The exhaustion of emotional components and the ego's alienation from the world of archetypal images result in its inability to react to sense-images at all, a fact which is particularly noticeable in modern man. Confrontation with an unconscious image, or even an unexpected situation, finds him immune to reaction. Contrasted with the instantaneous reflex action of the primitive, the interval between situation and reaction is extraordinarily prolonged, if it is not abrogated altogether. (Neumann)[35]

The ability to control our response to the world is one of the elementary steps in the emergence of consciousness—a masculine step by which we separate our experience from our response to it (repress instinct) and par-tition stimuli and emotion (objectify feeling). Neumann emphasizes here the enlargement of the ego as an inflation that restricts conscious participa-tion with our instinctual and emotional selves. The effects of this loss are as important morally as they are psychologically, for without authentic con-nection to feeling there is no internal motivation for ethical action or per-sonal change. O'Kane points out that in order for transformation to occur "images must be experienced emotionally rather than intellectually; their energy must touch the ego and provoke an affective reaction that will be a source of change."[36] If we have no feeling response to the events around us, we feel no urgency to respond to them and we certainly lack the motivation for changing how we think or looking closely at who we are. This process can be viewed as one of increasing abstraction of our experience, an ever-greater distancing of ourselves from our primal instinctual roots in which our aliveness and our moral self are planted. In this way it illustrates how in taking a step forward in consciousness a simultaneous rejection has been made of our nature and something crucial of ourselves.

Where Neumann's observation of the prolonged delay, if not abrogation, of our emotional responses to the world highlights the internal psychological condition separating us from emotional and moral engagement with the world around us, and Harding describes our loss of inner contact with the life-giving instinctual sources, Ulanov further notes how this emotional disconnection is reinforced by outer conditions in our culture. The psychological and moral discontinuity between image and our response is increased by the tremendous quantity of data to which we are exposed every day: "Post-modern globalization brings many benefits but it also bombards us with so much sensation and information that it is a cause of a kind of promiscuous arousal that knows no anchoring in a specific location, body, society."[37] Ulanov fittingly describes our arousal as promiscuous, for it is an anxiety that is present yet broken from the facts of actual experience, a kind of overstimulation that cannot find any ground within ourselves. Without the ability to participate emotionally with the content we come across, we cannot draw any meaning from it. Our success under the impetus of the archetypal masculine has effectively scrubbed the world clean of appreciation for the value of pursuing deeper meaning, for in this perspective all transcendent concerns are baseless, subjective acts of personal delusion without any *possibility* of being valid. Today the extent of our imbalance in favor of the masculine leaves a tremendous divide between the outer reality we know and the inner world we do not know. And it is much easier to lie to ourselves if we do not need to listen to our inner voice:

> [The] conscious ego may distort the facts and be self-deceived by desires and instincts for self-preservation, self-esteem, and the like. But in the unconscious, truth cannot be dissembled in this way. The unconscious can only mirror the actual facts and therefore cannot lie. For this reason a dream or fantasy may tell the expert more about a man's real character than anything he himself can say. (Harding)[38]

Our culture's masculine inflation has us soaring in a worldview that is unchained; knowing no limits or ground, we can imagine only unlimited forward movement. We maintain our grandiosity by not looking inside, but not looking at the context surrounds us in either the outer or inner world. What is most significant about the Western hero's journey into consciousness is our loss of the Feminine. We love reason above all else and express this love through science, religion, and an absolute devotion to capitalism and materialism. All of these things express our over-masculine imbalance that has us preferring distance and disconnection from the world. And so we have lost all those contexts that surround us and support us: we have lost the body for the mind's sake, lost the unconscious for the ego's sake, and lost the earth for the sake of our material compulsion—unconsciously we are substituting things (matter) for a real connection to Mother *(Mater)* and the archetypal Feminine. All of these disconnections serve to keep our inflation intact. We deny the existence of any other centers of creativity in the world or in ourselves. We deny the existence of any mystery.

> At present, our culture has rejected this world of symbology. It has gone into an economic and political phase, where spiritual principles are completely disregarded . . . Our religious life is ethical, not mystical. The mystery has gone and society is disintegrating as a result. (Campbell)[39]

We have lost our feeling for the infinite in our infatuation with ourselves. We deny the timeless inside ourselves and cannot imagine it to exist in the world. But the truth of who we are is never as linear as the Solar view would have us believe, and the Feminine can help us to receive "more possibilities than are contained in the realm of the established order."[40] If we are able to hold dynamically the tension within the psyche, we can break down rigid ego patterns and begin constructing the "tolerable paradoxes," in Jessica Benjamin's phrase, that express our ability to transform. At this moment, participating with this kind of consciousness can be understood as a curative to our culture's masculine imbalance. Constituent to this approach is a voluntary sacrifice of the ego in favor of a search for contents outside its present, narrow range. It is a movement toward participation with the natural generative function of the Feminine, with which we have lost touch. In the ego's sacrifice, we are opened, even if only temporarily, to a more holistic view of who we are. It is only through the ego's sacrifice, letting go of our little certainties, that we can regain an imagination for mystery.

Where the Feminine has been denied in its positive, creative form (relationships, eros, the body, the inner life, image, and dream), it will take us in its compulsive, negative form; where other cultures remain rooted in their relationship to the Feminine, "rooted in the soil of the matriarchal mother. Western culture is not; its mother *(mater)* is materialism—money and possessions that can quickly vanish." (Woodman)[41] Without contact with the Feminine, something of ourselves is missing, something of Nature is lost to us, something in the way in which we understand Creation and ourselves is incomplete. We deny the Feminine around us and inside ourselves and we know that something is missing, but we don't know what it is. "Something is amiss in the Western male psyche: Not only has he lost the feminine, but he is not interested—he doesn't even know that he has lost it."[42] Especially under the influence of a Solar imbalance, it is the Lunar path that can return us to contact with the natural meaning in the events of our lives and in who we essentially are, to walking hand in hand with the larger ground of Nature within us that has life beyond the Solar ego's daytime. Where we try to medicate it away or deny its existence and power over us, it nonetheless goes on producing symbols and symptoms. Jung recognized our cultural inability to symbolize as a psychological illness.[43] It allows the ego comfort, but robs us of connection to body, feeling, and meaning. Despite our illness and disconnection from it, psyche as Nature within us still speaks: "the unconscious, instinctive voice which refuses to be silenced. [It refuses] to adapt to ego demands" and where we have denied it conscious attention, it returns to haunt us in the form of our compulsions.[44] Saul advises that "to marginalize imagination in order to give comfort to rather simplistic linear methods and certainties is to undermine our strengths and discourage a dynamic use of our other qualities."[45] We've lost our receptivity to Nature's subjective, diffuse processes inside of us and given up the power to transform, having traded it for a vision of growth as ever-higher flying. Moore describes the difference between the two: "Linear thinking, so much a part of modern life, affects the way we understand our very lives. We evolve and develop, but we don't transform. We imagine growing like a skyscraper under construction, reaching to the sky, not like a caterpillar turning into a butterfly."[46] Yet, how can we understand the vital necessity of our use of this capability in us when we have lost our understanding of its value? How can we come to treasure the Feminine in Nature and inside us when we are impaired in our ability to make contact with it?

Despite their often perfect geometry, despite their eternal imagery, by their nature Crop Circles stand as a model of the sacrifice of the ego that is the antidote to the masculine inflation at the root of our current crisis. No matter how beautiful, grand, or complex they are, each formation is placed into a media that ensures it will be destroyed shortly after its appearance. We can speak of them in this regard as a kind of willing sacrifice, not an eternal monument but rather something accepting, from the start, its own upcoming destruction. Rather than the ungrounded, inflated, and precious self-image of our moment's "addiction to perfection," these constructs—which are indeed works of art—come forth as a movement into life, willingly accepting of imminent death. We can understand their character as related to the archetypal Feminine, not just through their association with grain, but also in the media and method of their appearance—offering none of the certainty and immortality that the inflated masculine associates itself with. They bring something for our imagination, something vivifying and fantastic but impermanent. Not susceptible to direct linear solution, neither distanced from us nor abstract, Crop Circles embody the qualities of the archetypal Feminine that stand and act in contradistinction to, and compensation for, the masculine. We can understand part of their purpose to be evoking our participation with them in just this way. Rather than insisting upon an exclusivity of interpretation, they stand before us simply and silently; rather than an egoic demand for agreement, they linger and only hint, offering an invitation. They beckon us toward the kind of consciousness that Jung, Woodman, and others understand to be vitally necessary in this moment, and in this way we can understand them as speaking to the specific context, crisis, and imbalance of our time. Our consciousness, lost in the illusion of its supremacy, cannot permit the existence of any error in its view, nor any deeper content living around it, nor the deflation of its unbound high gained from negating the eternal. Simply in standing silent, grounded in reality in our fields, Crop Circles demonstrate the insufficiency of this view. This phenomenon arrives unexpectedly and offers a new view that breathes life into us just by its being. Crop Circles deflate our mind's abstract possibilities and delusions of grandeur and point us back toward a broader vision of reality that is nonetheless focused on the present, on this world and the world around us. They both challenge us and offer us something we need, at a time when we need it. They reawaken us to a view of ourselves within a larger contextual whole. In these ways, they fit within and express the archetypally present return of our attention to the Feminine:

> The goddess myth needs to be made known not because it is superior to the god myth, but because it has been lost so long that we have apparently forgotten what it meant. For all the limitations of its over-identification with the natural world, it did at least give expression to the indissoluble relationship, even the identity that exists between part and whole and between visible and invisible in all orders of being. Above all, it gave emphasis to the wonder and delight of life, because it included all manifestations of life within the sphere of the divine. The question a study of the goddess myth invites us to consider now is whether (and, if so, how) we can participate in this relationship with the whole of life without sacrificing the consciousness for the sake of which we sacrificed the image of the divine in the natural world. (Baring & Cashford)[47]

We sacrificed our image of the divine as joined to Nature as a part of the evolution of our consciousness. Yet with the power of the discrimination and clarity that we have achieved by that sacrifice, can we now look honestly and openly at the kind of consciousness that we have today? What can we say about a view of ourselves that has no room in it for the Feminine, for Lunar consciousness? What can we say about a view of Creation that has no room in it for "the wonder and delight in life"? What can we say about a way of being that places itself so deeply into the center of its cosmos that it can no longer imagine anything else being out there or ever having been there? What can we say about a worldview that believes that Nature is best made our slave and that even seems angry at it? Baring and Cashford point out the purposiveness in our achieving masculine consciousness so it can be properly returned to focus upon our relation to the whole. They ask us to consider "whether and, if so, how" the powerful intelligence the human race has achieved through the sacrifice of our identification with Nature can be turned again to look toward it. Can we come to see ourselves within the whole of life? And is this question not dissimilar to the one posed by Crop Circles? Do they not also lead us to consciously wondering about our place and identity within the whole of Creation, within the "visible and invisible in all orders of being"?

> We cannot put new psychological wine into old philosophical bottles; new bottles need to be made by us and by coming generations. This task, however, will demand no less than a radical revision of our intellectual attitudes if we are to succeed in integrating into our view of the world those facts and findings which defy our rationalistic and positivistic frames of reference. (Whitmont)[48]

To begin to meet Crop Circles in a way that is more than intellectual, more than simply a continuation of the masculine imbalance we have inherited, requires both concrete apprehension of its facts and permitting the inclusion of our mythic imagination, our feeling responses and our imperfect selves. Even if our attitude toward them is entirely rational, one of seeking solutions to their causation and agency, there is still an element of emotion present unconsciously for us. Can we look not only at but *into* such emotional contents in our response? And are we further capable of allowing ourselves to feel some of the awe, and perhaps fear, that come with their arrival? What other emotions are there for you, dear reader? Can you—*do you*—feel any emotions in response to the formations?

> For our consciousness to appreciate a symbol which is new to us, we must have a symbolic attitude, an appreciation that the symbol allows a connection with our human level of reality and that of the objective psyche. No sacrament will work unless it is emotionally significant; defence or resistance prevent the symbol from having its effects. (Corbett)[49]

Through paying such attention, we may come to grasp "the inner meaning which until that moment lies concealed within the very texture of the concrete happening" that Harding speaks of as the moon revealing.[50] To give consideration to Crop Circles as a singular event, isolated from the facts and history of our time, is to continue to follow the masculine imbalance. Can we instead permit ourselves to imagine that they may be related to the rest of our moment? Might we recognize further that in the nature of Crop Circles, in their concrete mystery, in their close-at-hand fascination, and in their soft defeat of our ego's absolute certainties, in their invitation to us to use our lost ability to see symbolically, that they arrive to us, at least in some part, as a curative for the imbalance from which we suffer? In all of these ways they suggest the possibility that they may be related to our inflation, a prod into that dangerously too-large self-satisfaction that is leading us into ever-greater danger. Does such a recognition not necessitate our seeing a purpose in their arrival? Further still, does the existence of that purpose not direct our eye toward a purposiveness existing in the world beyond humanity, in Nature?

Regardless of their particular agency, to recognize these qualities in the nature of Crop Circles is to see behind the causation of the phenomenon something that is seeking to aid us. Being so deeply and unconsciously invested in an image of humanity as God-like and a corresponding picture of the world as voided of any living creativity, we resist any strange encounter that threatens our way of seeing. Despite our putting up fences to keep out the unknown, today banners fly in fields of grain proclaiming our self-involvement and grandiose self-inflation to be a childish oversimplification. Is it any surprise then that as our lack of connection to the inner world has us destroying the outer one, that something new would arrive, wearing the garments of the ancient goddesses in wheat and grain, pointing to the existence of something more "out there," reminding us of something more existing "in here" too, and most important, showing us that we are indeed a part of something larger than ourselves?

We usually assume that the future will look very much like the present—only more so. When we imagine what the changes ahead will look like, we do so through an imagination that is heavily invested in the present moment's biases. We construct images of the future that extend out of the ways of thinking that dominate our culture's psyche currently. However, despite our habitual and unconscious ideas about it, the future almost always defies our expectations. While there are periods of relative calm throughout human history, usually just as we are starting to feel settled something new and unexpected bursts into our reality. Sometimes our picture of the future is revised by violence—wars, disasters, and assassinations can do this. But perhaps it is most startling to us when the future defies our expectations for it in positive ways—delivering to us reconciliations and redemptions, freedoms delivered and walls torn down. As one member of the Beatles (the group itself is an example of an unexpected positive cultural phenomenon) has famously said: "Life is what happens while we're making other plans."[51]

Because we are used to moving in the direction that we are accustomed to, we usually assume that progress will mean even larger helpings of the same. For example, we have for some time imagined that in the future we will all live in a hyper-technological culture that may or may not involve jet packs but will almost certainly feature sterile, cold decor. In other words, we fantasize that we will move even farther away from Nature. However, Nature, it would seem, has other plans for us. Very few of us had imagined a world in which global warming and superbugs (that are not only resistant to our inventiveness but are actually caused by it), disease outbreaks, tsunamis, and storms *all serve to bring us closer to* Nature (whether we like it or not). The masculine impetus in us leads us to painting a rosy and orderly picture of a future full of greater separation from and control over Nature: "it is often assumed that the next stage of evolution will take the form of the last one, and achieve an even greater freedom from the given conditions of life in order to transform them still further."[52] Despite our vision of soaring into a spotless future full of sunshiney progress and ever-greater removal of ourselves from the dirty muck of *(feh!)* Nature, our moment pulls us down into it, down into unexpected consequences, uncomfortable demands, and imperfect compromises, out of comforting abstractions and into reality's pain and joy.

> We cannot live the afternoon of life according to the program of life's morning; for what in the morning was true will in evening become a lie. (Jung)[53]

Today, through suffering and newly met mysteries, we are encountering facts that poke away at our masculine inflation and our disconnection from any "unwelcome associations" to the world. Increasingly, where we have wanted to take refuge in our pre-existent certitudes, we are being forced to accommodate new facts. We are in a world in which spiritual dilemmas are being pressed upon us by down-to-earth crises, unexpected discoveries, and close-at-hand horrors—where the limits of the planet's resources and capacities are being reached and even exceeded. The zeitgeist of our era is one in which the shine is coming off of things we had imagined to be full of light: heroes, presidents, and priests are having their sins paraded out in public. They are being shown to be capable not only of incompetence, but of cruelty and crime. The unfortunate fact that no one comes without feet of clay is being repeatedly forced upon us. We are discovering that the people that make up our most sacred institutions are capable of the greatest crimes. Technological innovation has given us poisoned water and weapons of mass destruction, and even the most sacred cow of Western culture, materialism, has become complicated for us. Rising prices and falling values make us anxious and depressed—blind faith in markets is eroded and many people now realize that our unchecked greed and materialism are destroying the planet. Businesses too large to have any connection to a place never worry about destroying anywhere they have to in order to get all they can. Masculine institutions are losing their veneer for us—what once held the light for us is revealing its dark imperfection. The loss of shine on the objects of our veneration forces us into the pain of personal moral struggle: "How could they do that!" Through this process, in each of its minute movements, our gaze upon the world is made ever so slightly less naive, less distant, and we are drawn into closer relation to the world around us. While under the inflated spell of the masculine we have only been able to look "upward" for truth and meaning, today circumstances incessantly lead us toward discovering truth and meaning in places that are more down to earth. Despite imagining a future that is a continued extension of masculine knowing and controlling, our moment is turning us toward a Feminine participating and attentiveness, away from sterile distance and toward intimate, felt contact.

> I don't think spirit is up in the twentieth century; I think it's down. So that it affects the way that I experience my body, my images of God, what I'm willing to do and what I'm willing not to do. There is a kind of fierceness now, that's been souped up, if you like; an insistence. I'm with Simone Weil desiring God to come down. And I don't like the basic plan, I want an answer. So I'm in that mode which is very intense, very exciting. But it means every day not knowing.[54]

Here, Jungian analyst and professor of religion and psychiatry at Union Theological Institute, Ann Belford Ulanov, gives her words for the change that she believes to be present in our moment. She sees spirit as today being "down, down into matter and into what matters." Here the archetypal imperative that she is describing is different from the one that has driven our masculine rise out of unity with the unconscious upward toward abstract ideals. The direction Ulanov believes our moment is pointed toward is down—down into the present, into the concrete, material reality of the body, and into the pain and fear of losing things that matter to us. The insistence that Ulanov speaks of can be seen in the ever-increasing urgency with which we come to face our culpability in destroying our environment and its beings; in brutal acts of terrorism that refuse to leave us content in the satisfaction of our self-understandings; in the loss of idealized certainties that had provided us with comfort; in the loss of veneer from our institutions. No longer is it quite so easy to idealize one's nation or one's religion. This downward movement requires each of us to become *our own* moral authority.

Yet, while idealizations are coming down in the sea change of this special time's transition, this is also a moment, as Ulanov describes, of spirit coming down into matter, of our coming to embody consciously more of the best possibilities of humanity. Like never before, we are aware of and capable of responding to the plight of the fallen around the world—even if we cannot stop it, we are aware of each tragedy. Like never before, we are geared toward listening to formerly outcast and ostracized groups—even if we have not learned how to best respond to what they are saying. Awareness, not only of gender issues, but of all issues of disenfranchisement, display the archetypal Feminine emphasis upon relationship and a downward movement of spirit (we are aware of the rights and essential humanity of the "downtrodden"). A connection to Feminine images of God, the Virgin Mary, and Black Madonna figures—who are seen as protectors of the poor—are not only emblematic of this downward change, they are a part of its movement. The Catholic Church's Declaration of the Assumption of the Virgin Mary in 1951—the inclusion of Mary in the God-image psychologically—was an event brought about by people's protest (rather than by insight from the papal hierarchy). As Baring and Cashford describe, it is remarkable that "so many centuries after the Book was, as it were, closed . . . [we witness] the irresistible rise of Mary."[55] This event, along with the widespread worldwide renewed interest in Black Madonna images and the figure of Mary Magdalene, display the shift in impetus under this newly emergent archetypal zeitgeist. This shift lives both in the world and inside of us:

Now the archetype of the feminine, the archetype of the goddess, has become constellated in the collective unconscious. That's why all these different movements flare up all over the place. They all call for a recognition of matter, of nature of the irrational, of eros, of sexuality, of the importance of the physical. And this is also connected with the individuality of women, and her values with the values of eros, with the feeling relationship.[56]

Today the reemergence of the archetypal Feminine is visible in a large series of cultural changes. Hand in hand with political change that has liberated women, there has been growing within us a craving for the liberation of the Feminine inside ourselves. And so we find our new era's impetus expressed in us through what we feel called to do and what no longer satisfies us. Modes of physically embodying consciousness, such as psychotherapy, meditation, and yoga, are popular like never before and we speak more about feelings and sexuality than previous generations did. We see a sudden rise of female musical artists, who now dominate the charts as much as men do. Von Franz sees our time as qualitatively different from the time leading up to it. She describes the change in zeitgeist, much like Ulanov does, as a downward turn into matter, feelings, and body and away from abstraction. Both of them articulate a belief in the notion that our era is one of a change in story, a change in the narrative that we tell ourselves about who we are.

Ewert Cousins, Fordham theology professor and editor of the twenty-five-volume *World Spirituality: An Encyclopedic History of the Religious Quest,* echoes this understanding of our era, stating:

I believe that the human community is presently going through a Second Axial Period. . . . In the [original] Axial period the transformation of consciousness was mediated by great spiritual teachers who emerged in their pivotal regions. Confucius and Lao-Tzu appeared in China; the Upanishadic sages, Mahavira and Buddha in India; Zoroaster in Persia; the prophets Elijah, Isaiah and Jeremiah in Israel; and the philosophers Socrates, Plato and Aristotle in Greece. These teachers brought about a transformation from the mythic, cosmic, ritualistic, collective consciousness of primal peoples to the rational, analytic, critical, individual consciousness that has characterized the mainstream of human history since the Axial period. In the Axial period there emerged a sense of independent, individual identity. . . . This was a decisive moment in the history of spirituality, for with the emergence of individual identity, the spiritual core of the person came to consciousness. . . . But there was loss as well as gain. [They] lost their rootedness in the material and biological realms.[57]

Our epoch's entry into Ewert's Second Axial Period demands our rediscovery of "our rootedness in matter and the earth. This is seen in the emergence of the feminine, a concern for ecology, and in general a concern for a holistic spirituality."[58] Where the First Axial Period expressed our emergence up out of primal participation mystique with Nature into individual, rational masculine consciousness, the Second Axial Period expresses itself as a necessity of re-rooting ourselves down into Nature, both inner and outer, once again. Where we once had moved forward through our capability to act *upon* Nature, today we are being asked to act *with* Nature, and in that difference lies an archetypal shift from masculine to Feminine impetus.

Reflecting the Feminine nature of this change, it is being mediated not through singular figures but rather through a wider emergence of consciousness that is individually discovered and embodied. Thus the changes in which this Second Axial Period can be witnessed in our time all share one thing in common—they are available to each one of us as individuals: We can each experience Crop Circles for ourselves and need not take anyone else's word as authoritative about them. Previously hidden mystical practices are open to us all—yoga, meditation, and other esoteric arts are widely practiced, enabling personal explorations of grounding and embodying spirituality. Our era's discovery and dissemination of previously hidden religious texts brings them out of the dark and into the light, not only known but available to everyone. We can observe instances of synchronicity in our lives. Today we know more than ever before about the historical truth of religious figures, and esoteric practices and mystical ideas are in widespread use. In objective practices that enable individual embodiment of the sacred, and encounters with mysterious phenomenon that allow personal experiences but resist collective, objective solutions, there is a mixing of spirit and matter that is enacted in our time. This change in zeitgeist is *necessarily expressed personally,* and in our era we see, for good and ill, the elevation of the individual. Changes in media and culture since the turn of the millennium particularly emphasize the power of the individual. Our sources for information are democratic, and collective masculine authorities are being increasingly undermined with each new day. We no longer look to television news anchors to tell us what's important; outside sources (e.g., Wikileaks) and personalized news feeds now bring us the truth. Internet information sharing epitomizes the relational, individual-empowered nature of our new era. Reality television and contest-based shows emphasize a shift from celebrity worship to the rising up of the individual—the "every(wo)man" is being made a star. We are living in a time when the fantastic is being recognized as participating in the reality of the mundane. This change in the unconscious impetus that is driving us is found through our lives in our inner world and in outer events. While in some ways we are being brought down to size, in other ways we are being led—by the pain of suffering and the voluntary sacrifice of practice—to realize the precious value of each breath. We are being led out of grandiose masculine fantasies and into the reality of raw fact and blunt mystery. "Like someone parachuting out of a burning plane," we are dropping "out of [our] head[s] and into the truth."[59]

A movement in this downward direction is being provoked by our encounters with the new mysteries that are before us today. Will we participate with what is going on around us? Our culture resists looking at strange phenomena like Crop Circles, because admitting their reality into our consciousness would threaten the grandiose worldviews that we use to keep the world safely locked up in tidy, rational cages. Participating with Crop Circles leads inevitably to a confrontation with shadow. Eventually, especially early in one's exploration of them, a fear is constellated in us. Such fear may make us want to disavow the entire phenomenon and move into denial, or paint them with the shadow's brush and presume their agent to be threatening to us. The history of our responses to Crop Circles demonstrates our capacity for each.

Medieval categorization of them as Mowing Devils and later as "weather effects" shows us visions of our own capacity for shadow projection and defensive rationalization and reduction. These two responses continue to be the primary one's voiced in our culture. In the feature film *Signs,* M. Night Shyamalan characterizes the aliens behind the phenomenon as hostile creatures who must be violently overcome, depicting here the projection of the shadow from a masculine-dominated mindset. On the most immature level, the archetypal masculine wants to paint the enemy with all the qualities it rejects in itself; the psyche of a masculine culture "at least in its formative stage, tends to demand an opposite to secure its own identity and project the unresolved conflicts of its own tribe on to 'the Other.' This other, the alien, then becomes the enemy to be sacrificed—the 'evil' to be cast out from the good of the tribe."[60] We see this dynamic given voice in racism, wars, and political vitriol. Aliens are a natural vehicle for this kind of projection, and in a recent television documentary on the subject of extraterrestrial life, acclaimed physicist Stephen Hawking seemed to be expressing such a psychological dynamic. While he believes alien life is extremely likely given the size of the universe alone, his conclusive scenario is that if other forms of life were advanced they would certainly eventually use up all their resources and begin looking to "conquer and colonize any planets they could reach." He adds that if we should encounter aliens we can expect that it would not go well for us, as colonization has not gone well for those indigenous people conquered by other countries. Now whom does such a description fit? It fits *us;* it describes *our* relationship to *our* planet. Certainly such a categorization is based less on logical deduction than it is on individual psyche. Psychologically such a point of view expresses precisely the inner condition of the modern mind. Such a voice comes from the place in us that is rootless and insatiably limitless—the exact attitude that Hawking invests the Other with.

> He who is rooted in the soil endures. Alienation from the unconscious and from its historical conditions spells rootlessness. That is the danger that lies in wait for the conqueror of foreign lands, and for every individual who, through one-sided allegiance to any kind of -ism, loses touch with the dark, maternal, earthy ground of his being. (Jung)[61]

We need not choose to invest the Other with what we reject in ourselves, but the first step is to accept that our thoughts, visions, and attitudes about the Other are our own—they are issued from our psyche and it is there that we should wrestle with them. Can we own that our fear of the agent of Crop Circles is at least, in good measure, our own? If we can take ownership of some of our responses to the phenomenon we can begin to see that such material is actually *blocking our seeing what is really there.* If our response to the expansive and challenging mystery posed by Crop Circles comes from a place of shadow projection, then we risk seeing in them what we are failing to understand about ourselves. Hawking wonders aloud in his documentary whether "the real challenge is figuring out what might aliens actually be like." Yes! And how might we best begin to judge what they might actually be like? In this case, we have an opportunity to "know them by their fruits" (Matt 7:16). We can draw conclusions about their character based on their behavior as we would with any-human-one else. In this case we can judge them by their "artwork." By what they have demonstrated to us, we can see that they are not only familiar with advanced geometry, but they are inventive with its theorems, and we can see that they are beauty-loving, creative, and playful. The more we know about "the Other," the harder it is to remain in a consciousness that tars them with our own shadow qualities. Because we are at the end of the old masculine period and are capable of transformation, we can recognize this tendency and overcome our unconsciously oppositional stance. What is particularly difficult about dealing with a phenomenon of the scope of Crop Circles is that it bumps up against our masculine desire to categorize: "The danger is that, distanced from the unruly nature of actual experience, we tend to structure our thoughts in terms of our definitions, and so limit our perceptions to match the limitations of language."[62] Again we risk losing what is actually before us because of a desire in us to have the new fit into old categories—which is *by definition* impossible, as the genuinely new thing always exceeds our imagination for it. The choice that we have is whether or not to be conscious about our own responses, and from such a stance in reality move into authentic and direct engagement with the new.

> The old order based on innocence and unthinking allegiance to an outer authority is giving away to a new order based on questioning, experience and inner truth.[63]

Crop Circles exist outside of accepted institutions of authority—yet they are available to us all. In leaving their work unsigned, their author provides us with the opportunity to enter into a process of engagement. Our first question might be "Who is making those?" It might be followed by questions about what we really believe is "out there." Crop Circles invite us into a process of wonder—to once again staring up at the night sky both literally and metaphorically. We are invited back toward a relationship with the world that has awe and mystery and not knowing, but also subjectivity and "Other." Surely it is no accident that these cereal-formed artworks are made just as they are.

Crop Circles ask something of us and in so doing reflect a positive aspect of our moment's new impetus: they require that we come to meet the world close-up now; just as for two thousand years the zeitgeist has led us up and away toward ideals and abstractions. A new and different kind of future is unfolding and it seems to be characterized by a new intimacy between humanity and the "super"-natural, between earth, body, and spirit. The moral calling of the new day's reality cannot be met without the sacrifice of the ego—of *our* ego. Our discomfort, effort, and struggle are the cost of meeting it. In a time where both opinion and tradition are fractured and "where nothing agrees with anything else," it only makes sense that a truly new phenomenon would affect the deflation, not of one view, but of many. It seems necessary that this process requires something different from each one of us. The change of story in this moment's nature may be leading some of us to feel more awe and joy and others to break down old ways of knowing, but the paths seem to be singular and for each of us our own. Where those hardened into masculine approaches may have to realize with St. Augustine that "miracles do not happen in contradiction to nature, but only in contradiction to man's current laws of nature," the grandiose fantasies of inflated New Agers who are quick to say "You see, I was right the whole time" may have to settle for something more down to earth, discovering with Goethe that "mysteries are not necessarily miracles." While our experience of this time's change must—by necessity—be individual, this does not mean that it is directionless. We cannot hope to adequately come to face the mystery of Crop Circles through previously held abstract theories about the nature of our world. The new moral demand seems to be one that seeks that we look past our own preconceptions to see the complete truth of what *is actually* before us. It requires an attendance to what is, rather than to what we would like to be or what we believe there should be. Where the masculine has led us into identifying ourselves with light and being certain that our own view is the righteous one, today the boyhood of our self-investment must man up, let go of the shiny simplicities of his ego's fancy and begin to participate with the darkness, mysteries, and disasters that the world is showing him he has left behind. He must allow himself to feel the "unsettling spirit" of a startling new day.

> Feminine wisdom is bound to the earth, to organic and psychological growth, to living reality. It issues from one's instincts, from one's unconscious, from one's history and relationships. It is nonspeculative wisdom without illusions, and is not idealistic in its approach to reality but prefers what actually is to what should or might be. Feminine wisdom nourishes, supports and develops the strongest ties to reality.[64]

SEVEN   THE REALITY OF THE PSYCHE

Curiously, as the archetypal masculine impetus that has led our civilization for three thousand years seems to be nearing its zenith, discoveries made under its influence have begun to point us toward a view of Nature that is once again invested with elements of the archetypal Feminine. Since the beginning of the last century, discoveries in science and depth psychology have revealed a new understanding of the world we are just beginning to unfold today. Experiments in quantum physics that have shattered old assumptions stand beside the discovery of the unconscious, pushing together two seemingly incompatible worldviews, forever altering our understanding of reality and thereby how we may come to understand Crop Circles. Jung recognized that in unearthing objective archetypal contents at work within the human psyche in collective forms across cultures, depth psychology pierced our image of consciousness as entirely subjective, unique, and personal: within us breathes something shared. And where depth psychology found the fingerprints of an objective reality within the formerly exclusively personal domain of the psyche, discoveries in quantum physics and other areas of science revealed curious effects of consciousness upon physical, objective reality. Where our inflation under the influence of the masculine has left us believing in a world in which our internal state could never have any effect upon the objective world, if we are willing to look closely at the evidence of scientific experiments and psychological observation of the interaction of consciousness and the material world, today we are finding out something new about the reality of the psyche. From opposite starting points, Jung followed the same string that Einstein, Pauli, and other scientists found and each ended up holding one end of a paradox that remains sitting on the sidelines of our cultural awareness waiting to be considered. In proving the relativity of time and space, physicists shattered our most fundamental assumptions about the nature of the universe and we are now rediscovering what is an old idea, that a similar relativity exists between psyche and matter. Our model of Nature has become outdated and the hubris of the masculine view of the world as machine is today crashing into a new and ancient understanding of the world as innately something more.

> Pauli pursued the symmetries. The Chinese spoke of the yin and the Receptive in the Tao. The ancient Egyptians honoured the goddess Maat as an extended grid against which all could be measured and balanced. The Navajo imagine Changing Woman, who, with her bundles re-creates creation in space-time. Modern mathematicians write, Yes, God is a geometer. But never forget: She's better at it than we are. (Zabriskie)[1]

For many people today, science—that is to say, the belief in material realism (the impossibility of the supernatural)—is a core element of their belief system; it is maybe the only thing that they believe in. On the other hand, there are perhaps even more people, likely a majority in the West, for whom science and spirituality form a split across which their psyche stands straddling, propped upon two beliefs that do not seem to be reconcilable and that have opposing precepts. We may ascribe to belief in science but also be open to a spiritual reality existing beyond material reality; we may have beliefs about God, heaven, spirits, and signs, while also believing in the evolution of the human species, the validity of modern medicine and the value of technology. How many of us today struggle, on some level, to reconcile a spiritual or religious faith with science? The power of these beliefs to affect how we view the world and come to respond to it cannot be understated. Whether we have a strict belief in science as material realism, or stand unsteadily upon the split worldview of science and spirituality/religious faith, we are the products of a cultural moment in which this psychological division is acutely present. The modern worldview sees reality through the lens of a profound split between matter and spirit.

The fruit of three thousand years of the masculine impetus' increasingly objective relationship to reality is a tremendous amount of knowledge about the world around us. Viewing reality as a machine and investigating that perspective relentlessly has had the benefit of teaching us a great deal about how it does, in fact, operate mechanically. For the Western mind, matter is the only reality. Consciousness is an outgrowth of the machine-like piecing together of more complex biological pieces over time, which ultimately came to perform the trick of self-awareness. Simply an added feature to this version of the human, consciousness is also something that a machine, e.g., a computer, could have. In this understanding of the world, there is no soul, no magical entity that makes us conscious; we are strictly a product of biology (and history) and absolutely nothing more. Ample evidence supports this view. Take up a neuroscience text and you will see endless research of how matter—our brains—affect how we think, feel, and behave—in fact, how they *are* how we think, feel, and behave. Genetics too tells us the same thing again. Sociobiology, in particular, tells us that all of our traits are the result of evolutionary adaptation and the survival of the fittest. The amount of data collected to support and reinforce this view is staggering. How then, and by what, can this view be challenged?

Like foundation posts of our inner world, our core beliefs do not like to be challenged, and many of us will live and die with the same beliefs, prejudices, perspectives, fears, and automatic responses intact inside. Even if we have developed a degree of self-awareness, beneath its surface still lurk foundational contents upon which we have fashioned a framework of beliefs about the world. For each of us, there is an element of unconsciousness in our perspective on the world that makes us uncomfortable with challenges to our beliefs. Our identity rests on attachment to our beliefs, and if our beliefs are wrong our identity is endangered; and so, for most of us, believing as we do to some degree in the credo of material realism, challenges to that view are reacted to with an automatic resistance. Nonetheless, standing on the outskirts of the domain of accepted truth are facts about the world that profoundly challenge us, asking something of us before they are able to be welcomed in. Making room for consideration of these discoveries does not make material realism wrong, it simply suggests that we may have reached the limitations of its comprehensiveness as a worldview.

Since Galileo in the seventeenth century turned his telescope to the heavens, and Leeuwenhoek in the same century peered down through his primitive microscope at the minutiae, scientists have been delineating the forms of matter occurring in space and on earth with such impressive thoroughness that large numbers of people in our modern world have come to think of matter as the only reality. (Osterman)[2]

Through a series of observations that began with Einstein's quantum physics nearly ninety years ago, the orthodoxy of material realism—a bedrock of our worldview—has been undermined, although it remains the dominant view of academia and other institutions. These observations challenge the exclusivity of object and subject and point out ways in which the old view is incomplete. New observations point toward a view of the universe as an essentially interwoven fabric of psyche and matter, personal and impersonal, spiritual and material.

At the beginning of the twentieth century the house of classical physics was built on the strongest stuff imaginable—the impenetrable atoms which were the basis of the physical world. The location of each of these atoms was precisely fixed in the three-dimensional space of Descartes geometry. In a very few years, however, the house of physics was shaken to its very foundations. The atoms of its walls dissolved into abstractions. . . . It was assaulted by Einstein's general theory of relativity on the one hand and quantum theory on the other. Both new theories view the cosmos as an undivided whole. (Combs and Holland)[3]

In the traditional scientific worldview, all actions in the world, like billiard balls, come as a result of a prior act, and all reality is the outcome of the great "break" in the sky, the Big Bang (this neatly sidesteps the question of what existed before that).[4] Individual material objects are required to *come together locally* in order to affect causation; this is called "causal determinism." Another assumption of the scientific model is that by breaking down the world into its smallest observable parts we eventually come to discover the fundamental ground of reality. This approach, called "reductionism," is a natural expression of the material realist view in action. If matter is the only truth, then reducing that matter to its constituent elements must produce the ultimate source from which reality is constructed. Throughout the pursuit of science, this view accelerated in the speed by which it processed all the aspects of our natural world. Nature came to be known, not just microscopically, but eventually down into its atomic structure. However, in discovering the atomic building blocks of reality, several radical and unexpected observations were made. First, rather than reaching a solid bottom at this level, we instead reached its limit, described by some as an event horizon, at which we can no longer accurately predict with certainty. Second, and just as important, the operation of these smaller particles flew in direct contradiction to the governing assumptions of reductionist material realism.

The billiard ball view of the world in classical physics describes reality as being made up of matter, electromagnetic waves, and energy. These elements operate in a world that is characterized as possessing the following qualities: strong objectivity—the belief in a world made of material objects (upon which consciousness has no possible effect without physical action); causal determinism—by knowing the three-dimensional position of an object and the force (e.g., velocity) being introduced to it, we can always determine the outcome of the interaction; locality—objects can only be acted upon by local forces (no effect can be produced except by physical means); materialism—our interior experience of consciousness is entirely the product of our physical brain (consciousness is an epiphenomenon, an outgrowth, of matter). Each of these principles was placed in jeopardy by developments that would come to constitute the shift from "the physics that Isaac Newton founded in the seventeenth century and Albert Einstein completed in the first decades of the twentieth century."[5]

> Physics is a privileged form of coordinating experience with physical reality that has often obliged us to change our views of self and world. (Nadeau and Kafatos)[6]

In 1905, an unknown patent clerk named Albert Einstein began the process of radically revising our view of the world.[7] As a child, young Albert is said to have wondered "what would happen if he chased after a beam of light—faster and faster. When he himself was moving at the speed of light, what would he see?"[8] He would later discover the theory that answered this question and be rewarded for pursuing his curiosity with a Nobel prize.

While it is physically impossible, but mathematically certain, what the mover would "see" in such a case would be the lengths of objects in the direction of motion contracting and the appearance of a singular bright light into which both objects would appear to be moving. More important, as we approach the speed of light, designated by the constant, c, time would begin to slow down. Time is, in every real sense, stretched out by gains in speed approaching light speed. For example, if you take a particle and speed it up until it's moving incredibly fast, its internal rate of decay slows down. His famous equation, $E=mc^2$, expresses that time is, in fact, not constant, but is relative to other conditions. Confirmation of Einstein's relativity theory came during a solar eclipse in 1919, when the sun's gravitational field was observed bending the starlight around it. We know that atomic clocks run at different rates in different gravitational fields, and modern GPS, cell phones, and other technology require an equation that reflects this principle to function properly. The use of atomic clocks in a variety of locations has made this principle very well established. Einstein's discovery was the initial blow to material realism, but he failed to realize its significance (so too did the French mathematician Jules-Henri Poincaré[9] who simultaneously made the same discovery). Eventually, he came to recognize the vast equivalency, the essential universal wholeness that he had uncovered in his theorems:

> Einstein believed the universe is whole, that everything is ultimately equivalent to and transforms into everything else (depending on the relative motion of the observer): Matter is equivalent to energy, gravity to acceleration, space to time, it is all one unified field. (Briggs and Peat)[10]

Einstein's vision of the world as a unified whole would be filled out in deeper ways than even he was capable of imagining. In the 1930s, he and two of his students at Princeton, Podolsky and Rosen, conceived of a thought experiment (called the EPR thought experiment, after its founders) that was designed to disprove something that quantum theory predicted—that paired particles could remain correlated at a distance, which defies the classical rule of locality. In 1964, Briton John Bell deduced a mathematical theorem by which to begin devising methods of testing the EPR experiment.

The goal of all this was in fact to disprove the existence of nonlocality and thus insure the solidity of the classical view. Bell was personally convinced that the totality of all our previous knowledge of physical reality, not to mention the laws of physics, would favor the assumption of locality. (Nadeau and Kafatos)[11]

In nonlocality, two particles, after having been separated, are brought together and then split apart again, and display in their behavior a continued linkage to each other;[12] this linkage is maintained regardless of the distance and happens "in no time" (the term "instantaneous" would be scientifically not quite correct). Einstein was convinced that such "spooky action at a distance" was not possible and described the belief in it, which was shared by many of the colleagues that he respected most, as providing them with a "tranquilizing philosophy . . . so delicately contrived that, for the time, it provides a gentle pillow for the true believer from which he cannot very easily be aroused. So let him lie there."[13] Testing Bell's theorem required observation of particles after they had been split, and physical experiments capable of testing Bell's theorem were developed and perfected in the 1970s. In 1982, at the Institute of Optics at the University of Paris at Orsay, Alain Aspect and his colleagues successfully confirmed the existence of this nonlocality. In 1997, experiments on photons showed that even at a distance of seven miles these particles (quanta) continued to remain linked in their behavior and are spoken of as being "entangled." The successful results of both these experiments clearly reveal that "the character of physical reality as disclosed by quantum physics is nonlocal."

Broken down in this discovery are two of the most fundamental concepts underlying the modern scientific view of the world. Nonlocality undercuts belief in the material realist assumption of locality (its effect occurs regardless of distance) and causal determinism (its effect occurs without material cause). This truth is not simply theoretical idea but is an experimentally confirmed fact—Nicolus Gisin and team completed the 1997 experiments that made the existence of nonlocality certain at the University of Geneva. They observed that correlation in behavior between particles was not diminished at eleven kilometers. This convinced physicists that particles would retain their entangled linkage "where the distances between the detectors was halfway to the edge of the universe."[14] This fact does not point to information traveling across that span, as it is not communication that is occurring, but rather to a kind of shared consciousness between the particles, no matter what the distance—one particle knows and instantly responds to what the other has done. This fact points to a nonlocality or nonseparability that is certainly "a global or universal dynamic principle of the life of the cosmos."[15] This discovery is proof that two of the assumptions that reinforce the Cartesian divide of consciousness and matter are incorrect. Another strange discovery in quantum physics further reinforces the incompleteness of this widely held modern worldview.

Likely the most startling revelation witnessed in the operation of quantum mechanics, however, is the effect of conscious observation on the behavior of matter itself. It is found that matter exists as waves of possibility whose collapse into form is caused by our viewing of it.[16] Up until it is observed, quanta exists in wave form, "unless and until it is measured or observed," when it becomes a particle. Defined as "complementarity," this mystery is described by Goswami in reference to the double-slit experiment: "When we localize the electron by finding out which slit it goes through, we reveal its particle aspect. When we do not localize the electron, ignoring which slit it goes through, we reveal its wave aspect. . . . The formal cadence of predictive science that holds for either wave or particle is transformed into a creative dance of a transcendent wavicle."[17] Here psyche-matter interactivity in the quantum world shows us Nature as multivalent possibilities affected by us. Consciousness is also regarded as having an effect upon matter through another form of observation: "Quantum physics found that the act of observing a subatomic particle inevitably disturbs the particle, so that an exact knowledge of both its position and momentum is impossible to obtain (formalized as Heisenberg's uncertainty principle)."[18] Both of these effects point to inherent relatedness of psyche and matter in Nature.

The effect of conscious observation upon the behavior of matter is a longstanding source of controversy among physicists. The argument around the "observer effect" centers around what is an observation and what is a measurement, but for many of the founding fathers of quantum mechanics it was clear that matter was being affected by our conscious observation. Nobel laureate physicist Neils Bohr—discoverer of complementarity—has said that "those who are not shocked when they first come across quantum theory cannot possibly have understood it." In response to Einstein's desire for the certainty of a God "who does not play dice with the universe," that is, for a return to the now-shattered world of deterministic physics—the comfort of material realism—Bohr responded, "Einstein, stop telling God what to do."[19] In this dialogue one can see the interaction of the masculine-infused view and the new one: where Einstein wanted an entirely rational (and thus in some way controllable) world, Bohr insists upon leaving the nature of the cosmos to its own presentation of itself. Another Nobel laureate physicist, and longtime friend of Jung's, Wolfgang Pauli, felt that quantum reality could be seen to describe an essential irrationality in matter, irrational in the sense that it can no longer be predicted entirely casually or deterministically—the worlds of Newton's laws no longer applied. Pauli believed that the discovery of this irrationality forced one *to return to a humbler estimation of humanity,* to a view of Nature that included an element of mystery, and that "in probing the atom, science had encountered the need to "relinquish its proud claim to be able to understand, in principle, the *whole* world.'"[20] Here, a Feminine quality is being rediscovered in Nature and it brings with it a defeat for masculine views of Creation as existing within the intellectual control of humanity. Pauli says, "No, Nature here shows itself to us as a grander mystery than we can ever hope to control!"—and we can know that our grandiose inflation is an illusion. As Goswami points out, "we often resent being reminded" that the assumptions we have made about the world are *not actually facts;* and it is our tremendously deep unconscious attachment to being correct about our view of the world that keeps us from integrating, or even facing, the most difficult questions of the era (just as we have seen throughout the history of modern responses to the discovery of Crop Circle formations). In their *The Non-Local Universe: The New Physics and Matters of the Mind,* Nadeau and Kafatos ask: "Why has a discovery that many regard as the most momentous in the history of science received such scant attention?" They believe the answer to this lies in the degree of scientific literacy needed to come to grips with these experiments; however, our psychological attachment to masculine approaches to the world around us is the more likely culprit here—our belief in the world as rational, and in this way "conquerable" by us, is the "delicately contrived . . . tranquilizing philosophy" from which we "cannot be easily aroused." Instead we ignore the new thing, remain unknowing and "unshocked" and sustain our inflated high.

> Most of the creators of the new physics were acutely aware that the potential impacts of this new scientific worldview on our conceptions of the relationship between mind and world were nothing short of revolutionary.... Although there were a few [others] ... who vaguely understood these implications, they were largely ignored, until quite recently, by the vast majority of artists and intellectuals. (Nadeau and Kafatos)[21]

What these discoveries point toward is a world in which, at the most fundamental levels, *psyche and matter are entwined.* This view is, of course, extraordinary given the dominance in our world of the material realist worldview that believes this to be impossible. To the material realist, consciousness is an end result and by-product of matter; how can a by-product of matter be affecting it? This fact creates a paradox and tremendous tension for material realism—the worldview in which most scientists are psychologically invested. At the same time, however, the possibility that matter and consciousness are not exclusively separated lies at the root of nearly all of the world's spiritual and religious traditions and indigenous beliefs, and therefore discovery of scientific proof of this fact is tremendously exciting to those seeking ground upon which to base spiritual belief. While many in the science community do not accept the fact of this paradox, to others it is a source of comfort.

> When the new physics confronts us with a situation that seems paradoxical from the perspective of material realism, we tend to overlook the possibility that paradoxes may be arising because of the falsity of our unproven assumption. (We tend to forget that a long-held assumption does not thereby become a fact, and we often resent being reminded.) ... Concepts such as nonlocal and unitive consciousness and the idea of non-local collapse make the universe less comprehensible to the material scientist. These concepts also make the universe a lot more meaningful to everyone else. (Goswami)[22]

Like many other strange discoveries of our era, the evidence for the relationship between matter and consciousness witnessed in quantum mechanics has been received in a fragmentary way by us, predominantly ignored or denied and accepted only by a rare few. Yet for nearly a century, physicists have been observing these facts, and for longer still there has been an effort to scientifically study the ability of consciousness to affect matter. In his 2003 work, *The Sense of Being Stared At (and Other Properties of the Extended Mind)*, Cambridge biology professor and author of nine other books, Rupert Sheldrake, takes the reader across the last one hundred and fifty years of research into the ability of the mind to reach beyond physical constraint. Looking at thousands of studies completed in Europe and North America on telepathy, awareness of distant distress and death, card guessing, precognition, remote viewing (many of which were initially undertaken to *disprove* such effects), and animal sensitivity to these same effects, he found that "despite an impressive accumulation of evidence, psychic research . . . has been kept on the margins as a result of powerful taboos against the 'paranormal'" (p. 6). Resistance to this idea rests not on a lack of scientific evidence, but as is also seen in our responses to the Crop Circle phenomenon, on a lurking "archaic fear of witchcraft" (p. 9)—on our unconscious fear of the "irrational."

Broad and Wade point out that the scientific drive to resist being taken in by fraudulent ideas is often made a bulwark against nonfraudulent but profoundly challenging new ideas: "Acceptance of fraudulent results is the other side of that familiar coin, resistance to new ideas. Fraudulent results are likely to be accepted in science if they are plausibly presented, if they conform with prevailing prejudices and expectations. . . ."[23] It is in this way that the Crop Circle phenomenon was neatly swept under the rug with a one-word explanation: hoax. Such a pronouncement fits with our bias, soothes our unconscious anxieties, and was readily accepted—even though it was patently false. Kuhn wrote that "at any given stage in the history of science, phenomena that do not fit into the prevailing model or paradigm are dismissed or ignored or explained away. . . . Yet to the embarrassment of the reigning theories, they persist. Sooner or later science has to expand to include them" (p. 3). Our discomfort with the new, our unconscious resistance to the "irrational" coupling of matter and psyche, is often evident in the emotional reaction of those who do not want to believe that such possibilities, whether psychic phenomenon or Crop Circles, are true. As Sheldrake, who himself has been the victim of bitter responses, asks: "some people become angry at, or scornful of, anyone who takes these phenomena seriously. Why?" (p. 7)

Sheldrake's research (and summary of previous research) is important to our inquiry into Crop Circles, not only because, like quantum physics, it forms part of the context of our moment, but also because of peculiarities within the phenomenon itself. A biologist, Sheldrake sees the qualities of the extended mind as essentially natural (not supernatural) and as having a field quality: "trying to understand minds without recognizing the extended fields on which they depend is like trying to understand the effects of magnets without acknowledging that they are surrounded by magnetic fields. No amount of chemical analysis of melted-down magnets could explain the way magnets affect things at a distance" (p. 207–8). Sheldrake refers to this extended quality of the mind as a "morphic field."[24] One of his experiments on the sense of being stared at (which follows other research that showed statistically significant positive results) was done with one person acting as the starer and one as the target, where the target is asked in each trial whether or not they felt they were being stared at. Following a randomized list for staring or not staring, the accuracy of the target's responses were noted. Guessing randomly, people would be right 50 percent of the time. The nearly 14,000 trials completed by 1999 showed a 55 percent accuracy rate, which is "astronomically significant, with the odds against the results being due to chance more than 1,020 to 1." Sheldrake also notes there are many examples of particular individuals or groups being able to generate much higher rates of accuracy: "when twins worked in pairs as starer and subject, they did much better than non-twin siblings or unrelated children" (p.171). (Most of the trials completed here were done with unrelated people.) If the mind can reach out and "touch," so to speak, another person such that they feel they are being stared at, as is commonly experienced, then the effect here would have similar consequences to the observer effect found in the quantum physics: "If the sense of being stared at is real, as it seems to be, it throws into question some of the fundamental doctrines of rationalism. . . . It points toward a new understanding of the nature of the mind" (p. 183). The positive results of this experiment increased when one only considers the trials where one was actually being stared at, and has further interesting results: "Although novices tend to score best in looking trials . . . those who are tested repeatedly and given feedback tend to improve in both kinds of trials. It seems possible to *learn* to detect the difference between being looked at and not being looked at" (p. 175). This same experiment has also been done observing people through one-way mirrors, regular mirrors, and through closed-circuit televisions. A Dutch study completed 18,700 trials and had a positive significance of 10,376 against chance (p. 177).

Telepathy is among the most commonly tested aspects of the extended mind and there have been millions of trials completed in which subjects were asked to guess which card a person was looking at. Sheldrake notes that "between the 1880s and 1939, dozens of investigators all around the world published 186 papers describing a total of 4 million trials involving card guessing. . . . [Meta-analysis of these results showed that] the odds of these positive results arising by chance were more than 1,021 to one" (p. 46). Interestingly, some test subjects results were significantly "*below* chance levels" (p. 48). Negative test scores imply that subjects were actively going against a telepathic awareness that was present. A study by New York psychologist Gertrude Schmeidler found that this effect was particularly predominant among people who stated (prior to being tested) that they did not believe in the possibility of such effects (p. 48)—which illustrates the ego's tremendous capacity for denial. As with the staring experiments, telepathy experiments showed significantly better results when the sender and receiver were emotionally close: parents and children, siblings and lovers did better than people who did not know each other (p. 52). This difference was also observed by University of Virginia professor of psychiatry Ian Stevenson in his study of cases of telepathic intuition of distance death and distress—as was that emotional ties were more important than biological ones (p. 74). Positive results were also found in Sheldrake's (ongoing) testing of telepathic identification of incoming telephone calls (and emails)—the common experience of "I was just thinking about you when you called"—and here too "the difference between the scores with familiar and unfamiliar people was highly significant statistically" (p. 105). These results occur, of course, regardless of the physical distance between caller and receiver. Also of interest was the finding of *unconscious* awareness of being focused upon by another. In experiments where subject receivers had their skin resistance monitored, their guesses "were no better than chance. But their skin resistance was significantly different . . . showing that they were detecting the senders' intentions unconsciously, without knowing it" (p. 53). The ability to feel, even unconsciously, when someone is directing their attention toward us fits with common cultural traditions worldwide relating to the idea of the "evil eye."

Because of the success of these experiments, it should come as no surprise that the U.S. government has a longstanding interest in researching these effects (as did the former U.S.S.R.; and much of the formation on this research was made public during the Clinton presidency). Of particular interest was developing the capacity for remote viewing or psychic spying on distant locations. Physicists Puthoff and Targ, at the Stanford Research Institute, funded by the CIA and other U.S. government agencies beginning in the 1970s, developed a protocol for testing subjects on their ability to describe a place where a "beacon person" was located (p. 217). Sheldrake includes one vivid example of a Russian nuclear facility that was described in unique detail by a subject who found the specific details he had provided described in *Aviation Weekly* magazine three years later (p. 223). Further examples can be viewed online.[25] The experiments conducted at SRI went very well, and of over 25,000 separate trials conducted from 1973 to 1988 the overall results "were significant statistically, with odds against chance of a billion, billion to one."[26] The U.S. government then funded further controlled trials through the Science Applications International Corporation (SAIC, from 1989 to 1993, with further statistically significant success. Finally, Sheldrake reports:

> In 1995 the CIA commissioned a review of the results by an expert panel that included an eminent statistician, Jessica Utts, a professor at the University of California, Davis, and also a well-known skeptic, Ray Hyman, a professor of psychology at the University of Oregon. Both ended up agreeing that the results were "far beyond what is expected by chance." (p. 219)

Sheldrake also looks at another area of particular interest to him as a biologist, the curious extended mind behavior of animals. In the synchronized movement of flocks of birds and schools of fish, which happen too quickly to be consciously coordinated, he sees evidence of the evolution of the extended mind. Film studies by biologist Wayne Potts in Puget Sound, Washington, show the example of dunlins whose response time to stimulus (thirty-eight milliseconds) is more than twice that of the motion in concert of the flock (fifteen milliseconds). The same holds true of the high-speed defensive maneuvers of schools of fish whose "behavior has no simple explanation in terms of sensory information from neighboring fish because it happens far too fast for nerve impulses to move from the eye to the brain and then from the brain to the muscles" (p. 118). Sheldrake sees extended fields of mind as the best explanation for the coordination and profound beauty of these animals' movements. He also sees this as a possible explanation for the unity of mind that is widely seen in the insect world: "there is already evidence that coordination of the insects' activities depends on field-like influences that cannot be explained in terms of the normal senses" (p. 119). Evidence of the consciousness of other living creatures extending beyond their physical bodies and tying them to others is also seen elsewhere, in the behavior of wild animals and in those whom we keep as pets.

Hunters, trackers, and naturalists have long suspected that much of the anticipatory behavior that they have observed in animals pointed to their awareness of extended mental fields. Wolves have demonstrated an ability to find the rest of their pack across great distances while both are in motion, and their prey—elk and caribou—respond uniformly to a silent impulse to flee, both of which suggest the extended mind (Long in Sheldrake, p. 114). Sheldrake includes examples of many different animal groups (as witnessed by other scientists) displaying behavior that would seem to suggest their ability to sense predatory intent at a distance—which he points out provides an obvious evolutionary advantage. This quality echoes both indigenous hunting tradition, which sometimes calls upon the hunter to hide his thoughts of the prey (p. 153), and a common instruction given to fighter pilots in World War II not to look directly at the target they were sneaking up on (p. xxx). Hunters and wildlife photographers also describe their common experience of sensing that the animals know when they are being stared at, or themselves being the stared-at prey:

> I do not know, and therefore cannot explain, what brings it into operation. On this occasion I had neither heard nor seen the tigress . . . yet I knew, without any

shadow of doubt, that she was lying up for me among the rocks. I had been out for many hours that day . . . without one moment's unease, and then, on cresting the ridge, and coming in sight of the rocks, I knew they held danger for me. (Corbett in Sheldrake, p. 161)

Can we feel intention at a distance as our animal kin do? Many pet owners believe that a shared field of awareness exists. Sheldrake includes many tremendously powerful examples of the ability of pets to feel the intention of their owners at a distance (he describes many scientific tests performed on pets in his *Dogs Who Know When Their Owners are Coming Home* and on his website). His videotaped studies show dogs whose approach to the window (or other spot) comes in response, not to the nearing approach of their owner, but rather to that owner's intention to return, demonstrating a shared field of mind that many of us would not imagine to be possible.

At Duke University in the 1930s, J. B. Rhine conducted experiments focused on card guessing and showed statistically significant results, but positive results tended to taper off after a certain period of time—as the subject's interest in the game waned, so too did their accuracy. Without the energy of genuine feeling, the effect dwindled—this is, of course, similar to the common idea of "beginner's luck."[27] Novelty implies greater interest on the part of the subject, a level of heightened emotion also seen in synchronicity and other actions of the extended mind. Feeling when one is being stared at, the ability of loved ones to know when the other is calling, human and animal awareness of death, danger, or distress at a distance, and pet awareness of the owner's coming or going, are all aided by the presence of emotion: novelty, danger, fear, pain, and affection. Why? Why do such strange effects seem to require a certain amount of emotional charge in order for them to occur?

Feeling consciousness as a field quality that extends beyond the physical body of human and nonhuman creatures alike can be understood as a natural, but simply invisible, effect. As Sheldrake points out, one cannot understand magnets only through their physical qualities—it's through their effects that we come to understand electromagnetism. There are many qualities of the natural world we understand today (e.g., gravity, germs) that are invisible yet nonetheless present and natural; why then is it somehow unscientific to imagine that consciousness may work similarly? And what role might we understand feeling—authentic emotion—to have within this field? We know that the heart's magnetic field extends widely around the body, and here feeling plays a role in enabling these effects to take place at a distance—the other's real distress, danger, or interest heightens its action. Can we imagine the eros of genuine feeling to be quantitatively enhancing the movement of consciousness across space? Some think this to be the case and find a parallel in the kind of entanglement we see in the world of quantum mechanics.

> Some scientists suggest that the remarkable degree of coherence displaced in living systems might depend in some fundamental way on quantum effects like entanglement. Others suggest that conscious awareness is caused or related in some important way to entangled particles in the brain. Some even propose that the entire universe is a single, self-entangled object. (Radin)[28]

In the world of the relativity of time and space that Einstein revealed, it is implied that such effects may also have the possibility of existing in nonusual ways in relation to time as well. While it is commonly observed that moments of distress and death are felt across vast distances, such feelings can also arise prior to the tragedy's arrival, spanning not space but time. There are no shortage of historical accounts of friends and loved ones knowing when someone has died or claiming to have been visited by the spirit of the person at the moment of death, but it is something more to have had such a feeling before it occurs. Sheldrake includes a selection of these, several of which comes from Behe's 1988 work *Titanic: Psychic Forewarning of a Tragedy,* which describes the accounts of foreboding that led numerous individuals to cancel their trips (and some to continue anyway) and the account of one woman who was moved to cry out simply from watching the ship depart: "That ship is going to sink before it reaches America. . . . Don't just stand there staring at me! Do something! You fools, I can see hundreds of people struggling in the icy water."[29] Here is a similar modern account:

> I got to the airport and I just had a bad feeling. I started crying and couldn't stop. . . . I couldn't stop crying, so I bought a ticket for another flight and took off 10 minutes after that flight [TWA Flight 800, which exploded after takeoff in July 1996] did.[30]

One might choose to simply dismiss such accounts, but they are pervasive throughout our history. Interpreting dreams in association with future events (precognition) was a widespread part of human tradition, indeed a part of nearly every pre-modern culture, and plays a very significant role in the Judeo-Christian Bible. Sheldrake includes accounts of dreams relating to the tragedy of September 11, 2001, which came prior to that morning, and the recent death of one famous American political journalist was also felt prior to its occurrence by his spouse.[51] There is simply no end to such accounts if one is willing to look at them. In 1927, a British aeronautical engineer, J. W. Dunne, wrote a book called *An Experiment with Time* in which he observed future correlations between his dreams and future events. He believed that many people would have this experience if they more closely observed their dreams and that this phenomenon was behind the concept of déjà vu, whose meaning "already seen" reflects this idea.

Questions of matter's relation to time lead into a concept that Jung formalized the discussion of more than fifty years ago. Coining the term "synchronicity" to refer to the meaningful acausal relating of events, objects, and internal states of mind (commonly spoken of as "coincidence"), Jung had been observing these effects and discussing them for decades with Nobel laureate physicist Wolfgang Pauli and other leading thinkers, including Einstein (who was an occasional dinner guest). Through his discussions with them, he began to clarify a language for describing its operation. Where Einstein had found time and space to be relative to each other, Jung saw in synchronicity the relativity of matter to psyche. Just as the mystery of the effects of the observer on matter in quantum physics were demonstrating the relation of inner state to outer matter, so too was Jung observing, in the local, material occurrence of events related to inner states, this same emotionally laden interaction of material object to the consciousness of the human subject.

One of the earliest and most important personal encounters Jung had with synchronistic phenomena came near the end of a trip he and his wife, Emma, spent in Vienna at the home of Freud. Freud had come to view Jung as his heir-apparent and had specifically asked of him that he make of Freud's sexual theory "an unshakable bulwark," to which Jung replied "Against what?" "Against the black tide of mud," replied Freud, hesitating and then adding "of occultism."[32] During this visit in March of 1909,[33] which came at the midpoint of their relationship, Jung had felt himself experiencing physically the difficulty of withholding his criticism of Freud's overemphasis on sexuality as the root cause of all neuroses. Jung had hoped to interest Freud in a discussion of "spiritual events," but this is precisely what Freud had no interest in hearing about and Jung felt the sharp rebuke of his resistance. Jung felt Freud's attitude to be unscientific—"Shouldn't we at least look at evidence?" "For Jung, the 'occult' was a highly valued source of psychological data. . . . [For Freud it] was a menacing element seeking to bury once again all that he had worked so hard to uncover."[34] On the final evening of their time spent together on this trip, Jung would experience a synchronistic event that would point him in his own direction and toward a unitive view of psyche and matter.

> While Freud was going on this way, I had a curious sensation. It was as if my diaphragm were made of iron and were becoming red-hot—a glowing vault. And at that moment there was such a loud report in the bookcase, which stood right next to us, that we both started up in alarm, fear the thing was going to topple over on us. I said to Freud: "There, that is an example of a so-called catalytic exteriorization phenomenon." "Oh come," he exclaimed. "That is sheer bosh." "It is not," I replied. "You are mistaken, Herr Professor. And to prove my point I now predict that in a moment there will be another such loud report!" Sure enough, no sooner had I said the words than the same detonation went off in the bookcase. . . . Freud only stared aghast at me. I do not know what was in his mind, or what his look meant. In any case, this incident aroused his mistrust of me, and I had the feeling that I had done something against him. (Jung)[35]

This example not only demonstrates synchronicity as a material compensation for something unspoken in the psyche (and thus their inherent relatedness), but it also highlights the great difficulty that such experiences pose for those who are identified with worldviews that cannot abide them. Although he would later change his mind and conduct his own studies of psychic research, at this point Freud states his preconceived notions about such subjects plainly: "it strikes me as quite unlikely that such phenomena should exist."[36] Despite the difficulty of Freud's disapproval, Jung's openness to the ways in which the mind and matter interacted in his own life and the lives of his patients would continue to inform his study of the unconscious and his analytic practice. Although there are innumerable incidents of synchronicity in Jung's analytic work, one story provides a prime example of the phenomenon and its powerful relation to the psyche. For some time, Jung had been working with a young woman who, despite both their efforts, showed no progress. Her difficulty took the form of psychological one-sidedness, in favor of the masculine that Jung spoke of as an "*animus* complex." Where the male psyche is highly engaged by an inner female figure, the *anima,* the female psyche, similarly finds fascination in an inner male figure, the *animus.* Where a man can become lost in his inner Feminine in a variety of ways, so too can a woman become lost in her inner masculine, and Jung describes that in her case this left her domineering and always knowing better—an attitude that was advanced by the power of her bright mind and excellent education, all of which came together in a "highly polished Cartesian rationalism." Recognizing this imbalance, Jung sought to find a way to correct for it and connect her to her inner feeling function; he attempted to "sweeten her rationalism with a somewhat more human understanding [but failing, he hoped that] . . . something unexpected and irrational would turn up, something that would burst the intellectual retort into which she had sealed herself."

> I was sitting opposite her one day, with my back to the window. . . . She had had an impressive dream the night before, in which someone had given her a golden scarab—a costly piece of jewelry. While she was telling me this dream, I heard something behind me gently tapping on the window. I turned round and saw that it was a fairly large flying insect that was knocking against the window-pane from outside in the obvious effort to get into the dark room. . . . I opened the window immediately and caught the insect in the air as it flew in. It was a scarabaeid beetle, or common rose-chafer (*Cetonia aurata),* whose gold-green colour most nearly resembles that of a golden scarab. I handed the beetle to my patient with the words, "Here is your scarab." (Jung)[37]

With this experience, Jung writes, "her natural being could burst through the armor of her animus possession and the process of transformation could at last begin to move." Here the powerful effect of the breakdown of life's usual causality and its introduction of this meaningful synchronicity offered healing. It is important to note here that while there was a literal coupling of the dream event and the physically arrived scarab, the dream shows that the way was already being prepared for the patient to receive this new content. Although her conscious mind was trapped up with the animus and an exclusively rational worldview, the dream imagery demonstrated her unconscious preparedness for transformation. It was not the coincidence alone that struck the patient so profoundly; rather, it was *her need* for this specific kind of event, her need for its meaning that was present within her, that made her transformation possible. The dream struck the patient and the way had been readied for the fullness of its meaning to be received by her in the scarab synchronicity. Jung could not effect this change; he could only hold open his attention for the arrival of the irrational thing that "was needed" but "which was beyond my powers to produce."[38]

Synchronicity is by no means a modern phenomenon; it has been observed throughout our recorded history. In his groundbreaking opus *Cosmos and Psyche* (2006), Tarnas retells two wonderful, historic tales of synchronicity. Upon reaching the apex of his ascent of Mont Ventoux in April 1336—a climb that was rarely attempted in his time—Petrarch, one of the key figures of the Renaissance, looked down at the clouds, rivers, and valleys beneath him and the Alps and Mediterranean before him and opened at random his tiny pocket copy of St. Augustine's *Confessions* and read: "And men go abroad to admire the heights of mountains, the mighty billows the sea, the broad tide of rivers, the compass of the ocean, and the circuits of the stars, and pass themselves by. . . ."[39] Reading this moved him into a spiritual experience and "opened Petrarch's eyes to the complexity and mystery of the man-psyche relationship and moved him to write of the marvel of the soul," writes Hillman.[40] This epiphany, occurring through the synchronicity of a book opened at random, would lead Petrarch to become one of the leaders and most important figures of the Renaissance. But the wonder, complexity, and significance of this moment does not end there.

In the garden of Milan in 386, in a frenzy of spiritual crisis, he heard a child's voice from a nearby house mysteriously repeating the words "Tolle, lege" ("pick up and read"). Uncertain of their significance, he finally opened at random a copy of Saint Paul's epistles and there read words that spoke with uncanny precision to the nature of his lifelong conflict and its resolution, immediately after reading which "the light of certainty flooded my heart and all dark shadows of doubt fled away."[41]

For it was St. Augustine himself who had been led to the "revelation of his personal vocation"[42] through a very similar synchronicity twelve and a half centuries prior. Where Petrarch had read at random St. Augustine for the moment of truth that propelled forward the unfolding of his life, St. Augustine's spirit had found its peace in opening St. Paul in just the same way. Where "one revelation in the garden, pointed to Christianity and the Middle Ages, the other on the mountain, pointed to the Renaissance and modernity."[43] Petrarch wrote of his experience (in a letter to a friend): "I thought in silence of the lack of good counsel in us mortals, who neglect what is noblest in ourselves, scatter our energies in all directions, and waste ourselves in vain show, because we look about us for what is to be found only within."[44] Where these men had accepted these experiences and "waited for nothing more,"[45] they were transformed and fulfilled by them. What had happened to them became the source, not only for healing, but for psychological and spiritual rebirth.

If one takes an axiomatic stand in favor of causal determinism, one cannot find room for the possibility of meaningful coincidences. However, physical experiments have today demonstrated that effects can occur that are neither caused locally nor materially—it can be said that there are forms of causality in Nature that are not local or causal, and that our formerly held picture of the universe as a causally moved clock is a simplifying fantasy of the exclusively rational worldview.

In both the case of the observer effect and synchronicity, an event occurs that is related to a cause that is nonmaterial, nonlocal, and nonspatial (and sometimes nontemporal too). In a letter written near the end of his life, Jung advised that synchronicity and other paranormal events should be considered as "facts and not as supranormal perceptions. The uncertainty of the relation of time and space does not necessarily depend on a supranormality of our perceptions but rather on the relativity and only partial validity of time and space categories. . . . My emphasis lies on *reality of the event* . . . [and] is not 'miraculous' but merely extraordinary and unexpected and then only from our biased standpoint which takes causality as axiomatic."[46] We can understand such facts as demonstrating the relativity of causation (just as time and space are relative also) and conclude that what makes synchronicity possible is the very nature of the universe itself. It is for this reason that Jung spoke of synchronicity as stemming out of an acausal principle in Nature, in complement to causality, time, and space. Jung dubbed these occurrences as "acausal" because, while they often occur on the basis of an archetypal foundation and often with a strong affect being present, neither factor can be understood to provide cause. Rather than a cause-and-effect relation, we can instead see a preexistent field of potentiality that has become active due to the presence of a mix of factors, much like the collapse of the "wavicle" into either wave or particle form through our participation with it. We can understand the occurrence of synchronicity as pointing to an already present whole between matter and psyche that has been made active through our participation, but is not caused by that participation. This implies the necessity of a new worldview.

Where quantum physics found subject to be a nonmaterial causal agent in the objective world, depth psychology found objective contents in the mind's previously exclusive subjectivity. In discovering archetypal patterns in his patient's dreams, content that was were transpersonal, universal, and eternal, Jung found that the personal also has a connection to a greater objective whole built into our subjective inner world. If the universe can contain subjectivity on the outside, is not the inclusion of objectivity on the inside also a logical possibility, if not necessity?

> The inclusion of subjectivity in quantum observation was seen as complementary to Jung's assertion of the objective reality of the archetypes. . . . Matter and mind are both objective and subjective, complementary in their structure . . . reflective of each other.[47]

Jung observed that synchronicities occur most often where heightened affect or a highly charged emotional state is present: "Synchronistic phenomena occur for the most part in emotional situation; for instance, in cases of death, sickness, accident and so on. . . . We observe them relatively frequently at moments of heightened emotional activation, which need not however be conscious."[48] This same observation was made nearly 700 years ago by Albertus Magnus, a teacher of St. Thomas Aquinas:

> A certain power to alter things indwells in the human soul and subordinates the other things to her, particularly when she is swept into great excesses of love or hate or the like. . . . For a long time I did not believe it . . . [but] I found that the emotionality of the human soul is the chief cause of all these things. [49]

Belief in consciousness as an epiphenomenon of matter, that it is only an outgrowth of the physical brain, as well as belief in material realism cannot withstand the possibility of such effect. If the brain is an outgrowth of matter, how can it have an effect on material reality without material causation? It is not logically possible for consciousness to have an effect upon matter if it is an epiphenomenon of it—this possibility makes no sense in the material realist worldview and contradicts its central assumption. If consciousness can affect matter, the reductionist, billiard ball view of the world (including its view of ourselves) is made profoundly insufficient. The era of belief in the radical separation of objects and subjects is today beginning to come to an end.

> The assumption of locality that all interactions between material objects are mediated via local signals is crucial to the materialistic view that objects exist essentially independent and separate from one another. If, however, waves spread over vast distances and then instantly collapse when we take measurements, then the influence of our measurement is not traveling locally. Thus locality is ruled out. This is another fatal blow to material realism. (Goswami)[50]

What is amazing is that after millennia of digging at the edges of the natural world, of prodding and poking and constantly reinforcing our own assumptions in a reductionist direction, suddenly we noticed the edges getting blurry. Rather than finding more solidity in our picture of the world (the reassuring one in which everything could be understood by our rational minds), we start realizing that every question of "how" cannot be answered. Rather than an end to mystery, we have found its new beginning. It is very annoying to many folks that the clean, rational, scientific picture of the world is insufficient, and they may want to say, "Well, how does this work? How do synchronicity, the extended mind, nonlocality, and quantum entanglement all fit and work together?" Such a question seeks to restore our imagined control over Nature, which stems from the masculine inflation with which we are afflicted; it attempts to use a "how" question to overcome the truth of a new factual observation (the "what") and to avoid the more psychologically difficult questions of "Why?" and "What is the meaning here?" What can be said in answer to questions of "How does this all work?" is only that these new facts reopen us to questioning and force our re-estimation of the scope of our understanding about the nature of the universe, and, in parallel to the effect of our consideration of Crop Circles, we cannot necessarily know how these new discoveries work together, only that they point out that our imagined limitations of the world around us are too small, too neat, and too complete; and like Crop Circles they force us to re-inject a little mystery into our worldview and some humility into our ourselves. However, while these new avenues do not provide easy answers or solutions, they do point us in the direction of profoundly significant and meaningful new questions:

> In quantum physics—the new physics—we have found a theoretical framework that works; it explains myriad laboratory experiments and more. [It has] led to such tremendously useful technologies as transistors, lasers, and superconductors. Yet we cannot make sense of the mathematics of quantum physics without suggesting an interpretation of experimental results that many people can only look upon as paradoxical, even impossible. (Goswami)[51]

Whether in our innumerable observations of psyche's relation to matter in moments of synchronicity, or in clinical studies and anecdotal experiences of the effects of the extended mind, or in the discovery of the facts of the "spooky" behavior of matter in quantum mechanics, today the assumption of the truth of material realism, which lies at the foundation of most of our academic institutions, is profoundly challenged. Impeding us in such a humble acceptance of these new facts is our over-masculine consciousness. Our belief that consciousness is only ever a function of biological parts and not in any way related to anything outside of our brains or any greater whole makes it difficult to accept these new facts. Psychologically, this imbalance in favor of masculine thinking fosters our unconscious rejection of the very qualities of attendance and paradox that permit unfolding of these experiences—for where the archetypal masculine acts through juxtaposition and separation (qualities necessary to restrict our unconscious identification with these experiences), the archetypal Feminine acts through relating to and being with, and here it is the opening to our relation to the moment and its special "context and nuance," as Tarnas describes, that is necessary. As he describes further:

> The recognition of synchronicities requires subtle judgments made in circumstances usually pervaded by ambiguity and open to multiple interpretations. The suggestive patterning and often delicate precision of detail in such coincidences notoriously escape the net of objective assessments.[52]

While synchronicities are sometimes manifestly accessible to rational cognition because they reflect inner states and are acausally related to our genuine emotion, they are, by definition, in some way subjective—but they are not illusory or ephemeral. Instead, they speak to a view of Nature in which emotion plays a role in the behavior of objects, people, and events—and this is new. In this newness, in the inclusion of the subject in this new view's recognition of the psyche's relativity to matter, they arouse within us all of the fears that masculine consciousness has of the Feminine, our fear of the irrationality within ourselves and our emotions, and perhaps most of all they arouse our fear of our own moral and psychological capacity to transform, not just as an adjustment of the conscious mind, but in a whole-person reorientation. To understand that we are called upon to witness our own possibility of becoming more and of having more asked of us can be frightening and can draw from us a defensive reaction. We see this in the way that even secondhand discussion of the possibility of synchronicity or the extended mind can draw strong negative reactions from people *even before* they look at any evidence. This fear is, at least in part, rooted in a masculine culture's fear of the unconscious and the Feminine—having rejected the dark Feminine irrationality inside of us and assumed a masculine stance (which is often equivalent to the ego), we are threatened by this content, which has been neglected for so long. We fear being overwhelmed by the Feminine as Nature's unconscious ground within us or consumed by the instinctual beast inside. We are afraid we lack the ego strength to withstand the shattering of our identity, a necessary component of this kind of whole-person transformation. In such a fear is present the ego's desire to evade "the more complex and often painful emergence of the individual self that is in dialogue with the whole," which Tarnas describes. Petrarch, Augustine, and Jung's scarab dreamer were all, in their own ways, experiencing the pain of such a transformation before they reached the processes' climactic resolution (and the scarab beetle was taken by the ancients as a symbol of such transformation). Prior to their discovery, in the moment of synchronicity of meaning that was alive for them, and prior to finding the peace of their new self-emergence, they lived in the throes of flesh-and-blood discomfort, dissatisfaction, and the dying off of a previous way of understanding themselves and the world around them. Their struggle was in no way an abstract one, but rather was experienced empirically in their whole person and throughout their lives.

> The realization of "meaning" is therefore not a simple acquisition of information or of knowledge but rather a living experience that touches the heart just as it touches the mind. (von Franz)[53]

Accepting the possibility of such transformations requires a radical revision of our understanding of consciousness. Where Nature breathes in our emotion and breathes out meaning, fantasies, such as artificial intelligence being equivalent to psyche, are shown to be born out of our enchantment with our own genius. Where a computer can never truly *exceed* its own programming, human consciousness is *defined* by the ability to think outside the box, to be creative and authentically new.[54] As with another principle of quantum physics, a quantum leap or jump, in which "a quantum object ceases to exist here and simultaneously appears in existence over there; we cannot say it went through the intervening space," moments of human insight and creativity are not merely a placing together of parts piece by piece, but an arrival of something wholly new, a popping-up from one point to an entirely new one—just as we see in our leaps in which one belief system is left behind and another is radically burst into.[55] The possibility of the whole-person change, of psychological and spiritual transformation, is felt by those who experience it to be only possible because of the interrelationship of psyche and matter in Nature (or through the sacred in the world). The weight of these experiences was strong enough to change the lives of

Petrarch, St. Augustine, and Jung's scarab dreamer. In their special moment they each knew psyche's ground existed beyond the body and that we are not merely a collection of biological parts but exist in connection to a larger fabric. Synchronicity and these other new facts point to an understanding that has rightly given inspiration to spiritual belief. Yet, because we live in a culture that is enchanted with its own rational genius, we remain uncomfortable with and resistant to such a possibility.

Most of us today, in this era of rationality, have invested ourselves in ideas that provide a fantasy of control over both ourselves and the world around us. We have found ways in which to compartmentalize the chaos we feel into belief systems that provide a lens through which we can make sense of it all. These belief systems are as much lived, unconscious ways of responding to the world as they are consciously held ideas. Religion, skepticism, capitalism, consumerism, and apathy can all be routes by which we escape from anxiety through the presumed accuracy, completeness, and rationality of our own approach. Our masculine imbalance leads us to wanting to constrict and contain reality into a form that is easy for reason, the mind, and the ego to manage—we like to be able to say to ourselves "I am right," or "Our view is the right view (and they are wrong)." In this response we cut ourselves off from further participation with the Other, from the reality of the facts around us, and even from our own inner self. Blinding oneself to the complexities around one is the quickest fix, but in doing so we serve the ego and not the larger whole around us, not the Other person we meet nor the Other inside ourselves. Subtly, here we often even imagine we have got the sacred in a box too—we have figured It out, we *know* what is or is not going on in the heavens. One is just as likely to do this if one is religious as if one is not. Even the great Einstein was thought to have done this in his pronouncement of what was possible and impossible in physics, and was rebuked by Bohr to "stop telling God what to do." If we believe we have it all figured out, nothing is more threatening than to discover that the genie has escaped the bottle. In synchronicity, the mysteries of quantum physics, and the operation of the extended mind, we are shown a picture of the world that surpasses our rational formulas for it—we cannot know how it all fits together, only that our maps have become old. If we can look upon these facts not as a "black tide of occultism" but as occasions deserving of wonder, one moves out of the ego's inflated certainties and toward Creation. In these ways, we seem to be being led, as the Christian philosopher Paul Tillich questioned, toward wondering whether the broken split that we stand upon today might be bridged in our time:

> The question our century puts before us is: Is it possible to regain the lost dimension, the encounter with the Holy, the dimension which cuts through the world of subjectivity and objectivity and goes down to that which is not world but is the Mystery of the Ground of Being.[56]

If we can let go and "stop telling God what to do," we might see in front of us a wonder that calls on us to listen to it with a vocabulary from inside ourselves. In this day when our culture encourages us to forsake our interest in irrational mysteries, it would be easiest to leave these phenomena for others to consider and abdicate our power—we are quite certain that our own interest in them does not matter. They may then serve as a maze that we dare not enter, or in which we wander, seeking our own perfectly rational solution. However, these mysteries, and Crop Circles in particular by their form and arrival, speak to us in a dialect of symbols that call to our intuition; they appear before us with a scope and beauty that draws out feeling and our capacity to experience the numinous. But many of us struggle to come to terms with such a numinous reality. Torn between miles of factual scientific truth and a spiritual yearning that those facts seem to stand up against, we stand unreconciled, irresolute, and unable to summon the emotional conviction to run in another direction or jump across. At this time, we can hold onto the scientific method, but not to the promises of the absolute accuracy and completion made by material realism. Blending the Feminine back into our parched masculine consciousness does not mean a turn toward New Age slogans or old superstitions, but to opening ourselves to a more complex, less simplified, richer, and more heart-filled view of the world. While such a view is necessarily infused with mystery, including within it these new discoveries offers us the opportunity to join together the two loose strands of our psychological schism—belief in science and spirituality. Such a reunification is only possible if we are willing to consider our experience as it comes to us, without preconceived notions. Motivation for such an undertaking must ultimately come from that deepest wellspring within us—our desire to find meaning. This capacity, the one that defines us as human and is the strongest need in us, often leads to discovering something we did not know we were looking for. In seeking a meaningful understanding of our experience, we may find what Jung and his patient found in the scarab beetle at his window tapping, what Augustine was led to hear in a child's repetition of "Tolle, lege," and what Petrarch found in opening Augustine's *Confessions*. We may find that our struggle, our inability to draw conclusions, is a function of a difficulty that points to our preparedness for something greater—to an unimagined readiness to transform.

We have to come to know ourselves as a species and as individuals, as alone—ideas of any kind of consciousness beyond our brain are an illusion. Yet, in the strange, mysterious facts of synchronicity, quantum physics, and the extended mind, we find something that does not quite fit into the boxes we have placed around ourselves. Today we are being presented with the question of what it would mean to see ourselves within a larger picture of Nature. How might our view of ourselves (and our behavior) change if we were to realize that the world around is a flowing single garment of psyche and matter? While in these new discoveries there is a defeat for those masculine certainties that have comforted our egos on our journey here—and this means accepting too that material realism has been a myth we have clung to—at the same time these discoveries also provide a ground for truthful pursuit of facets of our highest aspirations.

For many of us, coming to see ourselves within such a view requires holding the tension of the masculine imbalance living on in us. However, as Barbara Hannah has pointed out, in the image of the mandala form we are provided with a "perfect expression of opposites being held together," and in the arrival of Crop Circles into this moment we are not only shown something suggesting the existence of an agency greater than ourselves living out there, we are also shown an image of tension held and provided with a symbol whose meaning we did not know we needed to find—one whose potency might help us to feel and understand ourselves to be living in connection with something greater. In this way, the phenomenon acts as an advocate for us in our movement toward this new stage, an agent aiding the solitary hero to make it back home to the sustaining mystery of the Feminine. For some of us, though, it points first to the hell that is the loss of our

ego's well-boxed rational ideas of what Creation is and should be, and toward our meeting authentically with what is. Yet, we should also remember that in choosing to reconcile ourselves to these new phenomena we are
not accepting belief in the fantastic—we are realizing that the myth of our
separation from something greater has been an inflating illusion. In this, I
am reminded of my friend who said to herself upon seeing pictures of Crop
Circles for the first time: "What a relief."

> Contrary to the strict division of the activity of the human spirit into separate de-
> partments—a division prevailing since the nineteenth century—I consider the
> ambition of overcoming opposites, including also a synthesis embracing both
> rational understanding and the mystical experience of unity, to be the mythos,
> spoken or unspoken, of our present day and age.[57]

EIGHT

GHOSTS OF ELECTRICITY

Suddenly my attention was drawn to a light that had appeared from nowhere. It was a few hundred yards away and directly in front of us. As soon as I'd registered its presence I alerted my colleagues. Amazed, we stood there gazing at this football-sized orange light as it hung motionless, about forty feet above the surrounding countryside. After an estimated five seconds the light began to slowly descend. Within another five seconds it had descended about ten feet and had faded into invisibility.

—J. RICHARDSON, 1992

Surprisingly, the account given above is from a member of an English formation hoaxing team out at night to create a fake.[1] It refers to the now-quite-regular sighting of translucent spheres of light, ten to twenty-four inches in diameter, moving with intelligence and intent in the area of or around a Crop Circle. Sightings of these Balls of Light (which I will capitalize here to respect and preserve their numinosity)—most often seen at night, but also witnessed in broad daylight—are so commonplace now that they have been caught on video by numerous English individuals as well as German, Dutch, and Japanese circle visitors.[2] Today nearly every Crop Circle researcher has had their own encounter with this phenomenon and one has spoken to nearly seventy eyewitnesses of it.[3] That so many people should have seen such a thing should be of little surprise in a region where the geography echoes a very long history of such encounters.

In the British Isles there is a widespread historic and geographic context within which to place sightings of Balls of Light. Place names display this association strongly, with the most obvious examples being Golden Ball Hill and Silbury Hill (where "Sil" is said to refer to the "people of light"). These sites are in the area of England where most of the world's Crop Circles are found, and there is an extensive history of folktales of such lights and their association with the sacred or "the Otherworld." Across this territory in the earliest part of the twentieth century, Walter Evans-Wentz traveled by foot collecting the people's tales of goings-on that could not be explained. He collected numerous stories of strange lights and spheres as well as of light-beings, pixies, or fairies coming at night to thrash or flatten a farmer's crop.[4] All across Northern Europe tales of the will-o'-the-wisp describe a spherical orb of light identical to what is now seen. In ancient mythology, light is associated with the afterlife, the divine, spirits, and spooks; in modern mythology it is associated with aliens and UFOs. What is the nature of these Balls of Light? How might they be related to the landscape that is named after them? Can we understand them as being alien or spiritual? Are these "shining visitors" "just another form of fairies"[5] as Shepard asked in the foreword to Evans-Wentz in 1966? Finally, how are they related to the agency, causation, and meaning of Crop Circles?

> Time and again strange lights are seen either coming down from the sky into fields where [crop circle] glyphs are subsequently found or spotted flitting around existing ones and the areas where they form. There is enough video evidence and eyewitness testimony to show conclusively that such lights exist, whatever they might be. (Thomas)[6]

It might be possible to dismiss both the geographic associations to Balls of Light and the modern eyewitness accounts of them, if it weren't for the presence today of so many different video recordings of this phenomenon. This footage is now widely available both online and in commercial documentaries. At least four different documentaries feature such footage: the earliest, *Undeniable Evidence* by Colin Andrews, features a Ball of Light being pursued by a British military helicopter;[7] *Contact,* a production of Dutch researchers, focuses on video footage of such lights; *Star Dreams,* a Canadian film, features Ball of Light footage from Sorensen and Fletcher; and *Crop*

Circles: Quest for Truth. Alexander's footage, as seen in *Crop Circles: Quest for Truth,* is particularly gripping because in it a farmer is seen driving his tractor underneath a moving Ball of Light. His vehicle stops just as it comes near to him—providing an interior self-reference to the phenomenon. The farmer later described to his family that when the light approached him the tractor's engine cut out. As we might expect, his family initially found his tale hard to believe—until they viewed the footage as well.[8]

Linda Moulton-Howe's *Mysterious Lights and Crop Circles* (2002) features frame-by-frame analysis of video footage taken by: Dutch researchers Kootje and de Bruyn in England on two different occasions—at night in 1993 and during the day in 1994; Dutch videographer Bert Janssen; Englishman John Fletcher; and others. Analysis of these videos shows similar-size translucent objects, seemingly "lit from inside," moving intelligently and seemingly with intent across the English countryside, in both day and night. Howe's book also features extensive presentation of photographic evidence of luminous Balls of Light in and around the formations. Such evidence is also available in other publications, but Howe's discussion with the photographers, along with the great variety of photographers whose pictures are included, makes her work particularly unique and valuable in this regard.

Farmers in the area of the greatest amount of Crop Circle activity regularly report seeing military jets and helicopters pursuing these lights. The Balls of Light blink in and out, disappearing when approached, apparently toying with their pursuers. Pringle (1999) includes one police officer's report of such a sighting, and Canadian archival documents include reference to such lights being seen by seen—on consecutive nights—in 1845.[9] This intelligent, intentional, and even whimsical interplay of the lights with humanity is one of its most common features—it is from this behavior that they have earned their centuries-old title of "Hermes lights," after the mischievous Greek-Roman messenger of the Gods.

I saw my first ball of light in 1986 while waiting for Dr. Terrence Meadan at a crop formation. The orb moved behind the only small cumulus cloud in that part of the sky and remained there. The moment I locked onto it with my eyes, it suddenly seemed to be aware of me and it began to move in a deliberate manner, almost as if it were toying with me. (Andrews)[10]

This account from Colin Andrews was, along with that of meteorologist Dr. Terrence Meaden,[11] among the first to be given publicly in relation to Crop Circles, and while the formations are often discovered the day after a nighttime sighting of Balls of Light, the lights themselves are not necessarily assumed to be producing the formations. Thomas (1998) writes of both a regional context for these lights and the breadth of possibilities that one might imagine for them within the mystery of the Crop Circle phenomenon:

> Since records began, folklore has spoken of "fairy folk" who would dance through fields and woods glowing brightly. Such luminosities have been seen without cerealogical connotations. . . . There are some who believe that the glowing points really are fairies, or Devas as more modernly described, nature spirits which tend to the planet's needs, giving off light as they go about their business. Some extra-terrestrial adherents are more militant about things and insist that any light in the sky must be a craft of some kind and that the balls of light are miniature "probes" sent down to create—or observe the creation of—formations.[12]

Thomas's description fits with the three general categories of causation described previously in Chapter Two. Sightings of these lights are thought of as related to UFOs, to spirits of some kind, and even to the consciousness of the Earth. There are descriptions and purposes for them that are related to technology and aliens, such as probes, or to spiritual concepts such as *devas* (which have an association to the Earth as well). I encourage you to view video footage of BOLs online or in a documentary DVD. Better still, if you are lucky enough to be able to afford it, head out into the English evening in search of them for yourself. It is also important in considering such sightings to remember that it only adds another piece to the larger body of fact, which is anchored in anatomical, cellular, biophysical, electromagnetic, and historical evidence. While Balls of Light may or may not be causally related to the phenomenon, these sightings do not exist in a vacuum.

One might expect that those viewing such objects would experience a degree of anxiety. To be walking or sitting in a field—especially at night—and to suddenly see something of this sort could understandably be frightening. Yet, in these encounters fear was often followed by something else. What began as tension and anxiety many times seems to ease into peace and astonishment. One witness said that after viewing it and its leaving, "he fell asleep immediately."[13] And while both devotees and hoaxers describe their sightings as amazing, the quality of their tone of voice, although varying, has a grounded, stable, and certain quality. In their words there is a down-to-earth quality—what they saw was simply what they saw.

Eyewitnesses of Crop Circle formations' construction, of which there are approximately fifty across the last century,[14] fall into four categories: causation by "wind" observed predominantly during daylight (the most common); causation by Balls of Light during both day and night (less common); causation by large, arching beams of light observed mostly at night (rare); and, in the very rarest cases, the beams of light are said to be connected to what is traditionally referred to as a UFO—but such observations are uncommon and, while not being ruled out, need to be weighted with regard to their infrequency. Witnesses of the daytime appearance of formations often describe a sort of airstream as multidirectionally causing the formations (blowing even the witnesses themselves around).[15]

> About 7:00 [a.m] the wind began to increase and swirl around. I paused and just happened to be looking across a shallow valley to the opposite side, the first crop ring appeared, then another and a third. After so many years I cannot be precise about the time interval between successive rings but think it was about four seconds, and the spacing between 1 and 2 was 100m, between 2 and 3, 80m, all in a straight line. I was working in the harvest fields on the Suffolk-Essex border, during a pause in our labours, I happened to be looking at a wheat field about 400m away and saw a crop circle form. "What's that?" I said to my companion, he replied "You don't want to worry about them boy, you often see them—the old men used to call them Devil twists". . . . . The farmer gave me a pitch fork and told me to try and raise the fallen corn. I stood in the circle but I faced a futile task, as fast as I raised the corn stalks they sprang back into place. (P. Germany)[16]

This account, which is typical of a daylight sighting of a Crop Circle's formation, comes from a gentleman who saw these formations appear in the English countryside in 1935 and 1937, the first sighting occurring when he was only ten years old. His detailed description fits precisely with the daytime descriptions given by many other modern eyewitnesses and includes reference to the distinguishing characteristic of modern formations—a central tuft of stalks being left untouched. Pringle provides numerous eye-witness accounts—the earliest of which are from 1947—including this account from a couple on a walk near Bryony Hill:

> Suddenly, in a matter of seconds, a band of mist rolled across and down from the top of the hill. It all happened so quickly. The wind pattern changed, the band of mist seemed to come between two trees at the end of the field; continuing on, it appeared to be pushing from two directions *and* surging forwards. At the centre of the mist the wind gathered force, sending strong waves as it went. The whirlwind seemed to appear at this point. It looked like a mist or light fog, and was shimmering.[17]

On May 17, 1990, Gary and Vivienne Tomlinson saw several small, perfectly formed circles in the field along the footpath beside them as they climbed up to Hydon's Ball at the top of Bryony Hill. As the wind picked up around them, a sound accompanied it—they were tingling all over and their hair stood on end. Simultaneously, they felt both sucked up and pushed down, then suddenly:

> All at once the wind scooped us off the path into the cornfield. We took a great buffeting. It was very frightening. Looking down we saw a circle being formed around us. It only took a couple of seconds. A spiral appeared anti-clockwise and grew outwards from the centre, about two meters in diameter.[18]

They go on to describe the whirlwind splitting into two, watching one zigzag as a shimmering mist across the corn and miniature whirlwinds gently laying down the standing corn and enlarging the circle. The second one gained the appearance of a "transparent glowing tube stretching endlessly into the sky."[19] Pringle's book contains diagrams of the formation that was left behind and also includes beautiful sketched interpretations of this episode completed by the couple's daughter. The couple suffered significant short-term health effects from their encounter, including lethargy and nausea, and her doctor diagnosed Vivienne as having suffered perforated eardrums. Pringle notes that more difficult, however, were the psychological effects of being unable to "to talk to anyone else who would understand what they have been through—for although other people have seen circles appear they have not actually experienced one forming around them—and consequently feel very isolated."[20]

The following account from Kathleen Skin of Cambridge is from a letter to the *Sunday Express* editor:

I witnessed a corn circle being formed in 1934. I was gazing over a field of corn waiting to be harvested when I heard a crackling like fire and saw a whirlwind in the centre of the field, spinning stalks, seeds and dust up into the air for about 100 feet or more. I found a perfect circle of flattened corn, the stalks interlaced and their ears lying on top of each other (some even pleated) on the periphery. The circle was hot to the touch. There was nothing to be seen in the sky—no wind, and no sound.[21]

Ms. Skin later described her experience:

Suddenly, Kathleen heard a crackling sound and saw there was a whirlwind in the centre of the field spinning out a circle in the corn and simultaneously spinning stalks and loose matter high into the air. She started running toward it, but within seconds the whirlwind had left its circle and was traversing the field. She reached the circle to find straw laying clockwise, interlaced, and pleated in the complex way now familiar to circles investigators. The air at the circle seemed hot, and she could feel the warmth of the corn through her shows, so she touched the lying wheat with her hand and was amazed at how hot the fallen crop was.[22]

Dr. G. T. Meaden, editor of the *Journal of Meteorology,* UK, also reports the following account from naturalist Sandy Reid, out studying foxes in Scotland, late August, 4:30 a.m., 1989:

Although it was still windless where he was, he saw that the corn over a circular area was being buffeted by a highly-localized movement of air. Indeed, this part of the field appeared to be waving about as if suffering from flowing air currents such as could be caused by a vortex vertically above it because the motion did not progress across the field but remained fixed to the same small area. This continued for some time, between half a minute and one minute. Then quite quickly the crop went flat over in a circular region, with a sharp perimeter, which he estimated had a diameter of 50 to 60 feet (15 to 18 metres). He remarked that it was extraordinary that the nearest part of the circle was no more than 15 metres distant, yet he felt no wind himself. He then entered the flattened circle noticing what he called "an unusual condition of the atmosphere." He could not express this in words but sensed a peculiar sensation in the air. Everything had gone quiet, the noise from the air and moving corn had ended, and the birds had stopped singing.[23]

Meaden also describes a large number of people viewing a formation appear near Starr Hill, in which no source is visible:

Dust sand, and other debris was lifted up in the air in a rotating motion and fell back on top of the flattened crop in the crop circle in a manner of seconds. . . . Suddenly the grass began to sway before our eyes and laid itself flat in a clockwise spiral, just like the opening of a lady's fan.[24]

In 1989, Meaden also published his own eyewitness account in the *Journal of Meteorology*. However, in his sighting, which occurred at night, the formation is apparently formed by the direct action of a Ball of Light. It occurred in Wilshire near Silbury Hill on the eve of June 28, 1989:

Soon after midnight the occupier of the roadside cottage by the path which leads to West Kennett Long Barrow noticed a large ball of light 400 metres distant in a wheatfield to the west. At the time of the observation he was walking from house to garage, and had a clear view to the illuminated part of the field through a gap in a hedge which borders his garden. He described the ball as orange in colour, adding that it was brighter around the periphery, and he guessed the diameter as 30–40 feet (say, 10–13 metres). When first seen, the ball was already low over the field and still descending. The witness watched the base of the ball "go flat" as it made contact with the crop and/or the ground. The ball then gave "a little bounce" and after a further "seven or eight seconds" disappeared in. Next morning on leaving the house the witness could see via the gap in the hedge a large circle at the place which corresponded to the position of the light source the previous night, and some smaller circles were evident as well. . . . A flyover the same day revealed a big circle with a ring around it plus smaller circles. [Meaden] arrived at the site on the morning of the 30th to find that a half dozen additional circles had joined the earlier ones. Five of these formed a quintuplet—a large central circle with four small evenly spaced outriders.[25]

A young Dutchman on whose property numerous formations have appeared, Robert van der Broeke, also witnessed the construction of Crop Circles through such a method. Although van der Broeke would go on to have a second somewhat different sighting (along with another eyewitness), in his first sighting he describes watching the creation of a formation occur directly through the activity of luminous Balls of Light—"spinning very rapidly through the crop"[26] and changing color as they went. Dr. E. Haselhoff[27] notes that such a variation in color from white-blue to orange-yellow could reflect the kind of changes in temperature necessary to create the noted anatomical changes to the plants, such as blown nodes, bent nodes, and dryness.

Haselhoff has observed a scientific correlation in the node length changes of plants in authentic formations that match precisely with the presence of a centrally present creative source. In a paper published in 2001 in the peer-reviewed scientific journal *Physiologia Plantarum*[28] he describes the presence of a central energy source that is detectable through circular, symmetrical changes in node length expansion. He also notes that data obtained from a handmade formation did not reveal the same characteristics.[29] His study concluded that:

> The node lengthening in several crop circles corresponds perfectly to the effect that would be created by a ball of light, heating up the crop during the creation of the crop circle. This is not the case for a man-made formation. The amount of node lengthening, and in particular its symmetry over the crop circles, lack any trivial explanation. Consequently, the study confirms the words of eyewitnesses, stating that they saw how crop circles were created by "balls of light."

> My paper does not attempt to explain where the balls of light come from, nor does it explain how the crop is flattened. It does, however, give a strong argument to take the "ball of light" phenomenon, as well as the words of eyewitnesses, very seriously, and I hope will stimulate further study.

> Finally, it should be mentioned that all these findings and conclusions have been published in "peer-reviewed" scientific journals. In order to guarantee a high level of reliability, such journals employ so-called "referees" (objective, anonymous experts), who accurately check each contributed paper for errors and

inconsistencies before it is published. Consequently, conclusions published in peer-reviewed scientific journals can not be simply dismissed as wild fantasy or pseuco-science. Therefore, it is fair to say that recent scientific findings have established considerable progress in understanding the crop circle phenomenon, although many questions still remain unanswered.

Further description of Haselhoff's investigation can be found in his excellent book *The Deepening Complexity of Crop Circles*. His investigation adds new depth to the scientific body of evidence. His work delineates a part of the process of construction of genuine formations and provides an additional factor by which to discern authentic formations from hoaxes. While such evidence does not prove that Balls of Light are responsible for the phenomenon's causation, production of the phenomena from a localized source is clearly part of what is pointed to by this evidence.

Scientific investigations of the phenomenon are wonderful because they provide anchors for our analytic understanding of this mystery, yet we must also note how reading such facts affects our thoughts about the nature of the phenomenon. Use of technical language—crucial as it may be to understanding Crop Circles—also tends to nudge us toward a more technological view of its agency, and in the process we often lose their numinous quality. Following such an in-depth analysis of the science behind the formations' construction—who or what do you now imagine is behind them? While the scientific terms that we use to label the effects of a formation's construction are crucial to our determination of the phenomenon's authenticity, in using such terms we run the risk of confusing our measurement for mastery. Being able to determine the exact scientific nature of the residual effects of the phenomenon's creation and being able to describe those effects in detail often causes us to begin to lose sight of the profoundly mysterious nature of what is being studied. Shepard describes this as our capacity for becoming "lost in the labyrinth created by [our] own practical skills."[30] As we proceed to consider further the nature of such effects it is important to remember the psychological hazards involved in the use of technical language. Speaking of their personal witnessing of Balls of Light, German authors Anderhub and Roth write:

Looking back, we can talk about all this very soberly. But taken in context it was a very startling experience that enlarged our worldview permanently. Even though it cannot be explained rationally, it set many things in motion for us. Reverence and amazement were indelibly and unforgettably impressed within us that night.[31]

In order to work toward (instead of away from) the potent psychological effect of the numinous quality of the phenomenon, one can use the same process of symbolic amplification that is applied to dream interpretation. Looking at Balls of Light through a mythological perspective reveals human culture's investment of light with natural mystery. Interwoven throughout our religious texts, ghost stories, and spiritual experiences is light's relationship to an "Otherworld"; sometimes even described as the source of spiritual life itself, it fills our picture of Heaven and of the soul's movement there. It is uniformly included in the description of the experience of near-death survivors. Throughout human mythology, beings of light, either sacred or profane, are distinguished in the nature of their otherworldliness by the quality of light that surrounds them. The idea that a saintly, glowing aura or halo is an indication of a figure's special spiritual quality is an idea found not only in Judeo-Christian tradition but throughout various world traditions. A special quality of light is said to give away the supernatural nature of something that is seen. As Aniela Jaffé describes:

> The frequent appearance of a light emanating from the ghosts, or of an illumination and transfiguration of its face or figure is an impressive detail. Sometimes only light is mentioned; again it may be a "glimmer" which announces the presence of the departed spirit without the latter becoming visible. In many other cases the great or even supernatural beauty of the ghosts is recorded as a kind of transfiguration.[32]

Jaffé observes that Jewish mysticism speaks of an eternal radiance that existed *even prior* to Yahweh's manifesting declaration of "Let there be light." *The Tibetan Book of the Dead* refers to the soul being met after death by a "dazzling brightness" called "the Bright Light," the "Primordial Light," or the "light of Dharma-Kaya," a term referring to perfect "enlightenment."

Jaffé also writes that this same Tibetan work refers to "the consciousness of those who have just died [as] 'radiant, void and inseparable from the Great Body of Radiance.' Indeed such a consciousness is the 'Immutable Light' it-self."[33] Freeman (2001) notes that in the folk tradition of the British Isles, light, the sacred, and the afterlife were tied together. In Celtic tradition, the Otherworld (which lies beneath and inside, rather than above and separate from the earth) is, in one form, called the "Land of Light," *Tír na Sorcha*; it is "a paradise whose landscape is suffused with an unearthly radiance." Many of the Neolithic sites around which Crop Circle formations appear, to which they are often geometrically referenced, and near to which Balls of Light are often witnessed are, in fact, ancient burial tombs,[34] and in some local traditions, Balls of Light were considered to be the spirits of the dead or the newly deceased. An account given by an elderly Welsh woman, and recorded by Evans-Wentz, makes this association direct:

> Here is the description of the death-candle as the aunt gave it in response to our request:—"The death-candle appears like a patch of bright light; and no matter how dark the room or place is, everything in it is as clear as day. The candle is not a flame, but a luminous mass, lightish blue in color, which dances as though borne by an invisible agency, and sometimes it rolls over and over. If you go up to the light it is nothing, for it is spirit.... I have seen more than one death-candle. I saw one death-candle right here in this room where we are sitting and talking." I was told by the nephew and niece of our present witness that this particular death-candle took an untrodden course from the house across the fields to the grave-yard; and then when the death of one of the family occurred soon afterwards, their aunt insisted that the corpse should be carried exactly the same route; so the road was abandoned and the funeral went through the ploughed fields.[35]

Other similar traditions echo the notion of the soul as a vehicle of light that can become related to a specific place. In European myth and folklore there is a linking of Balls of Light and ancient burial sites; such lights were "the souls of boundary-stone movers, usurers and swindlers become the Will-o'-the-Wisp in England, while the Italian *Fuochi Fatui* are said to be souls in Purgatory. The Swedish *Lygte* men are the soul's landmark movers as are the German *Lucthenmannekens*."[36] Freeman adds that in Irish tradition, posts or piles of rock were placed around the area in which a new home was to be built the night before construction was to begin, and "if they were found to be undisturbed in the morning, building could proceed, but if they were fallen or scattered, a new place must be found, for this was faery ground."[37] If this test was passed when the foundation stone was laid, an offering was placed beneath it. Here the spirit nature of certain places was given its due and while we might choose to think of such tales as fanciful, we would be wise to remember that universally throughout human folk tradition holy and unholy apparitions are noted to be bound to specific locations. This is particularly relevant to Crop Circles because formations often appear in reference to or nearby ancient tombs and sites of worship. Balls of Light are also frequently seen near such sites and often seem to arrive to demarcate tombs that have been recently or in recent years destroyed.

> In 1981 . . . two Corn Circles (a previously non-used number) appeared just off the A34 road, north of the village of Litchfield. The specific location was a corn/wheat field at a site known as "Seven Barrows." The construction of the A34 and a now disused railway line had erased five of the barrows. The two Corn Circles, each with diameters approximately 15 meters, were somewhat similar in size, shape, and location to the remaining round tombs. Thus, that year, it certainly seemed like the cosmic visitors were trying to draw attention to the megalithic tombs.[38]

The relationship between the appearance of Crop Circles and megalithic or Neolithic tombs can also be found in formations and sightings in North America. As noted in Chapter One, Canadian Crop Circle researcher Paul Anderson has observed the correlation between the frequent discovery of formations near Leeshore, Alberta, and that community's religious devotion. Formations on Vancouver Island, Canada, have also been found near a site of ancient habitation. Crop Circles in the United States have also been frequently found near ancient and modern religious sites in the United States, including near Serpent Mound in Ohio and at ancient sites in California, Oregon, and elsewhere.

To continue the symbolic amplification of light, regarding the soul as a vehicle of light that separates from the body at the moment of death is one of the most ancient and widespread beliefs of humankind. Jaffé (1979) notes that the history of this concept includes the Iranian mythological

Gayomart or "shining Yima," and the Egyptian concept of the *ba*—an inner being of light and immortal soul image. Hindu tradition also refers to the soul as leaving the body in such a form. As Barasch notes, "many traditions say that we commute to the invisible realm in an immaterial body capable of flight."[39] Jaffé also includes reference to the writings of Paracelus, a Swiss physician and philosopher, who described the inner being of light as the sidereal or star body. Connecting spiritual and extraterrestrial ideas, he wrote, "long after the dissolution of the elemental body in the earth . . . this sidereal body is gradually consumed by the stars."[40] Each of these speaks to a vision of the soul as existing and transiting to a heavenly afterworld following the body's death in a form of light. Author Marvin Barrett, describing his three such experiences—one as a child, one as a naval officer, and a third in his old age—says that in the first case, the image of the light faded but "not the memory of it." In the second, the light was blinding, "inexplicable, consuming, confirming the convictions that were falling into place"; it too receded, but remained present as a memory. Finally, in his third experience the light illuminated "a view of the ever-present future which has lasted me for nearly two decades."[41]

> And there was the light. The gentle intensity of that ambient light, and the green of the slope—the combination one sometimes finds on a clear morning where fertile fields grow close to the sea, in the Low Countries that my ancestors came from . . . it was the light and the peace accompanying it, that convinced me later, when I looked back, that I was indeed, for a brief interval, dead. Or if not completely dead, no longer conventionally alive; I was in another place, in another kind of time. (Barrett)[42]

Barrett's experience of an afterworld suffused with light was one and the same with his feeling of experiencing a different quality of time. And today we know scientifically that it is a fact of Nature that light and time *are indeed* related to one another (in $E=Mc^2$ the "c" refers to the speed of light). Human experiences of forms of timelessness are found in the writings of the mystics (many of which are also becoming available to us today for the first time in our history), in personal spiritual experiences, in meditative practices, and in folktales. The folktales of the English countryside are particularly full of stories in which the qualities of time and light are entwined:

In all fairy stories no mortal ever returns from fairyland a day older than on entering it, no matter how many years have elapsed. . . . People would be twenty years in fairyland and it wouldn't seem more than a night. (Evans-Wentz)[43]

Part of traditional fairy-lore is that one can be abducted into the Otherworld, becoming trapped there, losing time, or even disappearing permanently. An architect from Cornwall, England, recalled a story to Evans-Wentz, in which a pixie anoints a person's eyes, rendering them invisible, and "in the invisible condition thus induced, people were able to join the pixy revels, during which, according to the old tradition, time slipped away very, very rapidly, though people returned from the pixies no older than when they went with them."[44] (Evans-Wentz notes that the more common version of this theme is the anointing of a person's eyes by the fairy so that *it* itself is rendered visible to them.) He also includes an extensive selection of such tales that are widespread in Celtic and other mythologies.[45] Once again, attention to such stories is not without relevance to the larger inquiry at hand, for there is a particular abnormality that has been observed repeatedly in relation to Crop Circle formations: their unusual effects upon time.

Thomas, Pringle (1999), and many other researchers and visitors have observed such effects, most often experienced as time passing much faster than is later found to have been the case:

Many are the times when I have walked into crop circles to perform simple tasks requiring a few minutes, only to rendezvous with my colleagues nearby and find myself arriving hours late. Mine is not an isolated case, as many other researchers' furious wives will gladly tell you. (Thomas)[46]

Such experiences are reported by very many researchers and are thought to be related to other unusual physical effects reported in the formations. Particularly within new circles, visitors have reported subtle to gross feelings of loss of sense of direction (e.g., "Now where did I park?"), and unusual acute difficulty with linear thinking, which ceases immediately upon exiting the formation—such as entering a formation to take measurements only to forget why one has entered and only remembering after leaving again. I was particularly surprised to find myself having such an experience while investigating a Canadian formation in 2001. Although I am one of the most consistently well-oriented people that I know (and can always find the car), after a short period of time in a new, unexplored, and relatively small formation, alone on the Canadian prairie, I was startled to realize that I had utterly lost my bearings. Pringle has compiled the most extensive research into the experience of bodily effects among visitors to the formations, and her writing and website chronicle these findings.[47] Among the most unusual of these are people's experiences of time anomalies and losses.

Early researchers experiencing this phenomenon, along with other strange effects to electronic equipment, conducted experiments in the formations by placing clocks both inside and outside of them, with the second clock acting as a control. Thomas reports that results of such a test using calibrated digital clocks produced differences in the clocks on three consecutive nights, gaining thirty-one minutes the first night, twenty-one the second, and losing three minutes on the final night. Silva reports another shorter attempt at this experiment produced a difference of five minutes accumulating in only twenty minutes. Thomas and others claim that such time anomalies are evident in photos taken in and around the formations. In his book, Thomas includes a photograph taken by Holman in 1991 inside of a formation that appears to be double-exposed—but only in the center of the photo. The figures and background in the middle of the frame appear as they would in a double exposure: slightly delayed and clearly in two different positions. Yet at the frame's edge the objects are perfectly united, showing no distortion or separation of image at all. A second photo reverses the effect.

> It's as if time suddenly fractured in the localized area and leapt forward very marginally. . . . Both the photographs and the negatives were thoroughly checked over by laboratories at Kodak and by the president of the Photographic Society and both confirmed that this effect couldn't possibly result from double exposing or faulty processing. (Thomas)[48]

The presence of strong electromagnetic abnormalities in the area of formations was detailed in Chapter One. In both, various decades-old reports and current observations significant electromagnetic energies are found to be present in Crop Circles, particularly just after their creation. The

presence of powerful electromagnetic abnormalities in the area of a formation can be understood to potentially be responsible for the strange effects
upon time within the formations, due to our modern understanding of the
relativity of electromagnetism to time—yet how can descriptions of time
distortions be understood in relation to the larger context of the causation,
agency, and meaning of the Crop Circle phenomenon?

Biophysicist and Crop Circle researcher W. C. Levengood developed an
idea (initially suggested by Dr. Terrence Meaden) that postulated a connection between upper atmospheric ionic plasma vortices and the forces that
construct the formations. Some evidence for this kind of formation was
found in a 1993 Crop Circle that contained heavily coated, microscopic,
semi-molten meteoric iron particles. There was so much of this iron on the
crop that it could be held aloft with a magnet.[49] Since this time BLT Research has initiated regular soil testing of formations and "tiny 10–40 mi-
cron diameter spheres of unusually pure iron have been regularly found in
soils from crop circle sites."[50] The particles are sometimes found to be dis-
tributed in a pattern that follows Haselhoff's hypothesis of a central point
source (such as a BOL). Levengood put forth the ion plasma vortex theory
as a natural explanation, however natural causation fails to explain the directly displayed intention shown in Crop Circle timing and placement, as
well as the evolution of the designs themselves.[51]

The presence of atmospheric metal particles, Balls of Light, time distortions, and energy moving from the upper atmosphere to the surface of the
Earth suggests to many the possibility of extraterrestrial agency. As discussed in Chapter Two, the alien theory is among the most common responses of the modern age. Australian Crop Circles were first called "saucer
nests," and formations found and investigated in the 1970s in Canada were
attributed to aliens in Prairie newspapers. While Crop Circles were seen
as a natural phenomenon in the era of the Enlightenment and as the work
of the Devil in the time before that, in the modern era aliens are perhaps
the most popular agency thought to be behind the formations. In this scenario it is often assumed that beings come from outside of our earthly atmosphere and use superior technology (or other capabilities) to generate
the formations, the by-products of which might include the iron magnetite
particles and high electromagnetic radiation levels that are now observed.

Ascribing Crop Circles' agency to aliens makes sense in light of the scientific data that we have discovered about their construction process, however it might also, at least in part, reflect a culture that is enchanted by the wonders of technology.

When one speaks of "aliens" today there are a great many different pictures behind that one individual word. Some people use the term "alien" to refer to something similar to the alien creature of science fiction, including the common large-headed, dark-eyed Grays associated with Roswell and abductions; other people speak of aliens as being creatures that are not of the same dimension as we are, that live in some kind of alternative universe and are able to move into and out of ours; other folks think of aliens as spiritual, as beings perhaps closer to angels (and there is a school of belief that sees alien references in the Judeo-Christian Bible). Regardless of the truth or untruth of such various understandings and any alien relationship to Crop Circle formations, "alien" is a convenient way for a split-personality culture to hang a single banner across the phenomenon—we can ask to what degree does the word "alien" as a response to Crop Circles effect the relief of tension and keep us from really sitting with what we mean by that term. Do we say "alien" and forget it?

Faced with the enormous mathematical complexity and perfect construction of modern fractal Crop Circle formations, it is easy to say that aliens are the best, if not only, explanation for such work. However, can we picture too the vast history of the phenomenon, stretching back over centuries, and the slow evolution of those images across the years as being the handiwork of the same aliens? The term "alien" seems to have a measure of our modern, hyper-fast culture wrapped up in it. Can we think of them as also being that which has been patiently standing behind the origin of formations for centuries? Does use of the word "alien" bring us closer to the quality of the phenomenon's explosion in frequency in these decades, or does it remove us from it? Does such a labeling extend from a masculine-infused consciousness that sees a technological divinity above us somehow? Do we use the word "alien" to escape from the work of coming to consciousness with this mystery for ourselves? Do we make the phenomenon smaller or larger by claiming it is done by aliens?

The trouble here does not lie with whether or not aliens are constructing the formations, but rather with what we—*each of us*—means when we say "alien." It is possible that in using this word here one is grasping at a solution to this mystery that takes us out of all of the subtleties of its context. If this is the case, "alien" becomes a get-out-of-jail-free card that keeps us from having to think much further about Crop Circles; we just apply it and move on (imagining ourselves to be right, of course). If this is the case then we have extended our masculine illusion of mastery over Nature to the extraterrestrial as well. It would seem, in almost any case, that the word "alien" is simply a bottle cap placed upon a very big bottle of possibilities and ideas. Such an answer is both broad and vague. Do we even know what *we* mean when we use it? What do *you* mean by it? Are aliens spiritual beings? Are they other-dimensional? Are they patient? Are they capable of the kind of slow progress we see across the hundreds of years of Crop Circles' evolution? Can they be kind too or are they dark and threatening? Are they Grays? Do they come in a spaceship? Do the Star Children have a mother ship connection to make? When we say "alien" do we mean a creature or simply just "other intelligences in the galaxy"?

Removing the creature from the alien hypothesis and according the causation of the phenomenon to "other intelligences" makes the agent very similar to the other most popular one, that of causation by spiritual forces of some kind. Andrews expresses this common notion with the idea that the fundamental purpose of Crop Circles is to provide humanity with a "spiritual nudge." The channeler Isabelle Kingston speaks of the agency behind the phenomenon as the Watchers and believes that their goal is to raise "the consciousness of the Earth." The Watchers of Kingston's description provide a perfect example of a force that is interested in our receiving this "spiritual nudge." As described in Chapter Two, in this understanding of the agency behind the formation's construction, Crop Circles become the "vessels of communication between two worlds." Here Balls of Light can be seen as conscious entities with a spiritual nature that are active agents in affecting our growth in consciousness and perhaps in constructing the formations as well. The quality of light that they possess reflects all the associations our culture has made between spirituality and light. This theory also makes sense of the explicit depictions of religious symbols within Crop Circles. In addition, it may be possible to understand the spiritual agent hypothesis as being related to the human collective unconscious, as some authors have suggested:

> A major key to understanding current events is the collective unconscious: what humanity is unwittingly thinking, feeling, imagining and believing. . . . I work on the basis that life and events happen in order for us to *learn,* and are manifested by us—consciously or unconsciously—for the purpose of quickening our evolution. (Jenkins)[52]

Between Jenkins's understanding of the collective unconscious and Kingston's notion of the Watchers there is a great deal of overlap. In each, Crop Circles are understood to be vehicles for our growth, but in making the collective unconscious responsible for them, Jenkins folds humanity into this process more so than placing the agency into a group of beings "out there."

One could argue that since the very beginning of Crop Circle formations they have been drawing toward it those who are receptive to its mystery. From the carver of the infamous Mowing Devil woodcut of 1678, to Robert Plot's brilliant "wind" diagrams of the phenomenon in 1686, to Colin Andrews pulling over to the side of the road for the first time in 1983, the landmark moments in the history of Crop Circles come from individuals who had the best tools that their moment offered to respond to what they saw. United by their curiosity, each of these men did what they could to thread through to us a piece of the mystery as they discovered it. Were they meant to be the ones who received the phenomenon in their moment? Is the individual important or could anyone have passed on the phenomenon to us in the way that we have it today? As the agency behind the formations became more prolific in the 1980s, synchronicities occurring in relation to them increased too. Researchers dreamt about formations prior to finding them, wondered aloud about shapes only to discover them soon after (speak of the Mowing Devil?), and consciously meditated upon certain forms to find them realized shortly after. All of this leaves us to wonder whether the formations themselves draw together these synchronicities or their agent does—or are the synchronicities present somehow in the field between the formations, their agent, and ourselves?[53]

Andrews and Busty Taylor both tell the story of their flight over southern England during which Busty told Colin how much he would love to see a formation that incorporated all of the previous design motifs seen so far into one. The next day such a design was discovered—"precisely below where the aircraft had been when Busty had expressed his wish 24 hours earlier." Note here the presence of novelty—a felt interest in the new—present in Busty's request. As examined in the previous chapter, novelty is shown to be a factor in Rhine's experiments on card guessing and in the phenomenon that we call "beginner's luck." Where psyche and matter interact, affect—genuine feeling—plays a role. As Jung has pointed out, feeling is a quantitative measure of psychic energy—*where there is feeling there is psychic weight*—and that weight carries power in a world in which psyche and matter are entwined. Crop Circle–researcher interactions are most often found to occur where affect is heightened, just as is the case with synchronistic events in general. One finds that formations come when called—not by a researcher's ego—but by their genuine emotion, by their crying out for answers:

> I had laid in bed the night prior to this and had wished for a [Celtic Cross design] . . . to arrive at a location close to my home that would enable detailed investigation without the traveling across southern England that we were having to do at great cost . . . and to my utter amazement the following morning I received the phone call telling me of the pattern which I had visualized [having appeared] in this very field. I will never forget the emotion which came over me when I look down out of the aircraft and saw that Cross.[54]

Here Andrews sought a formation closer to his home so that the costs and time demands of traveling long distances could be reduced. He simply could not afford at this time to go the long distances that were being demanded of him by far-off formations. In his description there is a clearly present emotional authenticity, a genuinely felt need to be met by the phenomenon closer to home. Andrews explains how palpable his emotions were to him in this regard, especially in the days when he was one of the very few who were paying any attention at all to the phenomenon:

> I've often wondered why? Why me? Why did I find myself being one of only three people in the world, ten years ago, focusing my attention on these markings.

Other people were driving by, others weren't even giving these beautiful patterns a second glance. I had not only glanced, I had thoroughly looked, investigated, photographed and thought to the degree that I couldn't sleep for nights on end. Thoughts of possibilities and all the time, all the time, this pain—it was on the threshold of pain—this feeling in my stomach that I was looking at something of such magnitude. Why were other people passing it by?[55]

Another Crop Circle researcher undergoing an emotional conflict between his upbringing and new realities of the interactions of matter and mind, present today as a part of the phenomenon, had the following experience:

One of the strangest experiences I had so far was a very vivid dream I had one night in August of 2000, of looking down on a pattern in a field which appeared to have two circles in it, one a bit larger than the other. The whole "scene" was in vivid color, orange-red, like looking through an infrared filter or something similar. Inside each circle was what I could only describe as bright glowing "twisting bands of energy," like coiling snakes. I had many crop circle dreams before, even apparent premonitions in a couple instances, but nothing so vivid as this. . . . the next day I received a message from Nancy Talbott of a new formation at Moosomin, Saskatchewan, reported to her by a contact of hers. When our CCCRN Saskatchewan coordinator Dennis Eklund, in Saskatoon, went to the site shortly after, he was surprised to find that many of the plant stalks inside the formation, a 250 foot classic dumbbell with two attached circles in wheat, were deformed with "somatic developmental abnormalities"; the stems beneath the seed heads were twisted around, almost "knotted." Other seed heads themselves were bent at about a 90 degree angle. If a coincidence, a most unusual one. . . . I initially interpreted this as a basic premonition of sorts, although it is not known precisely when the formation itself was actually made (the condition on the ground did indicate quite recently however). Was this an indication that the phenomenon can and does interact with us, or that we are "tapping into it" somehow or both? The dream felt like a piece of the puzzle being viewed or presented for unknown reasons.[56]

Numerous Crop Circle researchers describe incredible experiences of such interactions with the phenomenon. Howe (2000) provides further accounts of this kind, as well as interactions between people, Balls of Light, and later discovered formations. As these people are experiencing for themselves, all of this leaves us wondering not so much whether such sightings of Balls of Light are real or not—clearly they saw something, something which has also been seen by country folk for centuries (so much so that they are literally part of the landscape), which we can now see ourselves on video—but rather how can we make sense of all this? How can we put together Balls of Light with old understandings and geographic contexts pointing to a relation to and concern for the dead and ancient tombs and new synchronicities that clearly demonstrate an interest in the living? Is there something that we are missing in our trampling willy-nilly over ancient burial tombs and sacred sites?

Greek culture spoke of their god Hermes as the soul's escort to the underworld of the dead, and in their mythology his role was not only one of guide but also of the soul's agent provocateur, the one through whom necessary psychological transformation is drawn forth. As mentioned previously, Balls of Light were called "Hermes lights" for centuries by English country folk because they understood Hermes as a boundary figure, the one who moves between worlds—messenger of the Gods. Hermes represents the threshold between normal consciousness and "the strange":

> Among the Hellenes, as the related word herma ("a boundary stone, crossing point") would suggest, Hermes embodied the spirit of crossing-over: He was seen to be manifest in any kind of interchange, transfer, transgressions, transcendence, transition, transit or traversal, all of which involve some form of crossing in some sense.

> In the myth, Hermes is born of Maia, a Titan Goddess, and Zeus, an Olympian god. He brings together the primordial, primitive nature of the Titans, who preceded the Olympians, and the Olympians, who represent more a sense of a higher, spirit nature. Thus from his inception Hermes has to do with between-ness, the bringing together of different realms. (Miller)[57]

Giving consideration to the origin and meaning of these events is itself a hermetic act, for it is from his name that we have the term "hermeneutics" for "the art of interpreting hidden meaning." In Crop Circles and BOLs, as with encounters with Hermes, the psyche is forced into a discipline of interiorizing. In myth, Hermes is known as a "psychopomp," an image carrying us more deeply into reflection upon ourselves.

> In the context of Greek consciousness, he stood as intermediate region neither divine nor human but as the principle of intercourse between them—Kerenyi points out that his link with Hermes emphasizes his role as communicator and psychopomp. As psychopomp he connects the personal to something beyond and brings the beyond into personal experience. He brings us a glimpse of the beauty and the horror of the Gods. (Miller)[58]

In our giving consideration to these phenomena we are flung into glimpses of the "beauty and the horror of the Gods." We are led into the frightening possibilities of alien causation—where we are deceived, toyed with, and ultimately made victim, as is fictionalized in M. Night Shyamalan's *Signs*. We are also led to grand, perhaps grandiose ideas about our involvement with Spirit: that in some way we may be moving closer to it, or that higher intelligences are coming to prevent us from the destruction that we are bringing upon ourselves and the planet. When we labeled them as "Devil's Twists" or "Witches' Rings," we were seeing them as something dark and wholly Other, from an unholy place. Locating their origin in a different realm may point to a projection, but not to a denial of their power; only in the modern era is the powerful Other nature of Crop Circles intellectualized and made into something tame. Scientific theories were our first step toward this, but in the modern era's dismissal of the entire phenomenon as a hoax it is made complete—utterly unthreatening and safe for consumption. And then again today we have become open to viewing them as something wilder: UFOs or spirits, a warning from Nature itself; once again its "different realm" is seen by us as *real* and *of the world*—and perhaps in this response it has escaped the cage of tidy rationalization and become free to roam our consciousness somewhat. And if our reception of these phenomena has some measure of wildness in it, then we have become capable of seeing—marvelously and frighteningly—something *new* before us.

To reflect upon our own theories and responses to Crop Circles is to allow ourselves to be placed into a triangulation between the phenomenon's facts and our own unconscious. In the movie *Signs,* as the news media is publicizing for the first time video footage of alien spacecraft all around the world, Joaquin Phoenix's character, wearing his pointy tinfoil helmet to protect him, exclaims: "Well, the nerds were right!" Aside from what may be *actually* making Crop Circles, in our involvement with them at this time we are led into confrontation with what *we believe* and *do not believe*, what *we feel* to be true and what *we project* out onto "the nerds." We may have a great capacity for imagining their spiritual agent and meaning but beneath this find an inexplicable need to deny their physical reality. We may cling to hoaxing as an explanation for the phenomenon, to deny its numinous reality (and the possibility of any numinous realities at all), and beneath this find fears that play out throughout our day-to-day lives. We may discover at times that our personal need to be right, to be valued for the correctness of our opinions, our attachment to our assertions about the character and purpose of the phenomenon, is a kind of grandiosity that comes as a counterbalance to denial of the phenomenon altogether (either within ourselves or by those around us). These psychological triangulations, particularly those between denial and grandiosity, blend down through us over time, giving room in the psyche to the possibility that we may be wrong in our denial first and in our theories second. It seems that many of us who have spent time studying and thinking about Crop Circles have gone through this cycle repeatedly, and no matter how far we go or have gone this process remains incomplete; just as the wholeness of our lives does not reach an end, nor does our unconsciousness ever become exhausted. Even if we should one day have an explicit and clear agency unveil itself, our integration of its meaning would remain incomplete. Do we imagine solving the mystery of Crop Circles' agency to be the goal of our inquiry? Could we, if necessary, separate the phenomenon's agent from its meaning for us? Often in our personal lives we experience things as meaningful for us. In these encounters, we do not equate the agent of the meaningful interaction with its meaning for us. If one gets in a car accident, one does not get out of the car and ask the other driver what the meaning of this accident is for one's life. Yet in theories about Crop Circles it seems often that the agent that is assumed to be behind them is made synonymous with their meaning for us. Realizing that the cigar in our dream was a Cuban doesn't take away the cigar's symbolic meaning to our life. We can see the need to equate agency with meaning in those individuals who insist that every formation is an authentic one. What are they afraid of? What would it mean for a formation to be a hoax? One might imagine that there is a measure of that person's sense of identity that is wrapped in the phenomenon, but beyond this it seems that there is a kind of kid-gloves approach taken to the agent behind the phenomenon, as if one single hoaxed formation could threaten the reality of what is making the genuine ones. As with alien theories, when we claim the phenomenon's agency to be a spiritual one, are we making it bigger or, in fact, smaller and easier for us? We would be wise to again follow Hermes here and remember to separate the message from the messenger. There is wisdom and stable psychological refuge too in remembering that Crop Circles have been appearing for centuries—transcending through that time the various theories that we have had for them. Mess-making facts are introduced into our interior world by the phenomenon's being real (or for others by the existence of hoaxes). Crop Circles lead us into our own most intimate and private questions about our spiritual beliefs and psychological natures (a form of inquiry that our over-masculine culture would prefer to sidestep with more easily consumed prepackaged systems of belief). The phenomenon, in fact, seems precisely suited to return us toward such questions.

It is not just the "out there" that is pointed to in the fact of Crop Circles' existence, in our experience of a synchronicity or in the mysteries of the extended mind, it is the "in here" of ourselves that is pointed to as well—we are led by the strange qualities of its appearance in relation to our interest to it, or perhaps forced even by these facts to question the way in which we view ourselves. Jaffé provides an example of Jung's interpreting of a patient's dream in which objects similar to Balls of Light are seen, which may be of service in our movement toward answering such questions:

One of his women patients dreamt that many shining spheres were hanging in the curtains of her room. . . . The patient always slept with a glass of water on the bedside table. One morning, just as she woke up, there was a loud sound and the upper part of the glass broke off in the shape of a perfect circle or ring. The edge was completely smooth. Jung interpreted the spheres of light in the dream as symbols of split-off fragments of psychic energy. This fragmentation was the result of a transference which had not become conscious. The dissociated quanta of energy seek to be reintegrated in the personality in order to restore the lost or "splintered" wholeness. But so long as they remain in a state of projection or "exteriorization," they can produce all kinds of parapsychological phenomena, for instance rappings inside walls and furniture, or psychokinetic movements of objects.

The most interesting point here is the symbolic analogy of the phenomenon: in the patient's analysis the restoration of the personality as a wholeness was at issue, and both the luminous spheres and the ring of glass can be regarded as circular symbols of wholeness. Further, it is as if, in the dream as well as in the parapsychological event, a meaningful symbolic image was presented. And this is indeed a healing factor, since the symbol is a means of transformation of psychic energies. To Jung's patient, the phenomenon appeared as if to prepare a transformation, by helping her to become conscious of the detached contents of her psychic wholeness.[59]

It is the constant desire of the rational mind to know with certainty what such things are—are they this or that? Spirits, aliens? While we cannot answer that question, Jung points us instead toward an inner direction in which we *can* find a meaningful context for them. He notes that in this particular dream Balls of Light represent psychic energy of the dreamer from which she is unconsciously separated. One can find a similar approach to such content through a mythic lens of fairies and their relationship to light—and this is an association that should not be dismissed lightly in relation to Crop Circles. For the Scots, beings of light are referred to as the *sidh,* or faeries. "In Scottish tradition this brilliant light illumines the *sithein* [pronounced sheen], or faery hills." Cirlot sees in fairies light-beings as a representation of psychic energy that is withheld, split off from consciousness, libido that is frustrated, just as Jung sees Balls of Light as "dissociated quanta of energy":

Fairies probably symbolize the supra-normal powers of the human soul, at least in the forms in which they appear in esoteric works. Their nature is contradictory: they fulfill humble tasks, yet possess extraordinary powers. They bestow gifts upon the newly born; they can cause people, palaces and wonderful things to appear out of thin air; they dispense riches (a symbol of wisdom). Their powers, however, are not simply magical, but are rather the sudden revelation of latent possibilities. Because of this it has been possible to link the legendary "forgotten fairy" with the Freudian frustrated act.[60]

While previous people who met with this phenomenon on the English plain were able to meet it without denial, today we are offered the possibility of going one step further—we can look at it with an objectivity of psyche that allows us to drop many of our primitive projections. We stand in a position where we cannot ascertain whether our cultural encounter with Balls of Light—which is now happening concretely and consciously—is a meeting with spirit, alien, or something else, but we can engage this development psychologically and ask what it is of ourselves that might be lost and seeking integration. What is it in our culture that is being unconsciously withheld in us? It is a function of our unique moment that today we are encountering, collectively and consciously, the participation of the fantastic with the mundane. We can watch video recordings of Balls of Light (or search them out for ourselves in the English countryside), we can look at the scientific evidence for the anomalous changes to the affected crop and soil in Crop Circle formations, and we can listen to the many individuals who testify of their own experiences of formations occurring in relation to their own authentic interest and wanting to know. What would, in previous times, have been declared impossible, "sheer bosh," or subtly dismissed as fantasy is today standing before us as concrete fact. From an archetypal perspective, we can see this same transition in the discovery of the psyche's relativity to matter in quantum physics, the scientific study and popular interest in the effects of the extended mind, and in our observations of synchronicity. We can also see this same story in our era's discovery and access to multi-millennia-old, lost mystical texts and religious artifacts from around the world. Today we can *know* something of these mysteries for ourselves, rather than be left simply to believe or not. We are capable of factually understanding a series of tremendous and new possibilities that are revealing themselves before us at this time. Although Crop Circles are not historically new, psychologically they are new—we are encountering them on a large scale and coming to recognize something consciously that we have not met previously in our history—we have never had quite this "dream" before. The meaning of this phenomenon, like the meaning of our dreams, can be true on many different levels; could Crop Circles be accurately understood as bringing information about the planet, the soul, and aliens? Certainly. The illusion that the answer can come only in linear pictures and singular solutions is part of what is being left behind in this transition. Here we are meeting Nature in an aspect that can be spoken of as archetypally Feminine and as capable of being multivalent: symbolically and literally meaningful at the same time. Yet this multivalency does not exclude the possibility of our getting it wrong, even if only for ourselves. We can become, and remain, stuck in our complexes in response to this phenomenon. In particular, we may choose to stop at, or focus upon, agency as the sole answer to the mystery. Clearly there is something greater here for us if we can allow ourselves to deepen into a more involved inquiry. What may be our greatest difficulty in drawing meaning from these events? Do we get stuck on believing or not believing these events? Are we capable of allowing their factual occurrence to affect us emotionally? Are we able to allow the story that we tell ourselves about who are to become changed by these new events, or do we go on barely noticing and unaffected? Jung believed that our full and conscious participation in this regard requires

the art of leaving the story just as it is, with all the trimmings that are so offensive to the rationalist. In this way the twilight atmosphere that is so essential to the story is preserved. An integral component of any nocturnal, numinous experience is the dimming of consciousness, the feeling that one is in the grip of something greater than oneself, the impossibility of exercising criticism, and the paralysis of the will. Under the impact of the experience reason evaporates and another power spontaneously takes control—a most singular feeling which one willy-nilly hoards up as a secret treasure no matter how much one's reason may protest. That, indeed, is the uncomprehended purpose of the experience—to make us feel the overpowering presence of a mystery. (Jung in Jaffé)[61]

NINE

NEVER MIND

> Like any idea, the idea of meaning has an opposite, which is that of non-sense, an absurd chaos.
>
> —MARIE-LOUISE VON FRANZ

Crop Circles are seen by some to be foreshadowing our planetary end, a "fair warning" given before our environmental self-destruction, before a Christian apocalypse. Most of those researchers, and others involved closely with the phenomenon, express some measure of this sentiment. As farmer Polly Carson, on whose property many of the first evolutions of form in the phenomenon have appeared, has said, "It is not as if these formations are saying to us 'Way to go human race!'"[1] Many different indigenous elders have said that they see an expression of the earth's destruction and suffering in their symbols; they are saying to us, "Mother Earth is crying."[2] Are Crop Circles an expression of the planet's own desperation, a warning of our approaching a self-made environmental collapse or biblical end-time?

We are right to recognize the apocalyptic in our moment—environmentally, economically, and internationally there are crises of tremendous difficulty and complexity right in front of our eyes. We face global warming, massive species extinction and other environmental dangers, terrorism, new diseases, and a host of economic problems, any one of which may be able to throw us into a frightening and potentially deadly time of chaos. Jung too felt that we were headed toward such a time of crisis and that it would be only our capacity to become more consciously aware of ourselves that would prevent it. He warned that "the world hangs by a thin thread, and that thread is the psyche of man."[3]

Confrontation with the possibility of apocalypse, especially one that is self-inflicted, should lead us into self-examination, into a consideration of our shadow. In ecological self-destruction, we might see our own narcissism, our need to let the planet go to hell, if stopping it would mean having to sacrifice any of our financial prosperity (death before disappointment). Our voracious need for consumer goods might speak to us, as it does for Woodman, of our loss of the archetypal Feminine inside us—an unconscious materialist compulsion outwardly expressing our longing for lived, creative spiritual participation with Mater (Mother), the archetypal Feminine. Some religious ideas of apocalypse do emphasize the importance of self-reflection, but most of these define the answer before asking the question (our sin or lack of adherence to their belief system requires a cleansing end-time). Despite our increasing awareness of the environmental dangers that we face, there is no call to look squarely at *how we might have gotten here,* and little call to take the radical steps that might ensure our own survival. Our response to the fact that we may be very near to ruining our own planet is a lukewarm "Well, we should probably do something." Why? Why is our response to the possibility of our extinction, like our response to Crop Circles, one of so little urgency?

One of the chief features of the movement into modern consciousness has been the gradual redirection of our psychic energy away from outer objects (Nature, God-images, etc.) into investment in ourselves. The awe and participation mystique that characterized our primitive ancestors' engagement with the world around them are today no more, and we sit unattached and anxious at the center of our own worldview:

> [Our] autonomy has been purchased at a staggering price: the disenchantment of the universe. The high cost has been a gradual voiding of all intelligence, all soul, all spirit, all meaning, all purpose from the entire world—now exclusively relocated in the human self, through what from this point of view can be seen as an extraordinary act of cosmic hubris.[4]

We have to come to see ourselves as alone in a clockwork universe. As a symptom of our masculine imbalance, our view of the world as clock shows our confusion of measurement with mastery—in measuring it we imagine somehow that we have actually created it. The clockwork illusion reflects our self-investment. We have purged out any mystery from our view of the world and today the ego sits enshrined in us unlike in any other previous human culture. We are lost in our own self-reflection, have made an idol of our own view, and believe that there are no other powers in the world (in parallel to the ego's view that there are no other forces in the psyche). We suffer from a "primitive grandiosity [that] does not want to acknowledge and respect any other center."[5] Our view of the outer world as cold, dead, and machine-like reflects the ego's relationship to the objective basis of the unconscious, from which it is distanced. The ego has usurped the power of that natural foundation within us for itself, and it is for this reason that Jungian analyst and professor at Chicago Theological Seminary Robert L. Moore understands us to have lost our ability to find the center, the axis mundi, the rejuvenating precinct where contact between the ego and the transpersonal takes place: "when you become truly modern psychologically and culturally, you cannot find the center anymore . . . it is [rendered] invisible."[6] Self-invested, we are blind to the larger forces inside of us and thus imagine none to exist outside of us either.

The objective basis of the psyche, the instincts and archetypes within us, are transpersonal and timeless. They are tremendously dynamic and powerful qualities, more powerful than the individual ego. Traditionally in human cultures, initiatory rituals were used to draw adolescents into a proper psychological relationship to these forces in us. Plato said of the initiatory rituals he underwent that they led "us back to the principles from which we descended . . . [to] a perfect enjoyment of intellectual [spiritual] good."[7] Initiation led one to have a proper relationship to the objective contents of the psyche, a proper relationship between the personal and the timeless, transpersonal ground inside of us. In initiatory rites personal grandiosity is brought into check against a larger whole. Spiritually one is led to the appreciation of the creature for the Creator, and psychologically the ego is brought into relation to the Self and the dynamic unconscious foundation of the psyche. However, as Saul has pointed out, our heroic yet tragic freedom from the primal paradisiacal unity has left us somehow angry at it. Our devotion "to absolute truths and linear progress" is fed by our "determination to deny mortality and timelessness."[8] We want to deny the existence of the psyche's objective basis and our need for contact with it. Woodman sees this played out in our addiction to perfection, our attempt to make the "temporal as perfect as the eternal that it rejects." She says further, "so long as conscious and unconscious are enemies, the ego experiences itself in constant danger of death. . . . That confrontation demands the surrender of the rigid, self-deceptive 'I.'" Where the ego cannot stand letting go of its inflation and "is hostile, then it experiences itself as the victim and sets itself up for self-murder."[9] When inflated ego is faced with the real power of the psyche's objective basis, it must either begin to transform or take on an "if I can't have it no one will" stance, seeing there an enemy—its own hostility reflected back to it. Where the ego is increasingly inflated and disconnected from the psyche's objective and timeless basis, the temptation becomes greater and greater to create a circumstance that will confirm "once and for all" the perfection of the ego's chosen worldview in an acted-out apocalypse. Ortiz Hill sees our "perverse literalization" of the ego's relationship to the Self as the root of our drive toward apocalypse. An acted-out apocalypse offers our towering unconscious grandiosity the opportunity to express itself in a perverse, unbounded, and malignant statement of its power. Moore points out that the enterprises of "unconscious gods have no limits in their fantasies. This is the satanic manifestation of the God image." (p. 28)

Seeing ourselves as having all the answers, as being right always and identifying ourselves with light psychologically, leaves the shadow in us unbound. Here, we risk falling prey to what Ulanov calls the "Devil's trick": "the Devil always tempts us in large terms . . . to make us let go of the good to fight evil, and even worse, to lead us to let go of an evil we could do something about to work for an abstract and idealized good that can never be realized."[10] As she describes it, the Devil's trick is to frighten "us with large abstract evils so that we let go of the little devils that live in us. And so we are seduced to forget our petty evils which are our specific and concrete ego tasks to meet. We see ourselves not only participating in the great production 'Evil and the Universe,' but starring in it!"[11] We live in a moment when this high-stakes showdown notion has no shortage of willing participants—each one certain that he or she is not only right but also righteous. So being, we are led to take any measure that will prove that it is true, that we alone exist in relation to the divine. Apocalyptic possibilities require this level of infantile grandiosity. This dynamic makes it seem right to threaten the entire planet with annihilation rather than admit to a truth existing outside the scope of one's belief. Our insistence upon having our own way "come hell or high water" becomes the road to our actual self-destruction.

In the past, human cultures were able to release some of their anxiety by redirecting their grandiosity as a group (with its totems, ideals, and God-images), and through the projection of our negative feelings onto other groups. "When the grandiosity is displaced onto a group, the ego can experience less anxiety and feel righteous and humble while sanctifying horrific, arrogant and hegemonic behaviors. . . . We turn our arrogant inflation over to social, religious, ideological, institutional or national structures, while our deep intuitions about the presence of an enemy [inside ourselves] cause us to demonize and dehumanize those other people outside our group."[12] This dynamic leads us into insatiable campaigns for safety that instead increase our exposure to danger. We saw this in a Cold War arms buildup that left us able to destroy the planet many times over, and in our endless drive for economic growth despite our potential self-destruction from it. As Grof points out, "We want to be so safe that we have actually created an unsafe world"[13];or as Jung described, it is "not nature, but the 'genius of mankind,' has knotted the hangman's noose with which it can execute itself at any moment."[14] The horror and insecurity of the circumstances of our moment remind us daily in new ways that absolute security is never possible—as people and as nations, we are always going to be vulnerable.

Where in the past we could simply say "We are right and they are wrong," today the nature of our global interconnectedness ensures that each culture is led into interaction, and thereby into questioning assumptions and thus into greater anxiety. "The increasing difficulty now is that everyone's grandiosity is bumping up against everyone else's grandiosity" (Moore, p. 148). The tremendous anxiety of the modern era leads to a compulsive desire to find a vehicle in which to place our grandiosity—to find a view that we can say with certainty is right. "If I don't know who I am, I want some hard facts or some fundamentalism real fast, to take away the anxiety of all the un-knowing" (Meade).[15] Whether it is a fundamentalist religion or a drive for the hard facts of a reductionist scientific view, the motive is the same, to keep us from having to actually face our grandiose self-investment and shadow. In this way, we are led down the road to hell by paving it in front of us with our own rational but abstract, good intentions. Our culture does not like to think about any shadow existing in our archetypal masculine certitudes that keep our world looking tidy and chaos-free, but it is through such denial that we coast toward apocalypse. The culture clashes and environmental crises that we face place our abstract notions about what the world should be into conflict with the concrete facts about what it is. Global warming and other human-made ecological damage require us to drop our vision of the planet as a body whose resources are best used up as quickly as possible for economic benefit. Conflicts between fundamentalist and nationalist worldviews—who see themselves in a heroic, righteous light and the Other as carrier of the world's evil—head us toward a "redemptive" showdown. Today our neat clockwork views of the universe are encountering the chaotic mess of all that we have denied in those views. Can we recognize our shadow and see, as Einstein did, that "it has become appallingly obvious that our technology has exceeded our humanity"? Can we understand our moment as qualitatively different from any that has come before? Certainly no human culture has ever been this close to ending life on this planet by its own hand. Can we recognize the tremendous anxiety and grandiosity that pressurize our culture's drive toward self-destruction? Only by our ego loving its own reason as much as we do could we get this far. Only when we have so completely denied the need for ego death in ourselves could we be so near to acting it out unconsciously.

> Some kind of great cleansing and spiritual transformation of Planet Earth seems guaranteed by the mounting pressure of grandiose energies in the human psyche. We see two alternatives: (a) the human species will act out its grandiose energies and get "purified" in a great fireball, a third World War, or (b) we will learn consciously how to sacrifice our infantile grandiosity and take conscious responsibility for making the changes we need to realize a great spiritual transformation.... The fundamentalist eagerness for Armageddon is simply an unconscious literalization of the imperative for transformation. (R. L. Moore)[16]

How then to escape our confinement within this tragedy? Before we break out of a pattern, we have to come to recognize the ways in which it is playing out through us, the ways in which we are unconsciously caught in it. Ironically perhaps, the gifts of the archetypal masculine can help us to do this—our psychological objectivity, our ability to discern with clarity and gain sight of our projections. The achievement of self-awareness and the possibility of nonidentification allow us to discover the story that we are playing out unconsciously. Only in coming to realize that one is caught in an unconscious pattern does one ever become able to break out of it. In looking at ourselves, and the way that we play out an old and unhealthy story, we become conscious enough to break out of it.

> We need to understand that the patriarchal symbolism permeating our culture results from being lost in a narrow band of the spectrum of the world's mythic imagination. (Moore)[17]

Under a now-over-masculine influence, we have managed to divide the world up into disconnected puzzle pieces and can no longer make emotional connection with context. The natural drive inside us to separate, which was once healthy for us, has now run amok and is keeping us from being able to construct any narrative for ourselves. We have been living in a story that has us, to a greater and greater degree, isolated from the world around us and dangerously satisfied with the righteousness of our own view. Our infantile grandiosity keeps us high up on the mountain and far from facing the imperfection in us, in our beliefs and in what we have done. Yet there is little clamor for change or self-reflection. In the biblical story of Jonathan, brother of King David and son of King Saul, it is understood that King Saul, as the first king of the Israelites, was the vehicle for the indwelling of the spirit of Yahweh, the Hebrew God. His reign was successful and blessed by God up until a certain point at which David's camp splits off from his father Saul's and Saul and Jonathan enter into a battle with the Philistines in which they are both killed. Prior to this battle, Jonathan's loyalty is split: he does not know whether to go with his father, Saul, or his brother David. He chooses his father and thus chooses death. The spirit of Yahweh had been with Saul, but it had abandoned him and was now with David. Thus, as Edinger points out, Jonathan's "residual dependence on the outworn state of being is what killed him."[18.] As with the biblical Jonathan, is our residual dependence on an outworn state of being leading us to our deaths? Is this masculine story of ours past its usefulness to us as the only narrative by which we understand ourselves? What might the cost be of remaining in grandiosity and habitual dependence when that mode now makes us unable to connect emotionally with the context in which we live? As one Jungian writer has chillingly described it, "At a time when our highest values, virtues and abilities are turning against us, the whole of humanity risks finding itself in God's shadow."[19]

There are many people who believe that our masculine imbalance has wounded us to a point that we experience life as though it were an abstraction, as though we were watching it "through a screen."[20] Andrew Harvey (1995) believes that the disconnection of our era has left us not only wounded but utterly passive, incapable of responding to our experience. He retells the story of a friend who survived a plane crash, describing the moments before the plane hit a mountain: "during the first few minutes, as people realized the end was coming, they screamed, sobbed and prayed out loud. In the next two minutes, the panic subsided; finally, in the end people just sat there, numb and frozen." Harvey feels that many people today are living in a state not unlike the people in those final minutes "too stunned even to cry out." He charges that much of our culture "conspires with this passivity. Its relentless trivialization of serious issues, its passion for distraction, its fanatical irrational belief in reason and the power of science to explain away everything, all prevent us from facing where we are and what we do."[21] Harvey believes that we are on the precipice of a human-made environmental disaster, essentially a mass "suicide" that we are moving toward swiftly, simply because we are too disconnected inside of ourselves to face squarely what we have done and what we need to do.

Might there be something in our condition today that has us petrified in our response to the world? Might it be that our psychological distance from Nature, both inner and outer, is what keeps our responses to the world around us lukewarm? As discussed previously in Chapter Six, might it be, as Neumann says, that where we have achieved in modern self-awareness the ability to split off our response from the images that we encounter, allowing us to choose our response, we now experience the world at such a distance that it has lost some of its reality for us and thus "confrontation with an unconscious image, or even an unexpected situation, finds [us] immune to reaction?"[22] Might it be, as Esther Harding describes, that the "little by little advance through the ages" of our ability to symbolize and abstract our experience—a great step forward—has also brought with it the danger that our consciousness, now cut asunder from the primal instinctual source of life inside us, cannot find it again? We are left with an "abstraction where reality used to be"—as Nietzsche screamed out at us? Maybe it is as O'Kane tells us, that images experienced without emotion have no power to transform us or to become a source of change or new action. Maybe it is as Ulanov says, that our postmodern globalization bombards us with so much sensation that we are now "promiscuously aroused"—unable to come to any conclusions—a process that necessitates our arousal being anchored in the present of our "specific location, body, society." Maybe it is as Washburn claims, that without being dynamically present in our bodies our experience has become "pale, distant and dull" and thereby "de-potentiated." Does this keep us from the horror potentially coming toward us as much as it does from the "ecstasy of the newness of the image" (Bachelard) that is present in Crop Circles? Can we live with environmental crisis and Crop Circles without thinking too much about either because neither one is very real to us? Do we not worry about the end of life on this planet because the possibility only exists for us as an abstract idea? Are we incapable of imagining *with feeling* what lies ahead? Have we intellectualized all of this and can now "live with it quite well," as Jung warned? Does this quality of our moment close us off from access to the voice of imagination inside us that would enable us to participate creatively with these new beauties and horrors? Is the spirit of our time most truthfully expressed in singing, "Well, whatever, never mind?"[23]

> Behind the "ecological crisis" and the "war on terror," there lies a crisis of meaning and a loss of the sense of the sacred in the immediate pulse of the world. . . . When "the End" seems near, how people imagine the world becomes more important; how people imagine humanity becomes of the utmost importance.[24]

Under the influence of our masculine imbalance, we have come to identify ourselves with light, and thus we require worldviews that enable us to keep that delusion intact. To do so, we hang on to ego-pleasing oversimplifications that keep us from fully participating with the truth that surrounds us, and especially from seeing the darkness in ourselves: the destruction that we do, the incomplete nature of our perspective, the dark mysteries that we deny. In his *Dreaming the End of the World,* Michael Ortiz Hill writes of our defenses against what's really happening around us as a kind of innocence: "As long as we drift innocently on the surface of things, like the uninitiated *Kore* picking narcissus in the Nyassan Meadows, it is almost inevitable that sooner or later the bottom will fall out and our innocence will be raped" (p. 86). In our culture, innocence is maintained by identifying oneself with light and coming to see one's own view and the view of one's group as not only correct but also virtuous—enlightened—and in such a state one's shadow is most definitely left aside. Here he is speaking of a self-satisfaction that is unconscious of its own unknowing, and where our ideas about the world around us and inside us are one-dimensional and sentimentalized, there is often a rejection of the world's depth, complexity, and mystery and our own. However intricate and complex our worldview is, our personal perspective can never be equivalent with the world around us and "the unimaginable presents itself in particulars, and attempting to relate to those particulars provokes the world's loss of cohesion."[25] Resisting the loss of our world's cohesion is accomplished through the denial of any crises or mysteries existing at all, through an inability to picture ourselves in the details of an ecological or other world-end, or through insisting that such an "unimaginable" future will happen under our terms—"I'll have my apocalypse done my way."

Letting go of an over-masculine worldview does not mean leaving one's religious faith, but it does mean becoming willing to put oneself into the tension that is present between our beliefs and reality—it means opening ourselves up to the "unimaginable." As author, paleontologist, and Jesuit priest Teilhard de Chardin describes it: "A constant spirit of inquiry directed toward the world and truth is an absolute duty." Such work will inevitably require a breakdown of something inside of us. Placing ourselves authentically into such an inquiry almost always requires some measure of ego death. Facing reality more fully requires a letting go of innocence and a willingness to go to hell.

The insight we obtain by looking at ourselves is generally very bitter, which is why so few people do it; it is *pikros*—bitter for it corrodes and is very disagreeable to the illusions of consciousness. That is why we speak of bitter truth, for self-knowledge is a bitter experience at the beginning. (von Franz)[26]

Jung recognized, in the process of movement into greater wholeness through ego death, a stage of medieval alchemy called *nigredo,* a blackening or decomposition, a breaking apart of the previous unity by which new growth is made possible. The term *nekyia* refers to a psychologically similar form of mythic night sea journey. In the decomposition of dark times, in suffering, pain, grief, or catastrophe, we are broken from the plans we had and snapped into voluntary or involuntary ego death. What this death looks like for each of us will be different; however, there are telltale signs of opportunity for such growth. Jung notes that the death motif here is real in that each of us will have a violent aversion to seeing through our projections[27] — that is to say, one does not move straight into the "lying down" of ego death; rather, we begin with rejection, refusal, being annoyed or offended. When we are experiencing such feelings, we can be certain that a root assumption of ours, one of our certitudes, is being challenged. Edinger writes of a response he had to a work of Jung's the first time he read it. He was strongly offended, and only after a period of time did he go through a deeper process: "I think each of you should ask yourself how you are offended, it will tell you something about the nature of your own unconscious assumptions and that can be a valuable bit of self-knowledge."[28] Such an understanding is vital to our engagement with the mystery of Crop Circles, because the magnitude of the questions raised by looking seriously at this phenomenon is sure to violate everyone's package of unconscious assumptions in some way. But it is only through such a loss that one comes to renewal. Such dark periods allow that which no longer serves us to die off, as Boznak explains: "In the *nigredo,* the process freed itself of the fixation in which it was long bogged down. In alchemy, the mortification, the dying of the old king, the grandfather, takes place. Outlived forms that have ruled us for too long rot away now, so that a solution can be found, and stuck psychic material disintegrates into its component parts."[29]

The egoic-masculine's voice inside us tells us that what needs to die is our subjectivity, our imperfection and weak, irrational feeling qualities. Where we are led by a search for perfection and an ever-brighter self-image, there is a correspondent denial that is ongoing, a rejection made—*a refusal to participate*—for "to move toward perfection is to move out of life, or what is worse, never to enter it."[30] Suffering and vulnerability can bring us more authentically toward life; in their process is begun a hollowing out that makes room for new fruitful growth. Here the ego defenses are broken down and we are brought closer to life. In suffering and helplessness, Ortiz Hill notes, "we are 'forced to live closer to the wounded earth'—which is to say our hearts' brokenness."[31] A culture that is bound up in shiny forward progress has an incredibly difficult time understanding that there might be something of value to be found in breakdown and vulnerability—the dark road of "union and death," of the psychological process of ego death and rebirth, runs counter to the masculine desire for straightforward linear approaches.

> The mystery of *nigredo* is very far from our patriarchal consciousness that values solidity, stability, constancy, and strength. For most people, it is a long and arduous path even to begin to appreciate the wisdom of this other way, the way of union and death. (Schwartz-Salant)[32]

It is very difficult for a culture that has been conditioned to reject and separate its awareness away from instinct, body, feeling, dream, and internal image to suddenly turn to look for value in these things. For thousands of years our cultural masculine journey has been one of separating away from this "dark background" of our internal experience and into the "light" of objective clarity. This way of knowing the world can only divide endlessly and does not know how to put back together:

> The question, as it is posed under the dominance of the hero archetype, excludes an answer from the beginning. Nothing can unite Heaven and Earth once they are defined as separated. We here encounter the tragedy of the heroic ego, which can only continue to separate, dissolve, analyze, and kill, but never again find connectedness, not because such connectedness is altogether impossible, but because it has no place within a myth aiming for separation. . . . It is not necessary for us here to enter into the question of to what extent this vision is responsible for the problems of the modern West (alienation, fragmentation, pollution, etc.) and specifically shapes the scientific mind. Our fate, however, may well depend

on whether we are able to move out from our confinement in the ultimately deadly hero myth.[33]

Jung warned us that our era's imbalance leads us to value "reason more than God's secret intentions."[34] We display our love of reason, above God and/or Nature's intentions, by holding on to old ways, through distraction and trivialization of serious issues, and by intellectualization and abstraction—the Devil's trick of substituting abstract pursuits for the good that we could do in the here and now. The voice of this imbalance in us insists that, not only is there no actual meaning in Crop Circles, or in the crises and discoveries of our moment, but that there *never could be any meaning in them* because meaning is only ever a subjective invention of the human imagination ("don't be irrational, silly"). This voice responds to the idea of our coming into a new story by saying that "things can never really change," that "things have always been this way and this is the way that they will always be." While many of us gaze in wonder and wrestle with the arrival of the Crop Circle phenomenon and its meaning for us, for the most part our culture has chosen to "love its own reason" and simply say "it cannot possibly be anything that we do not already understand." In doing so we most certainly do keep God's and/or Nature's secret intentions well away from our hearts. The possibility of meaning is excluded from the beginning in a view of the world in which all that we are is biological robots. As Marie-Louise von Franz has said, "Like any idea, the idea of meaning has an opposite, which is that of nonsense, an absurd chaos." The grandiosity of the era rejects the idea of meaning and leaves us only with the nonsense of hypocritical avoidance of reality and an absurd chaos in which nothing of real meaning is discussed.

Does a voice inside you say that Crop Circles having any meaning at all is absurd? That voice is our ego's resistance to the anxiety of not-knowing, our habitual attachment to preexisting certainties. Inside the egoic, archetypal masculine story, we can know that none of this really matters anyway, or if it does it could only ever matter within a well-defined masculine narrative. Our bias toward always needing to be correct and against not-knowing and ego death makes us resist meeting the new, both because it conflicts with our current worldview and because it endangers the broader, self-satisfied inflation. Today our culture sits puffed up and disconnected from the objective ground of Nature inside us. Most fundamentally, ours is a culture based upon the psychological denial of any timeless center in us. And if we do not believe that such a center exists, we cannot see any value in a breakdown that would reorient us toward it. That is why it is so difficult for us to understand that the dark journey we must undertake at this time is not a regression into unconscious participation mystique with Nature, but rather a conscious reunion with Nature's living foundation. The ground of the timeless within us as it is found on the other side of the ego's mature and conscious surrender. Do we have the necessary imagination to consider that, now, this is the way forward?

Our ancestral cultures knew this other way to be of value. As with many forms of initiation ritual, the Eleusian mysteries led one into a lived experience of the miracle of life and paradoxically through a psychological experience of death. Here one found that this miracle—the timeless in personal form—is the very ground of one's being. The ritual took the initiate out of the everyday profane time—the outworn state of mind—and led them into contact with the timeless, which provided renewal (and similar realizations can be understood to be at the root of all of the world's various mystical traditions). At Eleusis, through Demeter's recovery of her daughter Persephone from the land of the dead, initiates came to see that the ritual "contained the living idea—that, in motherhood, death and continuity are one"[35] and came to feel an experience of the unity of spirit and Nature, a quality of the world that could only ever be known *through feeling*. Here the ego's illusion that it is separate from Nature is overcome, the dark suffering of the initiate has opened the ego sufficiently to discover a profound truth that is fundamentally opposed to the ego's finite perspective.

The fact that people went back to the Mysteries in Egypt and Greece year after year (and that the Mysteries themselves last for thousands of years) suggest that the inevitable falling back into life in time needs a periodical dissolution into the timeless if the memory of the source is not to fade. Otherwise, the experience may become theoretical, an idea only, the inevitable consequence of knowledge divorced from being. (Cashford)[36]

Perhaps in no pervious human culture more than ours has the center been so lost. Not only is a "dissolution into the timeless" just an idea for us, it is a quaint one at that. Nearly every previous culture had a mythology, a ritual or series of rituals that enabled some degree of contact with the objective, transpersonal basis of the psyche. Only in our culture do we not only forsake such content and not believe in it, we actually resent the idea that we might need such contact. The ego has overturned the apple cart of our psyche and stands upon the mess proclaiming, "Thou shalt have no other gods before me" (and in America, "Thou shalt create no impediments to my profit"). We have no myth, no story, we are "unhistoric" in Jung's term and this is a psychological illness that is terminal. It is from this illness that a utilitarian view of ourselves, one another, and every living thing fills our perspective.

And then something that we did not expect to happen happened. At a time when we have lost contact with the part of ourselves that knows the center, that longs to touch the timeless, something appeared before us that speaks Nature's symbolic language. Formed in the same images that the psyche speaks when seeking or expressing wholeness inside of us, formations in grain and corn are appearing on Earth with ever-greater beauty, frequency, and complexity. In locations that emphasize our former land-based spirituality, we see images of geocentric and mandala form constructed in living grain. If one were to consider such images as one would a dream, what is shown here is the organic and biological side of the Self, the part of the urge for wholeness in us that becomes realized through the life of the body and through the living world—through personal feeling, seeing, touching, and sensing. Here, the quality of connection pointed to is embodied and present, immediate and Earth-bound, immanent and not at all abstract.

Today, when overheated masculine certainties hurry us toward Armageddon, when inflation and intellectualization keep us from really feeling the danger we face in destroying the environment, is there the possibility too that something else is being born in us? In the tremendous pressure that the psyche is under, in bearing the load of too much unconscious grandiosity and in its dangerously inflated present condition, is it possible that we can also discover that "danger itself fosters the rescuing power"?[37]

Perhaps it is only through approaching a precipice where we have both the means and psychological state necessary to destroy ourselves that we will come to look more closely inside and at "what we do." And perhaps it could be no other way.

Slattery has observed that the difference between tragedy and comedy is that in a tragedy the action always ends with not quite enough time (e.g., all Juliet needed was a few moments more), and in comedy there is always just enough time for a happy resolution.[38] Sufficient time allows "space" to be transformed into "place." Through emotional participation with a space over time, through the bonds of *eros,* feeling, and meaning, space is made into place in our hearts. One need only think of burial places or wedding tabernacles to know this is true. The difference in the two is like the difference between the way you look at the home you grew up in, filling it in with memories and emotion, and the way a geographer or real estate agent might look at that same property as a location, as space. It is the pause, the slowing down into being present that gives these places their meaning. Such archetypally Feminine approaches to the world around us are thoroughly degraded by our over-masculine culture that sees everything as only ever—and nothing more than—utilitarian opportunities. Space is made into place by our heart's real presence, through our lived attentiveness, through pain and joy.

> Space is more abstract than place. What begins as undifferentiated space becomes place as we get to know it better and endow it with value. . . . If we think of space as that which allows movement, then place is pause; each pause in movement makes it possible for location to be transformed into place. . . . [A]bstract space, lacking significance other than strangeness, becomes concrete place [only when it is] filled with meaning.[39]

Crop Circles lead us to pause again. This phenomenon is a mystery set into not just space but place, for the formations are not just set randomly into grain fields but placed precisely into landscapes, oriented toward ancient sites of worship, and can arrive in concert with individuals' emotional states. Through their precise placement into specific locations, Crop Circles run counter to the promiscuous arousal that Ulanov describes us as suffering from, that leaves us uprooted and unrelated to body, location, or moment.

Through their selectivity of location, through their mystery and aesthetic qualities, Crop Circles draw us down into a meeting of *this* location, *our* body, and into a pause for *participation* with place. This phenomenon leads us into fields that might have only been seen by us as spaces of utility— and in being led back into the fields we are given pause to look and wonder. Slowed down, we are offered an opportunity to make meaning, to look with new eyes, not only at the formation around us, but at the boxes into which we have placed our understanding of the world. We are given pause to consider how we view Nature, how we view God, and how we view ourselves. We are led back to considering spiritual questions in which spirit, the land, and ourselves are not separated. In the pause afforded to us by Crop Circles are we being led back toward recovering something of ourselves?

We are being brought back down to earth by the zeitgeist that is upon us. We are being cured of our ailment by being made to become reacquainted with our finitude. And, as Jung says of neurosis, we can go where it's taking us willingly and follow signs and dreams, or be dragged there unwillingly by symptoms and consequences. Our time is one in which we are being led back to relating to the context around us; we can choose whether to go creatively or destructively, consciously or kicking and screaming. If we are very lucky, we will manage to overcome that immature masculine voice in us that insists that it always knows best and bring ourselves to meet the world around us with emotional presence, experiencing both the horror and wonder that we have denied in it. If we are very lucky, we will have that kind of contact with the world and be transformed by it. That innate urge inside us toward transformation, the drive to become more wholly who we are, is being provoked by our encounters with the new mysteries that are before us today.

We are living in what the Greeks called the kairos—the right moment—for a "metamorphosis of the gods," of the fundamental principles and symbols. This peculiarity of our time, which is certainly not of our conscious choosing, is the expression of the unconscious man within us who is changing. Coming generations will have to take account of this momentous transformation if humanity is not to destroy itself through the might of its own technology and science. As at the beginning of the Christian era, so again today we are faced with the problem of the general moral backwardness which has failed to keep pace with our scientific, technical, and social progress. So much is at stake and so much depends on the psychological constitution of modern man. . . . Does he realize what lies in store should this catastrophe ever befall him? Is he even capable of realizing that this would in fact be a catastrophe? And finally, does the individual know that he is the makeweight that tips the scale? (Jung)[40]

Will we participate with what is going on around us? Will we see our moment with imagination and not be afraid of finding meaning and pattern there? In doing so we might see in this sequence of events that our coming to this point in the process is not only inevitable, but somehow natural (or at least necessary). In our leaving behind participation mystique and unconsciousness, was our reaching this extreme of disconnection and dissociation not an unavoidable eventuality? With consciousness came the loss of connection to the transpersonal basis of the psyche and a natural redirecting of our energy inward toward ourselves. What other course could we have taken and still made the journey out of unconsciousness? Was this movement not a natural progression and the result of our natural engagement with the archetypal masculine impetus? It is only now as this movement reaches its peak that it seems unnatural. One can protest that we "should know better," but it would seem that the root of this process lies in something necessary for the progression of human consciousness, and if so, should its *next phase* also not have a place in this progression? The description of our current moment as a part of an initiation process places the entire dynamic into an archetypal framework that, *even if unresolved, still provides a meaningful larger pattern by which to view it.* If our movement out of identification with Nature and into modern, fragmented, but sturdy self-awareness is a part of a natural process—then this current moment, in which we are so estranged from Nature and ourselves that we may destroy both, can also be understood as a part of a natural, if deadly process (not unlike a birth).

Seeing the story of our journey and its current crisis within such a frame suggests that we are experiencing a transformation not unlike that of the caterpillar to the butterfly. We are undergoing a process in which the smallness of our vision is broken down so that something larger can emerge. Bachelard observes that at times, what is required of us is a "melting into the basic element," a kind of "necessary human suicide for whoever wants to experience an emergence into a new cosmos."[41] Understanding our moment within the framework of initiation also suggests the necessity of our being willing and able to tolerate darkness—the darkness of doubt, the darkness of our not knowing, the darkness of letting go of familiar ways of understanding the world, the darkness of withstanding every voice that tells us that there is no point in looking for meaning in any of this; it requires our being able to withstand looking at the horror of what we have already done and are still doing. With crisis on one hand and Crop Circles and other new mysteries on the other, are we being led somewhere that we need to go, but do not know it? In both of these ways, can we recognize that the challenges we face today are challenges of the imagination, made so because of our inability to imagine our own darkness or to imagine that there might be something out there greater than ourselves? Can we imagine that our crisis stems from our inability to find ourselves *within* the story of the world?

> The problem isn't that the world might end completely, rather, the issue is how to act when it seems that way. . . . [W]hat's missing is the imagination necessary to hold end and beginning together. . . . Mythic imagination is a primordial resource of the human heart. . . . [W]hen times become truly tragic and dark with uncertainty what is missing is the touch of eternity and a mythic sense of being woven within the ongoing story of the world.[42]

Few better "miracles" could occur to help us to widen the band of our mythic imagination than Crop Circles. Not only do they fire the imagination, they demonstrate that we are moving through the masculine lens into a deeper, more whole view. They do this by exceeding the bounds of rationality that the old story places upon Nature and ourselves. In this way, we can understand Crop Circles as acting as an advocate for us in discovering a new and larger narrative for ourselves—and *not a simple return or regression* but a more conscious appraisal of such irrational realities. Looking squarely at the phenomenon's facts, uncovering its history, recovering our psychological projections, and moving forward from this concrete basis, we can proceed beyond where we have been before. Without such a bedrock by which to approach the phenomenon we would surely fall into primitive identification and participation mystique with it (as we likely still will).

Only from a grounding in the masculine principle could we turn to look upon the irrational mystery in the world without getting lost in it. In our consciously encountering the reality of these facts, one is offered a route by which to begin to look upon Nature with a broader imagination. The mysterious qualities of our world, which the archetypal masculine's bright Solar light had blinded us to, are today coming into focus again, offering not a return to the participation mystique of the past, but a new, mature, conscious encounter with Nature's living wonder. We can understand this transition as involving the reintroduction of our overly rational consciousness to the complex, multivalent, sustaining, and irrational nature of the cosmos as Feminine; the doubting ego meeting life's inexplicable meaningfulness.

Like a sunset, sunrise, birth, or death, Crop Circles may give us pause to consider the possibility of our connection to something greater. Times such as these are threshold moments—the sun's fading or arrival, a life's ending or beginning, a new phenomenon dazzling us with its entry into our world—and in our experience of such times we cross a threshold inside of ourselves. Here our inner world is able to breathe more deeply because the ego's theft of our inner authority is momentarily undone. For a moment consciousness sits with its inner order restored and we can experience the connection to the timeless that lives within us and know briefly the mystic's understanding. It is the nature of the psyche to bring about this reconciliation. In dreams and in other ways, the psyche leads us to a greater connection to our own capacity for depth. Finding it, we may discover we drop from our shoulders a burden that feels not entirely our own. When we surrender our grandiosity—relating to the spiritual power inside us without becoming identified with it—the ego drops an authority that is not its property. Experiences of the threshold, experiences that take us outside of the ego's confinement of our relationship to the world, help us to, even for a moment, find home again and make a connection with our inner transpersonal center.

The illness of the modern psyche has left us facing circumstances and crises that leave us hopelessly lost and crying out "Why?" But in those conditions, if we can look at them squarely, we will find something that will strike down our inflated self-satisfaction and return us to the "specific body, location, and culture" that is our own. Crop Circles too can defeat our inflated certainties and help us to leave behind the childish boxes into which we have stuffed all the magic and mystery in the world. Like the initiations of old, our transformation, through these encounters, roots us again into an earthy humility. By both the harsh and the fantastic, we are being led out of abstraction and into the reality that surrounds us. Each of these bring the "unconscious gods" inside of us into check by placing a limit on our fantasies about the perfection of our own view. The crises and mysteries of our age deflate our certainties and lead us toward a new understanding of our relationship to the world.

Through the simple act of our attendance to them, through our imaginative engagement with Crop Circles, we utilize a quality that we need to recover inside of ourselves. Meeting Crop Circles and our moment's crises in the fullness of our humanity requires our breaking through the mirror of our ego's notions. We require the heroism in which we are "broken for a new creation."[43] Through such an act, we may recover something we did not know we lacked. Anytime that consciousness is opened past the doors of the ego, a letting go of sorts, no matter how subtle, has happened. What has been sacrificed? The ego's illusion that we are something more than the imperfect but spirit-filled beings that we are. In becoming vulnerable to *what actually is* we defeat our grandiosity. For us today, reunion with the Feminine often requires a loss, a suffering of the ego—and its sacrifice cannot be substituted for. Ego death is the only cure for inflation, the only path to come into contact with the ground of actual experience, both inside and out. This approach stands in opposition to the certainty demanded of the masculine mindset, so here we must leave our old ways of understanding behind and search for something new. In searching, we may find that our moment of despair is also a time that is itself conspiring to defeat our grandiosity and seeking to help us make our way back home.

TEN

FIELDS OF WAVING CORN

> New points of view are not as a rule discovered in territory that is already known, but in out-of-the way places that may even be avoided because of their bad name.
>
> —JUNG

Our history has no shortage of figures who brought our attention to new points of view and were condemned for doing so. When a new step in our advance is put forward, it is very often immediately rejected. Researchers of Crop Circle phenomena know well that this can be the case. Too often the phenomenon's facts are ignored so that stories can be written that simply reinforce old thinking and collective prejudice. Both Crop Circle researchers and extended mind researcher Rupert Sheldrake find repeatedly that interviewers and critics frequently have little interest in actually looking at the tremendous body of scientific and historical evidence.[1] Not only is the data often ignored, but the researchers themselves are often defamed and given a "bad name." Meeting the new is often psychologically uncomfortable; a part of us would refuse its claim upon us and therefore must deny its reality. To receive a new point of view that conflicts with the status quo requires the courage to stand up to cultural taboos and to come to face the undiscovered taboos inside ourselves.

An intense gold-white glow came out of the clouds, descended slowly, silently, and majestically—brighter than the full moon. She took a brief look at the road ahead of her, then again at the mysterious shining object. At this moment a thin ray of white light appeared to come from it an angle of perhaps 65 degrees, and fell on the area in front of Silbury Hill. . . . On the morning of July 15, 1988, farmer Robert Hues discovered the first of five "Celtic crosses" that would appear that summer on his land in the area of Silbury Hill.[2]

In the night between August 7 and 8, 1997, at the foot of Milk Hill near Alton Barnes . . . [Czech researchers] observed a large bright light from which three successive sets of smaller lights emerged in the star-studded sky and made low passes over the field. The points of light flew directly to the field and after a short time returned to the object from which they came. At the break of day on August 8th, a huge, complex star formation was discovered at the foot of Milk Hill, a high point of the year 1997.[3]

Such accounts lead us to a threshold, to the limit of what we have been conditioned to believe is possible, to the edge of what is acceptable to our "reasonable" selves and to our egos. For some of us, eyewitness accounts of the fantastic such as these create a conflict between the constriction that our worldview places upon reality and our openness to expand that view, between our ego's desire to be certain about what it "knows" and our capacity to let go into a new experience. The ego works conversely too, when perhaps we jump toward the new too eagerly, denying the deeper process it asks of us. What happens inside of you when you read such an account? Does it exceed the territory that is comfortable to you? Is there some part of your response that gives the new thing "a bad name"?

Nancy Talbott is a Crop Circle researcher who focuses on documenting scientific evidence, including changes in the soil and the grain itself. She is the "T" in BLT research and she has pursued this phenomenon diligently for many years. She is a very grounded and objective woman. On August 21, 2001, she was in Holland at the farm of Robbert van der Broeke, a site where formations frequently appear. In her description of the evening she notes that she was thinking about all of the peculiar incidents that had been happening more and more frequently to her and other researchers. She was thinking too about all of the hard work that had gone into studying Crop Circles:

And it suddenly seemed to me that the phenomenon was just too complex, too elusive, too difficult to study. I suppose partly out of fatigue and partly out of frustration I decided to go up to bed, telling Robbert that I was tired of all this "pussy-footing" around and asking, "why can't this phenomenon be more obvious, more direct"?[4]

Genuinely overwrought and worn out with the mystery of all of this, she then went to bed. Staying up reading, at 3:05 a.m. she heard the cattle nearby bawling, "as cattle do when they are disturbed." But she didn't get up or look out the window. Then she heard them again at 3:10, and although she thought she should go to the window and look she did not: "again, I stayed put (in my notes from that night I have written that I was 'scared'). After a minute or so the cattle were quiet again." (I suspect that Nancy is not one who is easily scared.) Then, at 3:15 a.m. she saw "a brilliant, intense white column, or tube, of light—about 8" to 1' in diameter" flashing down from the sky so brightly that illuminated her bedroom and the surrounding area. After a second of darkness, the tube of light reappeared just to the left of where it had been. Then it went dark, and after a few seconds it reappeared. Within five to six seconds, a third beam of light was appearing and she yelled to Robert. He had seen the lights from the downstairs kitchen window and was running up the stairs toward her room. Together they stood at her room's glass doors looking and waiting. Both noted later that there was a spiral motion inside the tube of light. After a minute or so they stepped out the back door of the house toward the area into which the lights had shone. Just past the back fence, "barely visible in the darkness—was the new crop circle." Both Nancy and Robert were struck deeply by the sense that the incident was deliberate and on purpose. Nancy, for her part, struggled to overcome the notion that her meaningful understanding of the incident was just an anthropocentric fantasy,[5] but in the world that we are uncovering today we can be certain that such purposiveness is not an illusion.

One of the most astounding features of this account is that the Crop Circle seemingly came in response to Nancy's heartfelt emotion. She says, whether out of fatigue or frustration, that she had gone to bed "telling Robbert that I was tired of all this 'pussy-footing' around" and asking, "why can't this phenomenon be more obvious, more direct"? To this genuine calling out, a response came—dramatic and direct. How can we make sense of this? Rationally minded as we are today, we are conditioned to automatically intellectualize tales of the fantastic, keeping our experience of them abstract and distant, and it is therefore very hard for us to achieve an embodied acceptance of such a possibility until we have seen it with our own eyes. Nonetheless, they exist. Personally, because I understand Nancy to be extremely grounded and credible—she is by no means a flake—I have no doubt of the authenticity of this account. Helping me to accept this account, as well, is the fact that this kind of psychic coincidence, between researchers and formations, has been reported throughout the history of the phenomenon. Many otherwise normal researchers have reported formations occurring either when they thought of such shapes only the night prior, or had discussed such shapes while flying over a spot, only to find them there soon after;[6] others report successful attempts at asking for certain shapes to appear.[7] Andrews called for and received a formation close to his home when he could not afford to travel far away,[8] and there are innumerable minor synchronicities of researchers dreaming of formations prior to their arrival, and other less dramatic yet still "coincidental" occurrences.

Helping me further is my awareness of this kind of feeling-based psychic coincidence existing elsewhere in Nature. Jung observed synchronicity to be predicated upon the presence of affect, occurring "for the most part in emotional situations . . . we observe them relatively frequently at moments of heightened emotional tension, which need not however be conscious."[9] Because we know that synchronicity is a quality of Nature in which inner emotion and outer events are brought together, one can look upon the formation that Talbott and de Broeke saw arrive before their eyes as having come in relation to the authentic feeling that they had for the phenomenon. In this view, it is not anthropocentric (as Talbott wonders) to recognize meaning in the intermingling of event and emotion, but simply a quality of Nature that is ancient, well documented, and rationally recognizable. As documented throughout Chapter Seven, synchronistic coming-together of feelings and events is found throughout human history and reflects the extended mind qualities of Nature that Sheldrake has demonstrated exist. Such events are not supernatural, but natural. Again, the researcher's emotional involvement or intent is not assumed to cause a formation to occur, but rather, as with occurrences of synchronicity, affect is understood to be playing a part in a field dynamic of causation (we cannot know whether the phenomenon's agent is aware of the emotions present or not, but we cannot mistake that there is a correlation between the two).

We also know that a similar relationship between event and emotion occurs elsewhere in Nature: there are innumerable incidences of psychic coincidence in our historic record. This is found most commonly between loved ones, often in a moment of danger or death, when one person gets the feeling that something is wrong with another. This occurs in dreams or a daytime inspiration, by a feeling or "vision"—in the process of which one may become aware of the specific nature of the danger or wound. There are also experiences of a felt awareness of a vessel's journey being endangered prior to leaving, a phenomenon noted by *Titanic* passengers and a TWA Flight 100 passenger who was unable to board the flight (and in many other similar situations). Some may have a sense that someone else will be in danger on their journey, or one might dream of one's own death just prior to it, as Lincoln did.[10] Why do these cords of feeling extend across time and space? Do many of our religious and indigenous traditions not also share this belief—that in listening to our heart's voice we are sometimes led toward a saving grace? Such beliefs understand the world to be one in which human emotion transcends physical boundaries. While by no means equating the agency of Crop Circles with divinity, there are repeated incidents of correlation between the emotional state of researchers and the arrival of a new formation (a correlation that does not require them to be conscious of their emotion). In this case, after many years of dedicated research, Talbott says she felt overwhelmed by the magnitude and elusiveness of her task. She expressed this truth honestly—and then something she did not expect to happen happened.

While I believe this account, I also understand that many people cannot or have difficulty doing so. We find ourselves at the end of a long period of history in which we have become increasingly filled up with the awe and wonder that we used to project out into the world. Propelled by our masculine ability to separate and classify, we bask in the brightness of our glorious inventiveness, and are blind to the existence of any other centers of subjectivity in the world around us. Our possession by this masculine zeitgeist conditions us to reject the new phenomenon of Crop Circles by: insisting that all Crop Circle formations are necessarily fakes, because in appropriating "to itself all conscious intelligence in the universe" the modern mind is psychologically rooted in a cosmos in which there are no Others—no other agents who might produce them; believing in a reductive "scientific" point of view that believes (falsely) that the only kinds of causation are those that are mediated locally; believing that the conditions of the heart can never travel outside the body or have an effect on someone or something far away, and thereby necessarily insisting that all synchronicities are only figments of the imagination (despite all evidence to the contrary). In all three of these ways, the formation of a Crop Circle and its witness contradicts the rigid principles upon which our orthodox worldview stands. In addition to these direct and obvious conflicts, because we view ourselves through the masculine psychological lens there is also an undercurrent of unconscious psychological resistance to meeting any new reality that undermines our preexistent worldview.

The challenge today, for many of us, is to free ourselves from archetypally masculine patterns playing out unconsciously in our reactions to experience. Even in the face of solid scientific evidence, even after seeing such evidence with our own eyes in the fields, we may find that we are challenged to believe in what we have seen and know is true. Even if we do accept the evidence or the account intellectually, we may find ourselves challenged to incorporate it into our awareness in a deeper way—deeper than just a mental, abstract concept. Feeling the truth of such a profound new discovery may come for many of us only momentarily: it was there in my friend saying "What a relief"; it may contain awe and wonder; it may also hold fear of the Other. There is a long road between conceptual, intellectual belief and embodied experience, especially of something of this numinous magnitude. And again, not helping us to embody such content is the fact that we live, and have been brought up in, a culture that discourages acceptance of such extraordinary experience, despite fringe curiosity about it. Most of our institutions are founded on constricting the world to fit into well-defined rational boxes, and the exposure that we have to strange phenomena through entertainment by no means outweighs our cultural taboos against taking such stuff seriously. So what is the alternative?

As Talbott has demonstrated, participating in the fullness and imperfection of who one actually is can serve to bring about satisfying (if unexpected) outcomes. In some versions of the medieval Grail legend, it was not a heroic deed that recovered the Holy Grail and restored king and land, but rather the question of an innocent fool "carried by Eros, that brings new life." It was not "a pure, fearless knight endowed with a high degree of spiritual perfection who finds the Grail. It is a human, in his fool aspect, who by accepting the chthonic and irrational and by learning to use a new form of thinking . . . asks the question that will eventually transform the situation."[11] Here emotion and sincerity play a primary role. When the over-masculine impetus that we suffer from has dried us out, emptying us of curiosity and questions, we need to spend time attending to the moist darkness inside of us before we can know what we want to ask. It was only after she cried out in frustration "why can't this phenomenon be more obvious, more direct?" that Talbott was visited with an answer—that she no doubt found satisfying. If we allow the process to move us so that something emerges in us, out of that we may utter the right words, spontaneously and innocently. Doing so may lead us to discover on our lips the question that our situation requires us to ask.

Such a process is a heart-centered emotional gestation out of which the important new truth arrives into our awareness and, as such, it can be seen as archetypally Feminine. Such an approach contrasts the archetypal masculine drive for certainty and clarity that (particularly when holding us unconsciously) leads us to want to short-circuit meandering internal processes in favor of placing the new thing into an old, well-defined box. We usually do so by denying its reality altogether—as it's said, we cannot "place new wine into old bottles" (Matt 9:17). The Feminine makes room for the anxiety that is produced by meeting the new: it is that part of us that knows how to sit with uncertainty and in doing so is able to uncover in ourselves a new, authentic response.

> The Feminine mode gives us the wiles to live next to the gap, from which new symbols or refurbished old ones emerge. But when they come they are strange to us, full of ambiguity, with uneven edges, a crude power, an unsettling spirit. It is the feminine way to hover over this gap. . . . [We need to try to resist the temptation] to take the old or new part we know and feel at ease with and make it

substitute for the new whole whose dimensions we do not know or feel certain about. (Ulanov)[12]

Sitting with the "unsettling spirit" of the new thing necessitates that we are capable of holding tension and requires us to be able to withstand authentic emotional oscillation between the dark and light in ourselves, between our own hope and despair, between the best in us and the worst, between that in us which would make a space for the new and that in us which would rush to dismiss it, give it a bad name, and "shoo it out of town."[13] When we reject part of our responses to the world, the anxiety of meeting the new cannot be satisfactorily held and we collapse the process prematurely. "When a thing is new, people say: 'It is not true.' Later, when its truth becomes obvious, they say: 'It is not important.' Finally, when its importance cannot be denied, they say: 'Anyway, it is not new'" (William James).[14] All along the way, we missed it—something was happening but we didn't know what it was and never managed to make anything out of it. Allowing ourselves to proceed into the ego breakdown that is necessary for receiving the new is very difficult and is usually strongly resisted. Going forward into such a letting go of our inner road maps requires a well-rooted connection to our inner psychological ground. Only if we have an innate, instinctual trust of the world that comes through a secure connection to our emotional selves can we accept all of our responses and be present with them without needing to make them into anything else. Being able to meet the new without seeking to quickly dispel its ambiguity requires our possession of a dynamic, existential trust. This is present only to the degree that an individual "feels sufficiently contained in a fecund cosmos and who is able to trust in destiny, despite obstacles or misfortune. In other words, it requires a positive mother complex, a secure background."[15] When such a connection is possible, we are able to tolerate our process of gestation regardless of its ambiguity or irrationality; we require no assurance of outcomes; we can withstand our own anxiety and inner rational objections and can attend to ourselves with trust and a quiet heart, without any rationale for doing so.

The Conscious Feminine gives us the courage to love an acorn without knowing what an oak tree is. (Woodman)[16]

There lives inside of most of us, as a quality of our age, a knee-jerk needing to know, to understand, and to categorize. During each stage of a journey into understanding, we compulsively desire to conclude and to be sure. But we are not always at the end, where we can know for sure. If we can sacrifice our compulsive need to know, we can accord value to each stage of the process, holding steady in its darker phases until it emerges into clear form. This is what Woodman is speaking of when she describes the Feminine as the wisdom inside of us that can love "an acorn without knowing what an oak tree is." Where the over-amped masculine in us is compelled to be sure, the Feminine is the part of us that can live (and love) in doubt and without needing to know or to be certain. To return to the Feminine here is not a regression into childlike naiveté and participation mystique with the unconscious; it is not a surrender of the truth that the masculine helps us to see. It is instead a coming together of both principles in their highest form. At its best, the masculine in us is willing to let go of old theories and stand up in favor of newly arrived truth. Here, it can be "both the sacrificed and the sacrificer."[17] The masculine can help us recognize "the differences between symbols" and is all those discriminatory capacities that we must employ in order to understand what is true about this new mystery of Crop Circles. But when we are facing something that we do not yet know the answer to, it is the Feminine in us that allows us to stand straddling the gap out of which the new meaning arrives. If we are instinctively rooted to the foundational bedrock of our psyche and can handle the effects of our emotional responses without denial, rationalization, or projection, and allow ourselves to feel fear, frustration, and our spirit being "unsettled" without saying "to hell with it," then we can continually handle greater and greater "wattage" of experience. As we get closer to actually finding meaning in the new, we may hear the shadow masculine voice inside of us say something like "Why we are wasting our time with this nonsense?" It will throw up endless garbage to keep us away from the thing threatening the status quo (which also may bring out new life within us). It will provide innumerable models for us to compare ourselves against and fail by. At each step of the journey, it will see only literal losses or wins, and listening to it we will fail to gain sight of larger things ahead. Rarely looking at the larger picture, the shadow masculine can miss the relationship between subject and object, between action and story; the relationship that unfolds into meaning if it is allowed sufficient time and if an emotional attentiveness is held. On the journey toward meeting the new, it is only by having deep roots into the emotional and instinctual foundational ground of psyche that we can keep the masculine need-to-know from short-circuiting the unfolding. If we can sacrifice our compulsive need to know, we become able to find value in each stage of the journey, each step along the way—and in doing so, we keep alive the new thing growing inside of us. O'Kane speaks of this capacity as the wisdom of the fool, who

> instinctively knows that the shortest way is not always the best, and that quite often a circumambulation [proceeding around] will bring him closer to his unseen aim than a head-on approach. This aspect too is connected with the instinctive wisdom of Eros as opposed to the purposefulness of Logos: the path with heart is not as linear as logic and reason; it includes shadows and apparent failures. To follow it requires patience and the surrender of absolutes. . . . Because he manages to stand the chaos and even to be inspired by it, his unflinching exertion takes him further. Because Perceval shows heart, courage and the ability to forego measuring himself against a model, he finally succeeds and finds the Grail castle.[18]

The path of the heart leads to the unexpected treasure and the "unseen aim"—the thing that we need but do not know we need. Its path is noticed, not through the eye of discrimination or by comparison, but by listening closely to our heart in the present moment. When we can be steadily present with the heart, we discover the emotional truth that lives in us. These truths may not be pretty, they may be ugly and bitter—perhaps we may feel ashamed for our mistakes. However, whatever the truth is for us, the step of participation through the archetypal Feminine path of the heart is one of moving more closely toward *what actually is* in the fullness of its reality; it is a *whole* relating to the truth around us. Feminine modes help us to once again generate meaning by being present in the context that we are actually living—one does not need to conjure up meaning, it is already present in our lives if we can live with a heart that is present.

Increasingly today, where we have wanted to take refuge in our preexistent certitudes, we are being forced to accommodate new facts. Today we are experiencing a world in which spiritual dilemmas are being pressed upon us by down-to-earth crises, unexpected discoveries, and close-at-hand horrors, and where the fantastic (if not the sacred) is being consciously recognized as participating in the reality of the mundane. We can know that we are undergoing a shift in the zeitgeist by the nature of the difference in the questions we are facing today. How does an us-and-them point-of-view help us to respond to an environmental crisis that is global? What does belief not only in the rightness of one's view, but also in its righteousness, offer us when the new standing is before us in Crop Circle formations, in the nonlocality and indeterminism of quantum physics, and the operation of the extended mind and synchronicity? Accepting the truth of accounts of the fantastic is made easier if they can be recognized as having a place within a larger dynamic that is unfolding in our moment. They make sense if we can understand that we are living in the birth of a new story.

Where our advance has been fueled by upward momentum, toward enlightenment, pursuit of abstract values and advancements that demonstrate our capability to act *upon* Nature, today we are being asked to demonstrate our capacity to act *with* Nature. Where the burning candle of human genius—investing in our own perspective—has been the vehicle by which we have unfurled Creation's gifts and advanced consciousness, now we are being asked to advance through seeing ourselves in relation *to* others and *to* the world around us. Today, through suffering but also in newly met mysteries, we are encountering facts that poke away at our inflation. The discoveries of psyche's interplay with matter in quantum physics, synchronicity, the extended mind, and elsewhere in Nature defeat our grandiosity and show us that our labels for truth (such as objectivity) have sometimes been serving to keep us from it. Through this process, in each of its minute movements, our gaze upon the world is made ever so slightly less objective and we come to find ourselves in subjective relation to the world around us. While under the inflated spell of the masculine we have only been able to look "upward" for truth and meaning; today circumstances incessantly lead us toward discovering truth and meaning in places that are more down to earth.

This downward redirection of the zeitgeist is described by Ulanov as an insistence of spirit into our daily choices, requiring of us a step beyond conventional understanding into appreciating the presence of a natural spiritual quality in the mundane world. Irene Champernowne, an English psycho-therapist, describes her experience in a similar way:

> My experience, like many of this generation, is that we cannot manage to live any longer in this outer world with superficial values, and count life worth living. If one experiences strange and out-of-the-ordinary phenomena, and if one's life of outer reality is penetrated from time to time by the mysterious, religious, archetypal world, one is forced to accept the existence and power of these manifestations.[19]

As Champernowne describes, superficial worldviews will not satisfy us once we have come into contact with out-of-the-ordinary phenomena, and today it seems that such contact is happening ever more frequently. Like Talbott, whose witness of a Crop Circle's formation came on the heels of her expression of her heartfelt frustration with the phenomenon (thus exemplifying the out-of-the-ordinary being responded to both authentically and extraordinarily), Irene Champernowne found the fantastic in her life and held it as best she could.

I found her story in a small pamphlet on a lonely library shelf, quite by chance, while researching an entirely different subject. Irene Champernowne founded and directed a psychotherapeutic treatment center at a country house, Withymead, near Exeter, England, from 1942 to 1966 (she is revered today in the UK as a pioneer of art therapy). In the 1950s she was privileged to have as her analyst Antonia "Toni" Wolff. Toni Wolff was a very close companion of Jung's—earlier in her life she had been a patient of his, and later, during a time of crisis in his life, she helped him to explore a profoundly new level of depth in his own unconscious. By the time Irene began working with her, Toni had been analyzing dreams for more than forty years. In between her trips to Zurich to meet with Toni, Irene would send letters describing and discussing her dreams. She sent paintings of her dreams to Toni from 1950 until Toni's death in 1953. I am very proud to have arranged to have her record of this time, *A Memoir of Toni Wolff*, made available online for free distribution by its publisher, the San Francisco Jung Institute.[20]

> This memoir is an account of visionary experiences, represented in paintings (my art therapy) of a deep visionary kind, which I have not fully understood

even with Toni Wolff's help. Jung accepted it all . . . allowing it its inherent validity. Mrs. Jung wrote telling me how important she felt the material was. . . . I
am sure the pictures did their work in me. Some of the stages really made me feel
very anxious. But I could do nothing else but let these visions and dreams come,
record them honestly, struggle to add my thoughts and associations, and send
them to Toni Wolff when I was not able to see her. The whole happening was a
mystery, but I am sure I owe some of my peace and fulfillment of my life to this
fine Swiss woman and I am grateful.[21]

Irene had flown several times to Zurich in 1950 only to find that C. G.
Jung was unable, due to illness or absence, to meet with her. Due to his
unavailability, Jung referred Irene to Toni Wolff and they began to work
together. On her first night home from the second trip, she had a predominantly visual dream that she describes as "a vision, a dream of great power."
In it:

Two women were standing on the edge of the world, seeking. The older was
taller but lame, the younger was shorter and had her arm under that of the taller
as if supporting her. The older looked out with courage (I identified her in some
way with Toni Wolff) and the younger stood beside with strength, but feared
to look. Her head was bowed. I identified myself with this second figure. Above
was the crescent moon and the morning star, to the right the rising sun. An el-
liptical silvery object came flying (a flying saucer). . . .

It was peopled around its rim with figures which I think were men, cloaked
figures, all silvery white. The two women were awed and trembled in that unearthly cosmic space, their position untenable except at the moment of vision.[22]

Here at dawn, two women stand "at the edge of the world, seeking." The
younger with her head bowed, they tremble with awe in the presence of a
peopled flying saucer. Toni writes, "The dream is certainly an extraordinary
one, both in image and feeling. It has a cosmic and impersonal atmosphere."
In the dream, Toni saw a blend of personal and impersonal content and
imagery. She saw meaning present for Irene personally, and a spark of collective meaning—something in the dream was also speaking to the larger
whole that is all of us. In its mixture of personal and impersonal, the dream
is not unlike the nature of the Crop Circle phenomenon, in which a person

may be involved emotionally in the synchronistic-field dynamic of its arrival, but the formation is seemingly meant for the larger collective whole as well.

One key element in the dream is the presence of the older and younger women, which represent the inner figures of the Self and ego. In the psyche the Self seeks our individuation, the coming to maturity and full expression of who we uniquely are in our fullest possibility; and in the dream, the older is lame but looks out with courage, while the younger is strong but cannot look. Here the ego, as the younger woman, clings tightly to the present state of being, refusing to see the new thing. Such an interplay is typical of our own struggle with Crop Circles. Yet, when the older and younger can come to work together, as we see here, the birth of the new can be accomplished: "together the ego and the Self bring the new vision into life. That is a very beautiful and deep presentation of how things are in the psychological world, let us hope the one of the future. But even if the world at large does not see and know it, it is certainly the task of those who know to live it" (p.

14). "Living it" is certainly what Talbott did in her full-bodied engagement with her experience on the particular night of her eyewitness sighting—*she lived it!* She was present, simply with who she really was, feeling her own re-actions and not trying to be anything other than who she was, and a "new vision" arrived. Irene was doing this too—following her inner life as it al-lowed her to unfold something new, both for herself and for all.

However, Toni saw, in the dream's particularities of tone, action, and scope, qualities that she understood to have collective meaning. In the two women standing at "the edge of the world, seeking" and the sun just begin-ning to rise, she saw a visual representation of the change that is happening for all of us today, the change in the collective psyche:

> What happens then is the receding of night and of the moon and the coming of the sun, a new dawn, a new day, perhaps a new cosmic day, a new aeon, as is the case astronomically more or less, the sun being at the end of the Zodiacal sign of [Pisces] and . . . moving into the sign of Aquarius. So a cosmic year comes to an end (as was the case about the time of the birth of Christ, roughly when the sun moved from Aries into [Pisces]). This means, of course, tremendous upheaval, psychically and also concretely. The Christian era is coming to an end. So one can expect a new symbol to appear. It will, of course, not appear as a collective symbol . . . at first, but an individual one. The new symbol seems to be a round thing. As you know it is the symbol in dreams and visions of the Self, the com-plete man, the totality. That is probably the reason why "flying saucers" or discs as they are called in England are "seen." They are symbolic rumours or actually seen things unconsciously perceived as round things.[23]

While the idea of the dawning of the "Age of Aquarius" was popular in the 1960s, it is actually occurring in our time period today. Wolff points out that the change in era that is emerging in our time leads to the expectation of new symbols appearing. She suggests further that this new symbol may well be round. Here, Toni was expressing her own sense of the collective psyche and the interest in the "flying saucer" phenomenon at the time (that had led Jung to write a book on the topic).

Toni saw the meaning in Irene's dream to be profoundly connected to the reemergence of the archetypal Feminine in our time. In the very same year, 1951, the Vatican had announced the Assumption of the Virgin—a dogmatic inclusion of Mary within the God-image. This change came about not through papal initiative, but through parishioner insistence and petition. Jung and Wolff saw this alteration of dogma as a "tremendous happening because it accepts a new and earthly principle into the 2,000 year old masculine and exclusively spiritual principle."[24] They saw this change as emblematic of the emerging into consciousness of our unconscious need for the Feminine. Wolff describes the Feminine as coming in contrast to an "exclusively spiritual," unembodied masculine principle, and including feeling, *eros*, body and matter. While painting this first dream, Irene noticed the words "caught in the hollow of her hand" came to her, "as if the divine feminine deity had held out her hand and caught hold of me" (p. 10). Where feeling has been absent, life and spirit have been missing too. Two paintings produced by a patient of Irene's illustrate this:

> "The Flying Woman" was painted by an intellectual woman [who] lived entirely divorced from her feeling and was cut off from true human living. . . . In her picture, the woman flies far above the city with its pulsating life. . . . Her passion is in her head; her body . . . is bound by a golden cord . . . in self-contained system; mummified. (p. 35)

In the second painting, "The Woman of the Earth," a similar woman stands stretched between the earth and a heavenly sphere that touches her hand. Golden cords extend from the sphere to a star, around her and down her wrist, which rest on a bear, and to a tree beside. The tree has "some life: three leaves and a pear" (p. 35). Irene notes the connection here between Demeter, the Bear Goddess, and the Bear. Demeter is of-the-earth, and this dark Bear symbolizes the dark living matter that is archetypally Feminine. Irene says of this patient's creation: "She has begun her descent" (p. 35). Here the feeling is moving downward into the life of the previously "mummified," non-feeling woman.

Irene's second painting on the theme of the original dream and vision expressed further the idea of Feminine as spirit coming down into matter:

> Another picture emerged early in December . . . the peace and sincerity of the painting class drew it out of me despite the storm and stress of life. . . . In [it] the flying saucer seems to have come to earth and is like a flower. It contains two

women in its heart, and around the central seed box lie the stamens, faint pink-ish remains of the circle round the saucer's rim. . . . The picture gave me a feeling of peace; something had arrived and was settling down onto the earth. (p. 16)

In the center of the flower in this image sit the two women together, and the energy has "arrived on the earth and is still whirling around, but be-ginning to settle down, like a plant, therefore the green leaves" (p. 19). In "The Green Woman Crucified Between the Golden Wheels," the central woman stands "with arms outstretched holding two wheels apart" (p. 21). She writes further that in October 1951 she found herself drawing the same woman "bringing her arms together until the two wheels faced each other," and then:

Between them threads sprang up, joining them like silk or light, so creating two vessels which were revolving opposite ways, and touching at a central point where the strands met. (p. 25)

The image of a beam of light with two wheels revolving opposite each other is reminiscent of the spiraling beam of light that Talbott and van der Broeke witnessed creating the Crop Circle formation. This association is furthered by the next painting.

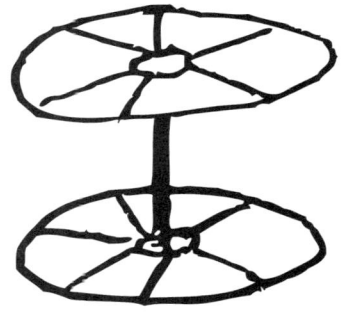

What had been two spiraling Golden wheels with a beam of energy in between them, here transforms into something that can fly off into the sky! And the image of the flying wheels would continue as an element throughout the image series. Also present here is the whirling energy seen in the second image (and others not shown). This kind of movement is strongly suggestive of the force that one imagines occurs in the creation of a Crop Circle, where grain is fanned and spun down softly to the ground. Such a connection might seem to be arbitrary if it were not for the fact of the original UFO image at the start of Irene's dream series, the flying off into the sky of the spiraling tubes of light and fact that the dreamer was then living in the English countryside—the historical epicenter of the phenomenon. These images make an explicit connection between swirling grain, UFOs, and the archetypal Feminine, in an astounding parallel to the kind of framework built here for approaching the mystery of Crop Circles. In making a connection between the Crop Circle phenomenon and these images, it is also important to remember that Toni Wolff, Emma Jung, and C. G. Jung all saw Irene's painting as expressing something that was emerging from our cultural psyche at this moment in time. I see them as offering a clue toward deeper understanding both of the Crop Circle mystery and of the nature of the change in the psyche at this time in general.

In the seventh, the woman "sinks to the earth, her face in her hands, relieved yet empty and broken, the wheels high up are flying away." In the eighth, the woman raises her head to find that she has been left with two little golden wheels "on her person, one at her neck and one at her waist. . . . She is terrified to see what she has acquired. . . . There is a sense of guilt as though she stolen the woman's equivalent of the Promethean fire from the Goddesses and has the impersonal stamp on her" (p. 27). The paintings

carry the woman into a forest and into a more person-focused image content. C. G. Jung spoke to Irene of these images as reflecting the conflict between the individual—as bearer of new consciousness—and the world around them.

Later images express that struggle and her achievement of a sense of a "knowing in the sense of experiencing" and the woman being "left with a value." Near the end, a cloaked figure in gray wrapped a dark green hooded cloak over her "and she shrank into it in thankfulness, hidden and withdrawn" (p. 30). Finally, in the twelfth picture, the broad landscape image returns: A storm sky, a sunrise at the center, a sea, or sea of clouds, a rainbow. . . . I could not see people on the earth and yet I knew it was not empty. . . . At the last moment . . . I suddenly saw three women, not two now but three, standing on the world . . . gazing up at the double wheel symbol flying away toward the rising sun. . . . I went away in peace. (p. 41–2)

Seeing the paintings together later, Mrs. Emma Jung (Carl's wife, herself an accomplished analyst) wrote that "your pictures have impressed me very deeply indeed; I feel there is something extremely important and valuable for woman in general [in them]" (p. 30).

A few weeks later, in early November, Irene met with Carl Jung and they went through her pictures together. They brought to mind for him the "conflict of opposites in life" and women's experience of that opposition. He showed her a wonderful antique manuscript written by Christian mystic Jacob Boehme, which illustrated his experience of the opposites. In Boehme's images two half circles were back-to-back with a heart in between. This image echoed a dream that Irene had nearly fifteen years prior, in which she and her mentor Peter Baynes each held a half-circle that became one as they passed through a fire. While speaking with Jung, Irene reflected on the difference between the opposites in life as she heard Jung describe them from a man's point of view, and how she experienced that opposition inside of herself. "I felt the 'essence' from the side of the flesh and Yin going over to comprehend the Yang. Up until then I had known what it felt like to be woman over against man (i.e., when the Yang principle comes down and becomes concrete in life through Yin). But this time I was quite separate" (p. 34). Toni Wolff had written of this idea to Irene, saying that "like the Chinese Yin, where the woman power or the feminine principle is the concrete principle which makes the ideas visible, when the masculine principle is hidden in the sky, so to speak, not yet formed. It needs the Yin principle to bring . . . [the ideas] down to earth, to give them birth in the concrete world." Of her experience Irene wrote further that:

> I felt something more, something new, namely the "essence" of the concrete principle of "being," Yin trying to rise up into Yang and find its meaning there. It was a tremendous experience, difficult to explain. I was trying to birth the experience from the side of Yin and via man. . . . The words of John Donne seem to explain this movement of woman:
>
> > . . . we understood
> > Her by her sight: her pure and eloquent blood
> > Spoke in her cheeks, and so distinctly wrought
> > That one might also say, her body thought.[25]

If one can hold the tension of inner struggle with an open heart, the two "half-circles" of light and dark are brought together. In doing so, a new wholeness is made inside of us, a new authority inside of ourselves is discovered. This is the bringing of spirit into matter through feeling.

Such an advance, however, cannot be completed without a firm foundation within the masculine principle. Our psychological return to the Feminine cannot be completed safely without the ability to discriminate between truth and falsehood, reality and illusion. Irene writes that the "'positive' regression to the mother and the woman, the womb, the body; the progression via the father; continuity and containment seems coupled with out-going risk and progressive evolution." Toni echoes this, writing that "she will not achieve it without the masculine principle of Logos" (p. 46). Our era's crises and mysteries challenge us to use both modes at once. And furthermore, while previously authority figures helped usher in the collective upward movement of spirit out of body, today returning the masculine to the Feminine requires the loss of authority figures and the bearing of the burden personally. "It all seems such a far cry from the simple religious life of my ancestors" (p. 54).

> The future marriage of the opposites is not only in our own lives but in the world. (p. 56)

Crop Circles leave us startled at having been met and spoken to by an Other. Yet who this Other is, we do not know. In this way, the phenomenon's mystery necessitates that we respond to it from a place of not-knowing. Following an initial masculine inquiry into its nature and authenticity, we are called to participate in a psychological struggle that necessarily includes attendance to our emotional and psychological responses. Within us are the most far-flung fantasies about what might be going on, and thoughts of the most fearful and dark characterizations of the phenomenon. Perhaps worst of all, at some point we will likely refuse to participate with it altogether. Even Talbott, after seeing the tubes of light in front of her—with another witness—was left wondering afterward whether what she had seen could really have been so deliberate. "What are the chances that this recent amazing display was coincidental?"[26] Experiences of the out-of-the-ordinary leave us oscillating between acceptance and denial, between the unsatisfactory, but familiar, old view and the newly emerging but still unformed one. Here mystery helps to break down the old rigid structures in us and the conflict with an unknown Other, and the physical nature of this phenomenon's mystery lead us down into the dark, unknowing place inside of us where vitality and new life might be found. This quality is both an outcome of Crop Circles and an innate part of their nature, for symbols of plant life, Jung says, lead us toward:

The downward way, the yin way . . . earth, the darkness of humanity.[27]

Where there is something that we need to know but we do not know that we need it, it is only out of darkness that it can come to us. This is why we speak of the shadow as dark, like soil; out of its blackness emerges the new life—unpredictably and uncertainly. Such new life cannot be found through direct, masculine pursuit. Solar approaches, upward toward ideals and clarity, lead away from what is needed, when the earthly, material principle is missing. When the Self archetype is symbolized through natural phenomena such as plant life "the instinctual or organic life of the Self is being stressed. This imagery tends to occur when the individual needs to re-establish contact with this level of being."[28] We daily take the miracle of life (the Mother) for granted in endless pursuit of more and more (the ego), and the wholeness and return to balance that we need will be found through the earthly and the vital.

We live in a moment in which mysterious realities are coming to visit whether we like it or not. Denial by our media and institutions has served to insulate us from this somewhat, but that is slowly giving way too. It is a quality of our age that these new mysteries want us to deal with them—clearly the Crop Circle phenomenon wants us to relate to it. Synchronicity, quantum physics, and the extended mind each show us a new vision of the world in which psyche and matter are of one fabric—Nature is revealing herself to us in a heart-entangled world. And we are ready for this. Two thousand years of the masculine path has left us with a solidly established ego that can withstand more "wattage" than ever before—we can handle more mystery, more life of spirit, more juju. These new mysteries point past clockwork worldviews toward something deeper, more complex, yet something that at the same time appears to be more intimate, seeking our fulfillment and engagement with it in the discovery of meaning every day. It is this newly emergent impetus that placed the mystery that Nancy Talbott had declared to be "too complex, too elusive, too difficult to study" right in front of her eyes. It is this same newly emerging force that led Irene to put her hand to a series of paintings that two seminal Jungian women felt to be of great collective value and that are indeed serving us today. It is this same newly emergent quality that led me to find a tiny pamphlet that offers us our best glimpse at what Carl and Emma Jung and Toni Wolff might have thought about Crop Circles. A part of this unfolding dynamic of era, Crop Circles both exemplify this change and embody it, simultaneously symbolizing and bringing us into a process that leads us out of our heads and *into* the miracle of life—a miracle that beats on every moment in each of our hearts. Answers now are being found in feeling—or rather, it is in following our feeling that the right questions are coming to be asked by us. Participation of the heart seems to be a requirement, not for someone else, but *for you and me.* These new phenomena are showing us a different picture of the world.

The God of Thunder, Thor, was seated in the sky; on his right hand was seated a great, black, ugly, almost obscene woman. I was observing this from a very small rocky island on which I was standing alone, naked, in the midst of the sea. Suddenly a raging wind and storm blew up and the sea beat all around me. Thunder and lightning followed each other in close succession. All was dark; one could not see. Equally suddenly after a tremendous clap of thunder all was hushed, the sky cleared. The woman had fallen from her heights by Thor and all I could see was a great black thigh sticking up like a rock out of the water. This rock I knew was she. The waves were gently lapping over it and a voice spoke saying, "Upon this rock will I build my Church." Then I saw below me, mirrored as it were deep down in the clear water, fields of waving corn with the wind passing over them. I knew that was the future.[29]

NOTES

PREFACE AND INTRODUCTION

1. While there are exceptions (a rare few researchers do *seem* to make something near a living, but I have yet to hear of anyone getting rich off of their work), most researchers of Crop Circles have put themselves into debt doing so or are barely making ends meet, having put their own money into their research. In many cases, even more costly is the toll that their curiosity has exacted upon their relationships and personal lives.
2. Carl Jung, *Collected Works 6,* trans. R. F. C. Hull (Princeton, NJ: Princeton University Press, 1953–79).
3. Irene Champernowne, *A Memoir of Toni Wolff* (San Francisco: San Francisco Jung Society, 1972), p. 30.
4. Tarnas, Richard, *The Passion of the Western Mind* (New York: Harmony Books/Random House, 1991), p. 4.
5. Carl Jung, *Collected Works 10,* trans. R. F. C. Hull (Princeton, NJ: Princeton University Press, 1953–79).
6. Ulanov, 1999, *Religion and the Spiritual in Carl Jung,* quoted from: C.G. Jung, *Letters,* 2 vols., eds G. Adler and A. Jaffé, trans. R. F. C. Hull (Princeton: Princeton University Press, 1973 and 1975), I, 30 January 1948, 492, and 23 September 1949, 537.
7. Ulanov, 1971, cited in Shuttle and Redgrove, p. 15.
8. Barasch, Marc Ian, *Healing Dreams* (New York: Riverhead, 2000), p. 48.
9. Nathan Schwartz-Salant, *The Mystery of Human Relationships: Alchemy and the Transformation of the Self* (London: Routledge, 1998), p. 195–6.
10. Ibid.
11. Corbett, *The Religious Function of the Psyche* (Chicago: Chicago Jung Society, 1986).

12. Jung in Harding, 1976, p. xi.
13. Ann Ulanov, "San Francisco Jung Conference: Depth Psychology and Spiritual Practice," San Francisco Jung Society Depth Psychology and Spirituality Conference, San Francisco Jung Society, San Francisco, CA, 2002. AUDIO.
14. Carl Jung, *Symbols of Transformation: An Analysis of the Prelude to a Case of Schizophrenia, Volume II* (New York: Harper & Brothers, 1962), p. 117)
15. Jung in Harding, 1976, p. ix.
16. R. A. Johnson, *Femininity Lost and Regained* (New York: HarperCollins, 1991), p. 3.
17. Rilke, 4/23/23.
18. Barasch, p. 361.

ONE **BODY OF EVIDENCE**

1. See Andreas Mueller, www.cropcirclescience.org; Canadian Crop Circle Research Network www.cccrn.ca; and T. Wilson, *The Secret History of Crop Circles* (Devon, UK: The Center for Crop Circle Studies, 1998).
2. See www.cropcircleresearch.com/articles/distribution.html and www.cropcirclescience.org.
3. See www.bltresearch.com for more on this.
4. www.bltresearch.com/plantab.html.
5. See Delgado (1992), p. 152–3, as well as www.bltresearch.com.
6. www.bltresearch.com.
7. www.bltresearch.com/otherfacts.html#growth.
8. See www.bltresearch.com.
9. See Colin Andrews' website www.colinandrews.net, or *Ultimate Crop Circles* (DVD).
10. *Crop Circles: Quest for Truth.* Dir. William Gazecki. 2002. DVD.
11. The occasional discovery of instrument variance is reported on occasion in the area of the formations. Nancy Talbott in personal communication (4/20/08).
12. Wilson, 1998, p. 33.
13. This account was originally published in CPR Newsletter, no. 3, p. 4; and CPR International newsletter v. 2, no.1, p. 6.
14. Wilson, 1998, p. 33.
15. See Andrews in 2002 video *Ultimate Crop Circles: Signs from Space;* and Pringle, 1999
16. Thomas, 1998, p. 21.
17. This is another experiment that could be easily carried out by amateur researchers, see online: www.cropcircleresearch.com/enigma/issue1/gizmo.html.
18. Similar results were also noted in Silva (2002), p. 123.
19. See Thomas, 1998, and also Silva, 2002.

20. Thomas, 1998, p. 21.
21. Delgado, 1992, p. 128–9.
22. See http://www.bltresearch.com/xrd.php.
23. D. M. Moore, "Presentation of the Roebling Medal of the Mineralogical Society of America for 2000 to Robert Coltart Reynolds, Jr., Am. Mineralogist," 86:943–45, 2001.
24. See www.bltresearch.com/xrd.html.
25. *Crop Circles: Quest for Truth.*
26. See www.sacredbritain.com/research-underground.html and also BLT Research, www.bltresearch.com/otherfacts.html#acquifer.
27. Pringle, 1999, p. 17.
28. Captured on video tape by Ulrich, using Peter Sorenson's video camera.
29. For more on the East Field, July 2009, see: www.silentcircle.co.uk/egf1.html.
30. See also Ohio formation, 2005: www.bltresearch.com/labreports/ohio.php.
31. Silva, 2002, p. 44.
32. Busty Taylor in Andrews' *Undeniable Evidence* (DVD), among others.
33. Pringle, 1999, p. 12. See also Busty Taylor in *Crop Circles: Quest for Truth* DVD.
34. See Busty Taylor, *Ultimate Crop Circles* DVD.
35. Pringle, 1999.
36. Pringle, 1999.
37. See Thomas, 1998, Wilson, 1998, Pringle, 1999, and Silva, 2002.
38. See Gazecki, 2002, and Martineau, 1993.
39. Most such white horses, however, are not ancient.
40. For an extremely thorough look at these formations in both years and the media accounts around them please visit: http://psiapplications.com/Treepad/.
41. Robert Plot's eighteenth-century diagrams do depict squares and other simple shapes.
42. Gazecki, 2002.
43. Barbury Castle, U.K. formation, May 1997.
44. Red Deer, Alberta, Canada formation, September 2, 2001.
45. Barbury Castle, U.K. formation, May 31, 1999.
46. At Glastonbury Tor there is a famous well-cover in the design of the Vesica Pisces.
47. Silbury/Avebury, 1992.
48. *Science News,* 382/1/92, p. 76.
49. Used with permission of the author.
50. See *Crop Circles: The Hidden Form* by Nick Kollerstrom or online at www.hypermaths.org/cropcircles/. Or see Bert Janssen's online geometry papers: cropcirclesandmore.com/geometries/geometries.html.
51. Silva, 2002, p. 195.
52. Silva, 2002, p. 197.

53. Jung, *CW 11*, par. 6.

54. CNN—2001 Milk Hill formations—U.S. broadcast of this formation's discovery.

55. National Geographic's series of television and written articles as well as much other reporting reflects this.

TWO **WITCHES' RINGS AND DEVIL'S TWISTS**

1. Fideler described them this way in 1991 in *Alexandria: The Journal of Western Cosmological Traditions*, #1, ed. by David Fideler (Grand Rapids, MI: Phanes Press, 1991).

2. Various, but see Hawkins, 1992.

3. Hawkins, 1992.

4. Various but see for example, Hussey, 2001: http://www.qtm.net/~geibdan/newse/croppic/huh.html.

5. This is a widespread and seemingly obvious interpretation mentioned throughout the literature. For a fictional interpretation, see the movie *Signs*, 2002.

6. See Hussey, 2001: http://www.qtm.net/~geibdan/newse/croppic/huh.html & Ruby. *The Gift*, 1996.

7. Nearly every Crop Circle book looks at this. See Martineau, 1992; Anderhub and Roth, 2002; Bartholomew, 1992.

8. See Martineau, 2003; Nick Kollerstrom, 2002; Bert Janssen, cropcirclesandmore.com/geometries/geometries.html and others.

9. See Neil Olsen's website www.cropcirclesdeciphered.com.

10. There are several other early accounts, including one from 1686, found in *A Natural History of Staffordshire*, written by Professor Robert Plot, LLD, the first "keeper" of Oxford's Ashmolean Museum and a professor of chemistry at Oxford. (For more on this, including illustrations, see bltresearch.com/otherfacts.html.) An additional earlier account, from 800 A.D. in Lyon, France, attributed to St. Agobard, Bishop of Lyon, has yet to be properly documented.

11. The pamphlet is subtitled *Strange News Out of Hartford-Shire* and is dated August 22, 1678.

12. Wilson, 1998, p. 145.

13. Robin Goodfellow is often depicted as a hoofed half man with a ring of revelers dancing in a circle behind him. Also known as Puck, a role in which he is featured in Shakespeare's *A Midsummer Night's Dream*, Robin Goodfellow is related to the figure of the Green Man, and is sometimes thought of as the King of Fairies (the Oberon role in *Midsummer*). In all of these forms, he is known as a trickster and a mischievous spirit who performs his deeds by moonlight. "The Mad Merry Pranks of Robin Goodfellow," a seventeenth-century ballad, describes his pranks and his mocking laughter as "Ho ho ho!" (Sound familiar?) "The Green Man is archetype for an androgynous, regenerative spirit connected with the earth and

its vegetation. . . . This archetype appears again and again as a striking contrast to the cultural mandate of perfection, often utilizing the easygoing laughter of regenerative naturalness. In these works, the archetype underscores the tension between masculine and feminine ways of knowing and being—the former characterized by single-mindedness and rigid control, and the latter by expansiveness and acceptance." Absher, p. 6.

14. Halifax, 1993.
15. Homeric hymn to Hermes.
16. *"Mercurius in the Cornfields," Cereologist* #1. See: http://www.sayer.abel.co.uk/cereol.htm.
17. Bartholomew, 1991, p. 125.
18. Michell in Bartholomew, 1991, p. 125.
19. Michell in Bartholomew, 1991, p. 125.
20. See, for example: http://herbarium.usu.edu/fungi/funfacts/ringsfct.htm.
21. Shakespeare, *The Tempest* (Act V, scene i).
22. Silva, 2002, p. 281; connection found by Sir Lawrence Gardner.
23. For more on Robert Plot see www.oum.ox.ac.uk/geocolls/plot/plothome.htm.
24. BLT Research: www.bltresearch.com/plantab.php.
25. Rediscovered by Peter Van Doorn and reprinted in the January 2000 issue of the *Journal of Meteorology* (Volume 25, p. 20–1). Mr. Van Doorn made this discovery while doing archival research on ball lightning phenomena. He heads the Ball Lightning division of the Tornado Storm and Research Organization (www.torro.org.uk).
26. The nine early categories of causation listed by Andrews were: Whirlwind Vortex, Plasma Vortex, Earth Energies [Gaia], Extra-Terrestrial Origin, Underground Archeological, Chemical Applications (no longer considered), Hoaxes, God Force, Military Experimentation. He believes that there are only three broad categories of explanation: Extra-Terrestrial, Gaia, or Spirits/Souls (Art Bell, radio broadcast, 2001).
27. Wilson, 1998, p. 33.
28. Noyes from "As Old As Adam?" in *The Crop Circle Enigma,* 1990.
29. Discovered by Andreas Mueller, this account from Barry Smith is in the BBC online archive "WWII, A People's War."
30. C. G. Jung, 1964, p. 31.
31. C. G. Jung, *Letters,* vol. 2, p. 259.
32. Leo Tolstoy, from: *What Is Art and Essays on Art* (Oxford, UK: Oxford University Press, 1930), trans. Aylmer Maude.
33. See Ted Koppel's reference to our overemphasis upon breaking news, on *Charlie Rose,* 11/21/05.
34. CNN, Milk Hill formation coverage, August 2001.

35. *National Geographic*'s commissioning of two formations in 2004 and one in 2007, and then presenting a television documentary that paid no attention to any of the scientific research done on the topic; for more on this see Lucy Pringle's article at www.kornkreise-forschung.de/textNatGeoHoax07 and BLT Research webpage: www.bltresearch.com/published/natgeo_cropcircleshow.php.

36. See "Bad News" Tom Stanton (2005), among others.

37. See Moore, 2004, p. 101.

38. Bartholomew, 1991, p. 10.

39. See Andrews, 1991, p. 160, for more on this.

40. This report is called the "Durant Report" or the "Robertson Panel Report." See www.cufon.org/cufon/robertdod.htm.

41. Wingfield and Delgado in Silva, 2002, p. 39–40. See also Taylor, "*What on Earth? Inside the Crop Circle*" DVD.

42. Silva, 2002, p. 36.

43. Andrews, 2003, p. 160.

44. Canadian Government files online, see www.JungAndCropCircles.net.

45. Government interest is also found in a Canadian report from the 1980s found in Andrews and Delgado, 1989.

46. http://psiapplications.com/Treepad/documents/220.html.

47. See both Taylor/Gazecki *Crop Circles: Quest for Truth* and Taylor *What on Earth? Inside the Crop Circle Mystery* (2009).

48. As listed above, Andrews suggested three broad categories of explanation for the phenomenon's agency in a 2001 radio interview: Gaia, Extra-Terrestrial, and Spirit/Souls. In 2003 he listed a broader range of possible agencies, many of which can be grouped together under one of these categories. In this publication, he also deemphasizes the suitability of the soul-spirit category due to the lack of evidence. See Andrews, *Crop Circles: Signs of Contact,* 2003. Despite Andrews's movement away from the third category, I believe that these three general categories provide a suitable response to the phenomenon and sum up the majority of the various explanations.

49. Andrews and Spignesi, 2003, p. 61–2.

50. Lovelock, James, *Gaia: A New Look At Life on Earth* (Oxford, UK: Oxford University Press, 2003).

51. In some descriptions this is attributed to a feeling that we are endangering the planet (Polly Carson, on video; Andrews, 1991; etc.).

52. Hussey, 2001, www.dreamscape.com/morgana/belinda.htm.

53. See Thomas, 1998, p. 103.

54. A technological example within this category includes Doug Ruby's 1995 book *The Gift,* in which he interprets the geometrical patterns of crop circles as two-

dimensional versions of three-dimensional technological models, which he believes were communicated to us as a gift from an extraterrestrial source.

55. Bert McKay, *Regina Leader-Post,* Regina, Saskatchewan, October 1974.

56. See Pringle, Andrews, others.

57. See www.bltreserach.com for the recent Polish account. See Pringle, 1999. See also Langenbrunner account from Manitoba, 1974.

58. Silva, 2002.

59. See later chapters for more on this.

60. *Ultimate Crop Circles: Signs from Space,* 2002.

61. *Undeniable Evidence* (film), 1991, ARK Soundwaves.

62. Silva, 2002, p. 268. See also Paul Anderson, CCCRN website, Moulton Howe, etc.

63. See Talbott interview, Taylor/Gazecki, *Crop Circles: Quest for Truth.*

64. C. G. Jung, *Mandala Symbolism* (Princeton, UK: Princeton University Press, 1972), p. 11. Here cites Caesarius of Heisterbach and notes additional references to this globe of light phenomena in Bozzano, *Popoli primitivi e Manifestizioni.*

65. See Silva, p. 271.

66. In Silva, p. 261, via a communication with Colin Andrews.

67. Taylor/Gazecki, *Crop Circles: Quest for Truth.*

68. Karen Alexander *nee* Douglas, 2000, online. For more of her writing see www.TemporaryTemples.com.

69. Anderhub and Roth, p. 123.

70. Jung, *Mandala Symbolism,* p. 3.

71. Jung, *Collected Works 13* (Princeton, NJ: Princeton University Press, 1983), par. 208.

72. Jung and Kerenyi, p. 13.

73. Jung, *Mandala Symbolism,* p. 4.

74. Jung, *Collected Works 10* (Princeton, NJ: Princeton University Press, 1970), par. 803.

75. Maria Szepes in Anderhub and Roth, p. 123.

76. Marie-Louise von Franz, "The Geography of the Soul," *In Touch* magazine, 1993.

77. See Holden and Scott in Bartholomew, 1991, and Silva.

78. Holden and Scott in Bartholomew, 1991, p. 94

79. Holden and Scott in Bartholomew, 1991, p. 99.

80. Jung, 1961, p. 334.

81. Holden and Scott, in Bartholomew, 1991, p. 101.

82. K. Alexander *nee* Douglas, 2001, online. This reference is outdated online but for more of her writing see www.temporarytemples.com.

THREE **GREENING CIRCLES**

1. Whitmont, in Zweig and Abrams, p. 14.
2. Von Franz, 1996, p. 39.
3. Psychology and mythologically, the power of naming is associated with making conscious. See for example the myth of Rumplestilskin. "Initiation consists in the act of learning to call the things of the world by those names which they bear in the spirit of their divine authors." (Rudolph Steiner)
4. The form of origin of the phenomenon worldwide and across centuries of reports is predominantly circular. Although there have been years in which the phenomenon displayed itself in insectograms and other natural nonconcentric images, the return of the form to predominantly concentric images for the last decades speaks to a coherent concentric patterning throughout the phenomenon's genesis. This evolution into greater complexity of form while maintaining (or returning to) a concentric pattern mirrors the form of the Self archetype in the psyche (as first observed by Jung), in which the circular form at its most basic and most complex (as in the mandala) serves in either case to be a vehicle for psychic reorientation and healing.
5. Jung, *Alchemical Studies* (Princeton, NJ: Princeton University Press, 1983), p. 25.
6. De Champeux and Sterckx, cited in Chevalier and Gheerbrant.
7. Chevalier and Gheerbrant, p. 333.
8. Hollis J., *The Eden Project: In Search of the Magical Other* (Toronto, ON: Inner City Books, 1998), p. 35.
9. Jung, *Collected Works 8* (Princeton, NJ: Princeton University Press, 1970), par. 507.
10. Paraphrase from Daryl Sharp's excellent, online Jung Lexicon: www.psychceu .com/Jung/sharplexicon.html.
11. Jung, *The Seminar on Nietzche's Thus Spake Zarathustra,* in Lecture VII, winter term, 1535.
12. Jung, *Collected Works 16* (Princeton, NJ: Princeton University Press, 1985), par. 470.
13. Samuels, Shorter, and Plaut, 1986, p. 139.
14. Whitmont, in Zweig and Abrams, p. 14.
15. Samuels, Shorter, and Plaut, 1986, p. 113–4.
16. See Chapter Two.
17. While the timing of Easter is related directly to the Hebrew Passover, its name is drawn from one of several possible similarly named goddesses, the Celtic Ertha, the Babylonian Ishtar, Astarte Babylonian, Goddess of the Sea, or Eostre, Anglo-Saxon Goddess of the dawn.
18. This shift is considered further throughout later chapters.

19. Jung, "Anima and Animus," in *Collected Works 7* (Princeton, NJ: Princeton University Press, 1972), par. 318.

20. Jung, *Collected Works 11* (Princeton, NJ: Princeton University Press, 1975), par. 131.

21. Sharp, *Jung Lexicon,* online.

22. Branden, in Zweig and Abrams, p. 281.

23. Whitmont, in Zweig and Abrams p. 17.

24. Von Franz, 1996, p. 158.

25. Branden, in Zweig and Abrams, p. 282.

26. Jung, *Aion* (Princeton, NJ: Princeton University Press, 1979), pp. 27–28

27. Bacon, "The Masculine Birth of Time," in *Advancement of Learning* (CreateSpace Independent Publishing Platform, 2013).

28. Von Franz, 1996.

29. Samuels et al, p. 11.

30. Jung, *Collected Works 9* (Princeton, NJ: Princeton University Press, 1981), ii, par. 15.

31. See Chapter Two.

32. Von Franz, 1996, p. 45.

33. Cirlot, p. 291.

34. Black Elk in Brown, 1971.

35. Gimbutas, *The Language of the Goddess* (London: Thames and Hudson, 2001), p. 282

36. Rector of Bardwell-on-Sea and chaplain of St. Peter's Chapel.

37. O'Donohue, p. xix.

38. Campbell, 1979, p. 42.

39. Judith, 2000, p. 32.

40. Fincher, p. 118.

41. Jung, 1964, p. 266.

42. Jung, 1997, pp. 318–319.

43. Young-Eisendrath, p. 320.

44. Jung, 1964, p. 803.

45. Fordham, 1953, p. 66.

46. In Edinger, 1972, p. 37.

47. Jung, *Collected Works 13* (Princeton, NJ: Princeton University Press, 1983), par. 25.

48. Von Franz, 1996, p. 82.

49. Chevalier and Gheerbrant, 1996, p. 196.

50. See the helpful entry on mandalas at en.wikipedia.org/wiki/Mandala.

51. Tresidder, p. 46–7.

52. Plato, *Timaeus, The Stanford Encyclopedia of Philosophy* (Spring 2014 Edition), http://plato.stanford.edu/archives/spr2014/entries/plato-timaeus/.

53. Cited in Chevalier and Gheerbrant, 1996, p. 120.

54. Tressider, 2005.

55. Chevalier and Gheerbrant, 1996, p. 29.

56. Jung, *The Seminar on Nietzche's Thus Spake Zarathustra,* in Lecture VII, winter term, 1935.

57. Both von Franz and Ulanov use this description of the activity of the Self archetype.

58. Artress, p. 15.

59. Artress, p. 14.

60. Joseph Campbell, *The Power of Myth* (New York: Anchor Books, 1991).

61. In Campbell, ed., *Mysteries,* Princeton University Press, p. 155, p. 161.

62. Jung, *The Seminar on Nietzche's Thus Spake Zarathustra,* in Lecture VII, winter term, 1935.

63. Robert A. Johnson, *Owning Your Own Shadow: Understanding the Dark Side of the Psyche* San Francisco, CA: Harper San Francisco, 1993).

64. Samuels, Shorter, and Plaut, 1986, p. 50–1.

65. Johnson, *Owning Your Own Shadow.*

66. Moore, T., *Dark Nights of the Soul,* p. 29.

67. Keats described this quality in a letter of December 1817.

68. Schwartz-Salant, 1998, p. 37.

69. Wilkinson, 1998.

70. A paraphrase of Wallace Stevens' "things seen are things as seen."

71. Jung, The Psychology of the Transference (Princeton, NJ: Princeton University Press, 1969), par 469, and Mandala Symbolism (Princeton, NJ: Princeton University Press, 1969), par. 634.

72. This is a paraphrase from T. Robbins, 1980, p. 229—much of this paragraph draws from that page.

73. Harris, p. 81.

74. Jung, *The Conjunction, CW 14* (Princeton, NJ: Princeton University Press, 1977), par. 706.

75. Jung, *Collected Works 9,* ii, p. 266.

76. Jung, *Psychology and Religion, Collected Works 11,* par. 134.

77. Antonio Machado, "Last Night As I Was Sleeping." Poem translated by Robert Bly.

78. Artress, p. 15.

79. Jung, *Collected Works 9,* par. 634.

80. Lawlor, *Sacred Geometry,* 1982.

81. Jung, *Collected Works 9,* par. 712.

FOUR **ANTIQUE PAGEANTRY**

1. While grain deities are found in both genders, worldwide the majority of agricultural deities are feminine, Goddesses as personification of the Earth as nourisher and sustainer.
2. Berger, *The Goddess Obscured,* p. 16.
3. Gadon, p. 3.
4. Patai, p. 15.
5. Ake Hultkrantz in Olson (Ed.), 1994, p. 202.
6. Brubaker in Olson (Ed.), p. 146.
7. Neumann, p. 261–2.
8. Harding, p. 159.
9. Harding p. 159.
10. Ishtar is related to nature even in her absence. When she is away, there is no desire to propagate.
11. Harding, p. 159.
12. Gadon, p. 143.
13. Baring and Harvey, p. 5.
14. Baring and Harvey, p. 6.
15. Baring and Cashford, p. 369.
16. Baring and Harvey, p. 78.
17. See Jung and Kerenyi, p. 137: "By entering into that figure of Demeter we realize the universal principle of life, which is to be pursued, robbed, raped, *fail to understand,* to rage and grieve, but then to get everything back and be born again."
18. Jung and Kerenyi, p. 142.
19. Jung and Kerenyi, emphasis original.
20. Here corn is being used to refer to grain. Corn is a New World plant and was not available in ancient Greece. Luke as cited in Gadon, p. 157.
21. Eliade, 1958, p. xv.
22. Eliade, 1958, p. 89.
23. Jeanne Groissant, *Aristotle et les Mystères* (New York: Arno Press, 1979).
24. Eliade, 1958, p. 89.
25. Eliade, 1958, p. 89.
26. Schwartz-Salant, p. 5.
27. Baring and Cashford, p. 8.
28. Judith, 2000, p. 386.
29. The New Jerusalem Bible, Proverbs 8:26–31.
30. The prior sentence also refers to Baring and Harvey; p. 22.
31. Baring and Harvey, p. 24.
32. L. L. Nelson (Ed.), "A History of Jonathon Adler" (2002).
33. Wilson, 1998, p. 140–1.

34. Sklar, 2001, p. 139.
35. Sklar, 2001, p. 140
36. See Leyland reference in Chapter Two.
37. Berger, 1988, p. 71.
38. Jones, 1990/1996.
39. Sjoo and Mor, p. 133.
40. Sjoo and Mor, p. 73.
41. Cited in Sjoo and Moor p. 133.
42. Dames, 1976, p. 12, as cited in Gadon, p. 76.
43. Baring and Cashford, p. 99.
44. Berger, p. 70.
45. Berger, p. 73.
46. *Imbolc* is also a Celtic term for "spring" and the celebration is thought to also re-
    late to the birth of ewes during this time. In each of these ways, *Imbolc* celebrated
    the Goddess' reawakening in spring and her renewed receptivity to seed.
47. In Berger, p. 21–2.
48. Berger, p. 22.
49. Berger, p. 21.
50. Berger, p. 19.
51. Berger, p. 71.
52. Gadon, p. 83.
53. James George Frazer, *Golden Bough* (Hertfordshire, UK: Wordsworth Editions,
    1998), p. 404.
54. Rickard in Noyes, *The Crop Circle Enigma,* p. 63.
55. Berger, p 2.
56. Berger, p. 66.
57. Berger, p. 66.
58. Berger, p. 66.
59. The New Jerusalem Bible, John 12:24.
60. Udo Becker, *The Continuum Encyclopedia of Symbols.*(London: Continuum,
    2000, p. 327).
61. Berger describes her life story, as found in Latin texts of the time, "the virtu-
    ous Radegund had been forced to marry the brutal Merovingian king Clotaire.
    When Clotaire murdered Radegund's brother, she fled, became a nun, and under-
    took to minister to the poor and sick. King Clotaire determined to recover her,
    set out in pursuit, but never actually captured her, and she went on to establish
    monasteries and continue her life of good works" (p. 55). Oral tradition would
    describe her pursuit and escape through the lens of the goddess and the Grain
    Miracle. As it is written in the fourteenth century, Radegund, traveling with two
    other nuns, is pursued by King Clotaire, when they come upon a farmer sowing

his field. She asks that he say that "neither man nor woman has passed by here" (p. 55). Upon entering the field, the wheat grows tall enough to hide them all and the farmer, when asked by the King if he had seen anyone pass by, responds, "No, not since [I] first sowed these very oats" (p. 55). The incorporation of the Grain Miracle into Radegund's legend cannot be located in written records, but by the tenth century ecclesiastical documents show an association of Saint Radegund with February sowing. Here actual events are brought to serve the psychospiritual tension between the old Goddess and the new God. Vernacular legend and oral tradition would make Saint Radegund into a transformation of the grain goddess—a process completed by the sixteenth century, when she is depicted in church-approved art (Berger, p. 56; Breviary of Anne de Pris, abbes of La Trinité at Poitiers, 1480–1505). Well before this, the practice of worshipping Saint Radegund through offering of oats had begun, continuing until the twentieth century, as did reports of her miraculous healing with them. English calendars begin recording an oats festival in her honor in the tenth century. No doubt these local practices influenced the decision of the Bishop of Poitiers to consecrate a special festival in her honor, "Saint Radegund of the Oats, to be celebrated on February 28th." Her official Saints day is August 13, the date of another very popular pagan Christianized grain ritual, further reinforcing the association to the pagan Goddess.

The lives and legends of four other female saints would carry forth the same process in different regions. Macrine in western France, Walpurga in southern Germany, Milburga in Anglo-Saxon England, and Brigid among the Celtic peoples, would each effect this transformation locally. Macrine, to whom a traditional version of the story is attributed as well, in a particularly colorful form of the legend, is said to be pursued by a giant Gargantua or ogre. After Macrine is hidden by the wheat's miraculous growth and saved by the farmer, the ogre cleans the mud from his clogs and flings it into the countryside, creating the hillocks near where the chapel of Saint Macrine now stands (p. 61). Again, the Goddess is intertwined with both grain and landscape. The eighth-century nun Saint Walpurga traveled on a mission of conversion with her two brothers, from England to Germany. In her version of the Grain Miracle, she is hidden in the back of a farmer's wagon, loaded with the harvest, "when the fiendish white rider came by." Safely protected, she departs, enjoining the farmer to keep a close eye on his grain. Arriving home the next morning, the farmer finds that his grain has turned to gold. The final verse of this tale includes reference to the fashioning of St. Walpurga corn dollies and her association with sheaves—the author takes for granted the listener's familiarity with this custom. In England, St. Milburga would provide a provisional cross-over figure for pagan farmers unwilling to give up goddess worship. The previously quoted planting charm comes from the same time, from

Anglo-Saxon culture in which Milburga rode the countryside. A classical version of the Grain Miracle myth is attributed to her and this association is reinforced through the date of her festival, February 23, in the midst of spring sowing in England.

62. Berger, p. 55–61.
63. Berger, p. 71.
64. Berger, p. 73.
65. Berger, p. 74.
66. Richard, in Noyes (ed.), p. 62.
67. Richard, in Noyes (ed.), , p. 136.
68. Berger.
69. Baring and Cashford, p. 553.
70. "De Barende Vrouw," meaning "woman giving birth to," given to Crop Circles in Belgium. From a 1938 account in T. Wilson, *The Secret History of Crop Circles,* p. 36.
71. Tarnas, 1991, epilogue.
72. Jung, *Collected Works 16,* par. 344.
73. Groissant, Aristotle et les Mystères.
74. Eliade, 1958, p. 110.
75. Jung and Kerenyi, p. 117.
76. Jung and Kerenyi.
77. Jung and Kerenyi, p. 106.
78. Jung and Kerenyi, p. 116.
79. In the *Anthologia Palatina,* XI, 42, cited in Jung and Kerenyi, p. 144.
80. Hesiod, Homeric Hymn to Demeter.
81. Eliade, p. 217.
82. Eliade, p. 217.
83. W. Otto, "Meaning of the Eleusinian Mysteries." in Campbell, *The Mysteries,* p. 25; see also Mylonas, p. 305–10.
84. Jung and Kerenyi, p. 117.
85. Jung and Kerenyi, p. 153.
86. Jung and Kerenyi, p. 152.
87. Woodman, 1980, p. 105–6.
88. Corbett, 1996, p. 48.
89. Moore, p. 139.
90. Eliade, 1958
91. Harvey, p. xiii.
92. In Harvey, *The Essential Mystics: The Soul's Journey Into Truth* (Castle Books, 1998), p. xv.
93. Cited in Baring and Harvey, p. 31.

FIVE **REASON ALONE**

1. Baring and Harvey, 1996, p. 8.
2. Jung, *Collected Works 16,* p. 319.
3. Jung, *Collected Works 8,* p. 451–4.
4. Baring and Harvey, 1996, p. 8.
5. Hafiz, "The Subject Tonight Is Love," poem, trans. D. Ladinsky.
6. Tarnas, "The Great Initiation," pp. 24–31, 57–59.
7. This patriarchal emergence has its roots in Zorostrianism and other previous religions.
8. Neumann, 1954, p. 5.
9. Neumann, 1954, p. 138.
10. Neumann, 1954, p. 121.
11. Stein, p. 22.
12. Stein, p. 25.
13. Stein, p. 26.
14. Neumann, 1954, p. 127.
15. Raff, 2000, p. 102.
16. Ulanov, 1971, p. 146.
17. E. F. Edinger, *Anatomy of the Psyche* (1994), cited in Raff, 2000, p. 191.
18. A complete and precise clarity of definition of the archetypal Masculine and Feminine is never completely possible, as both concepts by definition extend past our ability to be consciously aware of them. Our descriptions of the qualities and differences provide guidelines nonetheless.
19. Neumann, 1954, p. 286–88.
20. Certainly there are contra-stereotypical examples to be found in certain cultures of females leaving tribes, however this pattern remains a viable way of understanding the ego's requirement of a heroic advancement at this stage.
21. Bachofen, 1948, as cited in Neumann, 1954.
22. Neumann, 1954, p. 115.
23. Neumann, p. 47.
24. Neumann, p. 115.
25. Jung, *Symbols of Transformation,* par. 415.
26. Jung, *Collected Works 5,* par 415.
27. Jung, *Collected Works 5,* par. 457.
28. Baring and Cashford, p. 437.
29. Tarnas, 1991, footnote from p. 94, points out the interpretation of YHWH remains controversial.
30. Baring and Cashford, p. 417.
31. Exod. 20:3–4.
32. Baring and Cashford, p. 440.

33. Patai, p. 23–4.

34. Patai, p. 21.

35. Ulanov, "San Francisco Jung Conference: Depth Psychology and Spiritual Practice."

36. Tarnas, 1991, p. 4.

37. Tarnas, 1991, p. 3.

38. Tarnas, 1991.

39. Tarnas, 1991, p. 8.

40. Or the birth of the individuated ego within human consciousness.

41. Samuels, Shorter, and Plaut, 1986, p. 86.

42. Joseph Campbell, *Creative Mythology* (1968), cited in Johnson, *Femininity Lost and Regained,* p. 3.

43. Tarnas. "The Great Initiation," pp. 24–31, 57–59.

44. Rouselle, in Campbell, 1979, p. 118–9.

45. Tarnas, 1991, p. 117.

46. Copernicus found that computing planetary orbits in a heliocentric (sun-centered) model made the mathematics simpler and more natural. He did not believe that the Creator would be so inelegant as to produce a world in which the heaven's orbits were so awkward. Initially, Copernicus's work was accepted by the papacy and taught in their schools of astronomy. Only later, after Protestant rejection of his idea, did the Church turn to reject the theories of Copernicus (and his later adherents Bruno and Galileo). The proposition that the Sun, and not the Earth, stood at the center of God's universe was a radical undermining of the Christian conception of humanity as the focus of Creation. Would the central drama of the universe's unfolding, God's plan for salvation, unfold on a planet that did not lie at the focal point of the cosmos? Up until this time the Catholic Church had been particularly tolerant of rational inquiry; Copernicus himself had been hired by the Pope to help solve the difficulties with the calendar created by the geocentric system (which he could not solve under the old view). His publication on the new heliocentric model, *De Revolutionibus,* was dedicated to the Pope, but due in part to difficulty with publishing in a repressive Protestant climate, Copernicus would not see it published until the final day of his life. Eventually, the Catholic Church would also reject his theories, bringing Galileo before the Inquisition, and forcing Copernicans within the Church from their positions. The threat to belief recognized in the heliocentric view was considered greater even than that of Protestantism (Tarnas, 1991, p. 254). Under this new pressure, the former accommodation available to science within the Church was no longer to be found—and all efforts to deny the validity of such teachings were undertaken with ruthless authority. "With the Copernican theory, Catholicism's long-held tension between reason and faith had finally snapped." Tarnas, 1991, p. 254.

75. Sussman, *Speech of the Grail,* p. 202.

76. Ulanov, *The Wisdom of the Psyche,* p. 5.

77. Saul, *Voltaire's Bastards,* p. 339–40.

78. Jung, 1957, p. 112.

79. Vycinas, *Earth and Gods,* p. 250.

80. Vycinas, *Earth and Gods,* p. 251.

81. "A respectful stand in face of reality allows this reality to appear in its own way, undistorted by approaches. In one of his latest works, Heidegger states that modern man has lost this ability to face things as they are. He takes the example of a blossoming tree, which we, modern men, no longer face the way it is in itself, but in fully distorted form. A scientific approach does not see reality the way it is. As far as science is concerned, to stand in front of a tree is an event which occurs in our head rather than in reality. By trying to explain the blossoming tree strictly scientifically, we end up with brain circuits" (Vycinas, 1969, p. 29). Vycinas is a follower of Heidegger.

82. Vycinas, *Earth and Gods,* p. 270.

83. Nietzsche, *The Philosophy of Nietzsche* (New York: The Modern Library, 2000), p. 11.

SIX **A CALLING BACK DOWN**

1. Harding, E. M., 1971, p. 150.

2. Monick, 1987, p. 102.

3. Bill McKibben, "The Christian paradox: How a faithful nation gets Jesus wrong," www.harpers.org/archive/2005/08/0080695.

4. Saul, *Voltaire's Bastards,* p. 583.

5. Interview sessions at Jung's Zurich home in 1957. Conducted by Dr. Richard Evans of the University of Houston.

6. Jung, *Modern Man in Search of a Soul,* p. 219.

7. I first heard this image via Tarnas, public lecture.

8. Harding, 1971, p. 20.

9. Herbert Marcuse, *One Dimensional Man,* quoted in Absher, p. 100.

10. Woodman, *Addiction to Perfection,* p. 179.

11. Jung, *Collected Works 13,* pp. 456.

12. Harding, p. 82–3.

13. Nichols, S. p. 322.

14. Harding, 1971, p. 151.

15. Scott London, radio program. See also Robert Johnson, audio interview, *Insights and Outlooks.*

16. O'Kane, 1994, p. 52.

17. Jung, *CW 14,* par. 672–3.

18. Harding, 1971, p. 7–8.

19. O'Kane, 1994, p. 34.

20. Elizabeth Dodson Gray, *Nature As an Act of Imagination,* in Nicholson, *The Goddess Reawakening* (Chennai, India: The Theosophical Publishing House, 1989), p. 274.

21. Woodman, *Addiction to Perfection.*

22. Primo Levi, cited in Tarnas, 2006, p. 30.

23. Saul, *Voltaire's Bastards,* p. 187.

24. Savoyard , Emile, pp. 354–55, and Foxley, p. 254., cited in C. Taylor.

25. Saul, *Voltaire's Bastards,* p. 582.

26. Tarnas, *Cosmos and Psyche,*p. 34, p. 32.

27. Saul, *Voltaire's Bastards,* p. 178.

28. Woodman, 1982, p. 52.

29. Ulanov, *The Wisdom of the Psyche,* p. 36.

30. Ulanov, *The Wisdom of the Psyche,* p. 3.

31. Washburn, *The Ego and the Dynamic Ground,* p. 121.

32. Judith, A., 1996, p. 96.

33. Scott London radio interview of Johnson.

34. Jung, *Collected Works 13,* par. 528.

35. Neumann, 1949, p. 386–7.

36. O'Kane, 1994, p. 43.

37. Ulanov, "San Francisco Jung Conference: Depth Psychology and Spiritual Practice."

38. Harding, *Women's Mysteries,* p. 67.

39. Campbell, *Myths of Light,* p. xvii.

40. Absher, *Men and the Goddess,* p. 94.

41. Woodman in Harris, *Jung and Yoga,* p. 7.

42. Robert Johnson, 1983, p. 76.

43. Interview sessions with the famed psychoanalyst at Jung's Zurich home in 1957. Conducted by Dr. Richard Evans of the University of Houston.

44. Woodman, p. 37.

45. Saul, *On Equlibrium,* p. 162.

46. Moore, *Dark Nights of the Soul,* p. 24.

47. Baring and Cashford, p. 484.

48. Whitmont, 1969, p. ix.

49. Corbett, 1996, p. 106.

50. Harding, 1971, p. 151.

51. John Lennon, "Beautiful Boy."

52. Baring and Cashford, *The Myth of the Goddess,* p. 662.

53. Jung, *Modern Man in Search of a Soul,* p. 111.

54. Ann Ulanov, "Faith and Doubt at Ground Zero," *PBS Frontline,* www.pbs.org/wgoh/pages/frontline/shows/faith/interviews/ulanov.html.

55. Baring and Cashford, *The Myth of the Goddess,* p. 669.

56. "The Geography of the Soul," interview reprinted in *Touch,* Summer 1993.

57. Cousins, *Fires of Desire,* p. 140–141.

58. Cousins, *Fires of Desire,* p. 141.

59. Lee, *Writing from the Body,* p. 74.

60. Baring and Cashford, *The Myth of the Goddess,* p. 66.

61. Jung, *Collected Works 10,* par 103.

62. Jung, *Collected Works 10,* p. 675.

63. Woodman, 1990, p. 211.

64. Ulanov, *The Feminine,* 1971, as cited in Absher, p. 191.

SEVEN **THE REALITY OF THE PSYCHE**

1. Zabriskie, 1999, p. xlv.

2. Osterman in Wheelwright, 1961, p. 14.

3. Combs and Holland, p. 11.

4. "Sheldrake has pointed out that even if quantum physicists are successful in deriving the ultimate force, the one which supposedly was responsible for the big bang that gave birth to the universe 15–20 billion years ago, they will still be faced with an insurmountable problem. The ultimate seed force would necessarily be the first law of nature. But where did this first law exist before the Big Bang? The answer to that question, Sheldrake says, must be metaphysical. He believes that hard-nosed mechanists who claim to reject all metaphysical assumptions are unwilling to recognize that their own theory is based on the vague philosophical idea that an eternal law of nature can exist even before nature herself is said to exist" (Briggs and Peat, p. 79).

5. A. Goswami, IONS article, *Quantum Yoga,* issue 56.

6. Nadeau and Kafatos, 2001.

7. Said to have been born December 14, 1900, with arrival of Planck's constant, quantum physics.

8. John Briggs, *Looking Glass Universe: The Emerging Science of Wholeness* (New York: Simon & Schuster, 1986), p. 57.

9. Nadeau and Kafatos, p. 22. The simultaneous and independent discovery of new revelations is a frequent, odd recurrence throughout history and has been seen as implicating an archetypal and holistic view of the unfolding of knowledge as a non-local and psychically unified event unfolding as part of a whole.

10. Briggs and Peat, p. 67.

11. Nadeau and Kafatos, p. 2.

12. This linkage is also called "quantum entanglement."

13. Alfred Einstein, *Letters of Wave Mechanics* (New York: Philosophical Library, 1967). Cited in Briggs and Peat.

14. Nadeau and Kafatos, 1999, p. 79.

15. Nadeau and Kafatos, 1999, p. 79.

16. The propensity for a particle-wave function to collapse at the moment of observation is a subject of debate among the scientific community, as one might expect. In the Copenhagen interpretation of this experiment by great Danish physicist Neils Bohr, the wave function collapses at the moment of observation (Wigner's view, see also Goswami, Capra, etc.). There are other interpretations that exclude the necessity of a human observer in the determination of this result. The quote following this is from Nadeau and Kafatos, 1999, p. 13.

17. Goswami, 1993, p. 73.

18. Lindorf, p. 93.

19. At Brussels, October 1927, Fifth Solvay International Conference on Electrons and Photons.

20. Pauli in Lindorff, p. 89.

21. Nadeau and Kafatos, p. 9.

22. Goswami, p. 45.

23. Sheldrake, 2003, p. 8.

24. For more on morphogenetic fields, see en.wikipedia.org/wiki/Morphogenetic_field.

25. See www.biomindsuperpowers.com/Pages/CIA-InitiatedRV.html.

26. Sheldrake, p. 217.

27. Jung, *Collected Works 8,* par. 846.

28. Radin, *Entangled Minds,* p. 2.

29. Behe in Sheldrake, p. 240.

30. Elsa Benitez in *Sports Illustrated,* Winter 2004, p. 17. There are literally hundreds of such accounts throughout our social historical records. They are, of course, most common during war, when more people are in danger or dying, but also come at times when relatives have no context for their fears at all.

31. See Tim Russert: www.people.com/people/article/0,,20207591,00.html.

32. Jung, *Memories, Dreams, Reflections,* pp. 150–1, as cited in Aziz, p. 94.

33. See Aziz, p. 237, for a discussion of the dating of this conversation.

34. Aziz, p. 94.

35. Jung, 1961, 155–6.

36. McGuire, cited in Aziz, p. 96.

37. Jung, *CW 8,* par. 982.

38. Jung, in Aziz, p. 79.

39. Cited in Hillman, *Revisioning Psychology.*

40. Hillman, *Revisioning Psychology,* pp. 196–97.

41. Augustine's confessions, cited in Tarnas, 2006, p. 53.
42. Tarnas, 2006, p. 53.
43. This is a change in verb tense paraphrase, but otherwise direct quote from Tarnas, 2006, p. 53.
44. J. H. Robinson, cited in Tarnas, 2006, notes p. 496.
45. J. H. Robinson, cited in Tarnas, 2006, notes p. 496.
46. C. G. Jung, *Letters, Vol. 2*, pp. 537–43.
47. Zabriski in C. A. Meier (ed.), *Atom and Archetype* (Princeton, NJ: Princeton University Press, 2001), p. xxxviii.
48. Jung, *Letters, Vol. 2*, pp. 537–43.
49. Albertus Magnus, *De mirabilibus, Incunabulum,* undated (circa 1200–1280). Here Magnus is following the thought of Avicenna (980–1037).
50. Goswami, p. 46.
51. Goswami, 1993, p. 9.
52. Tarnas, 2006, p. 95.
53. Von Franz, 1988, p. 257.
54. Goswami, 1993, p. 225.
55. Goswami, 1993, p. 9.
56. Paul Tillich, Hillel Society, Harvard University, 1956.
57. Pauli, in Kafatos, p. 215.

EIGHT **GHOSTS OF ELECTRICITY**

1. www.circlemakers.org/amber.html.
2. Thomas: ". . . Taken by German students at Manton, Wilshire in August 1991," p. 71; Japanese tourists see Silva, p. 143; Steve Alexander video in Gazecki, *Crop Circles: Quest for Truth* DVD; and others.
3. Andrews claimed in 2002.
4. See p. 483 and also Evans-Wentz, *The Fairy Faith in Celtic Countries:* The pisky thrasher, p. 172, and p. 88. See p. 143, 151, 172, 181, 184 for references to fairies' circular dances.
5. Evans-Wentz, p. xiii.
6. Thomas, 1998, p. 71.
7. See Andrews, *Undeniable Evidence* DVD. Helicopters chasing BOLs away has also been repeatedly reported by eyewitnesses.
8. See Gazecki, *Crop Circles: Quest for Truth* DVD, among other sources.
9. CBC Archives online: archives.cbc.ca/science_technology/unexplained/clips/4395/
10. Andrews, p. 164.
11. Which can be read further in his 1991 publication, *Circles from the Sky*.
12. Thomas, 1998, p. 74.

13. Taylor, *What on Earth? Inside the Crop Circle Mystery* DVD.

14. There are approximately twenty-five historical accounts, pre-1989, of eyewitnesses seeing Crop Circles form (see T. Wilson, 1998), and an additional twenty-five in the modern post-1989 era (various sources).

15. See Pringle.

16. Paul Germany, crop circle eyewitness.

17. Pringle, 1999, p. 3.

18. Pringle, 1999, p. 3.

19. Pringle, 1999, p. 4.

20. Pringle, 1999, p. 5.

21. Letter to the *Sunday Express* editor, on August 12, 1990.

22. As reprinted in Meaden, p. 180.

23. G.T. Meaden, "Nocturnal Eye Witness Observation of Circles in the Making, Part 2," *Journal of Meteorology,* U.K., 29 June 1989, 15:3. This account can be viewed online at: www.science-frontiers.com/sf070/sf070g18.htm, p. 122–3

24. Meaden is describing the account written by A Shuttlewood, in the magazine *Now!,* 29 August 1988, reprinted in the *Journal of Meterology,* Vol. 9, 137–146. 1984: "Some years earlier the formation of a circle was watched by a large number of people as it appeared in long grass one summer's evening near Starr Hill, also known as Middle Hill, in West Wiltshire. 'Suddenly the grass began to sway before our eyes and laid itself flat in a clockwise spiral, just like the opening of a lady's fan. A perfect circle was completed in less than half a minute, all the time accompanied by a high-pitched humming sound. It was still there the next day.'"

25. Meaden.

26. Eltjo Haselhoff, "Scientific Studies Confirm: Crop Circles Made by 'Balls of Light,'" *Physiologia Plantarum* (111:123–125), 2001, p. 21. To download a pdf copy of the *Physiologia Plantarum* article, see: www.ecn.org/cunfi/Haselhoff.pdf. To view an online explanation of Haselhoff's work, see: http://psiapplications.com/Treepad/documents/70.html.

27. Haselhoff, 2001.

28. Haselhoff, 2001.

29. Haselhoff, 2001.

30. In Foreword to Evans-Wentz, *The Fairy-Faith in Celtic Countries.*

31. Anderhub and Roth, p. 212.

32. Jaffé, p. 56.

33. Jaffé, p. 72.

34. www.wiltshire-web.co.uk/history/barrows.htm.

35. Evans-Wentz, p. 155.

36. Arrowsmith and Moorse.

37. Freeman in *Parabola,* Fall 2003, p. 32.

38. Wilson and Delgado, 1989, p. 19.

39. Jaffé, p. 288.

40. Jaffé, p. 67.

41. Barrett, in *Parabola,* Summer 2001, p. 65. His second experience of this light did not occur during an NDE.

42. Marvin Barrett, 1999, p. xiv–sx.

43. Evans-Wentz, p. 296n and p. 95.

44. Evans-Wentz, p. 175. See also p. 88, 176.

45. Evans-Wentz, see pp. 113, 135, 145, 149, 154, 162, 329, 339, 350, 354.

46. Thomas, p. 127.

47. See Lucy Pringle's website: www.lucypringle.co.uk.

48. Thomas, p. 99.

49. See Gazecki/Taylor, *Quest for Truth* DVD.

50. Or see www.bltresearch.com/magnetic.html.

51. The difference between intelligent design and intentional design in Crop Circles, as evidence for its creation by a conscious agent, would be its interior design reference and location near ancient stone circles and other geographic features. Other qualities of intention could of course also be found in reference to other aspects of the phenomenon and could be seen further in this work.

52. Jenkins in Bartholomew, p. 44.

53. As with a quantum holograph.

54. Andrews, *Undeniable Evidence* DVD. Formation is 1988 Celtic Cross of Longstock.

55. Andrews, *Undeniable Evidence* DVD.

56. Used with Anderson's permission, for more see: www.cccrn.ca/circular conciousness.html.

57. Miller, p. 221.

58. Miller.

59. Jaffé, p. 75–77.

60. Cirlot, p. 96.

61. Jaffé, p. 78

NINE **NEVER MIND**

1. Andrews, *Undeniable Evidence* DVD.

2. Bartholomew, 1991.

3. Jung, 1977, p. 303.

4. Tarnas, "The Great Initiation," pp. 24–31, 57–59.

5. Moore.

6. Moore, p. 66.

7. Plato in *The Eleusinian and Bacchic Mysteries,* trans. Taylor, 1891.

8. Saul, *Voltaire's Bastards,* p. 178.

9. Woodman, *Addiction to Perfection.*

10. Ulanov, *The Wisdom of the Psyche,* p. 22.

11. Ulanov, *The Wisdom of the Psyche,* p. 54.

12. Moore, p. 222.

13. Grof in Kohley and Mann, *EntheoGenesis* DVD.

14. Carl Jung, *Answer to Job* (Princeton, NJ: Princeton University Press, 2010), par. 734.

15. Meade, Audio Interview with NPR: www.mosaicvoices.org/page.cfm?id=20 [audio].

16. R. L. Moore, p. 54.

17. R. L. Moore, p. 139.

18. Edward Edinger, *Creation of Consciousness* (Toronto, ON: Inner City Books, 1984), p. 25.

19. C. T. Frey-Wherlin in O'Kane, p. 8.

20. Quoted in Taylor, *What on Earth? Inside the Crop Circle Mystery* DVD.

21. Harvey, 1995, p. 13.

22. Neumann, 1949, p. 386–7.

23. Nirvana, "Smells Like Teen Spirit," song lyrics, K. Cobain.

24. Michael Meade, interview with NPR: www.mosaicvoices.org/page.cfm?id=20 [audio].

25. Ortiz Hill, p. 85.

26. Von Franz, 1980, p. 90.

27. Jung, *Collected Works 14,* par. 674.

28. Edinger, 1992, p. 24.

29. Boznak, 1996, p. 69.

30. Woodman, *Addiction to Perfection,* p. 52.

31. Ortiz Hill, p. 71.

32. Schwartz-Salant, p. 128.

33. http://web.utanet.at/salzjung/ontogeny.htm.

34. Quoted in Adler, "Aspects of Jung's Personality and Work," *Psychological Perspectives* 6 (Spring 1975), p. 12.

35. Jung and Kerenyi, p. 142.

36. Cashford, p. 359.

37. Holderlin quoted in Edinger, p. 37.

38. Dennis Patrick Slattery, lecture, Pacifica Graduate Institute, 1999.

39. Quoted in J. Z. Smith, *To Take Place* (Chicago: University of Chicago Press, 1992).

40. Jung, *Collected Works 10,* par. 585–6.

41. Bachelard, *Poetics of Reverie.*

42. Meade, interview with NPR: www.mosaicvoices.org/page.cfm?id=20 [audio].

43. Perera, p. 53.

TEN FIELDS OF WAVING CORN

* Image use: Champernowne paintings are used courtesy of Julian David.

1. There are innumerable examples of this on the Crop Circle front. Most television and newspaper stories do not feature any of the science, even when provided it. Recent *National Geographic* articles are one example. In Sheldrake's experience, one such example was when he entered into a television debate with Richard Dawkins, in which Dawkins replies that "he isn't interested in looking at the evidence:" www.sheldrake.org/D&C/controversies/Dawkins.html.

2. Hesemann in Anderhub and Roth, p. 112: Mary Freeman of Marlborough in the evening of July 13, 1988.

3. In Anderhub and Roth, p. 115.

4. See BLT Research: www.bltresearch.com/eyewitness/eyewitness1.php.

5. See BLT Research: www.bltresearch.com/eyewitness/eyewitness1.php.

6. Busty Taylor and Colin Andrews, see *Quest for Truth* film.

7. Silva, 2002, p. 266–271.

8. Gazecki/Taylor, *Crop Circles: Quest for Truth* DVD, Extra features.

9. Jung, *Letters, Vol. 2,* pp. 537–43.

10. Dreaming of one's own death just prior to it is perhaps the most-widespread historically documented kind of psychic coincidence. Published account of this famous dream from 1911: www.worlddreambank.org/L/LINCOLN.HTM.

11. O'Kane, p. 88.

12. Ulanov, 1988, p. 133.

13. See O'Kane, p. 97.

14. William James, 1896.

15. William James, p. 101.

16. Woodman.

17. Schwartz-Salant, p. 201.

18. O'Kane, p. 258.

19. Champernowne, *A Memoir of Toni Wolff,* p. 7. *A Memoir of Toni Wolff* can be downloaded for free, courtesy of the San Francisco Jung Institute: www.sfjung. org/about/other_institute_publications.asp.

20. www.sfjung.org/about/other_institute_publications.asp.

21. Champernowne, p. 5–6.

22. Champernowne, p. 10

23. Champernowne, p. 10.

24. Champernowne, p. 13.

25. John Donne, *The Second Anniversarie: of the Progresse of the Soule* (1612), p. 243–246, as quoted in Champernowne, p. 34.
26. Talbott, http://www.bltresearch.com/eyewitness/eyewitness1.php.
27. Jung, *Visions Seminars* (Putnam, CT: Spring Publications, 1976), p. 118–9.
28. Corbett, 1996, p. 46–7.
29. Champernowne, p. 34.

RESOURCES

GLOSSARY

To help with the Jungian terminology used in this book, I recommend Daryl Sharp's online Jung Lexicon at www.psychceu.com/jung /sharplexicon.html.

WEBSITES

www.bltresearch.com
www.cropcircleconnector.com
www.cropcirclemovie.com
www.JungAndCropCircles.net
www.sfjung.org (*A Memoir of Toni Wolff* is available for free download on the San Francisco Jung Institute's website at www.sfjung.org/about/other_institute_ publications.asp)
www.temporarytemples.com

BOOKS

Alexander, Karen. 2006. *Crop Circles: Signs, Wonders and Mysteries.* New York: Chartwell Books. If you are looking for a single visual introduction, I would highly recommend this book.

Haselhoff, Eltjo H. 2001. *The Deepening Complexity of Crop Circles.* Berkeley, CA: Frog Books. Recommended for a look at some particular qualities of the science of the phenomenon.

Howe, Linda Moulton. 2000. *Mysterious Lights and Crop Circles.* New Orleans: Paper Chase.

Pringle Lucy. 2000. *Crop Circles: The Greatest Mystery of Modern Times.* London: Thorsens Element/Harper Collins. Lucy Pringle's books and aerial photography are highly recommended and I find her writing on Crop Circles to also be both insightful and balanced. This book is my favorite of hers on the subject.

Thomas Andy. 2002. *Vital Signs: A Complete Guide to the Crop Circle Mystery.* Berkeley, CA: Frog Books. Very good.

VIDEO

Gazecki, William. 2002. *Crop Circles: Quest for Truth.* San Francisco, CA: Open Edge Media. DVD, 115 min. Academy Award–nominated director Gazecki and producer Suzanne Taylor provide the best visual introduction to the science and depth of complexity found in this phenomenon. Available on DVD, Amazon, iTunes, and at www.cropcirclemovie.com.

Taylor, Suzanne. 2009. *What on Earth? Inside the Crop Circle Mystery.* Los Angeles: Mighty Companions. DVD, 81 min. Perhaps the best way to quickly gain an understanding of Crop Circles. Available on DVD, Amazon, iTunes, and at www.cropcirclemovie.com.

SELECTED BIBLIOGRAPHY

Absher, Tom. *Men and the Goddess: Feminine Archetypes in Western Literature.* Rochester, VT: Park Street Press, 1991.

Anderhub, W. and H. P. Roth. *Crop Circles.* New York: Lark Books, 2002.

Andrews, Colin and Pat Delgado. *Circular Evidence.* London: Bloomsbury, 1989.

Andrews, C., J. O'Donnell, S. Shalofksy, P. Robbins, and T. Werenko. *Ultimate Crop Circles: Signs from Space?* New York: Central Park Media, 2002. DVD, 115 min.

Andrews, Colin. *Undeniable Evidence.* Glastonbury, UK: ARK Soundwaves. Video. 1991.

Andrews, C. and S. J. Spignesi. *Crop Circles: Signs of Contact.* Franklin Lakes, NJ: New Page Books, 2003.

Artress, Lauren. *Walking a Sacred Path: Rediscovering the Labyrinth as a Sacred Tool.* New York: Riverhead Books, 1995.

Arrowsmith, Nancy, and George Moorse. *A Field Guide to the Little People.* New York: Pocket Books, 1978.

Aziz, R. *C. G. Jung's Psychology of Religion and Synchronicity.* Albany, NY: State University of New York Press, 1990.

Bachelard, Gaston. *Poetics of Reverie.* Boston, MA: Beacon Press, 1971.

Barasch, Marc Ian. *Healing Dreams.* New York: Riverhead, 2000.

Baring, Anne and Jules Cashford. *The Myth of the Goddess: The Evolution of an Image.* New York: Penguin, 1993.

Baring, Anne and Andrew Harvey. *The Divine Feminine: Exploring the Feminine Face of God throughout the World.* London: Godsfield Press Ltd., 1996.

Barrett, Marvin. *Second Chance: A Life after Death.* New York: Parabola Books. 1999.

Bartholomew, Alick, ed. *Crop Circles: Harbingers of World Change.* Bath, UK: Gateway Books, 1991.

Berger, Pamela. *The Goddess Obscured: Transformation of the Grain Protectress from Goddess to Saint.* Boston: Beacon Press, 1988.

Boznak, Robert. *Embodiment: Creative Imagination in Medicine, Art, and Travel.* Chicago, IL: University of Chicago Press, 1996.

Briggs, J. and F. D. Peat. *Looking Glass Universe: The Emerging Science of Wholeness.* New York: Cornerstone Library, 1984.

Brown, Joseph E., ed. *Sacred Pipe: Black Elk.* New York: Penguin, 1971.

Campbell, Joseph. *Creative Mythology.* New York: Viking, 1968.

Campbell, Joseph. *Myths of Light: Eastern Metaphors of the Eternal.* Novato, CA: New World Library, 2003.

Campbell, Joseph, ed. Papers from the Eranos Yearbooks. *Eranos 2. The Mysteries.* Princeton, NJ: Princeton University Press, 1979.

Champernowne, Irene. *A Memoir of Toni Wolff.* San Francisco, CA: San Francisco Jung Society, 1972.

Chevalier, J. and A. Gheerbrant. *The Penguin Dictionary of Symbols.* New York: Penguin Books, 1996.

Cirlot, J.E. *A Dictionary of Symbols.* Mineola, NY: Dover Publications. 2002.

Combs, A. and Holland, M. *Synchronicity.* Washington, DC: Marlowe and Company, 1996.

Corbett, Lionel. *The Religious Function of the Psyche.* Chicago: Chicago Jung Society, 1986. Audio tape.

Corbett, Lionel. *The Religious Function of the Psyche.* London: Routledge, 1996.

Cousins, Ewert. *The Fires of Desire: Erotic Energies and the Spiritual Quest.* Edited by Fredrica R. Halligan, John J. Shea. New York: Crossroad, 1992.

Delgado, Pat. *Crop Circles: Conclusive Evidence?* Bloomsbury, UK. 1992.

Edinger, Edward F. *Anatomy of the Psyche.* La Salle, IL: Open Court Publishing Co., 1994.

Edinger, Edward F. *Ego and Archetype.* Putnam. 1972.

Eliade, M. *Rites and Symbols of Initiation (Birth and Rebirth).* Translated by W. Trask. London: Harvill Press, 1958.

Evans-Wentz, W. Y. *The Fairy-Faith in Celtic Countries.* London: H. Frowde, 1911.

Fideler, David, ed. *Alexandria: The Journal of Western Cosmological Traditions, #1.* Grand Rapids, MI: Phanes Press, 1991.

Fincher, Susanne F. *Creating Mandalas.* Boston, MA: Shambhala, 2000.

Fitzgerald, F. Scott. *This Side of Paradise.* New York: Charles Scribner's Sons, 1970.

Fordham, Frieda, *Introduction to Jung's Psychology.* New York: Penguin, 1953.

Gadon, Elinor. *The Once and Future Goddess: A Sweeping Visual Chronicle of the Sacred Female and Her Reemergence in the Cult.* San Francisco: HarperOne, 1989.

Gazecki, W. (director). *Crop Circles: Quest for Truth.* Produced by S. Taylor, D. Hughes, and M. Zinn. Los Angeles, CA: Open Edge Media, 2002. DVD, 115 min.

Goswami, Amit, with R. E. Reed and M. Goswami. *The Self-Aware Universe: How Consciousness Creates the Material World.* New York: Penguin Putnam Inc., 1993.

Hafiz. *The Subject Tonight Is Love: 60 Wild and Sweet Poems of Hafiz.* Translated by D. Landinsky. Myrtle Beach, SC: Pumpkin House Press, 1996.

Halifax, Joan. *Fruitful Darkness: A Journey Through Buddhist Practice.* San Francisco, CA: HarperOne, 1993.

Harding, Esther M. *Way of All Women.* C. G. Jung Foundation Books. 1971.

Harding, Esther M. *Women's Mysteries: Ancient and Modern.* New York: Harper & Row, 1976.

Harris, J. *Jung and Yoga: The Psyche-Body Connection.* Toronto, ON: Inner City Books, 2000.

Harvey, Andrew. *The Return of the Mother.* Berkeley, CA: North Atlantic Books, 1995.

Haselhoff, E. H. *The Deepening Complexity of Crop Circles: Scientific Research and Urban Legends.* Berkeley, CA: Frog Books, 2001.

Hawkins, G. *Probing the Mystery of Those Eerie Crop Circles.* Cosmos Journal of Emerging Issues. Vol 1, No. 2, pp. 23-28. 1992.

Hillman, James. *Revisioning Psychology.* New York: William Morrow, 1992.

Jaffé, A. *Apparitions.* Dallas, TX: Spring Publications, 1979.

James, William. *William James on Exceptional Mental States: The 1896 Lowell Lectures.* New York: Scribner: 1983.

Johnson, Robert A. *We.* New York: Harper Collins, 1983.

Johnson, Robert A. *Femininity Lost and Regained.* New York: Harper Collins, 1991.

Judith, Anodea. *Wheels of Life.* Llewellyn Publications. 2000.

Jung, C. G. *The Undiscovered Self (Present and Future).* New York: American Library, 1957.

Jung, C. G. *Memories, Dreams, Reflections.* Edited by A. Jaffe. New York: Vintage Books, 1961.

Jung, C. G. *Collected Works.* Translated by R. F. C. Hull. Princeton, NJ: Princeton University Press, 1953–79.

Jung, C. G. *On Synchronicity and the Paranormal.* Translated by R. F. C. Hull. Princeton, NJ: Princeton University Press, 1977.

Jung, C. G. *Modern Man in Search of a Soul.* Translated by W. S. Dell and C. F. Baynes. London: Kegan Paul Trench Trubner, 1933.

Jung, C. G. and C. Kerenyi. *Essays on a Science of Mythology: The Myth of the Divine Child and the Mysteries of Eleusis.* Princeton, NJ: Princeton University Press, 1969.

Jung, C. G. and M. von Franz. *Man and His Symbols.* New York: Doubleday, 1964.

Kollerstrom, Nick. *Crop Circles: The Hidden Form.* Salisbury, UK: Wessex Books, 2002.

Lawlor, R. *Sacred Geometry: Philosophy and Practice.* London: Thames and Hudson, 1982.

Lee, J. *Writing from the Body.* New York: St. Martin's Press, 1994.

47. Tarnas, 1991, p. 277.

48. C. Taylor, 1992, p. 365.

49. Descartes believed that evidence for God was found in humanity's own consciousness being capable of discovering the presence of the divine in the forms of the world, and our finitude inferred a container of consciousness greater than itself as existing somewhere—for "how can something come of nothing?""How can there be an effect (consciousness) without a cause (God)?" Practically, however, Descartes's philosophy emphasized the validity and authority of *res cogitans,* human perception, over *res extensa,* the objective, material world, and this reinforced the growing tendency towards objectification of human experience, reductionism, etc.

50. Tarnas, 1991, p. 279.

51. Cited in C. Taylor, p. 463, quoted in Ricardo Quiñones, *Mapping Literary Modernism* (Princeton, NJ: Princeton University Press, 1985), p. 93.

52. Tarnas, 1991, p. 327.

53. Tarnas, 1991, p. 280.

54. F. Scott Fitzgerald, *This Side of Paradise* (New York: Dover Publications, 1996).

55. Tarnas, *Cosmos and Psyche,* p. 12.

56. C. Taylor, p. 459.

57. Edward Edinger, *Ego and Archetype* (Boston, MA: Shambhala, 1992), p. 15.

58. Krishnamurti in Corbett, *The Religious Function of the Psyche,* audio, tape 9 of 9.

59. Saul, *Voltaire's Bastards,* p. 581.

60. Mamet, *Bambi vs. Godzilla.*

61. Jung, *Modern Man in Search of a Soul,* p. 199.

62. One of the defining characteristics of our zeitgeist, and of the history of this century and the last, is the emergence into the political-social dialogue of those groups that were formerly excluded.

63. Edinger in Segaller, *The Wisdom of the Dream* (Boston, MA: Shambhala, 1990), p. 164.

64. Quoted in Tarnas, 1991, p. 409.

65. C. Taylor, p. 317.

66. Quoted in Saul, *Voltaire's Bastards,* p. 474.

67. Saul, *Voltaire's Bastards,* p. 476.

68. Saul, *Voltaire's Bastards,* p. 476.

69. Saul, *Voltaire's Bastards,* p. 477.

70. Jung, *Modern Man in Search of a Soul.*

71. Neumann, 1994, p. 28.

72. Tarnas, *Cosmos and Psyche,* p. 31. Emphasis in original.

73. Rainer Maria Rilke, *Duino Elegies.*

74. Saul, *Voltaire's Bastards,* p. 339–40.

Lindorf, David. *Pauli and Jung: The Meeting of Two Great Minds*. Wheaton, Illinois: Quest. 2004.

Lovelock, James. *Gaia: A New Look At Life On Earth*.Oxford, UK: Oxford University Press, 2003.

Mamet, David. *Bambi vs. Godzilla: On the Nature, Purpose, and Practice of the Movie Business*. New York: Pantheon Books, 2007.

Martineau, John. *Crop Circle Geometry*. Glastonbury, UK: Wooden Books, 1992.

Monick, Eugene. *Phallos: Sacred Image of the Masculine*.Toronto, ON: Inner City Books, 1987.

Moore, R. L. *Facing the Dragon: Confronting Personal and Spiritual Grandiosity*. Edited by M. J. Havlick. Wilmette, IL: Chiron Publications, 2003.

Moore, Thomas. *Dark Nights of the Soul: A Guide to Finding Your Way through Life's Ordeal*. New York: Gotham Books, 2004.

Moulton Howe, L. *Mysterious Lights and Crop Circles*. New Orleans: Paper Chase Press, 2000.

Nadeau, R. and M. Kafatos. *The Non-Local Universe: The New Physics and Matters of the Mind*. Oxford, UK: Oxford University Press, 2001.

L. L. Nelson, ed. *A History of Jonathon Adler*. Akron, OH : University of Akron Press, 2002.

Neumann, E. *The Origins and History of Consciousness*. Translated by R. F. C. Hull. New York: Pantheon Books, 1949/1954.

Nietzsche, Friedrich. *The Philosophy of Nietzsche*. New York: The Modern Library, 1950.

Noyes, Ralph, ed. *The Crop Circle Enigma*. Bath, UK: Gateway Books, 1990.

O'Donohue, John. *Anam Cara: A Book of Celtic Wisdom*. New York: Harper Collins, 1997.

O'Kane, Francoise. *Sacred Chaos: Reflections on God's Shadow and the Dark Self*. Toronto, ON: Inner City Books, 1994.

Carl Olson, ed. *The Book of the Goddess, Past and Present: An Introduction to Her Religion*. New York: Crossroad, 1983.

Ortiz Hill, Michael. *Dreaming the End of the World*. Dallas, TX: Spring Publications, 1994.

Patai, Raphael. *The Hebrew Goddess*.Detroit, MI: Wayne State University Press, 1967.

Perera, Sylvia Brinton. *Descent to the Goddess: A Way of Initiation for Women*. Toronto, ON: Inner City Books: 1982.

Pringle, L. *Crop Circles: The Greatest Mystery of Modern Times*. London: Harper Collins, 1999.

Radin, Dean. *Entangled Minds*. New York: Paraview Pocket Books, 2006.

Raff, Jeffrey. *Jung and the Alchemical Imagination*. Newburyport, MA: Nicolas-Hays, 2000.

Robbins, Tom. *Still Life With Woodpecker.* New York: Bantam Books, 1980.

Ruby, Doug. *The Gift: The Crop Circles Deciphered.* Cocoa Beach, FL: Blue Note Publications. 1996.

Samuels, A., B. Shorter, and F. Plaut. *A Critical Dictionary of Jungian Analysis.* London: Routledge, 1986.

Saul, J. R. *Voltaire's Bastards: The Dictatorship of Reason in the West.* Toronto, ON: Penguin Books, 1992.

Saul, J. R. *On Equilibrium.* Toronto, ON: Penguin Books, 2005.

Schwartz-Salant, N. *The Mystery of Human Relationships: Alchemy and the Transformation of the Self.* London: Routledge, 1998.

Sheldrake, R. *The Sense of Being Stared At, and Other Aspects of the Extended Mind.* New York: Crown Publishers, 2003.

Silva, F. *Secrets in the Fields: The Science and Mysticism of Crop Circles.* Newburyport, MA: Hampton Roads, 2002.

Sjoo, M. and B. Mor. *The Great Cosmic Mother: Rediscovering the Religion of the Earth.* San Francisco, CA: HarperCollins, 1991.

Sklar, Deirdre. *Dancing with the Virgin: Body and Faith in the Fiesta of Tortugas, New Mexico.* Oakland, CA: University of California Press, 2001.

Stein, M. *Solar Conscience, Lunar Conscience.* Wilmette, IL: Chiron, 1993.

Sussman, L. *The Speech of the Grail: A Journey Toward Speaking that Heals and Transforms.* Great Barrington, MA: Lindisfarne Books, 2000.

Tarnas, R. *The Passion of the Western Mind.* New York: Harmony Books/Random House, 1991.

Tarnas, R. "The Great Initiation." *Noetic Sciences Review,* Vol. 47 (Winter 1998): 24–31, 57–59.

Tarnas, R. *Cosmos and Psyche: Intimations of a New World View.* New York: Viking, 2006.

Taylor, C. *Sources of the Self.* Cambridge, MA: Harvard University Press, 1992.

Taylor, Thomas. *The Eleusinian and Bacchic Mysteries.* New York: J. W. Bouton, 1891.

Taylor, S. *What on Earth? Inside the Crop Circle Mystery.* Los Angeles, CA: Mighty Companions, 2009. DVD, 81 min.

Thomas, A. *Vital Signs: A Complete Guide to the Crop Circle Mystery and Why It Is Not a Hoax.* Berkeley, CA: Frog Books, 1998.

Tressider, J. *The Complete Dictionary of Symbols.* San Francisco, CA: Chronicle Books, 2005.

Ulanov, A. "San Francisco Jung Conference: Depth Psychology and Spiritual Practice." San Francisco Jung Society, San Francisco, CA, 2002.

Ulanov, A. *The Wisdom of the Psyche.* Cambridge, MA: Cowley Publications, 1971.

Ann Belford Ulanov, *The Feminine in Christian Theology and in Jungian Psychology.* Evanston, IL: Northwestern University Press, 1988

Von Franz, Marie-Louis. *On Divination and Synchronicity.* Toronto, ON: Inner City Books, 1980.

Von Franz, M. L. *The Interpretation of Fairy Tales.* Boston, MA: Shambhala, 1996.

Vycinas, V. *Earth and Gods: An Introduction to the Philosophy of Martin Heidegger.* The Hague: M. Nijhoff, 1961.

Wasburn, Michael. *The Ego and the Dynamic Ground: A Transpersonal Theory of Human Development.* Albany, NY: SUNY Press, 1987.

Wheelwright, Joseph, ed. *The Reality of the Psyche.* New York: Putnam, 1961.

Whitmont, Edward. *The Symbolic Quest.* Princeton University Press. 1969.

Wilkinson, T. *Persephone Returns: Victims, Heroes and the Journey from the Underworld.* Tulsa, OK: Council Oak Books, 1996.

Wilson, T. *The Secret History of Crop Circles.* Devon, UK: The Center for Crop Circle Studies, 1998.

Woodman, Marion. *Addiction to Perfection.* Toronto, ON: Inner City Books, 1982.

Woodman. Marion. *The Owl Was a Baker's Daughter.* Toronto, ON: Inner City Books, 1980.

Woodman, Marion. *The Ravaged Bridegroom: Masculinity in Women.* Toronto, ON: Inner City Books, 1990.

Young-Eisendrath, Polly, and Terence Dawson. *The Cambridge Companion to Jung.* Cambridge, MA: Cambridge University Press, 1997.

Zabriskie, B. *Atom and Archetype: The Pauli/Jung Letters, 1932–1958.* Edited by C. A. Meier. Princeton, NJ: Princeton University Press, 1999.

Zweig, Connie, and Jeremiah Abrams. *Meeting the Shadow.* New York: Tarcher, 1991.

ACKNOWLEDGMENTS

Throughout my long journey on this work, many friends and family members have supported me and I greatly appreciate it. Thank you.

In the Crop Circle world, I would like to especially thank Paul Anderson. As director of the Canadian Crop Circle Research Network for many years, Paul has championed this phenomenon tirelessly. He generously welcomed me to his treasure trove of research and our many discussions were particularly helpful when I was just getting my feet wet in this exciting world. My consideration of this topic was made possible by the pioneering work on the science of this phenomenon done by BLT Research. I strongly encourage you to consider donating to help them continue their efforts (www.bltresearch.com). I would also like to thank Andrew Harvey, Suzanne Taylor, and Andy Thomas, whose warm reception of my work has been very meaningful to me.

It is profoundly life-giving to find oneself being seen by others who understand and appreciate who you are and what you are trying to do. To my dear friend Shannon O'Neill, colleague and classmate, I am so thankful for all of your help during this effort and every other one. I am proud to be able to be there for you too. I was fortunate, midway through the writing, to befriend Sarah "Jung Girl" Stevenson, who was the first to read the chapters as they were completed, one by one. Your support and enthusiasm filled me up when I needed it most. Thank you.

Finally, I have been gifted to have a wonderful partner at the final stage of this book's birth into the world. Your genius for the psyche and passion for graceful expression helped take this book to the next level. Even more important to me, words cannot express how grateful I am to be understood by someone whom I so deeply respect and care for. Thank you, Dr. K. D. Farris.

ABOUT THE AUTHOR

Gary S. Bobroff, MA, has been pursuing the enigmatic beauty of Crop Circles since the 1990s and has been privileged to visit Crop Circles in Canada, the U.S., and the U.K. Born in the land of wheat—the jewel of the prairies, Saskatoon, Canada—he studied philosophy at the University of British Columbia and psychology at Pacifica Graduate Institute in Santa Barbara, California.

He writes and speaks internationally, exploring the ancient themes that draw us further into engagement with life's deep mystery.

His primary website is www.gsbobroff.com. His website for this topic is www.JungAndCropCircles.net. He is also the developer of the Archetypes of the Feminine and Masculine workshop series (www.YourMyth.com).